IS NOW!

URBAN SCRAWL

the written word in street art

LOU CHAMBERLIN

Hardie Grant
TRAVEL

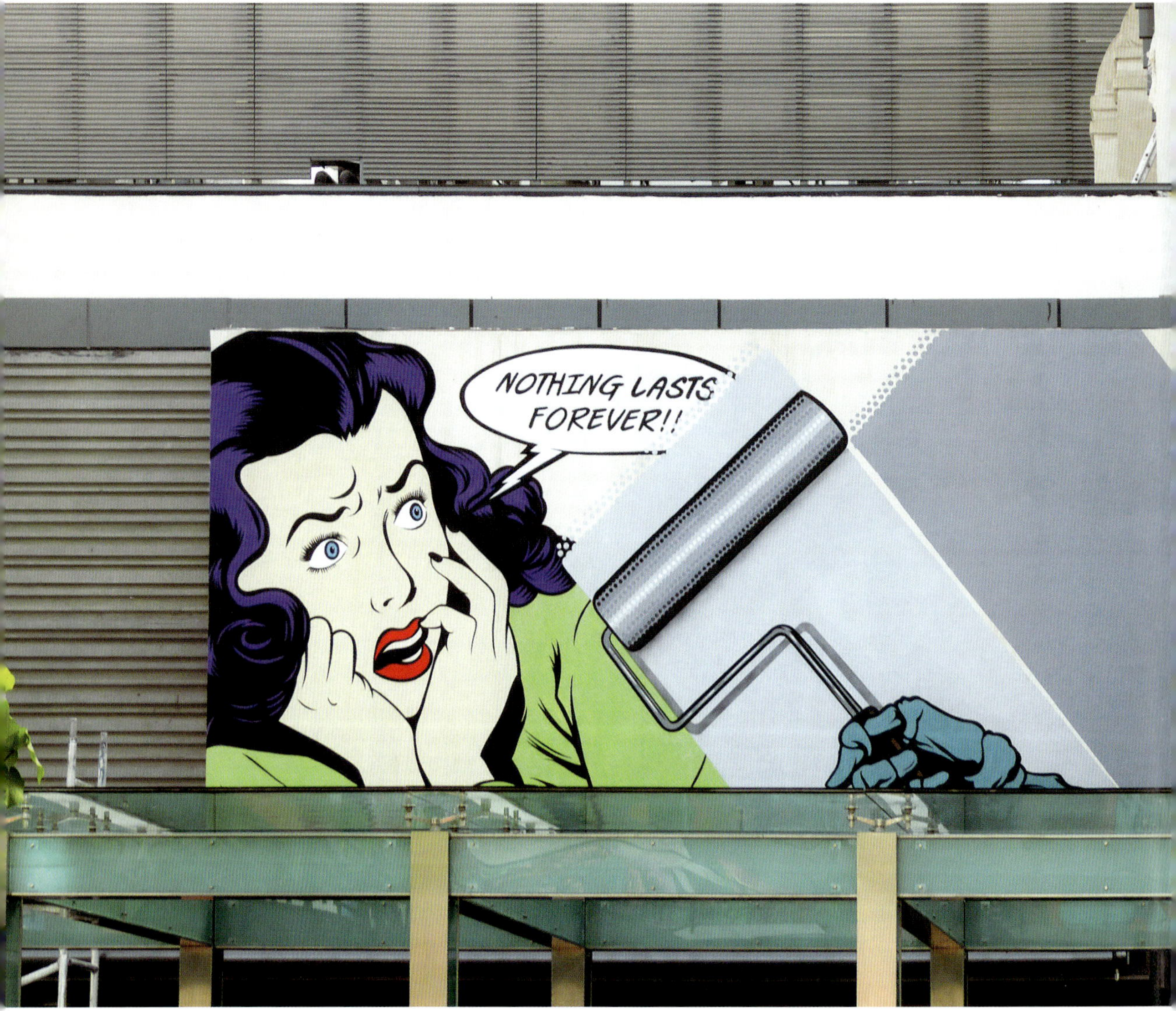
NOTHING LASTS FOREVER!!

Contents

FRONT COVER Mau Mau, *Get Rich or Try Sharing*, London, UK, 2016

BACK COVER WRDSMTH, Melbourne, Australia, 2015

END PAPERS Lana Hughes and Rory Elphick, Animaux Circus, *The Time is Now!*, Melbourne, Australia, 2018; Jesse Harris, *You've Changed* (2012), Toronto, Canada, 2018

CONTENTS OPPOSITE D*Face, Dubai, United Arab Emirates, 2016

FOREWORD Blu, Aarhus, Denmark, 2016

INTRODUCTION SLICK, *Big Slick Aloha*, Honolulu, Hawaii, USA, 2017

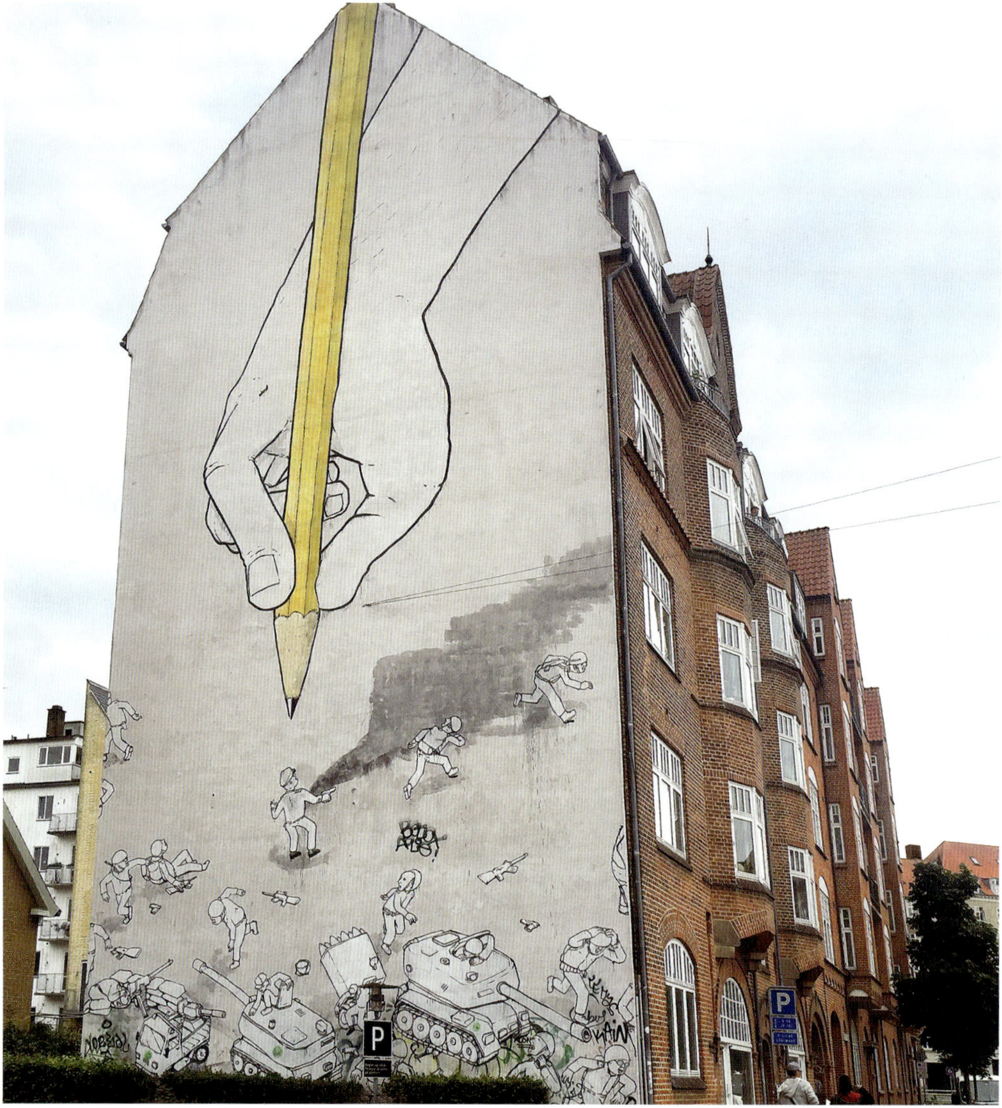

Foreword

During our lives, we pass through many different stages. As children, for example, we discover the world around us and see every day as a new adventure. From the moment we start school, however, the structure and the patterns become more and more demanding. Work, social life, expectations; maybe we're even being sucked in – sucked into an organised, fast-paced, highly demanding life. You know what I mean, right? Honestly, I was, and maybe still am, stuck in this kind of life as well, working really hard to pay the rent, doing my chores after a long day and even making a serious attempt at having a social life. I sometimes even succeed at having one ;) So, what has this got to do with street art? Well ... everything!

Street art can get you out of your daily routine, even if it's only for a few minutes. Street art is everywhere. The best thing about it is that it's available 24/7 for everyone and you don't even have to pay for it. It can speak to you through images and text and take you to new places where you can meet interesting artists and other like-minded people. How can you not like it?

To me it's like a gust of fresh air in cities often dominated by concrete, glass and corporate ads. So just open your eyes while walking the dog, shopping for groceries or taking your kids to school. All these colourful walls have a story to tell; sometimes the message is left for you to imagine for yourself, but often the artist offers clues by adding carefully chosen words. I have to admit that it can be a bit difficult for the untrained eye to interpret these works in the beginning but luckily for you, this amazing book, *Urban Scrawl*, will guide you in the myriad ways that text can be used in the world of street art. But I also have to warn you – street art can be addictive. Look at me and Lou: we are among the dozens of 'hunters' worldwide who contribute to the *Street Art Cities* website and mobile app, searching for beautiful murals in our own towns and travelling the world to see more. The wall opposite is one such example, the oversized hand and pencil dwarfing the images of warfare testament to the power of art and the written word to overcome conflict.

Maybe all I'm trying to say is that the world has so much beauty to offer, so many stories begging to be told, discovered and shared. Just open your eyes and explore. Grab your camera, go out there and hunt for treasures. Love the back alleys, skip the high streets and let the city and its street art seduce you with its stories. The artists will guide you.

Enjoy!

Sanne Gijsbers, Heerlen
Co-founder *Street Art Cities*
www.streetartcities.com
www.streetartcities.com/app

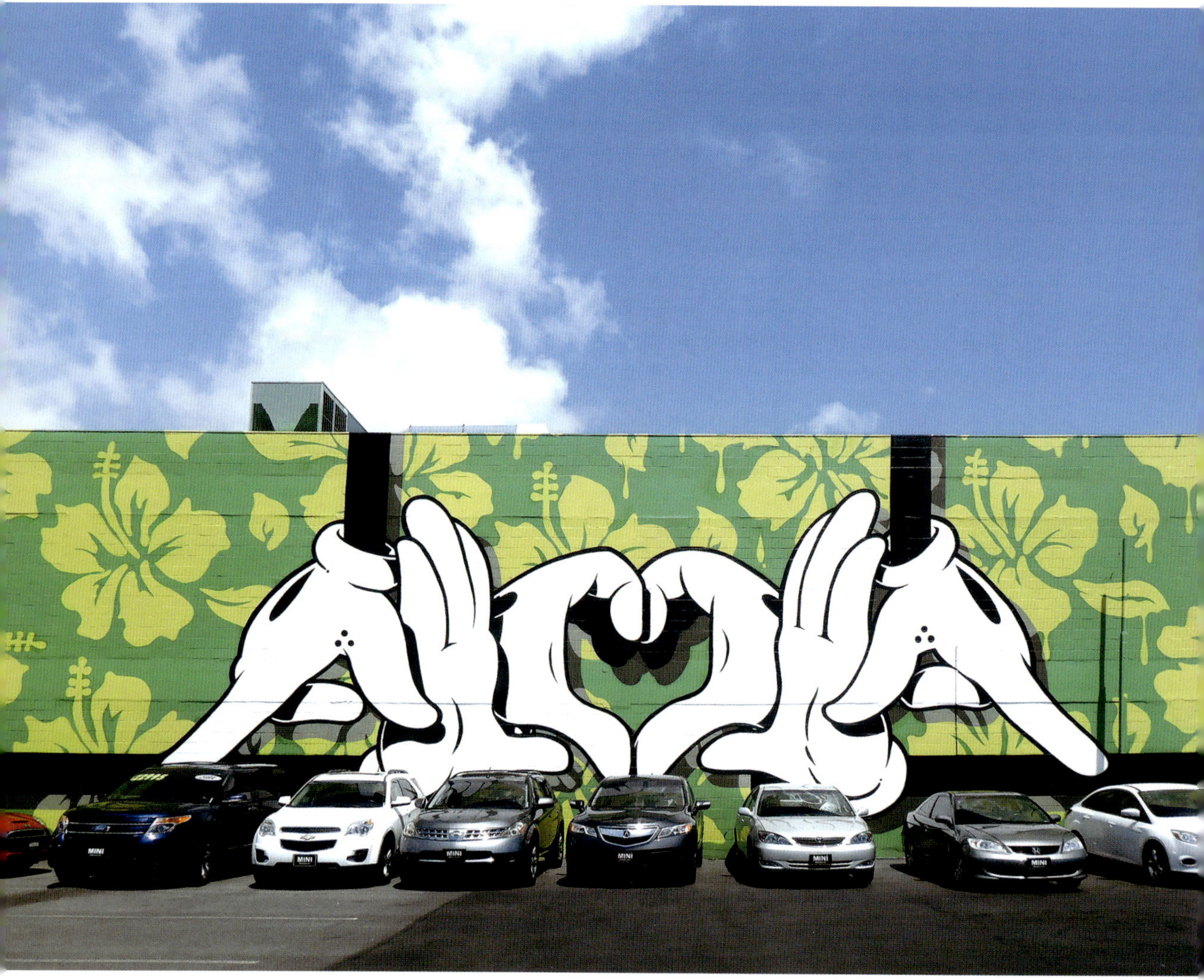

Introduction

We are bombarded by words. They pass through our urban landscape on the sides of buses and trains. They sit on billboards and posters as we drive to work or walk to a meeting. They are even more intrusive when they sneak up on us from the screens of our smart phones.

But what a pleasure it is when these words are placed on the street by artists rather than advertisers, especially when they are presented with such wit and joie de vivre as SLICK's *Aloha* opposite! Although usually used as a simple greeting, 'aloha' means much more to Hawai'ians. It also expresses feelings such as gratitude, affection, compassion and love, so like street art it can say much more than a superficial reading would suggest.

Living in a visually stimulating environment is a source of enjoyment for many and it's not surprising that creative individuals will 'colour our city' with images and ideas. Their work can act as a dynamic antidote to a dreary urban landscape and give a voice to a range of common themes.

Text is an integral part of the imagery that appears on walls. Sometimes the art and the text are big and beautiful, the result of organised festivals and paint jams. In their humbler form the works are small and often easy to overlook, but they celebrate free speech and allow anonymous protest.

From formal typography to angsty scrawl, the text can be playful or profound. It can express beliefs and fears and pleasures. It can be gentle, touching and unpretentious, or openly assertive, subversive or downright aggressive. Whether it's been sprayed, stencilled or pasted onto a surface or simply scribbled onto the footpath, it can share a heartfelt message or be boldly poetic. It can inspire, amaze and offend. It will always be more abrasive when life is more difficult, such as during times of political or social unrest.

The images on these pages have been captured in cities large and small. Many of the walls have been photographed in Melbourne, Australia, because that's where I live. Others have been photographed on my travels, the earliest taken in India in 2001. The dates in the captions refer to when the artworks were captured. Many of the walls had already begun to weather – this reflects the grittiness and transience of our ever-evolving world. Some of them show evidence of additions and subtractions by passersby who engage in the conversation begun by the artist.

But wherever these images call home, they are part of a conversation that crosses international boundaries and circles the world. Sitting side by side on most pages are images from different countries and cultures. They are often very similar, in content if not in appearance. Many of the same thoughts and concerns are expressed, transcending language and culture, just as human desires and needs express universal truths. They are shaped not only by the vision of the artist but also by the social pressures and tensions of time and location. The meaning of such imagery is enhanced by where it is found.

To reflect these broad themes, this book has been divided into chapters that reflect a diversity of subjects, from love, laughter and words of wisdom to subversion, defiance and protest. The images haven't been selected for their beauty, but rather because of what they say. After all, this is a book about communication. While many of them ARE beautiful, others have been created at speed, perhaps even under cover of darkness. They speak to us, they tell us secrets and remind us of truths.

I hope that within these pages you find messages that speak to you.

Aloha!

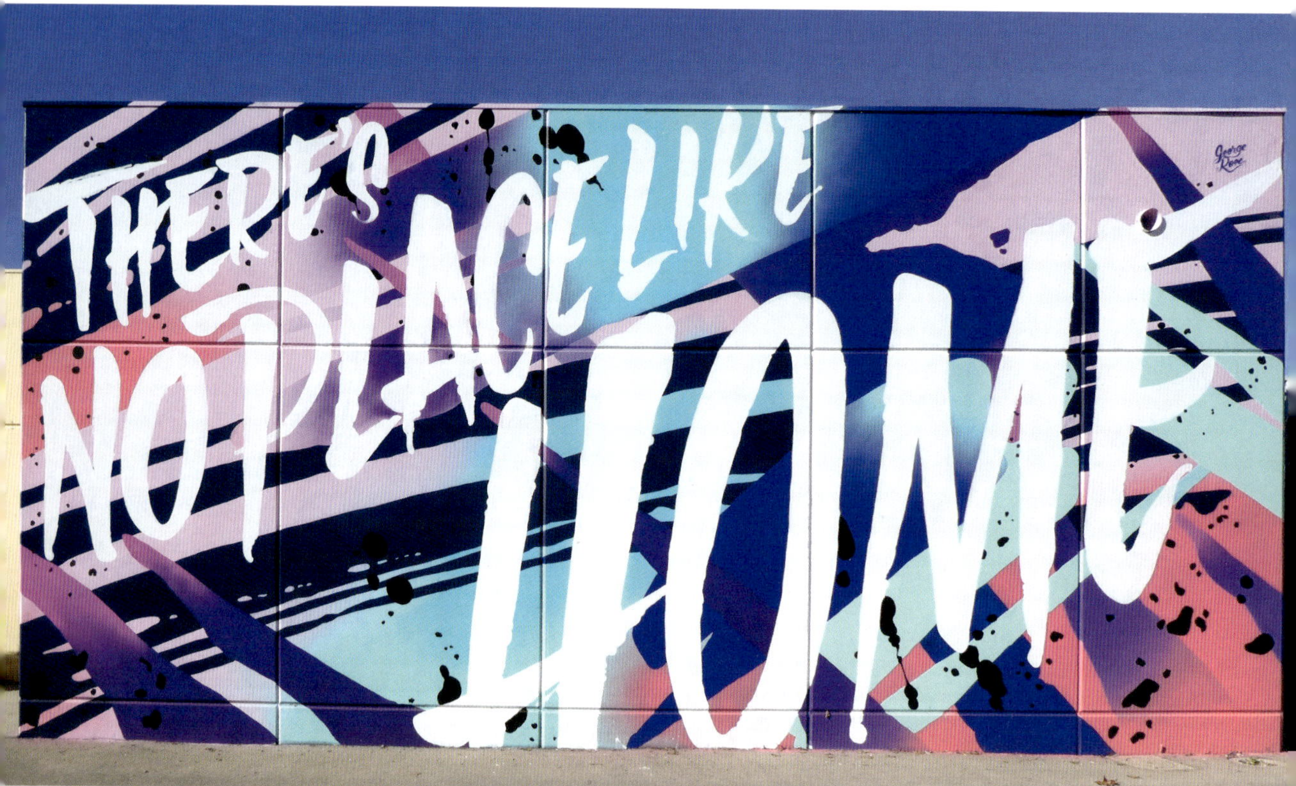
THERE'S
NO PLACE LIKE
HOME
George Rose

Big and Beautiful

Text on a grand scale can inspire and motivate or it can simply brighten an ordinary day by making us smile. The messages painted on the walls on the following pages are thought-provoking and at times inspirational. Their scale has an impact, as does their urban context, both enhancing the meaning of the text. Sometimes the message is ambiguous because the artist wants the observer to interpret it in a way that is relevant to them and their lives.

Some of these walls bear examples of formal typography, like the street poetry of Robert Montgomery. Alternatively they may only carry sufficient words, small and discreet, to add a layer of meaning to a powerful image, as with the walls of Axel Void and Ricky Lee Gordon. There may be speech bubbles, such as D*Face often adds to his images, or complex layers of text and imagery, as in Tristan Eaton's work.

Sydney-based George Rose and New York graphic designer Andrea von Bujdoss (aka Queen Andrea) both love powerful phrases and intense colour. There's visual movement in their compositions, too. These two images are perfect examples of the way in which painted walls can draw attention to themselves in an otherwise grey urban environment.

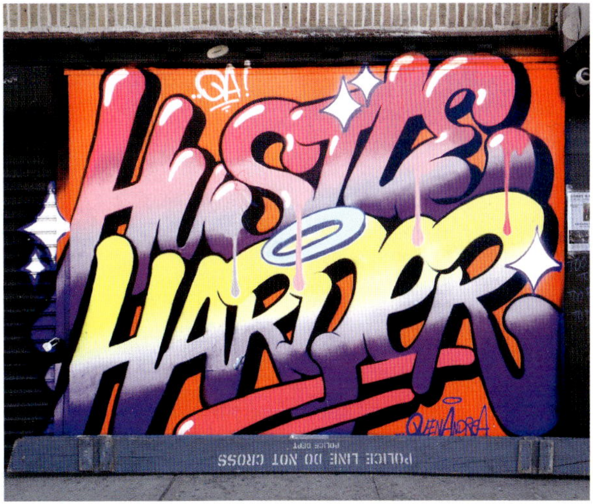

OPPOSITE George Rose, *No Place Like Home*, Benalla, Australia, 2017
RIGHT Andrea von Bujdoss, *Hustle Harder*, New York City, USA, 2018

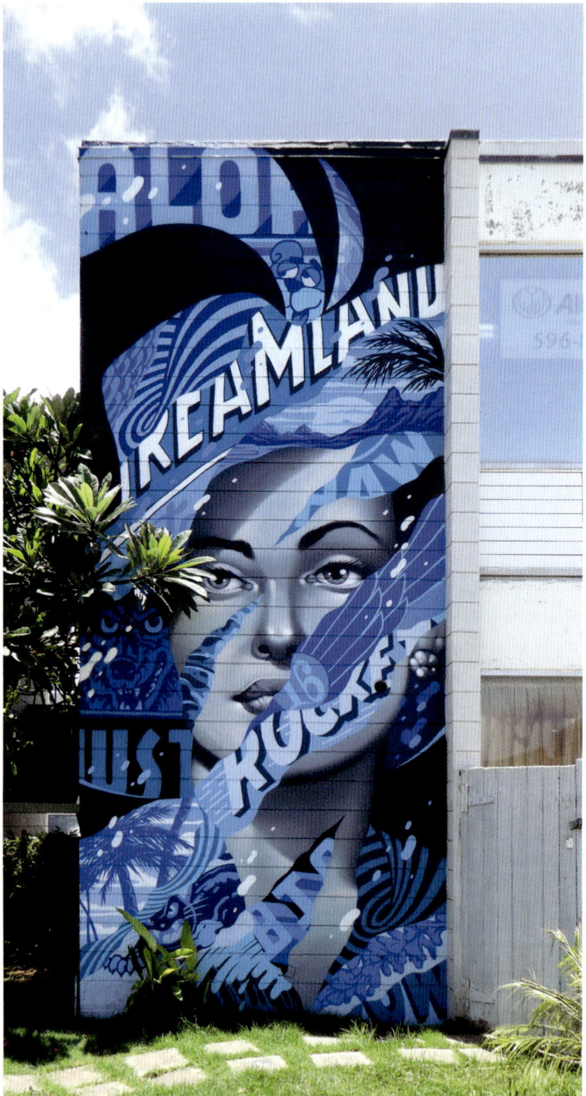
REAMLAND

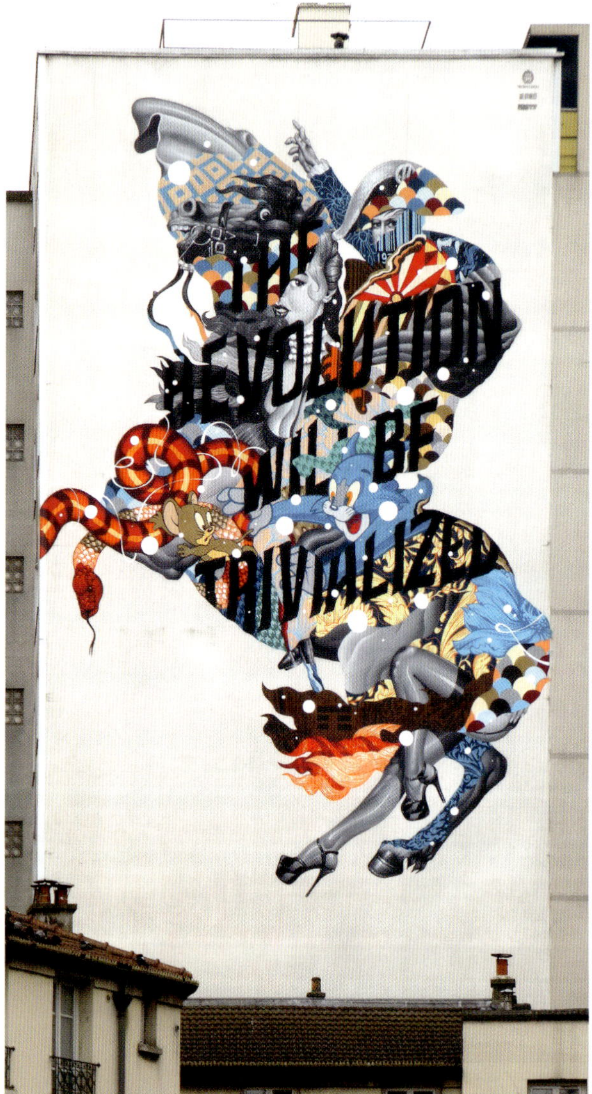
THE
REVOLUTION
WILL BE
TRIVIALIZED

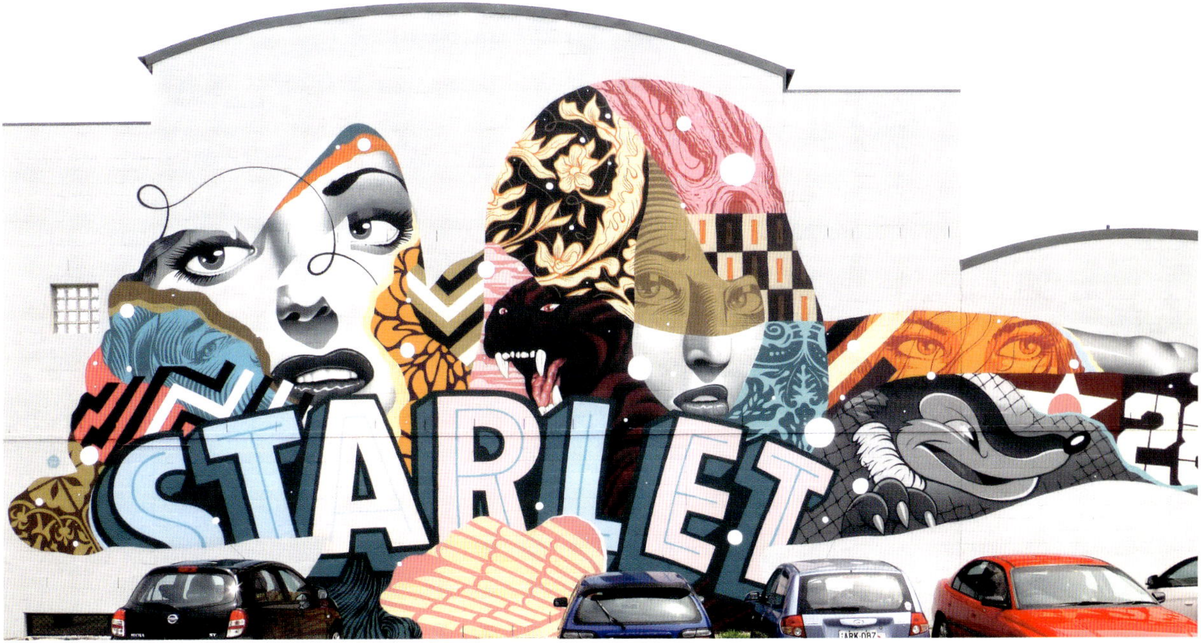

OPPOSITE LEFT Tristan Eaton, *Aloha Dreamland*, Honolulu, Hawaii, USA, 2017

OPPOSITE RIGHT Tristan Eaton, *The Revolution Will Be Trivialized*, Paris, France, 2015

ABOVE Tristan Eaton, *Starlet*, Newcastle, Australia, 2015

TRISTAN Eaton maintains a studio in Los Angeles but his large-scale murals in cities around the globe give him an international presence. His walls are detailed collages, with layered juxtapositions of text, pattern and Pop Art imagery. *Aloha Dreamland* is a patchwork of lush blue landscapes and text superimposed over the face of a 1950s pinup–style beauty. *The Revolution Will Be Trivialized* subverts the meaning of the 1803 painting by Jacques-Louis David that inspired the silhouetted figure of Napoleon on horseback. The combination of cartoon characters, illustrative pattern and camouflaged text creates a lively composition in the heart of Paris' 13th arrondissement.

Starlet was painted in Newcastle in 2014. The vivid colours, comic-book characters and pinup-style faces tell a story of love found and love lost.

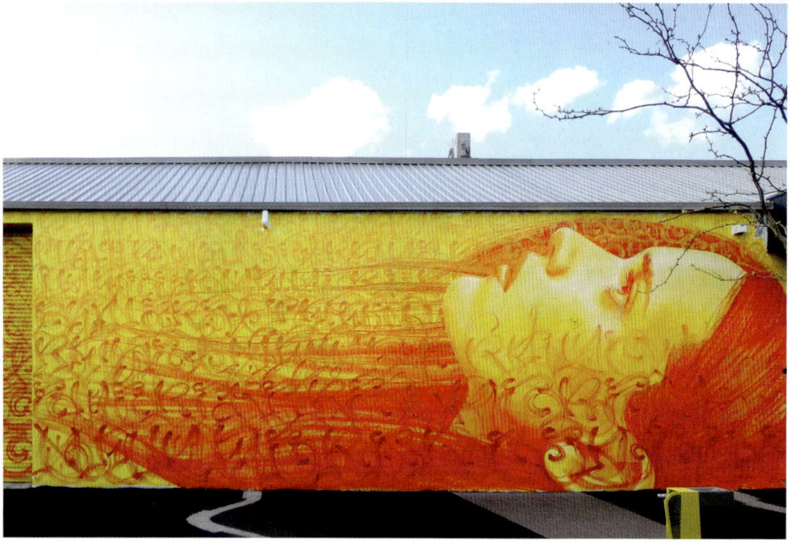

TOP Rone and Mayonaize, Melbourne, Australia, 2015

BOTTOM Rone and Wonderlust, Melbourne, Australia, 2014

OPPOSITE D*Face, Los Angeles, USA, 2016

RONE'S haunting faces are often found in visual collaboration with text. At left we see the flowing calligraphy of Mayonaize creating a veil that gently envelops the face, and below, the powerful text work of Wonderlust adding meaning to the straightforward gaze. All three artists work in Melbourne.

Popular culture is reflected in D*Face's iconic images that remind us of the Pop Art of the 1960s. The characters recall comic book heroes and heroines, and the plots are often inspired by love. Sometimes speech balloons, as here, suggest stories of conflicting emotions.

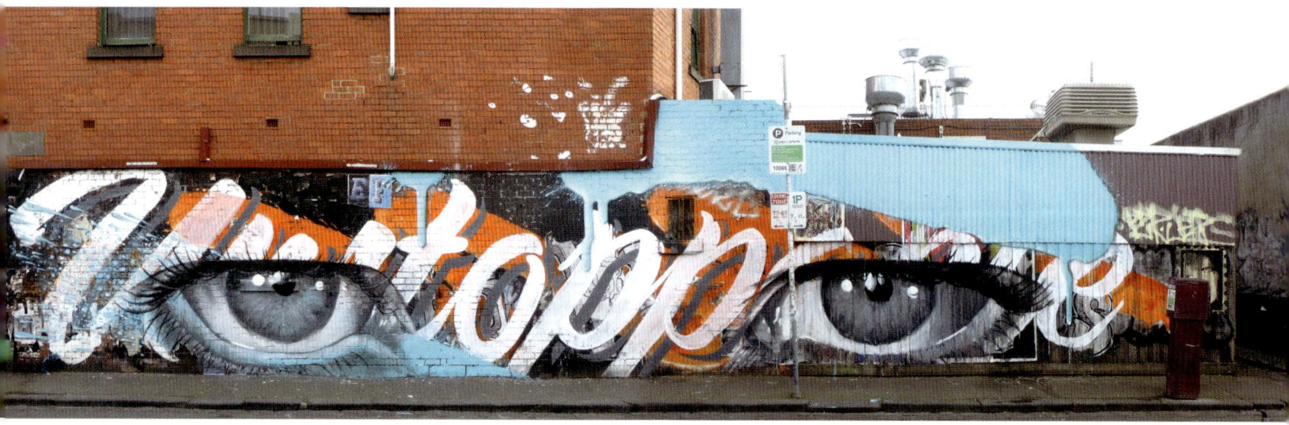

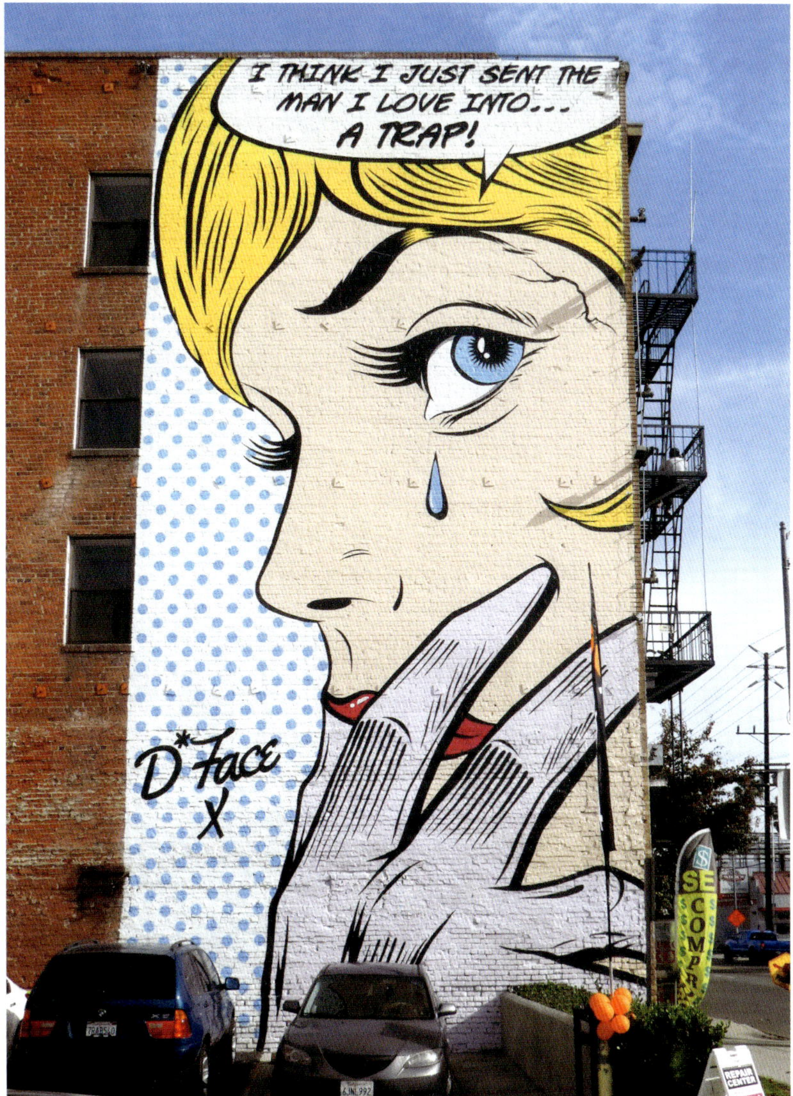
I THINK I JUST SENT THE MAN I LOVE INTO... A TRAP!
D*FACE
X

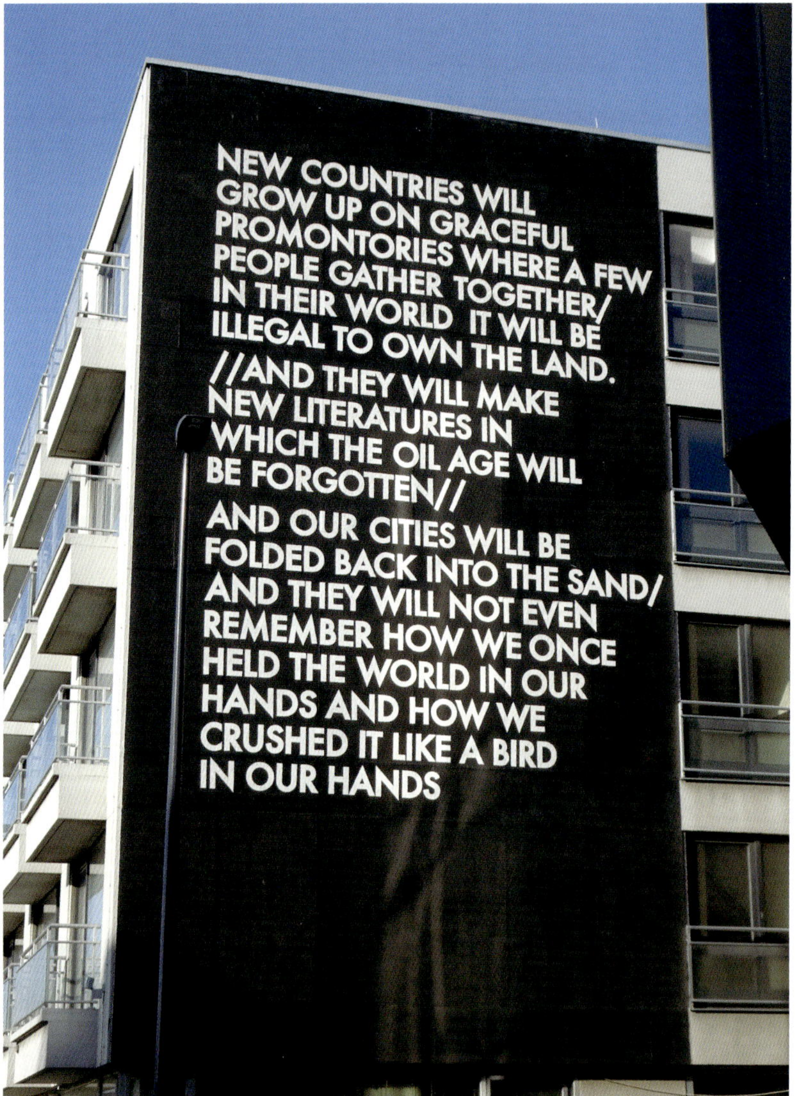
NEW COUNTRIES WILL
GROW UP ON GRACEFUL
PROMONTORIES WHERE A FEW
PEOPLE GATHER TOGETHER/
IN THEIR WORLD IT WILL BE
ILLEGAL TO OWN THE LAND.
//AND THEY WILL MAKE
NEW LITERATURES IN
WHICH THE OIL AGE WILL
BE FORGOTTEN//
AND OUR CITIES WILL BE
FOLDED BACK INTO THE SAND/
AND THEY WILL NOT EVEN
REMEMBER HOW WE ONCE
HELD THE WORLD IN OUR
HANDS AND HOW WE
CRUSHED IT LIKE A BIRD
IN OUR HANDS

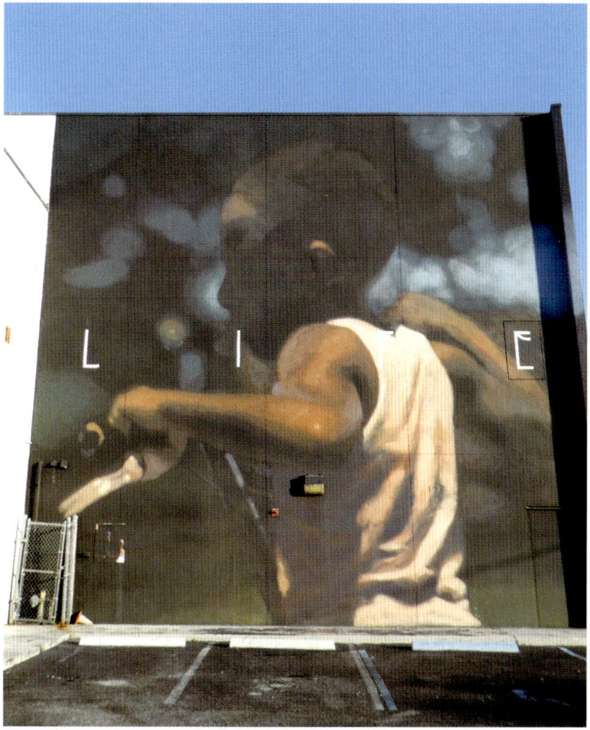

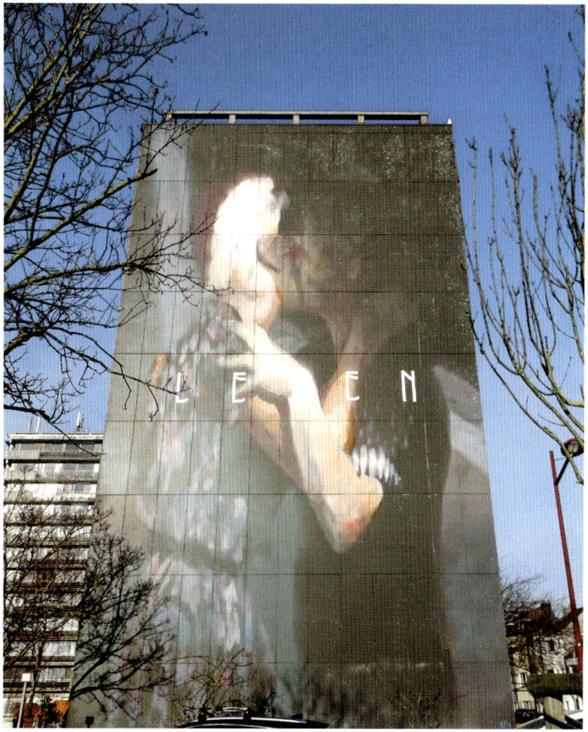

OPPOSITE Robert Montgomery, Ostend, Belgium, 2018

LEFT Axel Void, Miami, USA, 2017

RIGHT Axel Void, Ostend, Belgium, 2018

SCOTTISH-BORN, London-based conceptual artist Robert Montgomery is an urban poet who creates light poems and fire poems as well as enormous murals such as the one opposite. He explains that he likes to work with words because they slow us down at a time in history when life is increasingly fast-paced. He uses a simple font in white on a black background because he wants his work to be easily read and understood.

Miami-based artist Axel Void's work clearly reflects his background in classical painting and drawing. He believes that art should be thought-provoking. His walls always contain a back story, one not easily interpreted but with its own haunting sense of tender poetry. On the two walls above, the word 'life' is inscribed in different languages over characters of different ages.

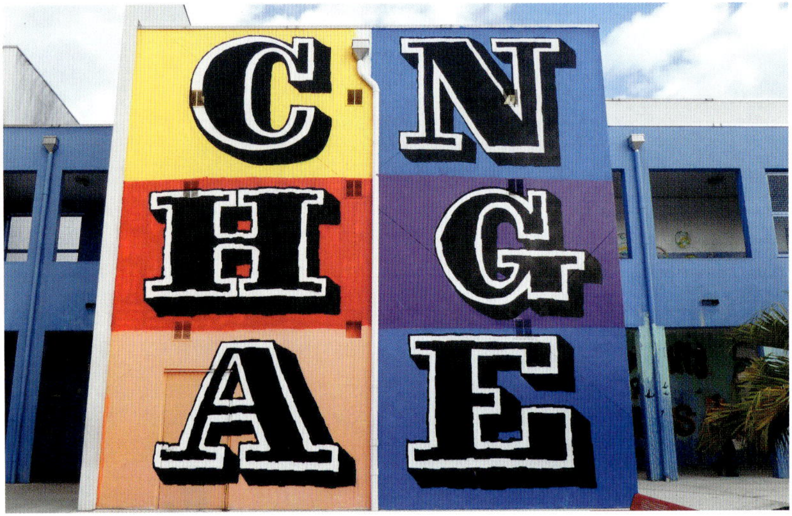
C N
H G
A E

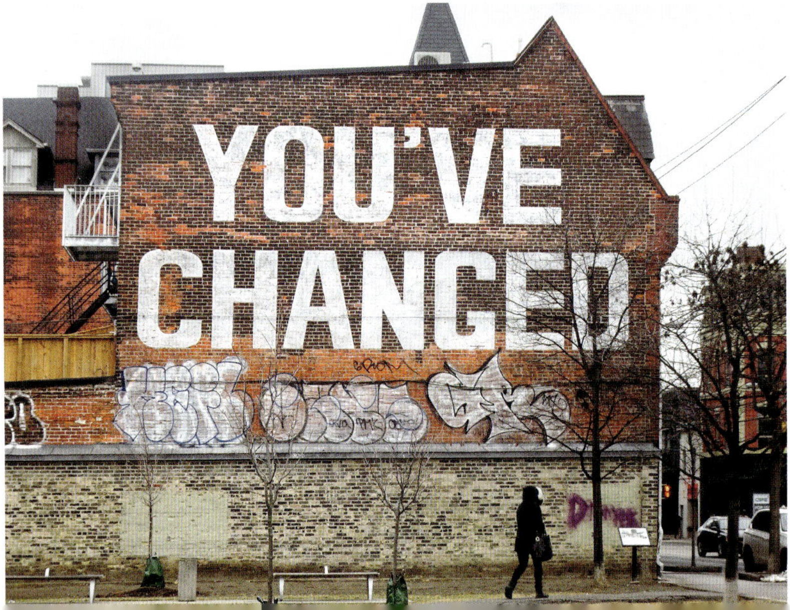
YOU'VE
CHANGED

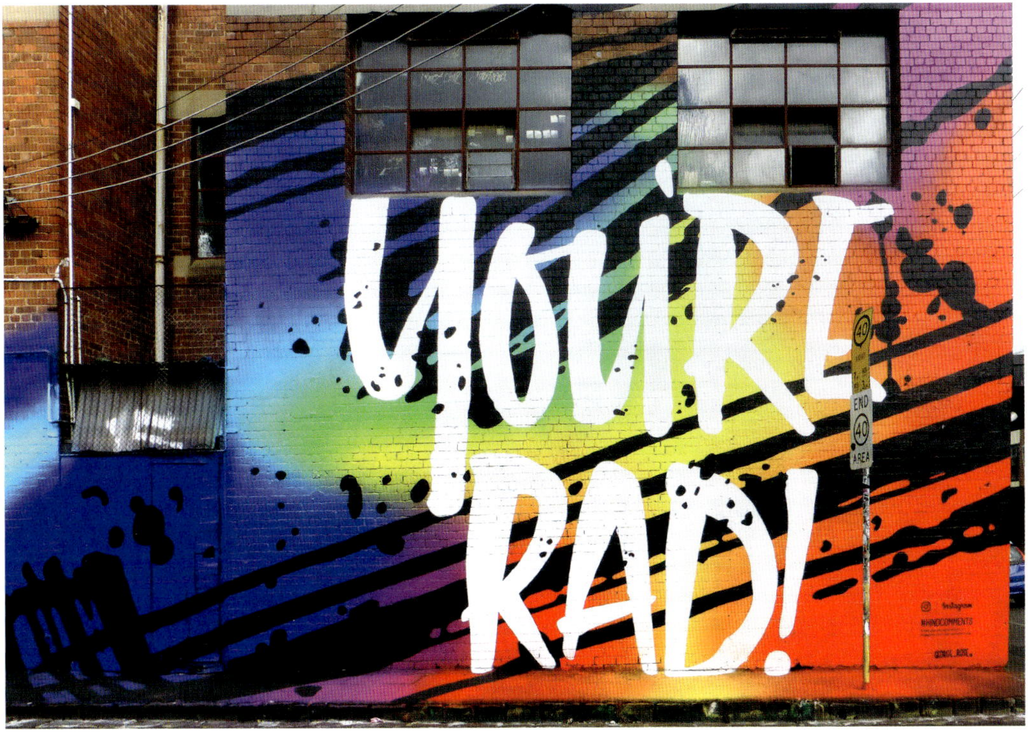

OPPOSITE TOP Ben Eine, *CHANGE*, Miami, USA, 2017

OPPOSITE BOTTOM Jesse Harris, *You've Changed (2012)*, Toronto, Canada, 2018

ABOVE George Rose, *You're Rad!*, Melbourne, Australia, 2018

THE two large walls opposite, one in a high school in Miami and the other in a small neighbourhood park in Toronto, speak of change. Modest or substantial, passive, transformative or revolutionary, change is the stuff that creates the future. Ben Eine's confident typography at top and Jesse Harris' giant uncomplicated letters at bottom warn, encourage and affirm.

George Rose's wall is a dramatic expression of approval. The eye-catching waves of spectrum colour with the superimposed white text and black slashes and splashes are a welcome burst of love on a grey day.

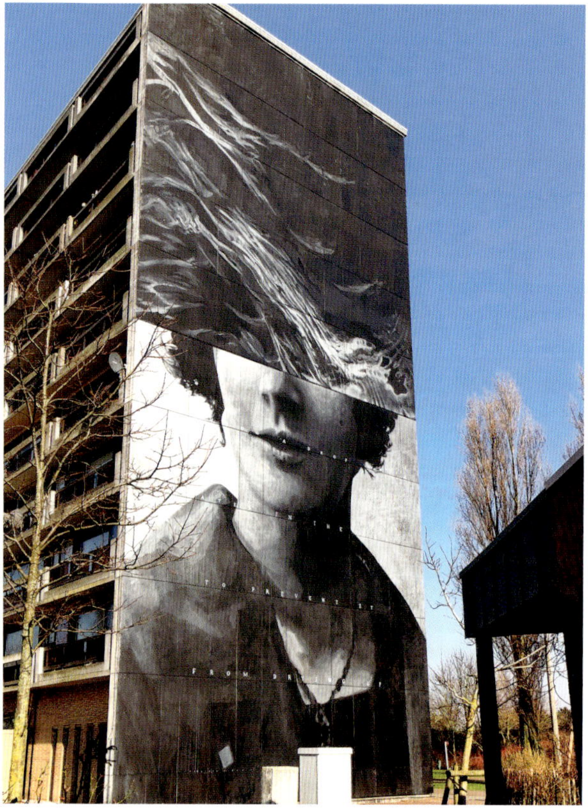

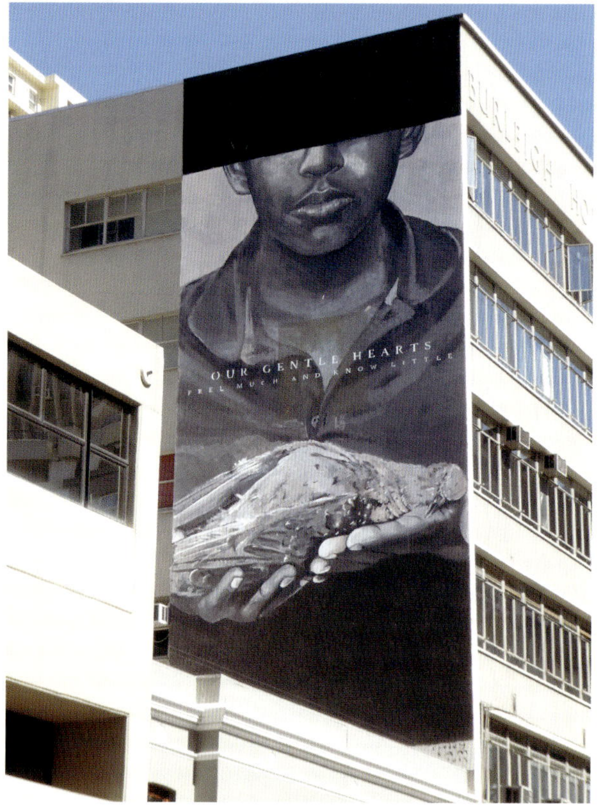

LEFT Ricky Lee Gordon, Ostend, Belgium, 2018

RIGHT Ricky Lee Gordon, Cape Town, South Africa, 2017

OPPOSITE Shepard Fairey, *Peace Waratah*, Sydney, Australia, 2017

SOUTH African artist Ricky Lee Gordon creates large-scale and thought-provoking murals with a meditative quality. He often crops faces, as here, to suggest the universality of the human condition, removing the emphasis on individuality. Gordon sees the wall (above left) as a homage to memory. The figure of the woman was based on a photograph found in a family album belonging to one of the residents of the building. The absence of colour, combined with the unobtrusive text, lends both walls a pensive air.

Shepard Fairey added *Peace Waratah* to Sydney's skyline in 2017. The woman, with flowers in her hair and her eyes closed in introspection, holds a stylised image of the waratah, the state flower. This work is a perfect example of the clean lines and strong design typical of the artist.

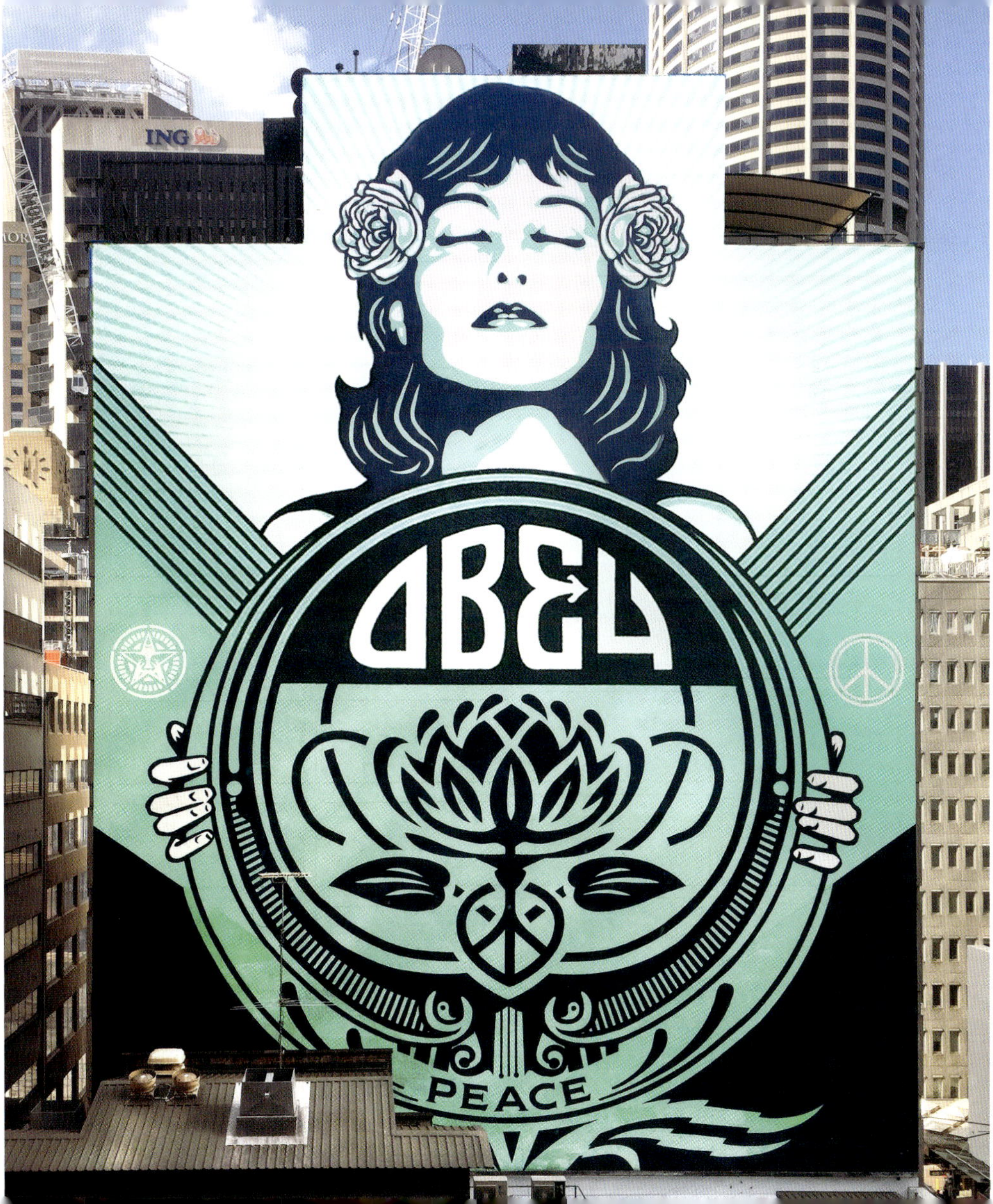
ING
OBEY
PEACE

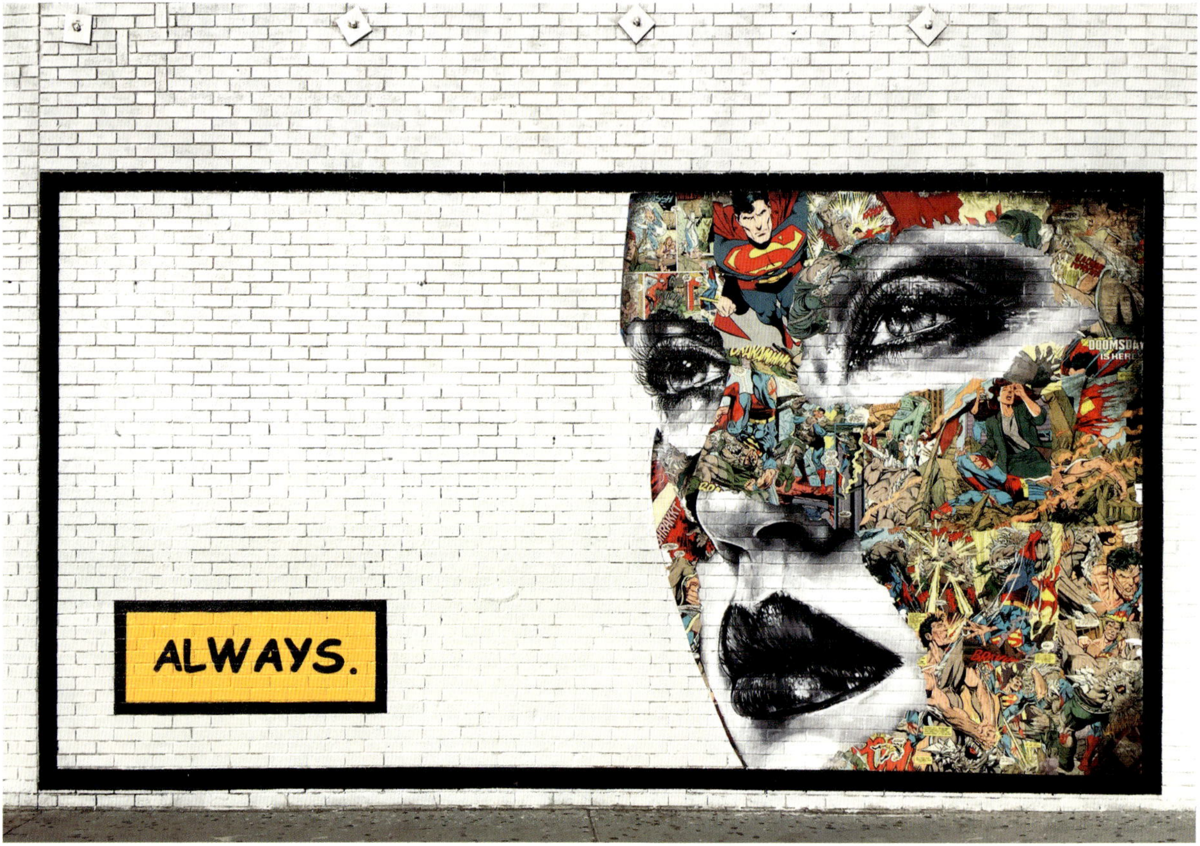
ALWAYS.
DOOMSDAY IS HERE

OPPOSITE Sandra Chevrier, *La Cage, pour toujours*, Los Angeles, USA, 2016
TOP Georgia Hill, *Ever and Ever*, Perth, Australia, 2017
BOTTOM Georgia Hill, *Always*, Newcastle, Australia, 2015

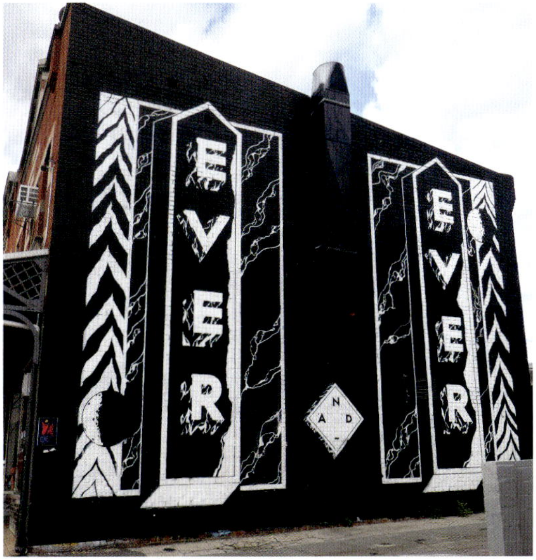

THE individuality of the woman's face painted by Montréal-based artist Sandra Chevrier (opposite) is obscured by a collaged mask of finely detailed comic book heroes engaged in action-packed drama. Part of her series *Cages*, this work sees Chevrier use the contrasts of open space and densely packed detail, order and chaos, and heroism and vulnerability to draw attention to the social limitations and controls that lock women into narrow identities.

Text and time-based language are ever-present in the bold black and white walls painted by Sydney-based illustrator and typographer Georgia Hill. Her clean lettering style is enhanced by symmetry and repetition as well as texture and contrast. The words themselves allow for personal interpretation shaped by the viewer's experience.

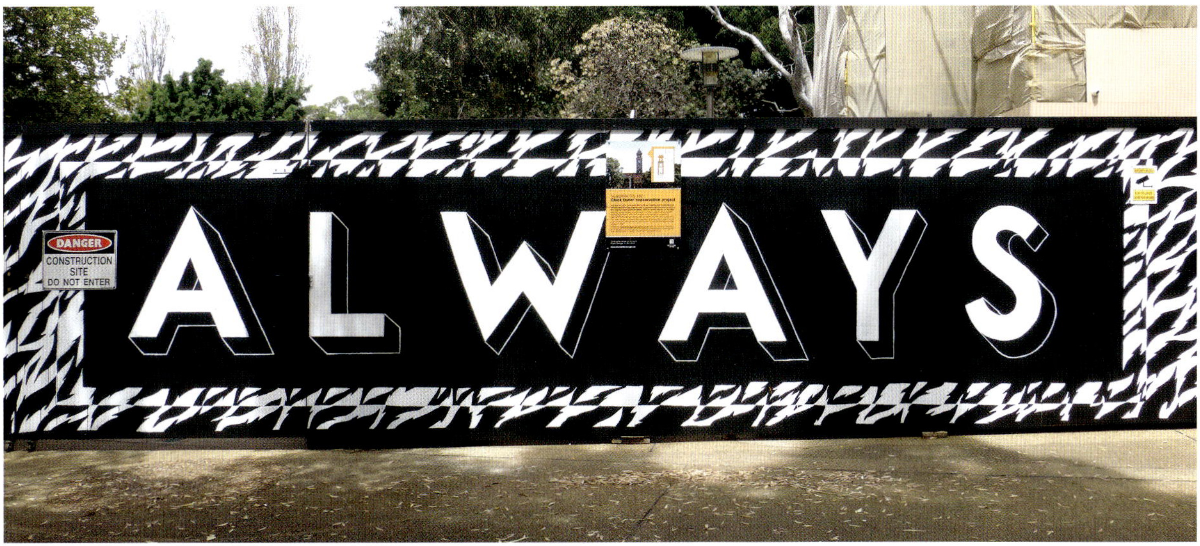

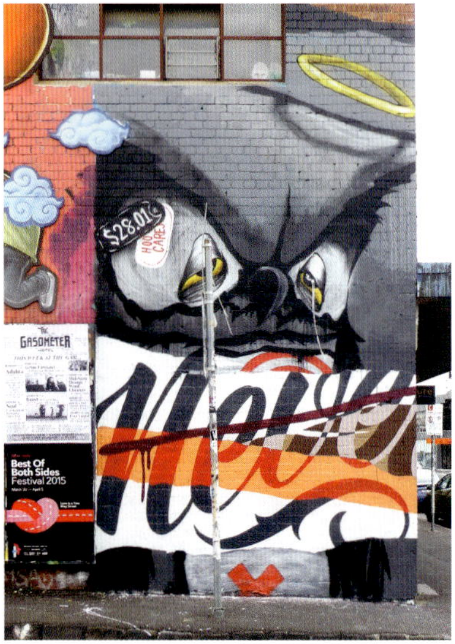

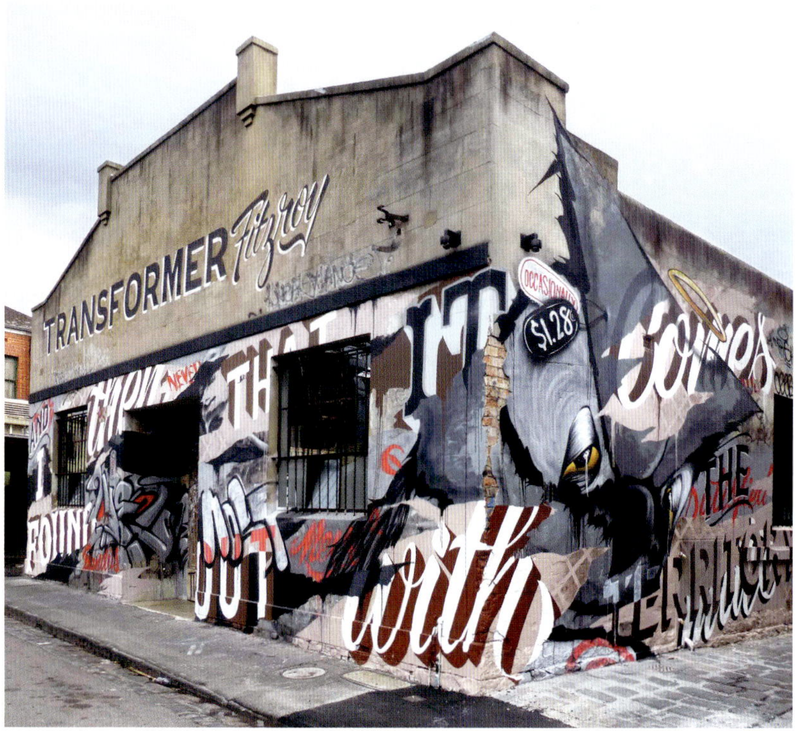

LEFT Mr. Never Satisfied, Melbourne, Australia, 2015

RIGHT Mr. Never Satisfied, Melbourne, Australia, 2015

OPPOSITE Elliott Routledge, Sydney, Australia, 2017

WHEN Mr. Never Satisfied visited Melbourne in 2015, he left behind a number of his signature 'sad' walls, including the two above. His unhappy owl, with its price tag of $1.28 or $28.01, is always accompanied by text that reflects its sadness. The words 'never' and 'occasionally' encourage our curiosity.

References to time take on different meanings when they're painted near public transport. Elliott Routledge painted an enormous 'Never Too Late' on a wall adjacent to a train station in Sydney's Inner West. It is typical of his bold, clean, uncluttered graphic style.

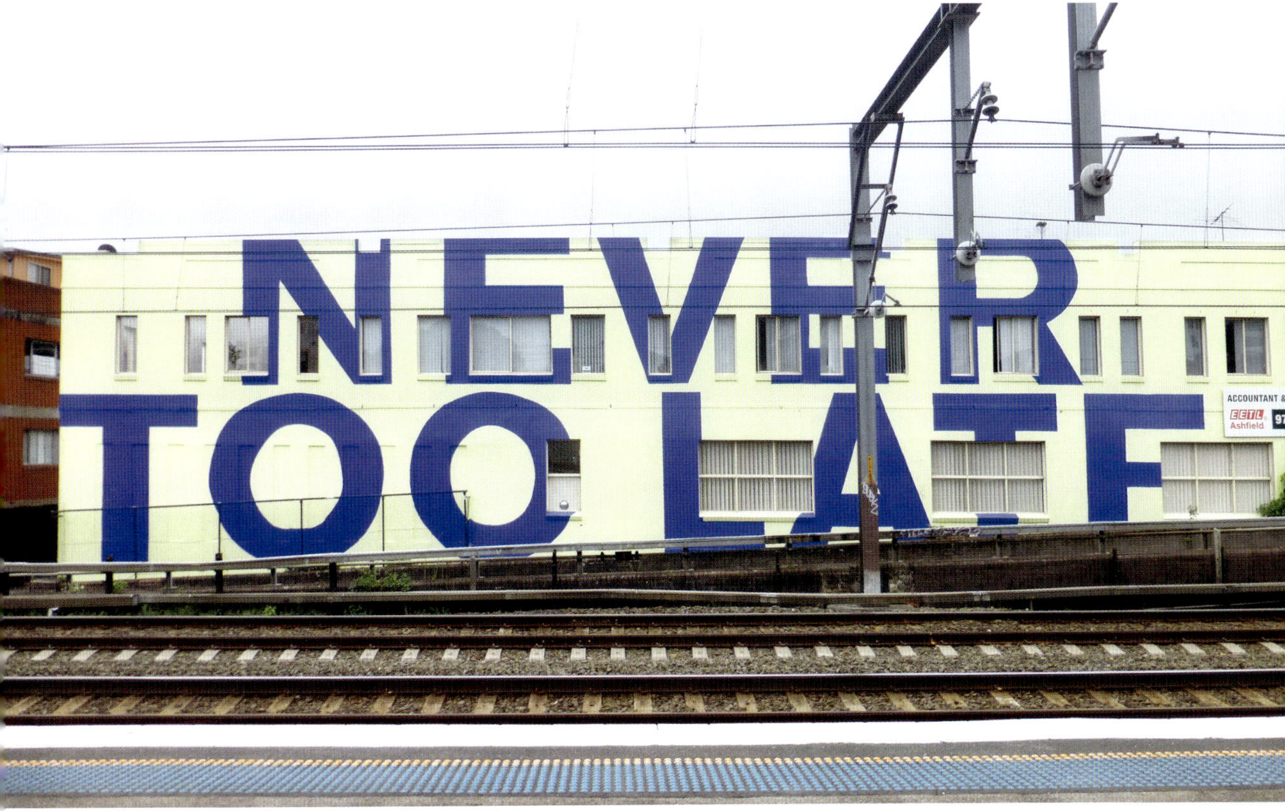
NEVER
TOO LAT
ACCOUNTANT &
Ashfield
97

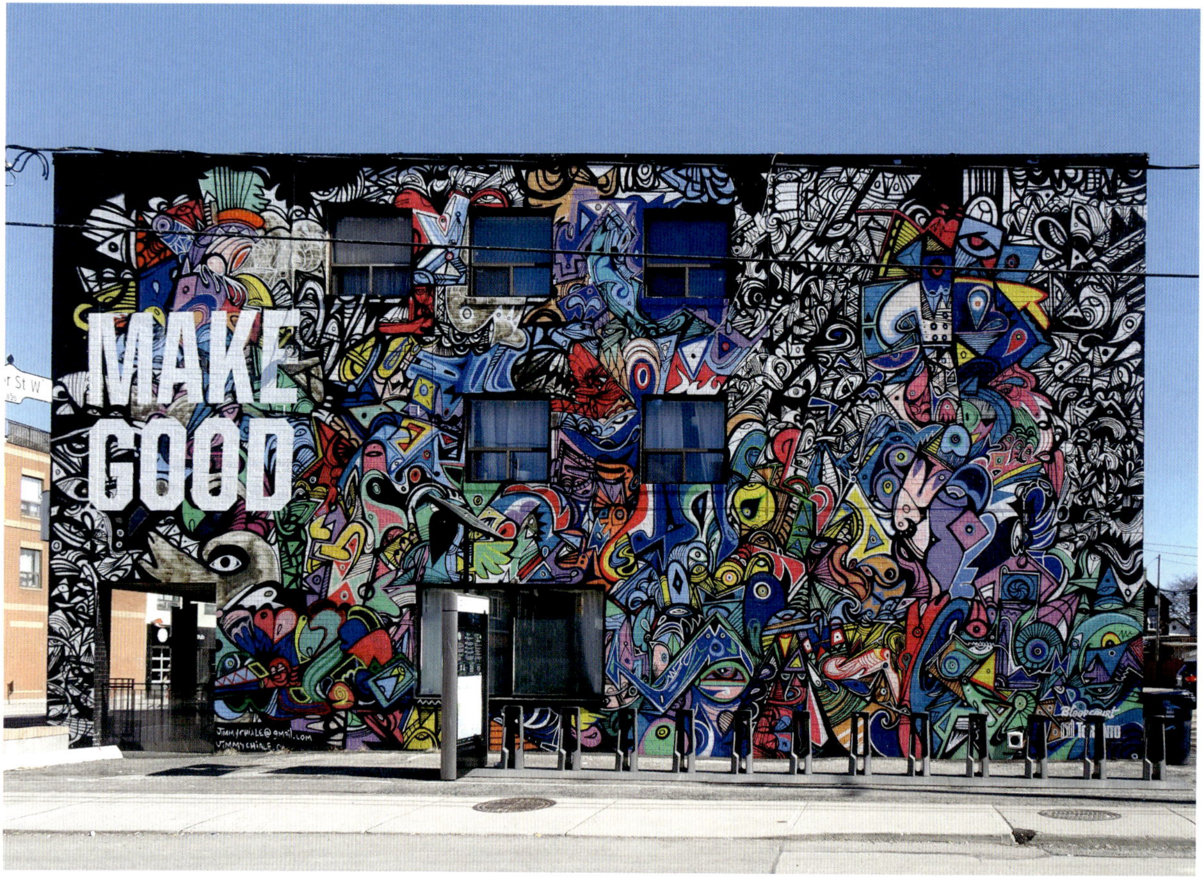

ABOVE Jimmy Chiale, Toronto, Canada, 2018
OPPOSITE TOP Huge, Stockholm, Sweden, 2016
OPPOSITE BOTTOM Fanakapan, Los Angeles, USA, 2017

THE *Make Good* mural in Toronto was painted by Paris-born, now Toronto-based, artist Jimmy Chiale. The playful abstract shapes and the rich bright colours interspersed with black and white patterns are exactly what could be expected of a self-described 'compulsive doodler'.

Huge and Fanakapan both paint photorealistic foil balloons. Huge's blue helium balloon letters were painted on a wall at Snösätra, a street art hub with constantly changing walls in an old industrial area some distance away from the centre of Stockholm. Fanakapan's *Star* was painted outside the Venice, Los Angeles, studio of fellow artist Christina Angelina, who is also known as Starfighter.

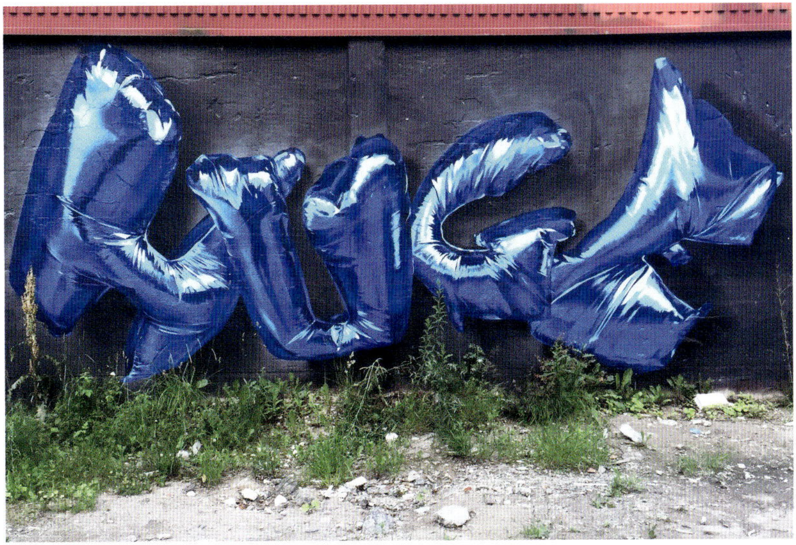
HUGE

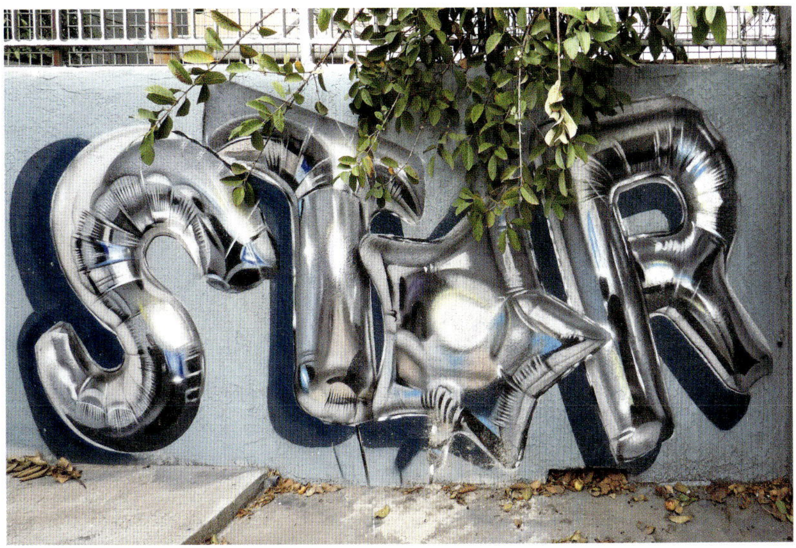
STAR

OPPOSITE TOP Lushsux, Melbourne, Australia, 2018

BOTTOM, BOTH PAGES Tom Dean, Toronto, Canada, 2018

THIS *Is Paradise* was painted by Tom Dean in 2011 on a long wall of Cameron House, a Toronto live music venue with a well-known visual identity. The phrase, on a field of yellow and blue, both right way up and inverted, echoes a placard inside the bar.

Upside down is also the motif for the small wall at opposite top painted in Melbourne by the anonymous artist Lushsux. It makes sense as a 'cheerio' to the rest of the world from the land Down Under. It's a clever, although very tame offering from an artist whose work has been variously called provocative, bawdy and licentious.

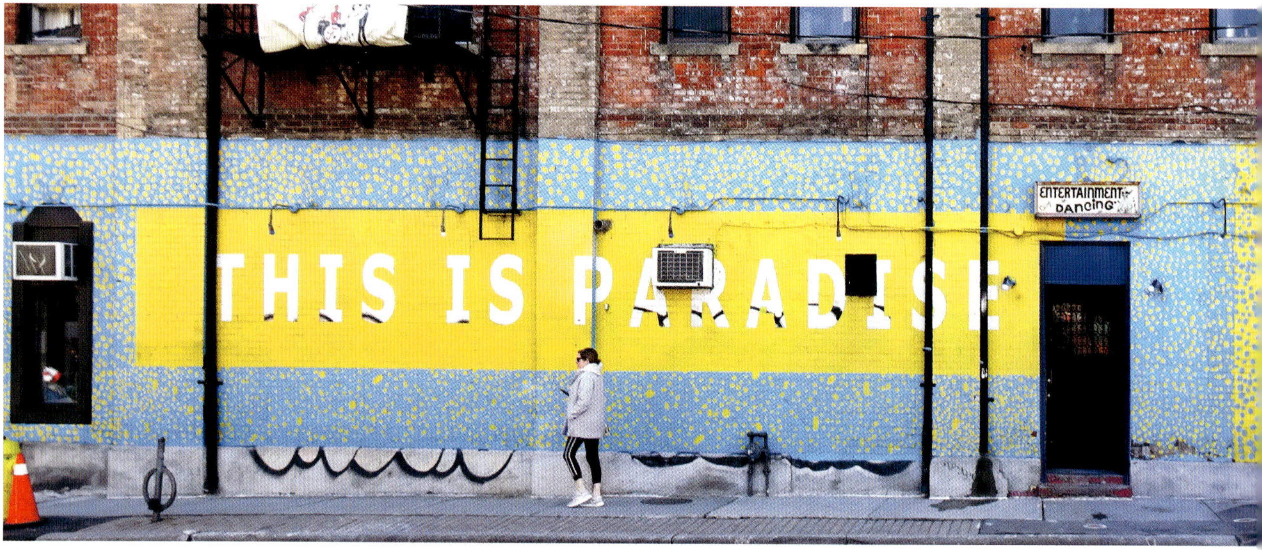

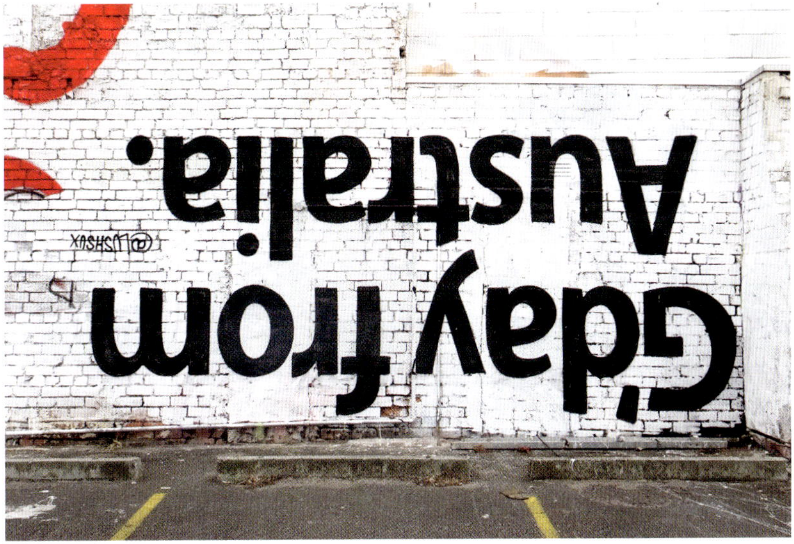
G'day from
Australia.

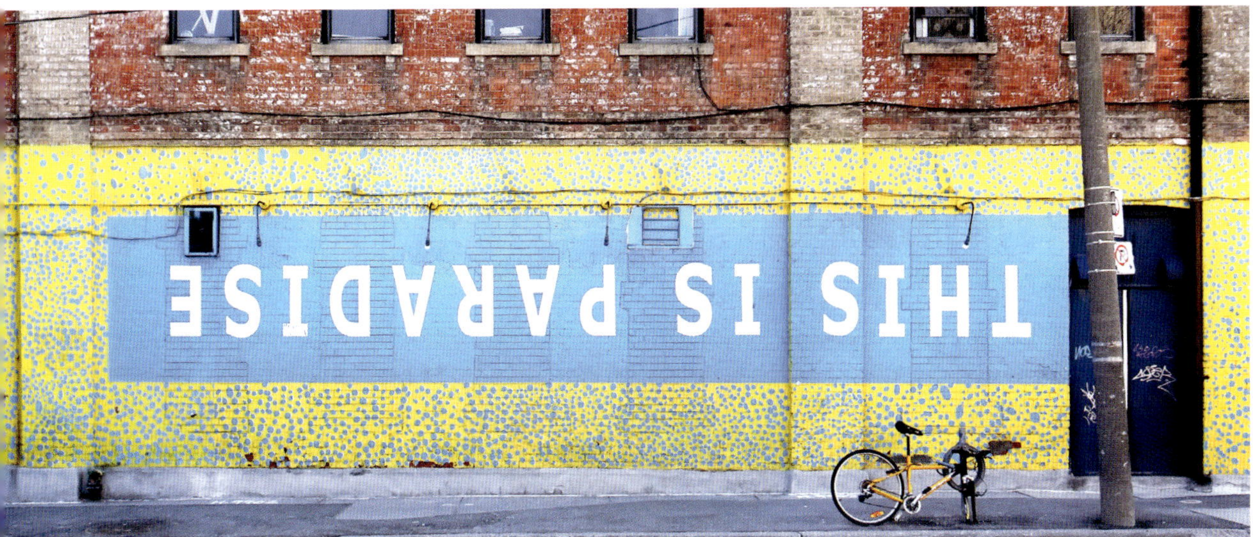
THIS IS PARADISE

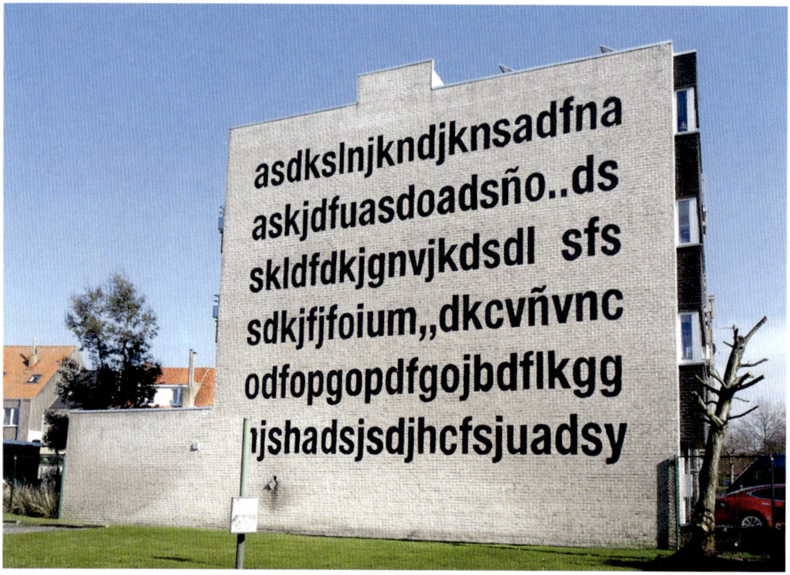
asdkslnjkndjknsadfna
askjdfuasdoadsño..ds
skldfdkjgnvjkdsdl sfs
sdkjfjfoium,,dkcvñvnc
odfopgopdfgojbdflkgg
jshadsjsdjhcfsjuadsy

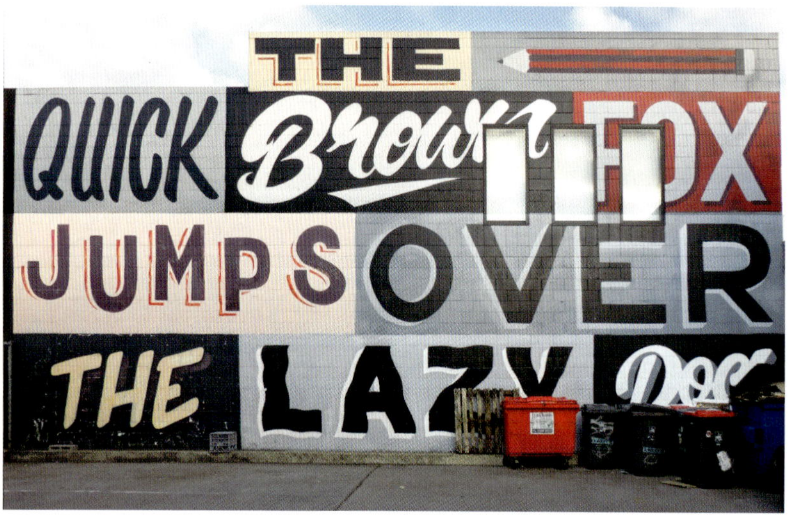
THE
QUICK
FOX
JUMPS
OVER
THE

OPPOSITE TOP SpY, *Letters*, Ostend, Belgium, 2018

OPPOSITE BOTTOM Elliott Routledge, Roach and Joel Birch, Brisbane, Australia, 2014

TOP 1AM, San Francisco, USA, 2017

BOTTOM Rolando Venegas, *Today Was a Good Day*, Honolulu, Hawaii, USA, 2017

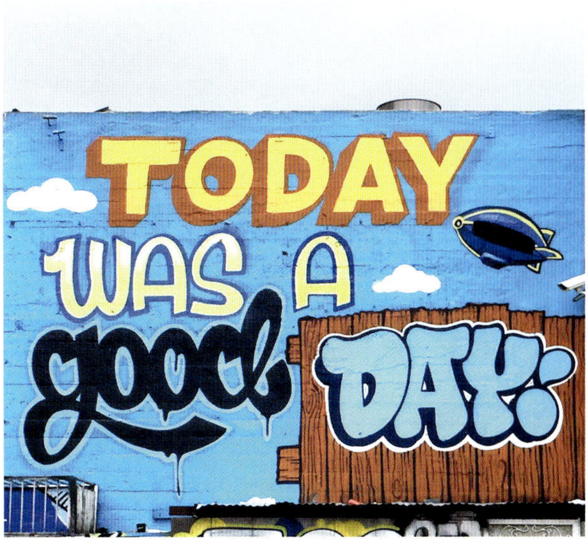

SpY'S urban interventions are always thought-provoking and often humorous. However, there is no profound or hidden meaning to the sequence of the letters he painted on a wall in Ostend (opposite top). It's as if random letters were thrown against the wall before being lined up in military order. He is happy for viewers to find their own meaning. Elliott Routledge (aka Numskull), Roach and Joel Birch also used type as the subject matter of their collaborative wall (opposite bottom), showcasing their mastery of typography with the well-known pangram.

'Today was a good day.' What a happy sentiment! It prompts us to be mindful of the here and now. The version at right was painted by the San Francisco-based collective 1AM, short for First Amendment – the right to free speech. The one below is the work of Rolando Venegas in Kaka'ako, the street art hub of Honolulu.

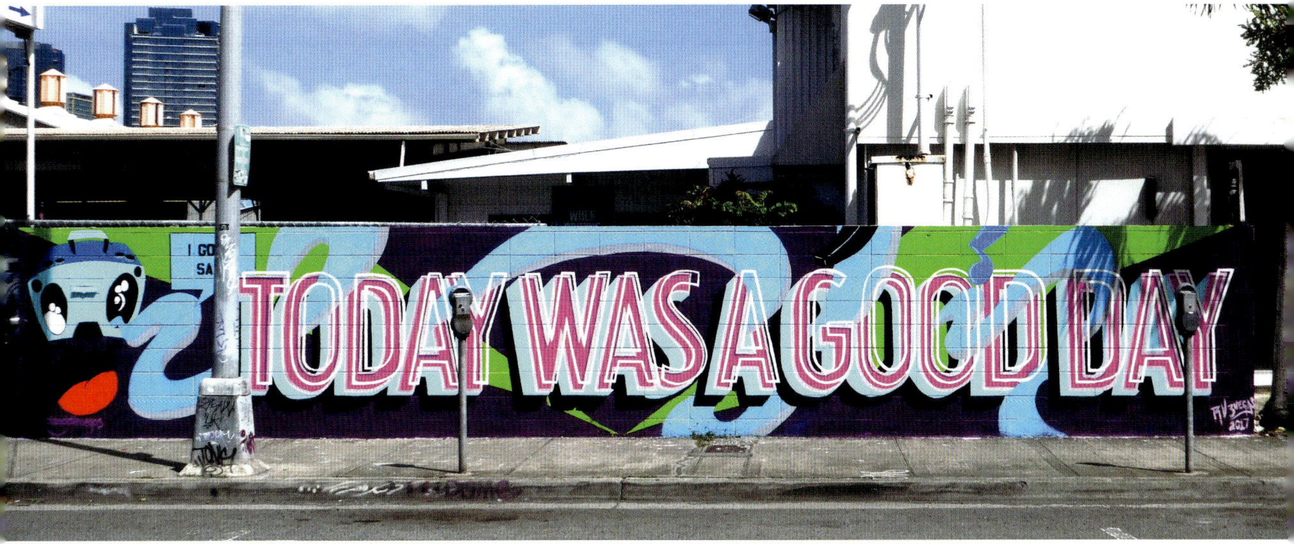

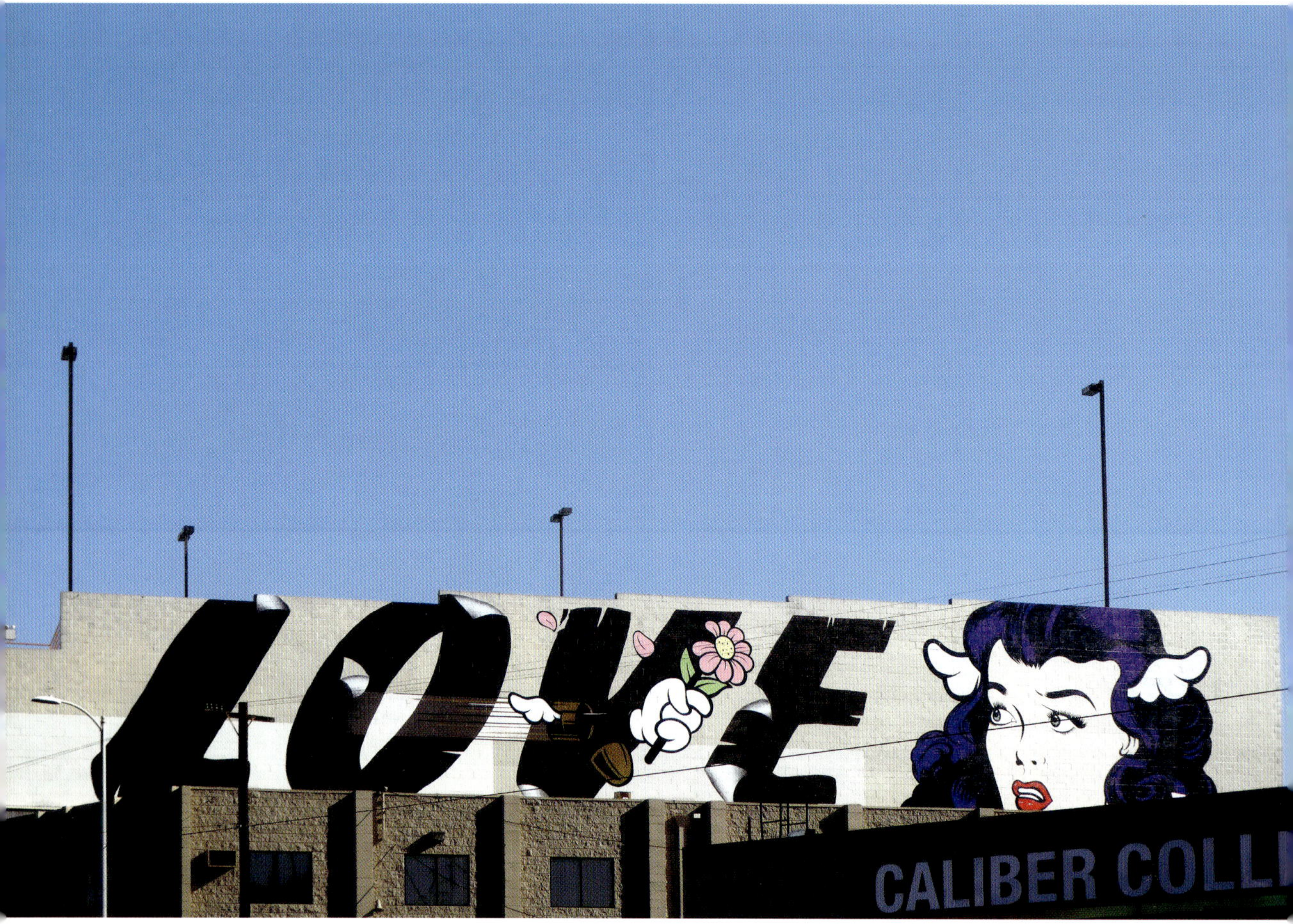
LOVE
CALIBER COLL

Love and Hate

Love is a complex set of abstract emotions and a central theme in the creative arts. It ranges from affection and romance to passion, and from compassion to an appreciation of life's simple pleasures, such as a good meal. In its simplest visual form, love can be expressed by the classic red heart shape that has been used as a metaphor for the concept of love, especially romantic love, since the 19th century.

Expressions of love have a place on walls everywhere, not just in the most romantic cities in the world, but also in ordinary places, amid the grime of everyday life. Artists show us the gentleness of being in love (seen in the meandering love vines painted by in love street art in Paris, p. 32) and celebrate the way love can effect change (Jason Naylor's *Love Can Change the World*, p. 27). And of course, there is the pain of love withheld or withdrawn (WRDSMTH's melancholy message about borrowed love, p. 36).

Sadly love and hate can co-exist, and dying love can become dislike and hatred (cleverly suggested by Dolk's grenade-headed figures, p. 39).

The enormous wall on the opposite page was painted by D*Face and is a single example of the way in which street artists, like others who work in the creative arts, can be inspired by love.

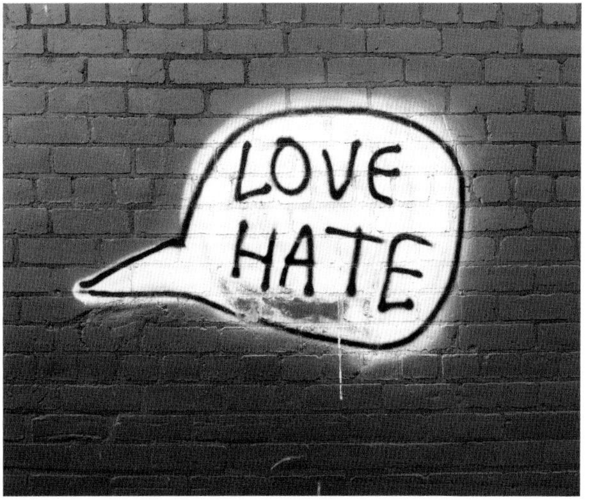

OPPOSITE D*Face, Los Angeles, USA, 2017

RIGHT Unknown artist, Geelong, Australia, 2017

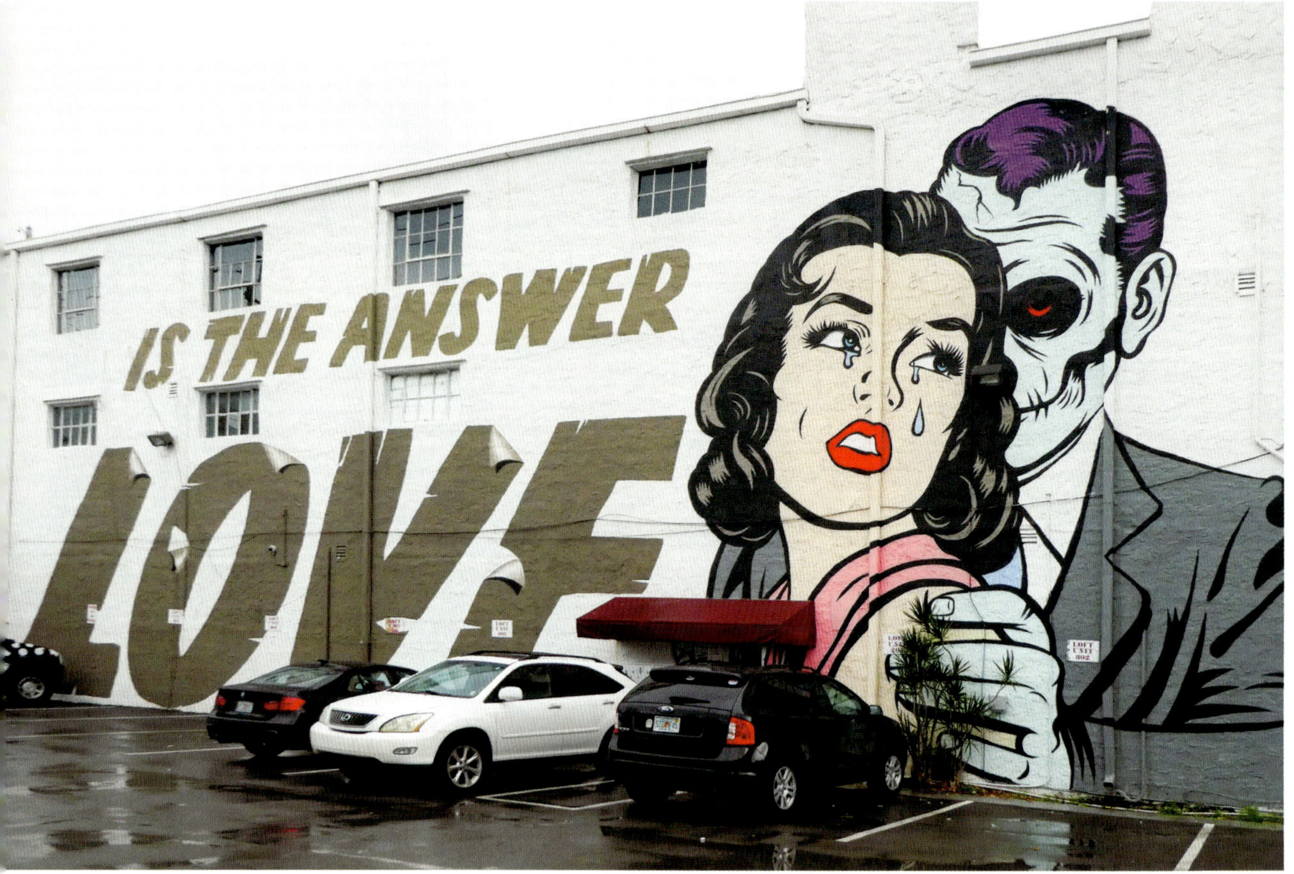
IS THE ANSWER
LOVE

OPPOSITE D*Face, Miami, USA, 2017
TOP Ruben Rojas, Los Angeles, USA, 2017
BOTTOM Unknown artist, Sydney, Australia, 2016

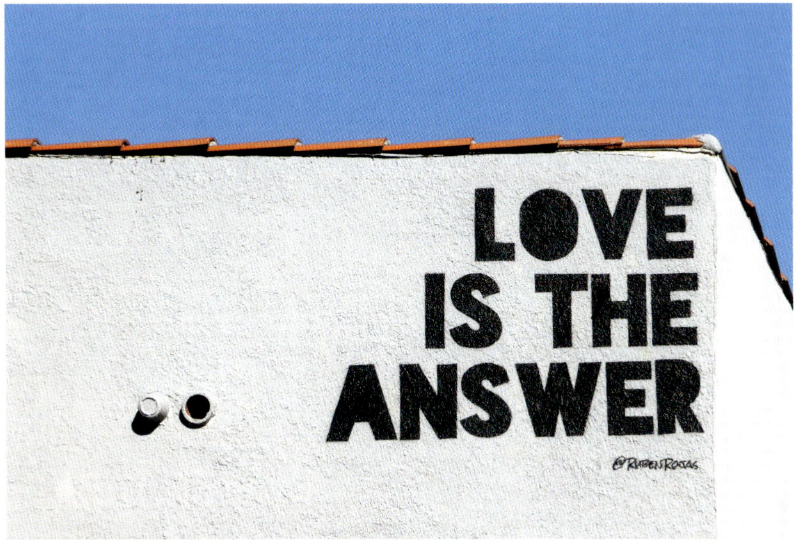

'IS the answer love?' Well, that depends on the question, doesn't it?

Love is a common theme in the enormous works by D*Face, as are the characters in the work opposite, which also explores the theme of death in the midst of life, both sad and romantic.

The two walls on this page have answered his question the same way. At top, Ruben Rojas, a co-founder of Beautify Earth (an agency in Los Angeles that encourages social responsibility through art) uses maximum contrast to add strength to the simple statement. The version at right in Sydney is gutsy and raw.

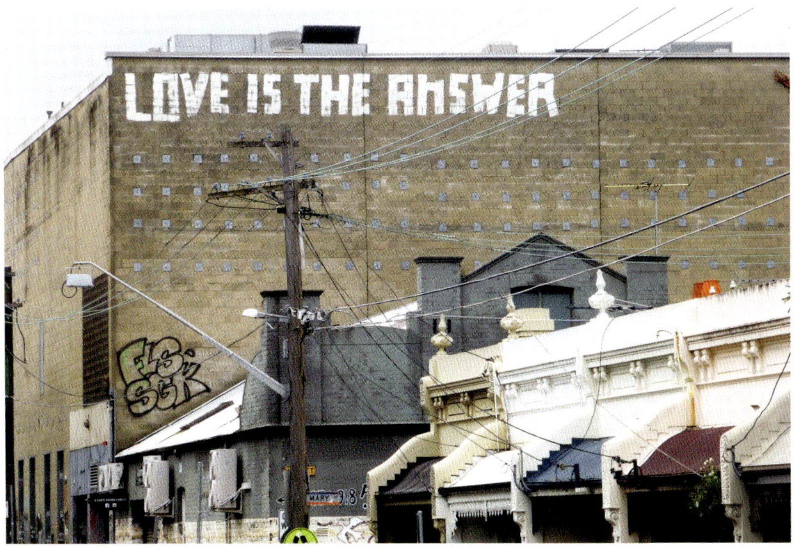

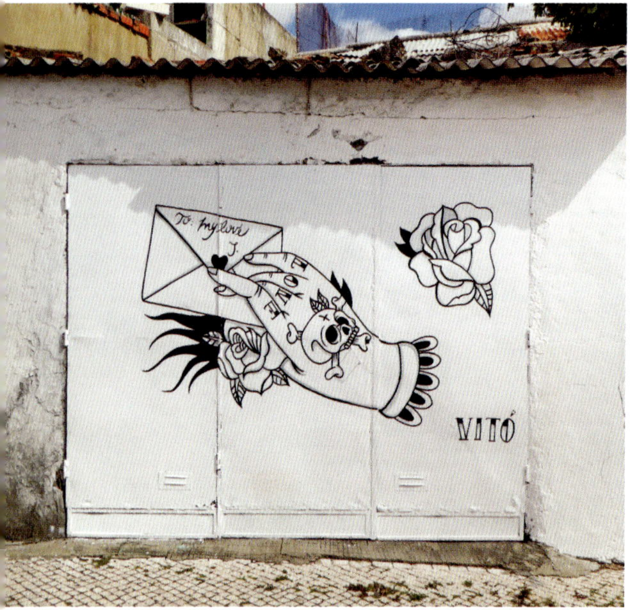
To: my love
J.
VITÓ

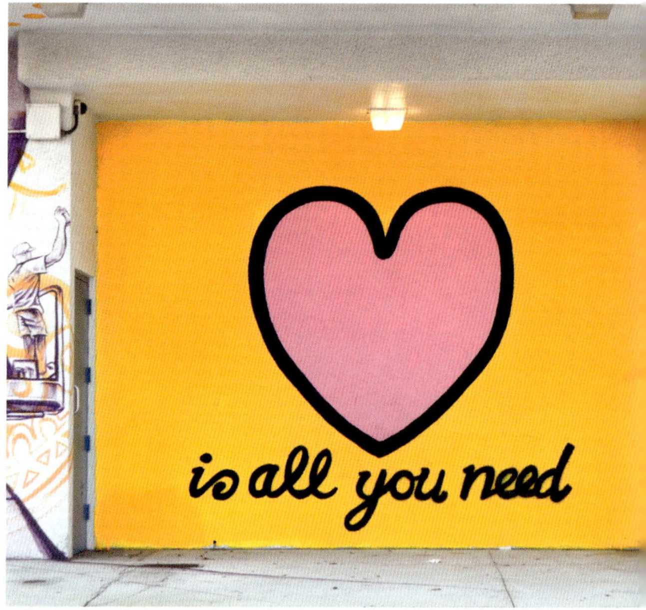
is all you need

EXPRESSIONS of love can be found in every art form, from oil painting to theatre, from poetry to tattoos. At opposite left, Vitó Julião has used distinctive designs such as finger tattoos and the rose to tell a story of 'love' on his painted doors in Lisbon. At opposite right, Briton Ryan Callahan replaces the word love with the universally understood heart symbol and uses clean colour and simple black text to share his positive message, one that echoes the lyrics of the famous 1967 song by the Beatles.

Protestations of love come in all sizes, from the simply drawn white figure at right bearing a small heart that was scrawled quickly onto an already image-saturated wall to Jason Naylor's heart-warming message below, with its vibrant colours emerging from a rich black background.

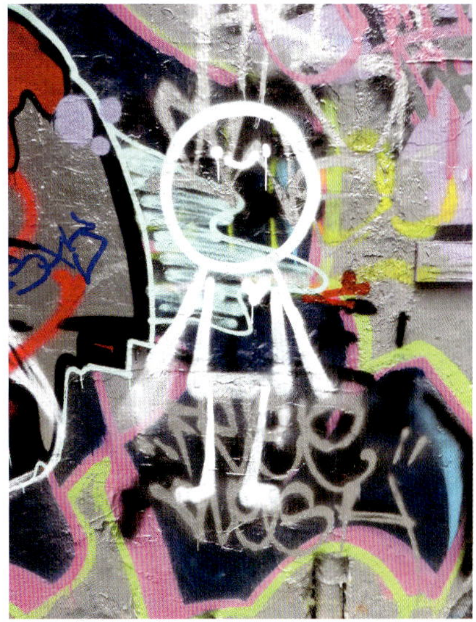

OPPOSITE LEFT Vitó Julião, *To: My Love*, Lisbon, Portugal, 2016

OPPOSITE RIGHT Ryan Callahan, Miami, USA, 2017

TOP Unknown artist, Melbourne, Australia, 2017

BOTTOM Jason Naylor, New York City, USA, 2018

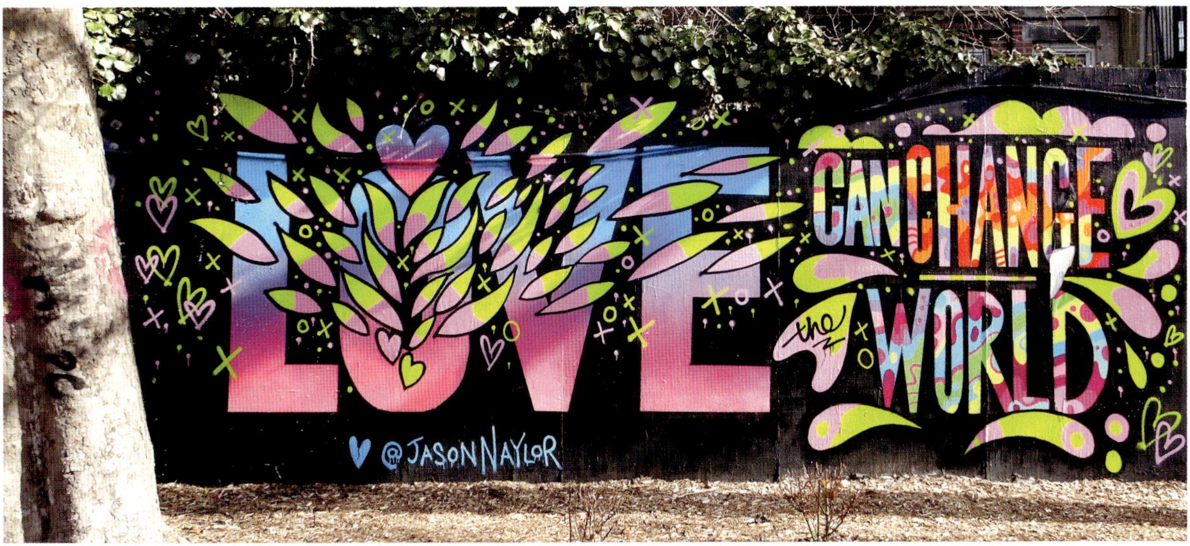

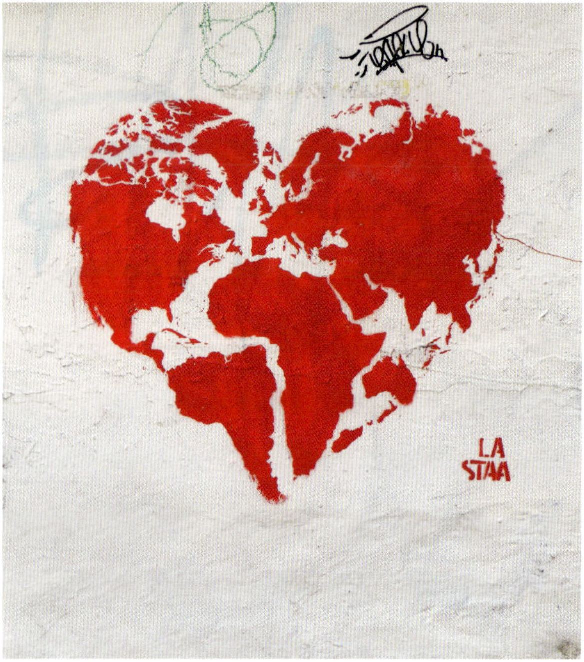

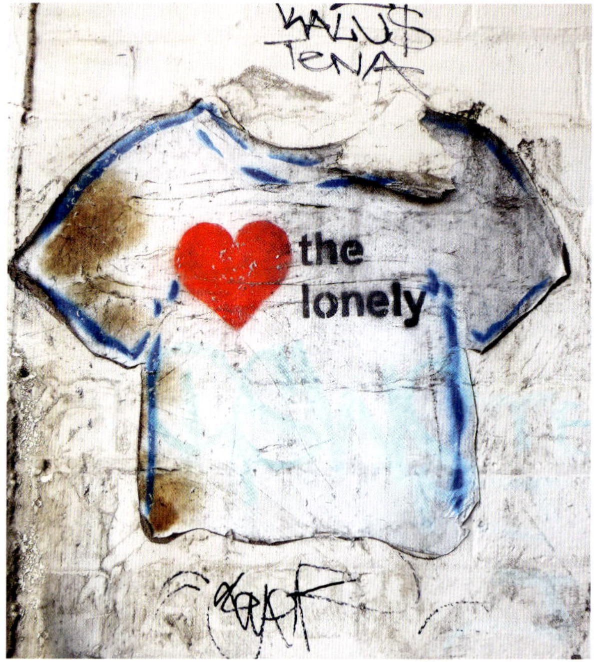

LEFT La Staa, *One*, Bergen, Norway, 2016

RIGHT Unknown artist, Melbourne, Australia, 2014

OPPOSITE TeneT and drsc0, *Love Is a Serious Mental Disease*, Melbourne, Australia, 2016

THE Norwegian street artist La Staa combined the heart symbol with a map of the world in a striking red design. Is it broken or coming together? As with all street art, our reading will depend on our perspective. The heart stencilled on the sprayed t-shirt reminds us that we all need love.

A big pink heart sits behind TeneT and drsc0's paste-up of Plato and his saying 'Love is a serious mental disease'. Plato's adage reinforces how difficult it can be to remain objective and rational when emotions are in control.

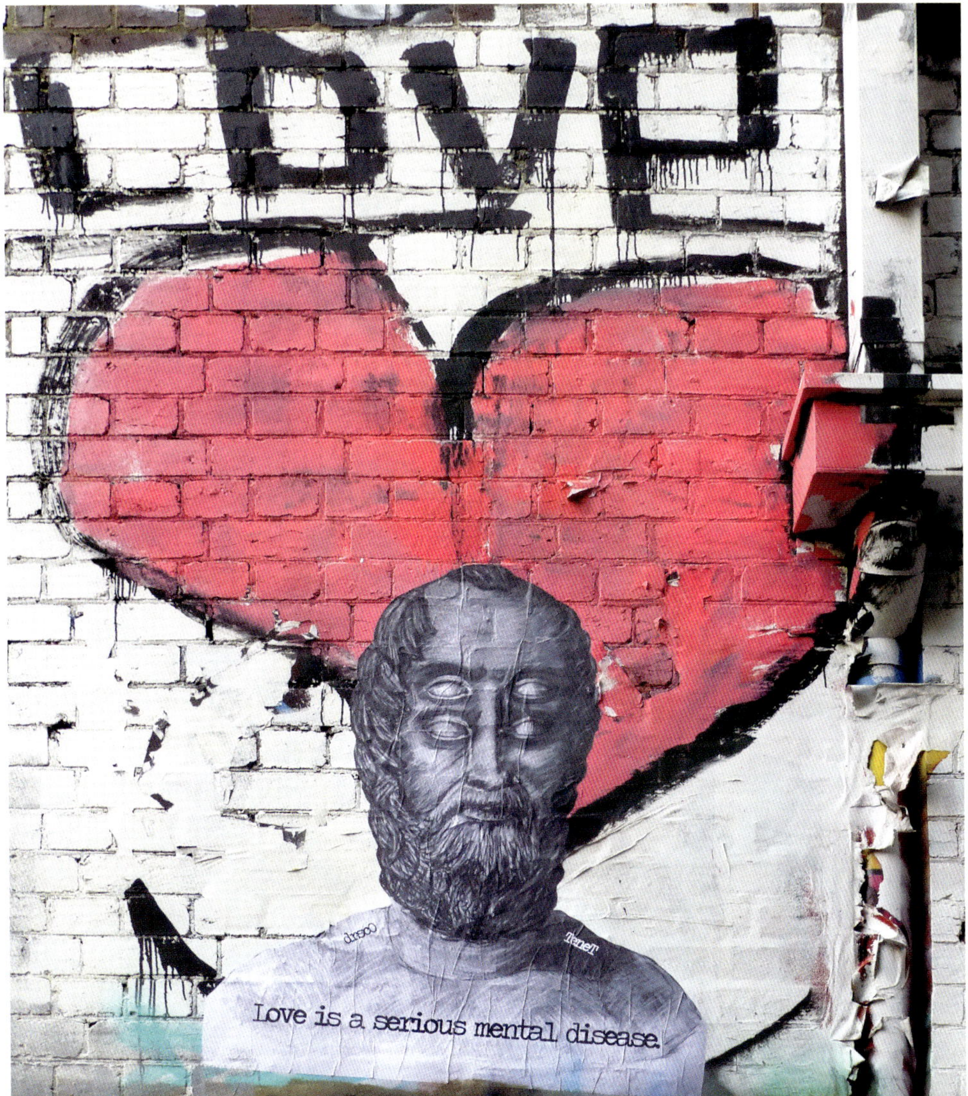
Love is a serious mental disease.

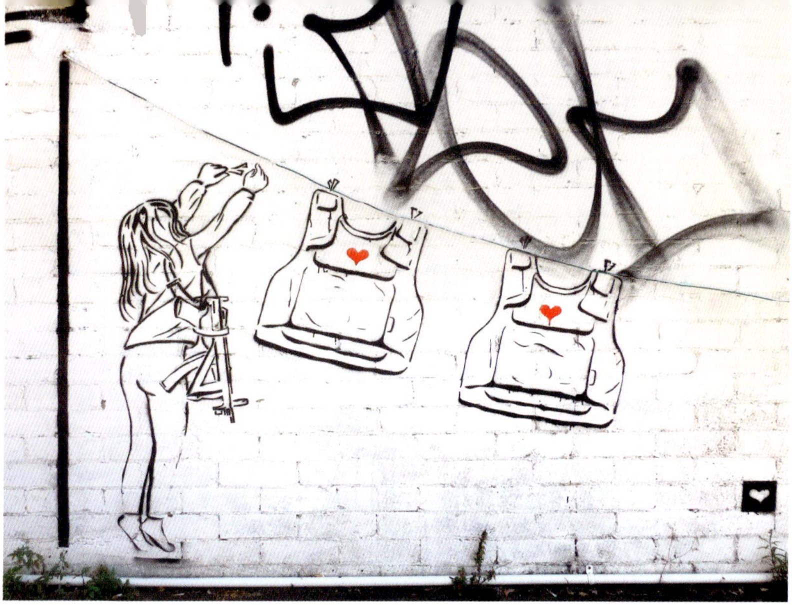

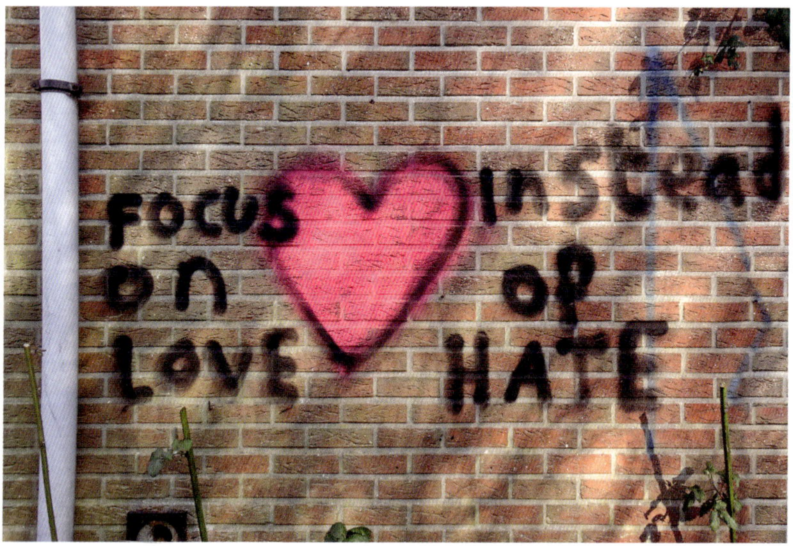

TOP Unknown artist, Sydney, Australia, 2017

BOTTOM Unknown artist, Doel, Belgium, 2018

OPPOSITE Boa Mistura, *Undying Love*, Zaragoza, Spain, 2016

THE universal symbol for the heart has been used in the two works to the left. There is ambiguity in the hearts stencilled onto the flak jackets being hung out to dry by a machine gun–toting child. If you look closely you will see that the artist has used a wire on the wall as the clothesline. There is, however, no doubt about the meaning of the message sprayed on a wall in the town of Doel. Slated for demolition to expand the port of Antwerp, the ghost town has become a haven for street artists.

Boa Mistura declares undying love with a combination of reality and symbolism, but here, too, there is uncertainty in the message, due to the fusion of images that reflect both life and death. It was painted on a wall in Zaragoza that abuts a disused and neglected urban space being rehabilitated as part of a project called *Esto no es un solar*.

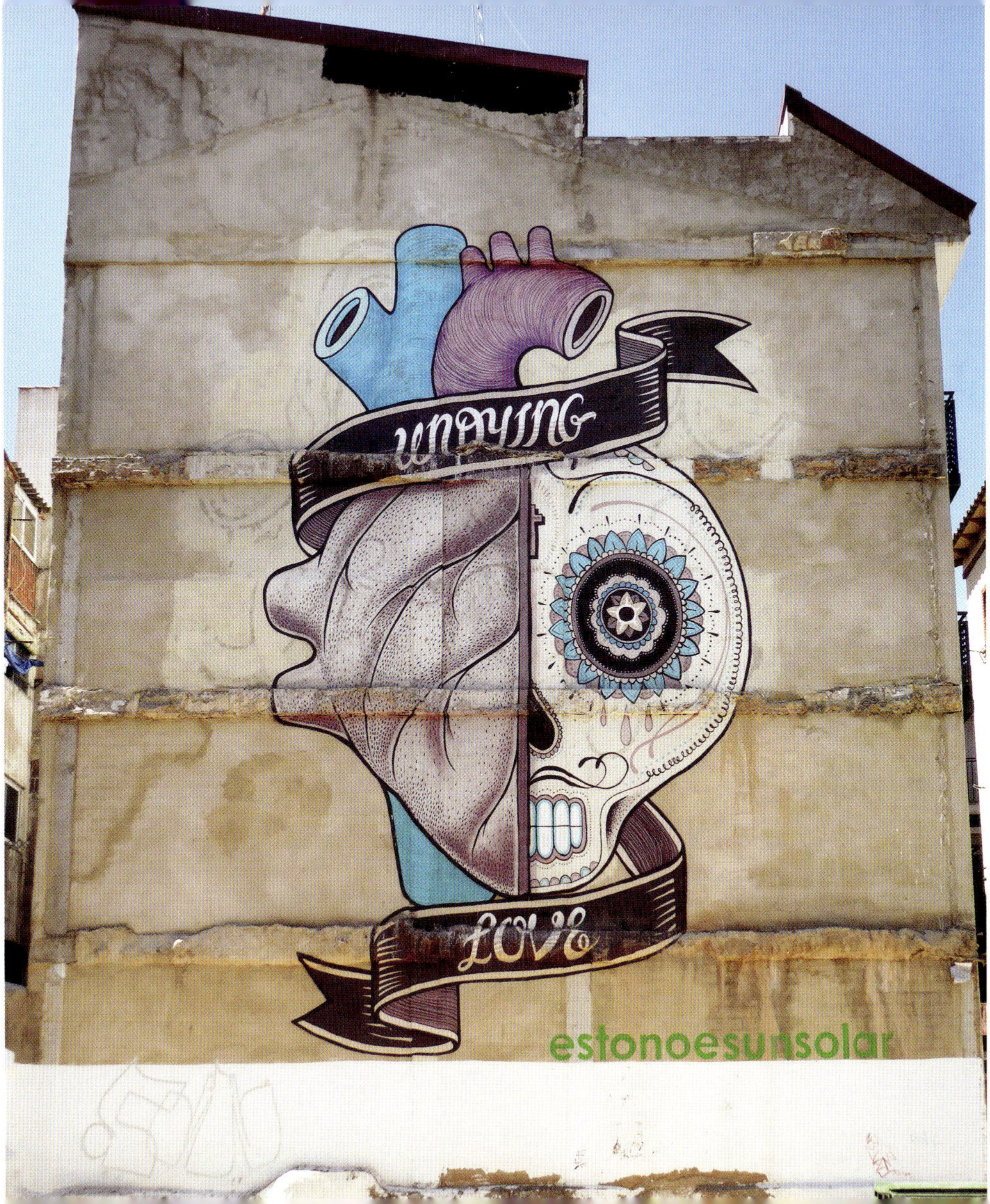
undying
love
estonoesunsolar

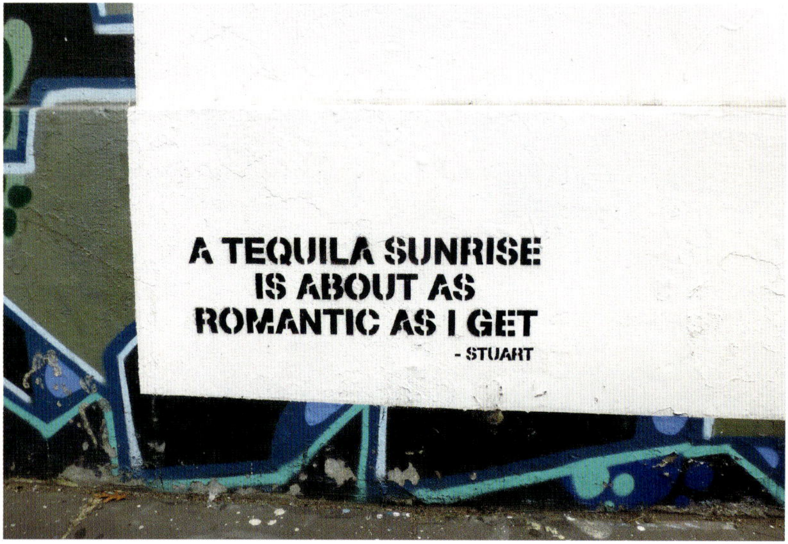

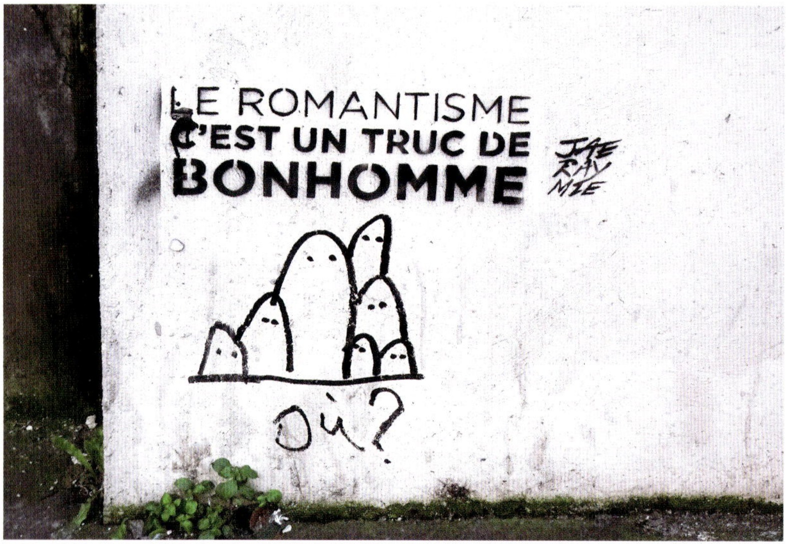

TOP LEFT Stuart, Melbourne, Australia, 2015

BOTTOM LEFT Jaeraymie (text only), Paris, France, 2018

RIGHT in love street art, *Arbres Coeurs*, Paris, France, 2018

OPPOSITE LEFT Unknown artist, Barcelona, Spain, 2016

OPPOSITE RIGHT Unknown artist, Rio de Janeiro, Brazil, 2012

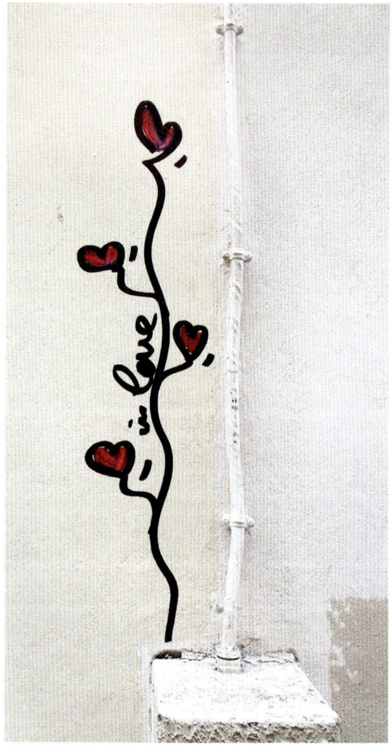

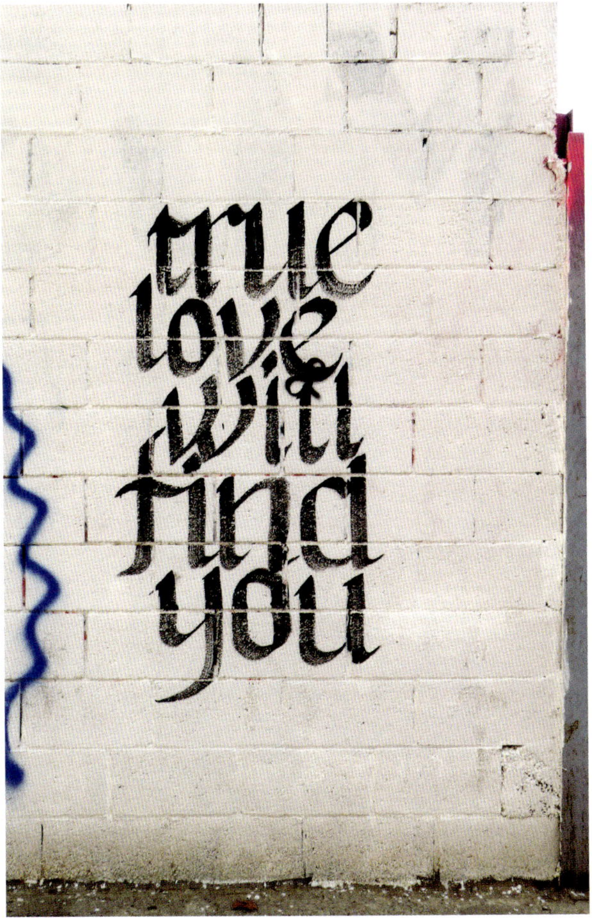

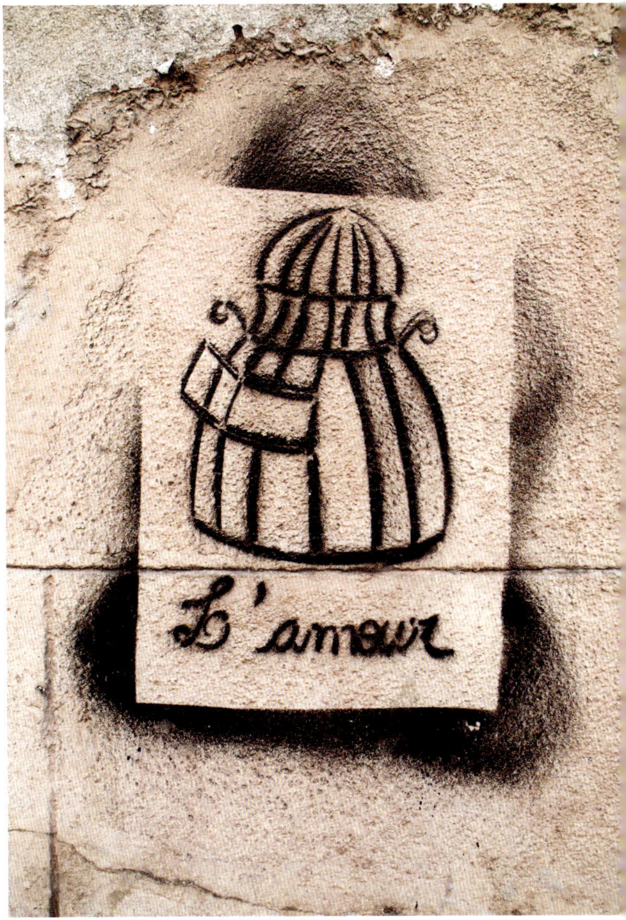

THESE pages contain simple text that talks about universal concepts and feelings. One interpretation of Jaeraymie's quote at opposite bottom left is 'romance is a guy thing', a sentiment that could be questioned by many women. And a tequila sunrise – yes, it may be romantic for some. Both remind us that there are no hard and fast rules about what IS romantic; surely love and romance are in the heart and mind of the lover. The gently climbing vine bearing love hearts is typical of the meandering lines painted by the anonymous Parisian love activist named *in love street art*. It recognises the simple joy of love.

The open cage above could be interpreted as an injunction to 'set your heart free' or alternatively to 'let love go'.

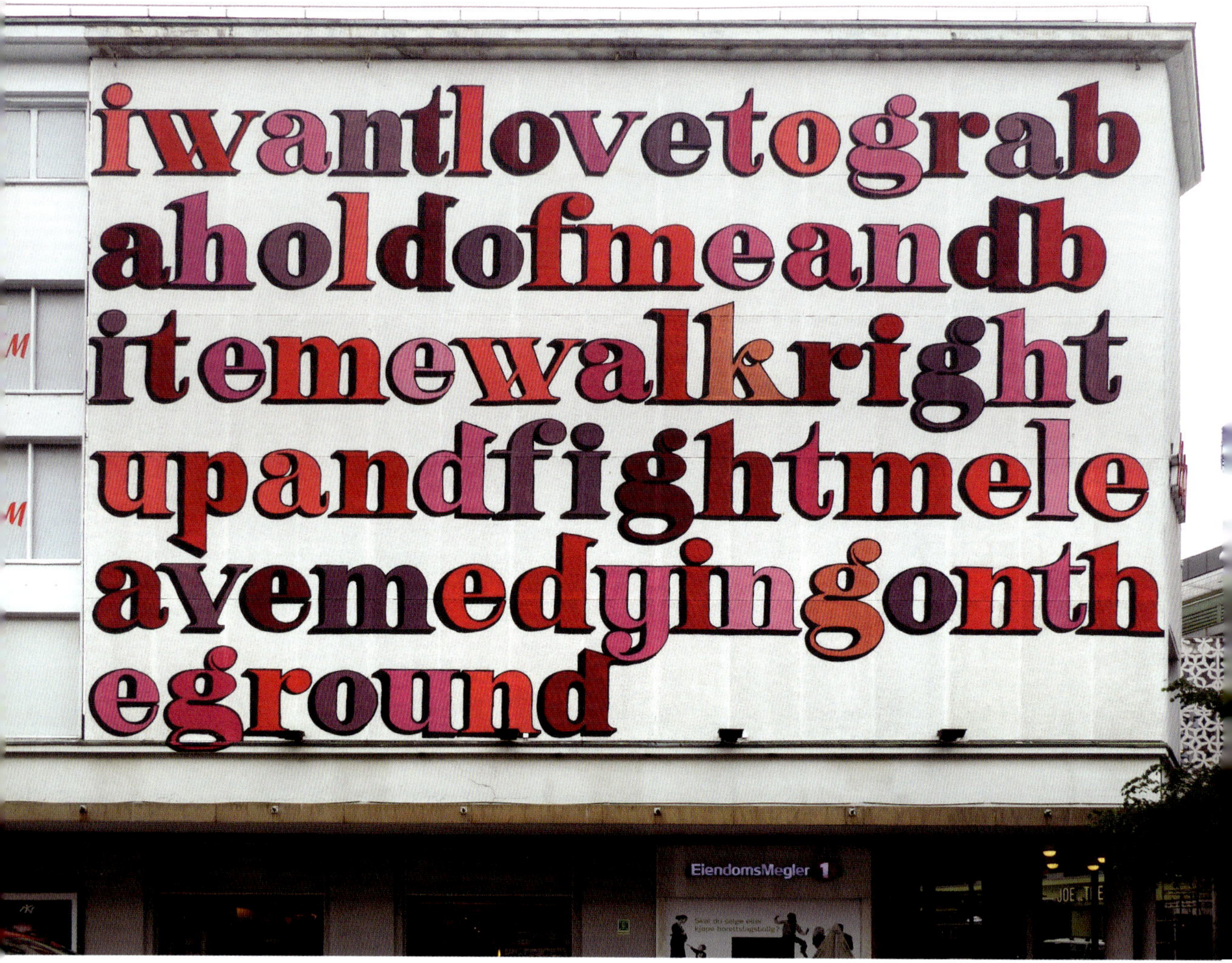
iwantlovetograb
aholdofmeandb
itemewalkright
upandfightmele
avemedyingonth
eground
EiendomsMegler 1

OPPOSITE Ben Eine, *Love Interruption*, Stavanger, Norway, 2016
LEFT Unknown artist, Melbourne, Australia, 2014
RIGHT Lov3 and Baby Guerrilla, Melbourne, Australia, 2014

BEN Eine used the lyrics from 'Love Interruption' by Jack White as the text for his typographical work in Stavanger (opposite). His technique of running the letters together forces the viewer to stop and concentrate before being rewarded by understanding. The bold colours and shadowed serif font add a further layer of strength to the compelling statement of the power of love.

The unofficial collaboration (at right) between Lov3 and Baby Guerrilla combines text and image to share a similar message. The same protestation of love is expressed below in a rather less romantic manner and on a much humbler scale.

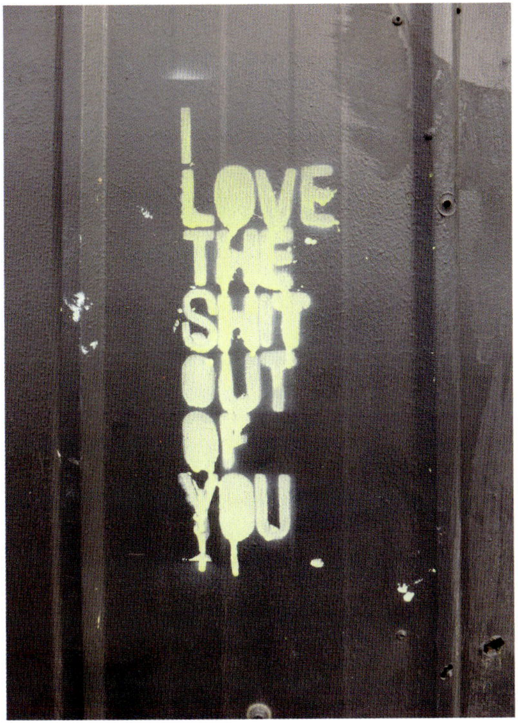

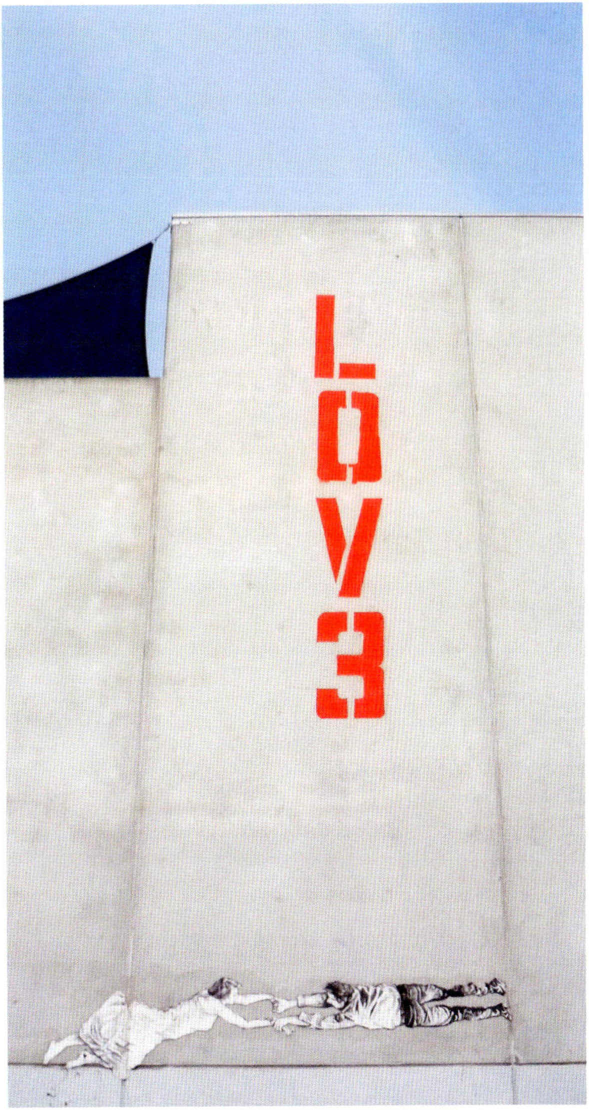

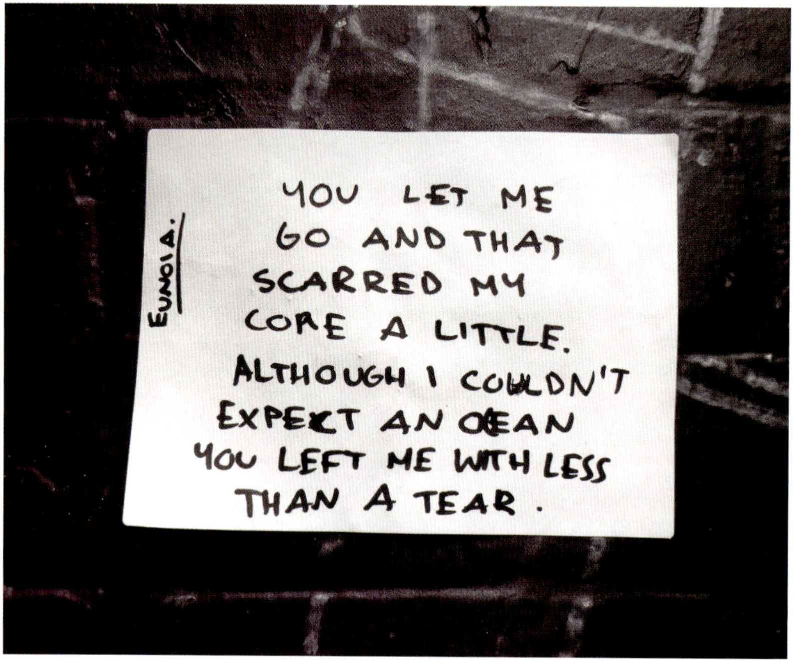

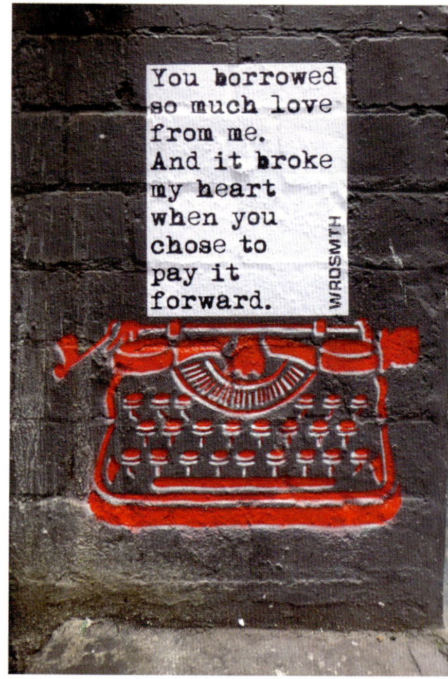

THE experience of love ranges from joy and euphoria to heartbreak and desolation. This makes it an inspirational theme for poetry and its street cousin. From stardust in the eyes to the depths of despair, thoughts and feelings can be distilled by the poet into a minimum of words. This applies particularly to heartbreak – one of the favourite subjects of poetry and the inspiration for the two works above.

The pain of fearing that love isn't permanent can be felt in Cept's Pop Art–inspired image, opposite left, of the superhero and his heroine. In cel out's paste-up, the redacted words add an extra touch of pathos to the message that eludes Joe.

LEFT Eunoia, Melbourne, Australia, 2013

RIGHT WRDSMTH, Melbourne, Australia, 2015

OPPOSITE LEFT Cept, London, UK, 2015

OPPOSITE RIGHT cel out, *Love Redacted*, Melbourne, Australia, 2014

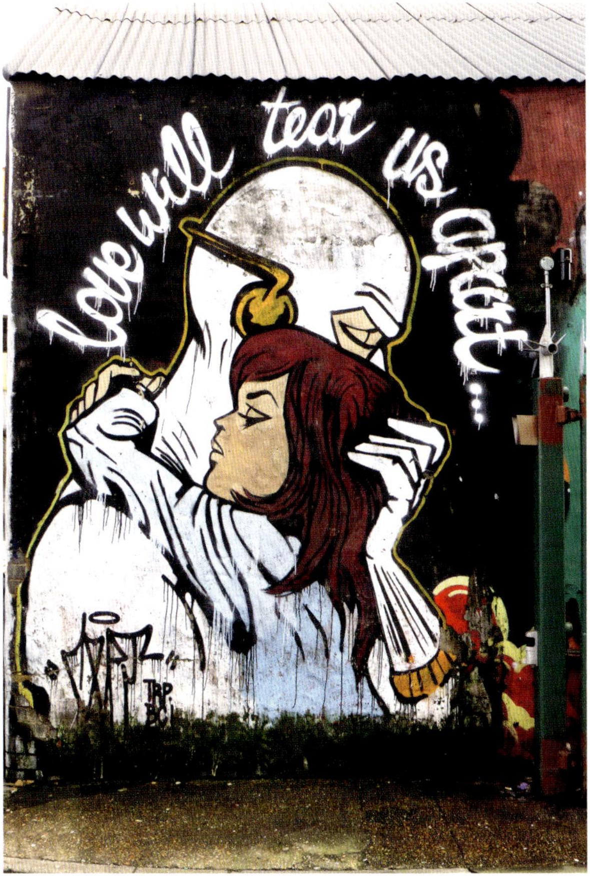
love will tear us apart...

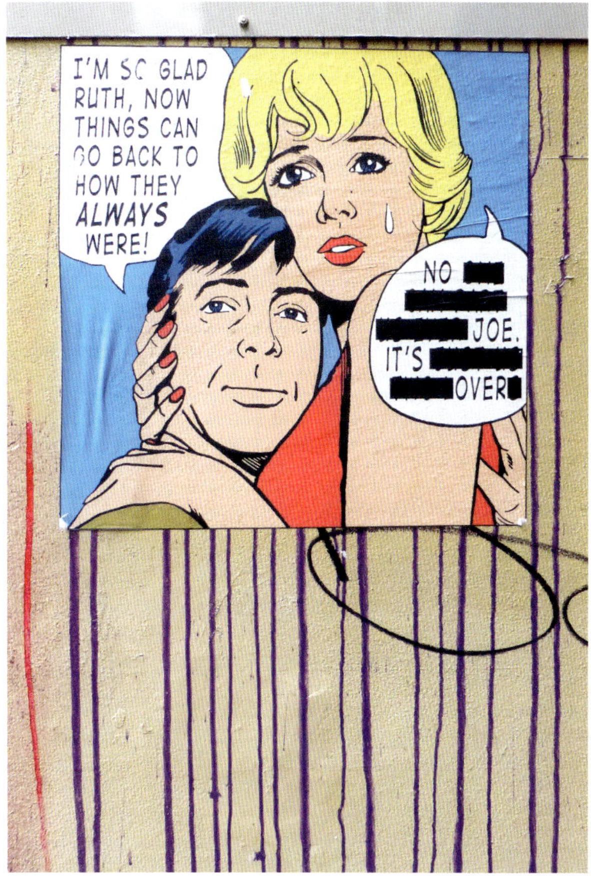
I'M SO GLAD RUTH, NOW THINGS CAN GO BACK TO HOW THEY ALWAYS WERE!
NO JOE. IT'S OVER

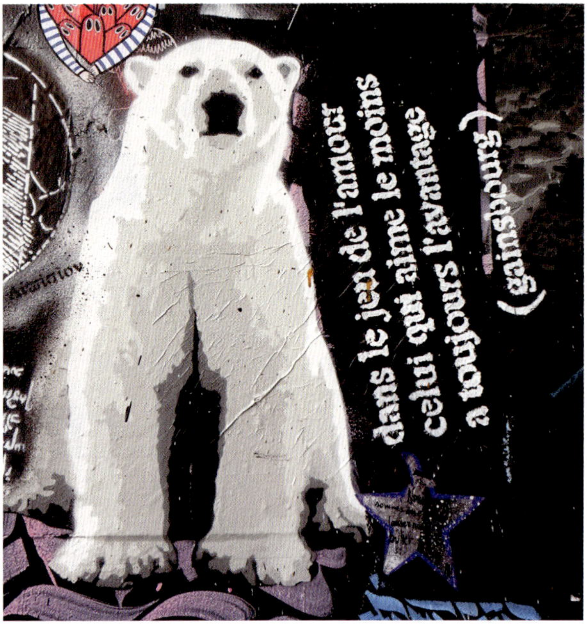

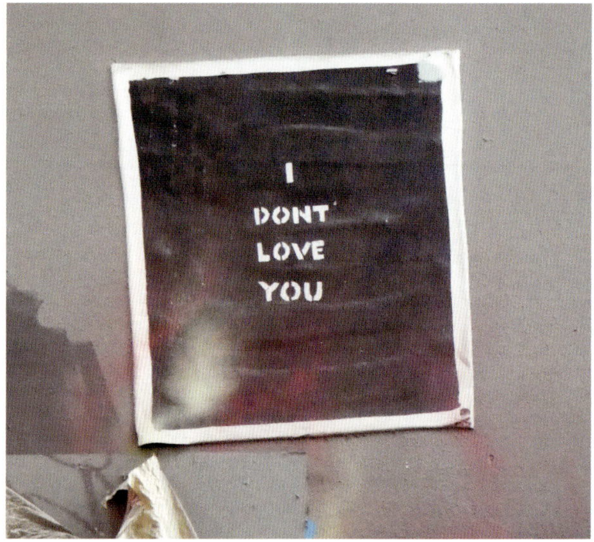

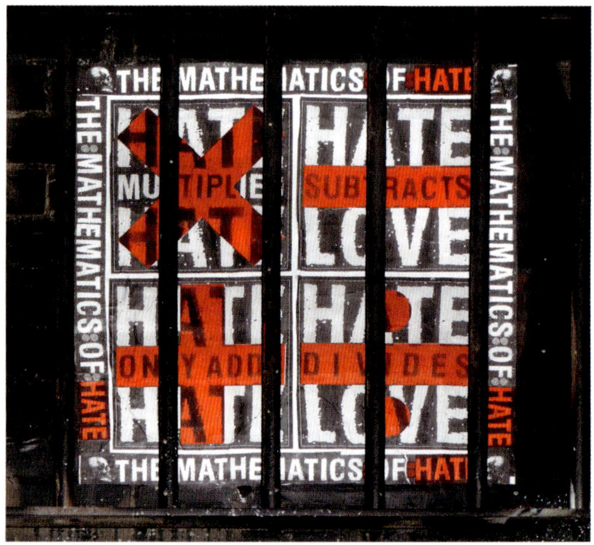

THE downside of love is expressed in each of these images. The quote attributed to Serge Gainsbourg above translates from the French to 'in the game of love, the one who loves the least always has the advantage', while the anonymous paste-up *I Dont Love You* (above right) is all the sadder for its lack of explanation. Phoenix's paste-up (at right) is a work from his series *The Mathematics of Fear*, one of a number of series collectively titled *In the Land of the Blind*.

Dolk (whose street art name is the Norwegian word for dagger) is a stencil artist who uses humour in his observations of life. The message behind his grenade-headed figures is obvious. Its unexpectedness may even make us smile. Love CAN be like a grenade, ready to explode.

LEFT SST Division (text only), Paris, France, 2018

TOP RIGHT Unknown artist, Melbourne, Australia, 2017

BOTTOM RIGHT Phoenix, Melbourne, Australia, 2012

OPPOSITE Dolk, Stavanger, Norway, 2016

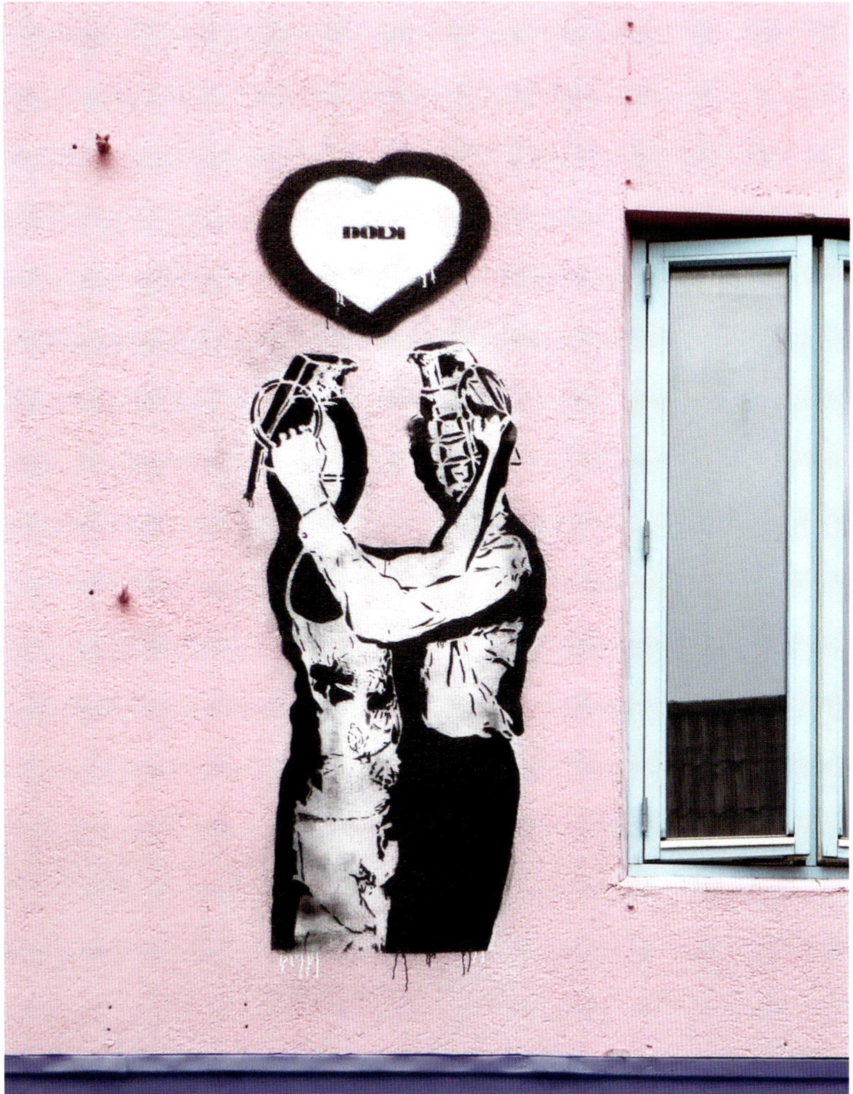
DOLK

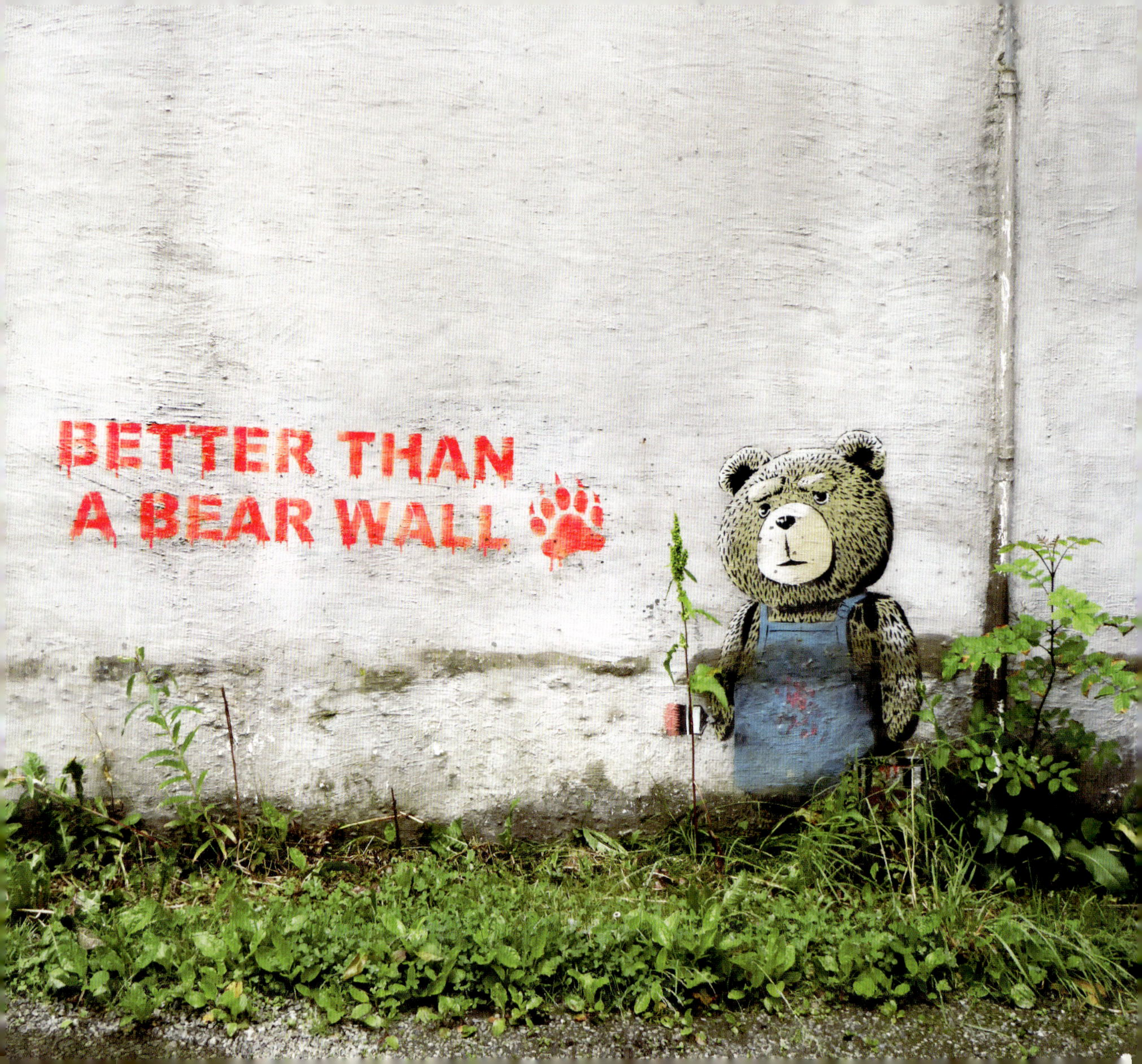
BETTER THAN
A BEAR WALL

LOL

No – LOL doesn't mean Lots of Love. It also doesn't refer to the online video game League of Legends. In this context the acronym stands for Laugh Out Loud. LOL binds this collection of laugh-out-loud funny images and those that are light-hearted, quirky and uplifting.

Humour has been an important element in art since the Dada and Surrealist artists of the early 20th century encouraged the viewer to think in terms of irony, satire and subversion of meaning. That trend has continued and we see it in much of the work painted or pasted on walls, fences, hoardings and the backs of street signs.

In the context of street art, humour can be based on familiar imagery taken out of context, like Falko One's *Enjoy a Joke* parody of Coca-Cola advertising (p. 48). It can be witty word and image play, such as *Better than a Bear Wall* by JPS (opposite), or it can engage with its physical location, like the Fruit Tingles lamppost (p. 50). It often laughs at life. We can see this in Zabou's *Have Some Fun!* (p. 67). It could simply be gentle and whimsical, like Hayley Welsh's fanciful characters (p. 59). Juxtaposition, ambiguity and visual puns may make us chuckle or indeed laugh-out-loud as they satirise or criticise the world we live in. Humour can also be used to access difficult themes, presenting a softer approach to issues that test us.

Scribbles by people who have passed by before us can add humour to an otherwise serious work or even to an object in the streetscape, like the faces we might see drawn or sprayed onto unexpected surfaces.

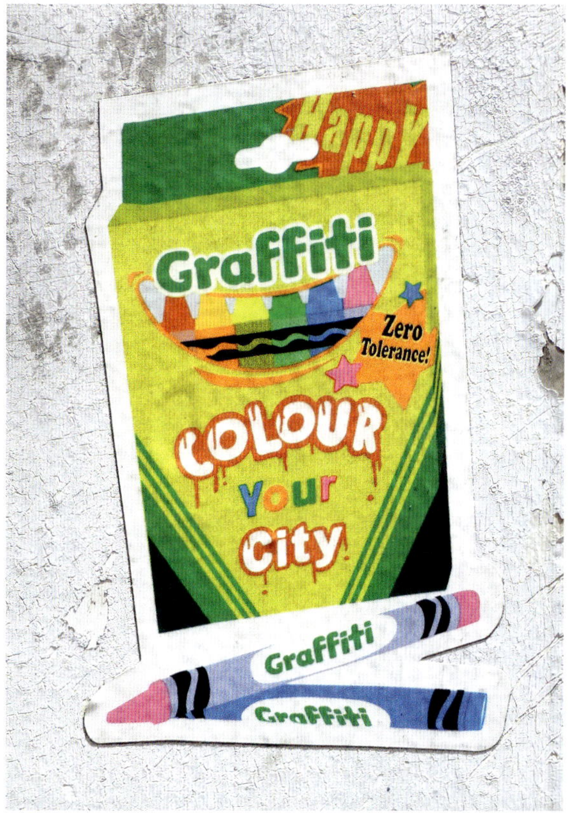

OPPOSITE JPS, Stavanger, Norway, 2016

RIGHT Happy, Tokyo, Japan, 2014

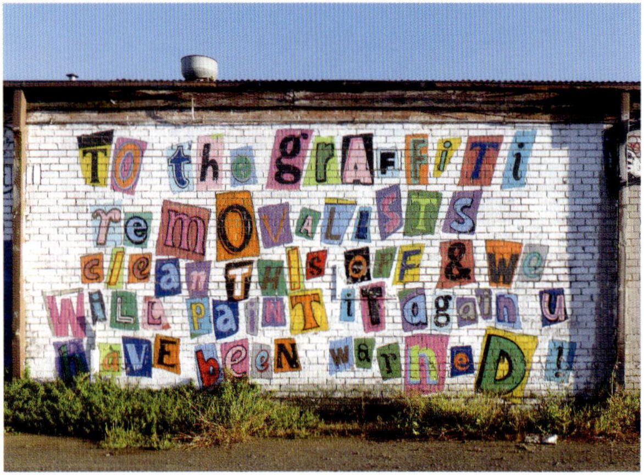

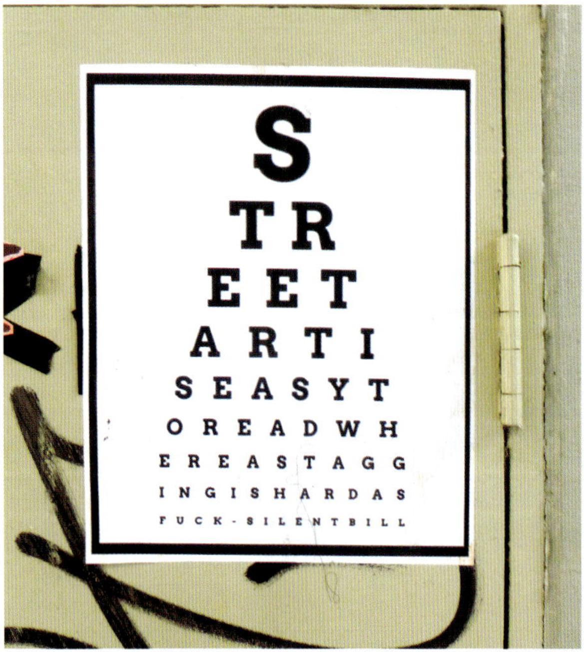

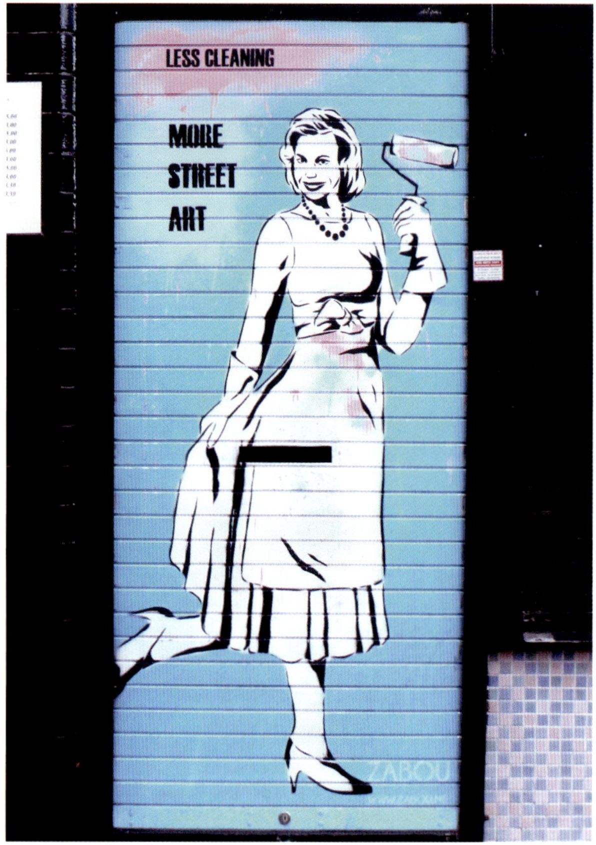

TOP LEFT Lushsux, Melbourne, Australia, 2018

BOTTOM LEFT Silent Bill, Melbourne, Australia, 2018

RIGHT Zabou (2014), London, UK, 2015

OPPOSITE LEFT Unknown artist, Sydney, Australia, 2016

OPPOSITE RIGHT Banksy (1999), Bristol, UK, 2015

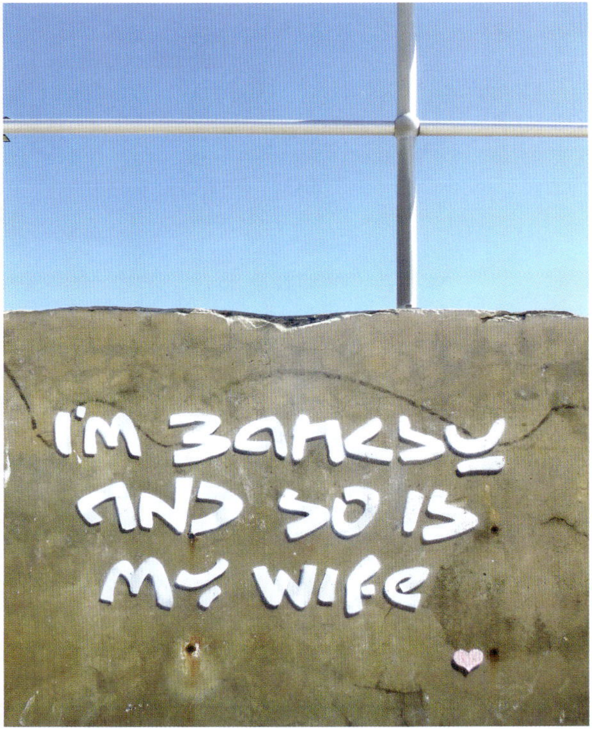

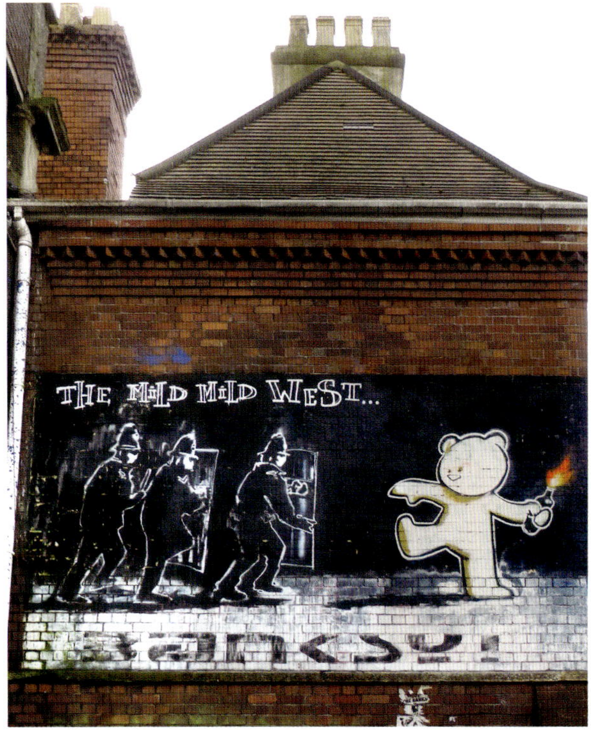

THESE images show us that street art doesn't always take itself seriously. On the opposite page, we can see three artists make statements in their very different styles. Like Banksy, Melbourne-based artist Lushsux prefers to remain anonymous. His warning to graffiti cleaners at top left uses a collage technique we recognise from crime fiction. Silent Bill is the founder of an international artists' collective known as The Secret Society of Super Villain Artists and is the self-proclaimed 'People's Artist'. The collective utilises humour in their paste-ups to draw attention to community issues and attitudes. French artist Zabou is based in London and creates aerosol work with a wry vintage quality such as the retro housewife wielding a roller.

While Banksy is using dark humour for serious social commentary in his home town of Bristol, above right, the unsigned stencil on Sydney's Bondi Beach Graffiti Wall (above left) reflects the street art community's appreciation of Banksy's anonymity and sense of humour.

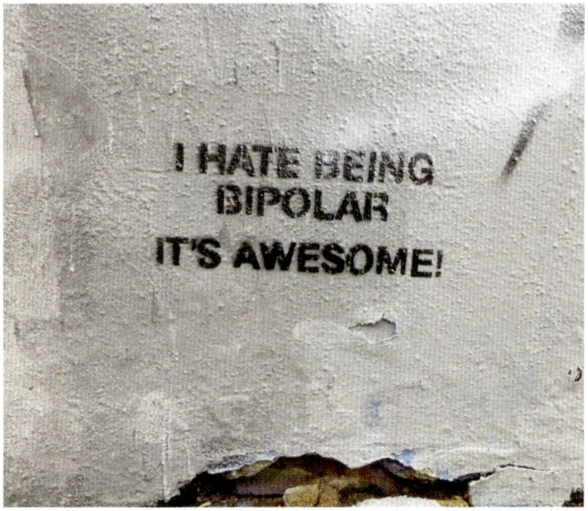

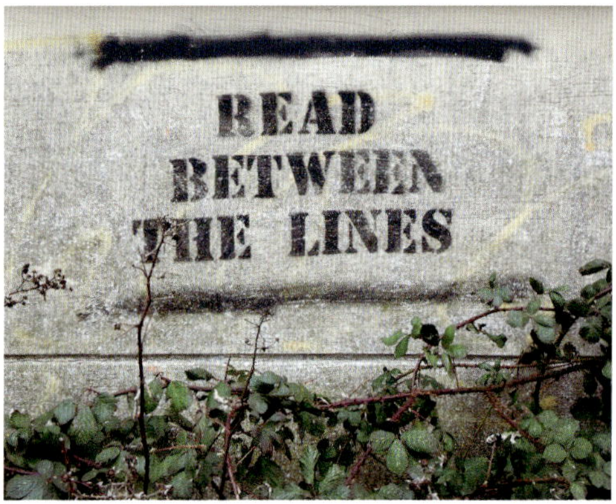

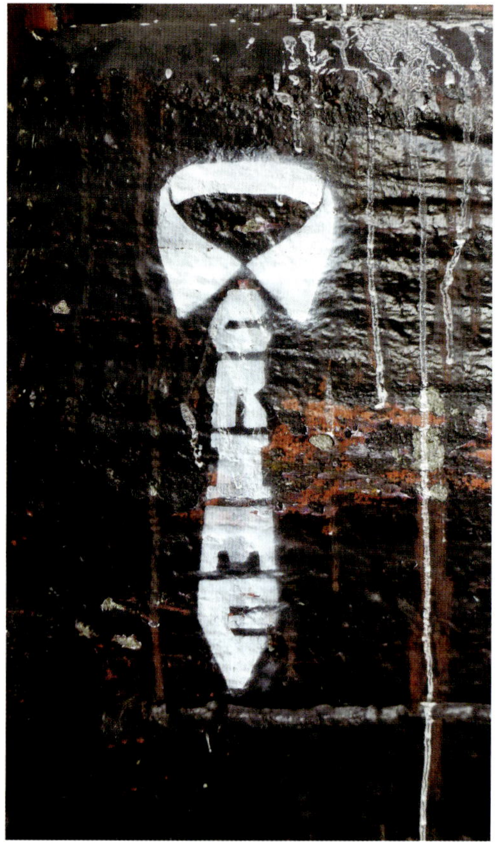

TOP LEFT Unknown artist, Melbourne, Australia, 2014
BOTTOM LEFT Unknown artist, Ghent, Belgium, 2018
RIGHT Unknown artist, Dunedin, New Zealand, 2015
OPPOSITE Rigo 23, San Francisco, USA, 2017

PLAYING with words and phrases that are part of everyday language can be fun. The obvious contradiction in 'I hate being bipolar It's awesome!' depends on our understanding of bipolar disorder. 'Read between the lines' has been sprayed onto the wall – between lines, of course. And a minimal image coupled with one simple word is enough to evoke the concept of white collar crime.

Rigo 23 is well known for his huge and witty murals which use the conventions of street signs. Opposite they add to the cleverness of the clearly accurate directions painted above a private carpark in San Francisco's Mission District.

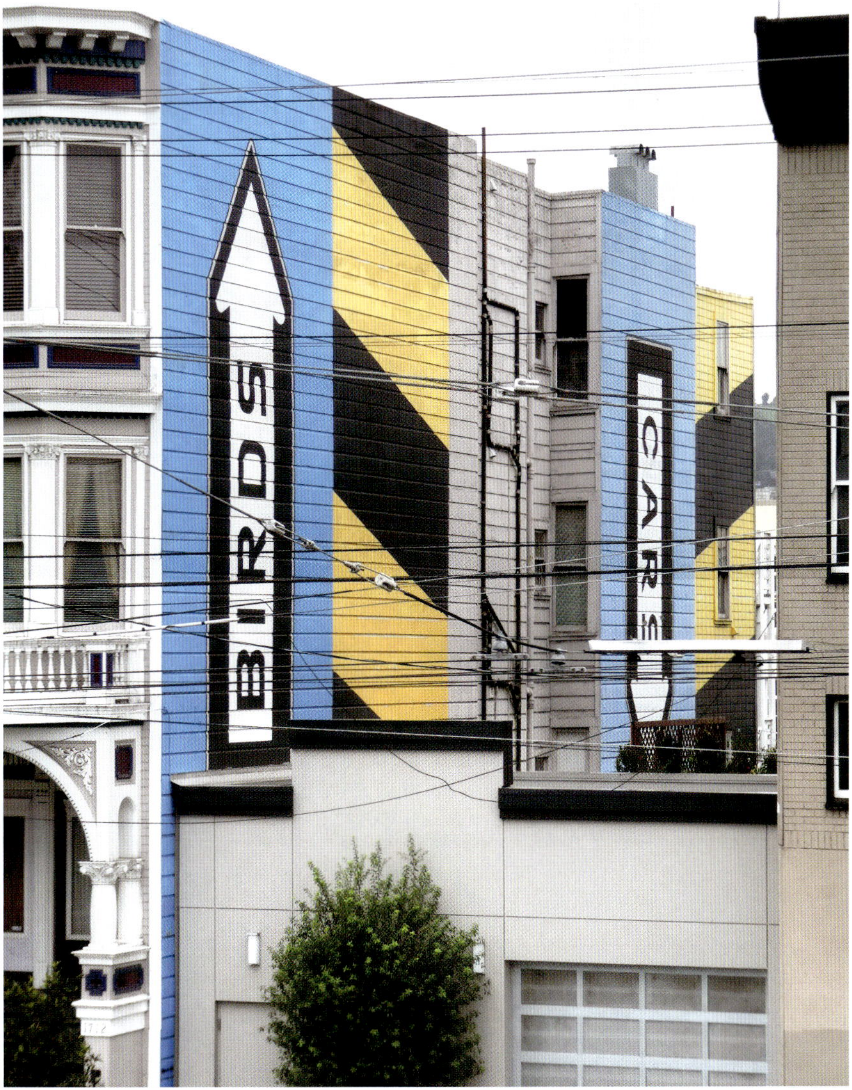
BIRDS
CARS

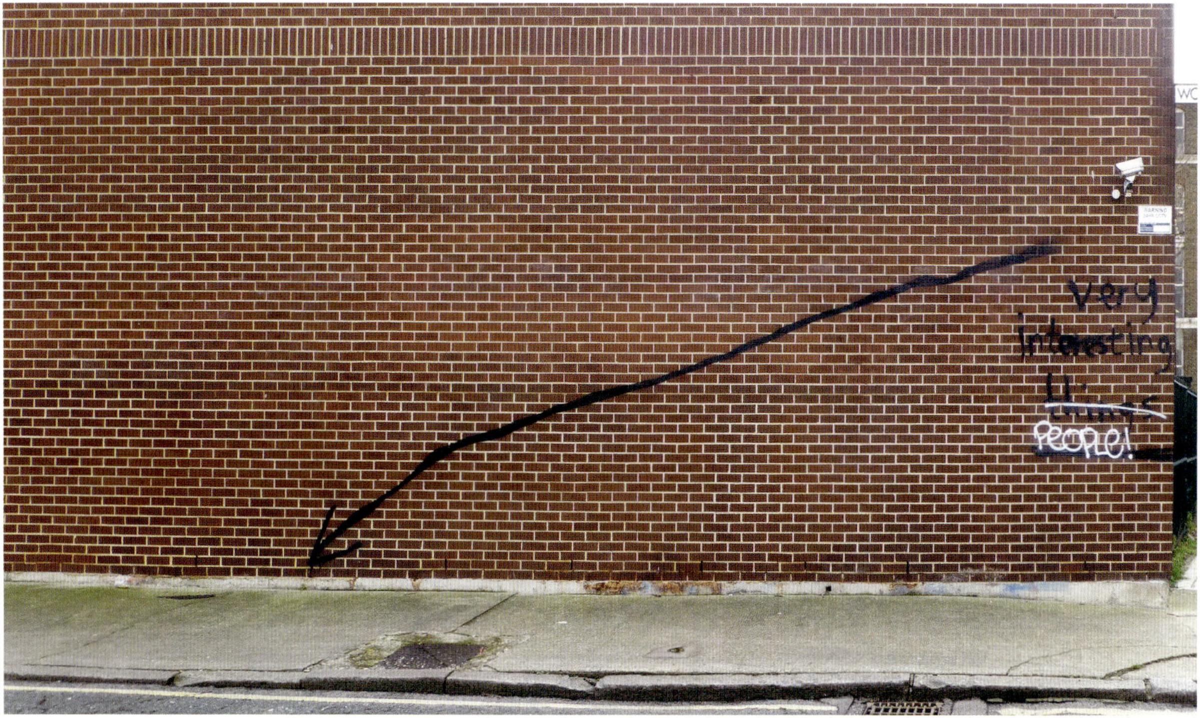

ABOVE Unknown artist, London, UK, 2015

OPPOSITE TOP LEFT cel out, *Neighbourhood Watched*, Melbourne, Australia, 2017

OPPOSITE TOP RIGHT Unknown artist, Melbourne, Australia, 2012

OPPOSITE BOTTOM Unknown artist, Melbourne, Australia, 2013

CCTV is an increasingly intrusive part of life in our cities – we ARE being watched. While it may make us feel safer, the concept and practice of surveillance also compromises our privacy. It has been a source of commentary and humour for artists for many years. On the opposite page we see works that show contemporary reality in a way that makes us chuckle, including cameras zooming in on bill posters, watched by Bill Gates and Bill Murray.

The same message is shared by the intervention above on a wall in London, where the camera is watching 'very interesting ~~things~~ people!' On the other side of the world, paste-up artist cel out created a meme of the Australian Neighbourhood Watch program logo, opposite top left, that included a closed circuit camera as another 'watcher'.

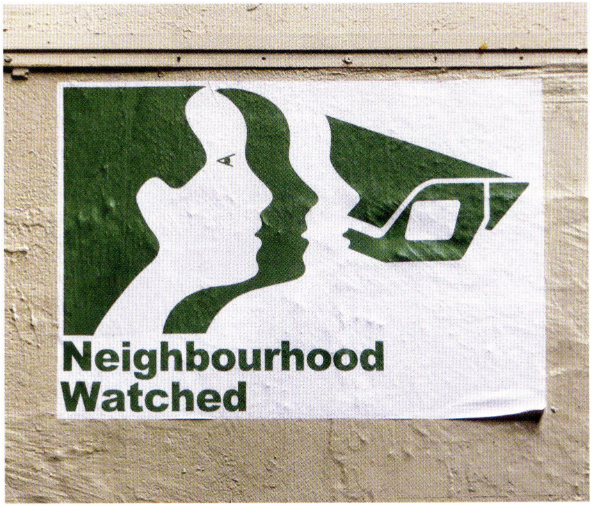
Neighbourhood
Watched

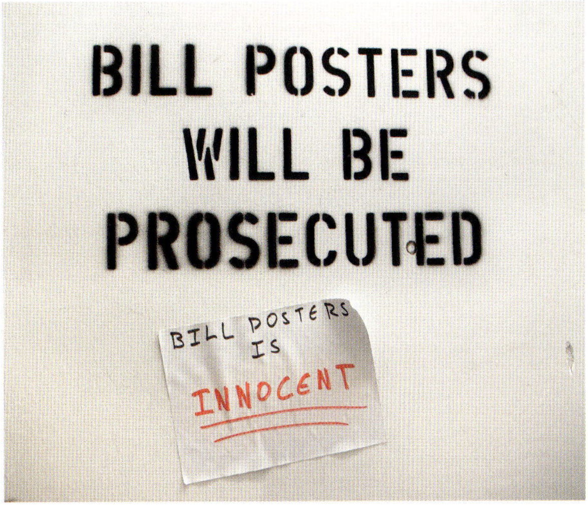
BILL POSTERS
WILL BE
PROSECUTED
BILL POSTERS
IS
INNOCENT

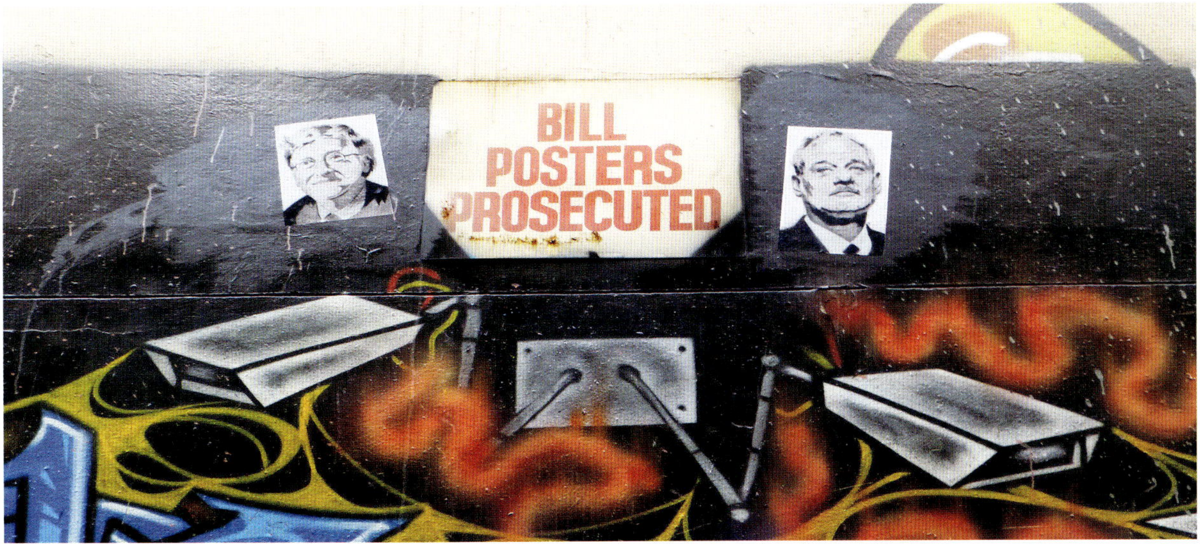
BILL
POSTERS
PROSECUTED

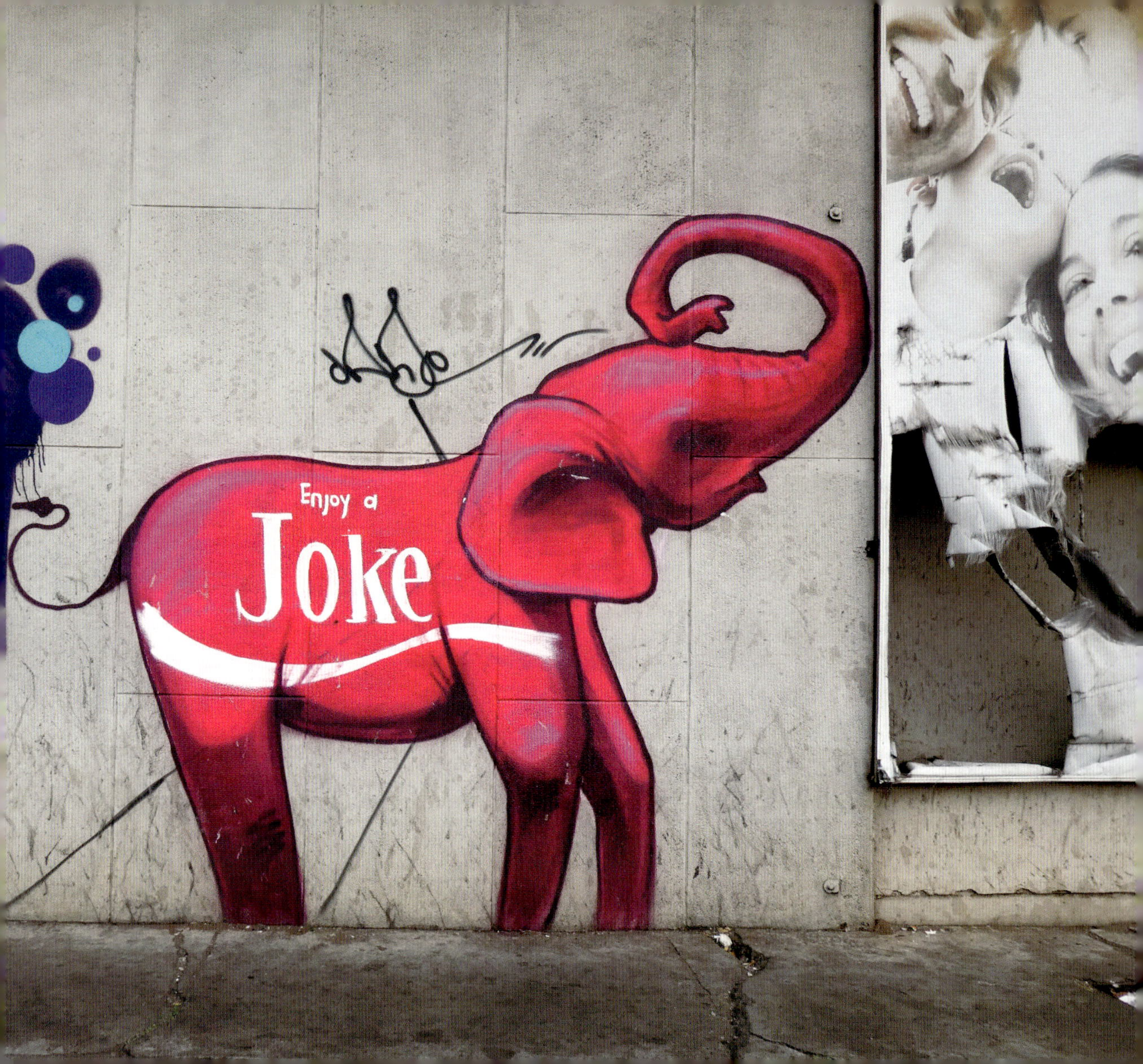
Enjoy a
Joke

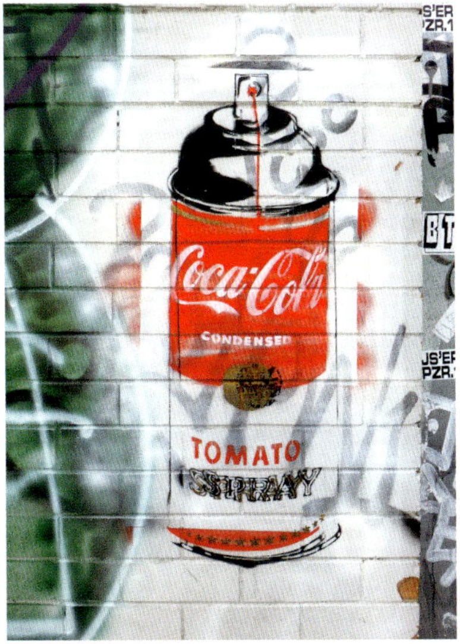

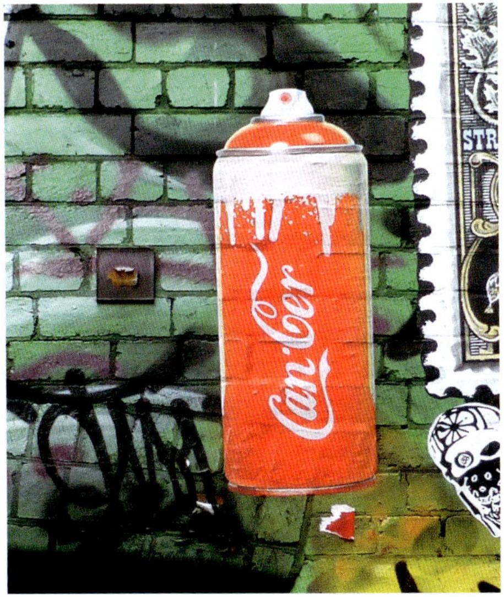

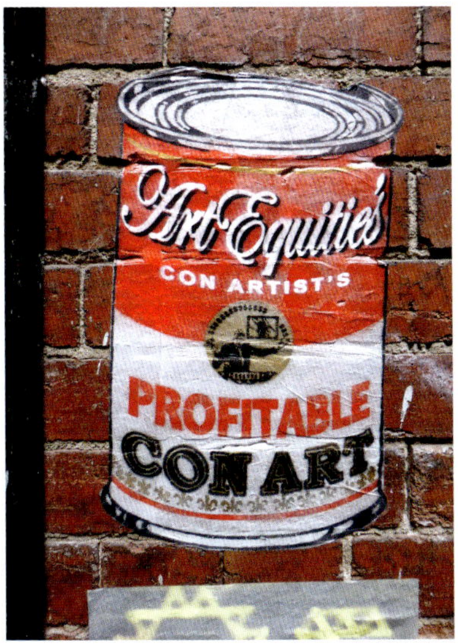

OPPOSITE Falko One, Johannesburg, South Africa, 2017
TOP LEFT Unknown artist, Melbourne, Australia, 2014
BOTTOM LEFT Sunfigo, Melbourne, Australia, 2016
RIGHT Unknown artist, Melbourne, Australia, 2015

IT'S easy for artists to have fun with labels and brands. These examples laugh at two of the big ones – Coca-Cola and Campbell's Soup. The easily recognisable red and white labels and the distinctive fonts lend themselves to an infinite number of variations.

South African artist Falko One has melded readily identifiable elements of Coca-Cola's advertising program with his signature image, the elephant. The combination is so clever that it takes a moment to catch on to the wittiness of the word play.

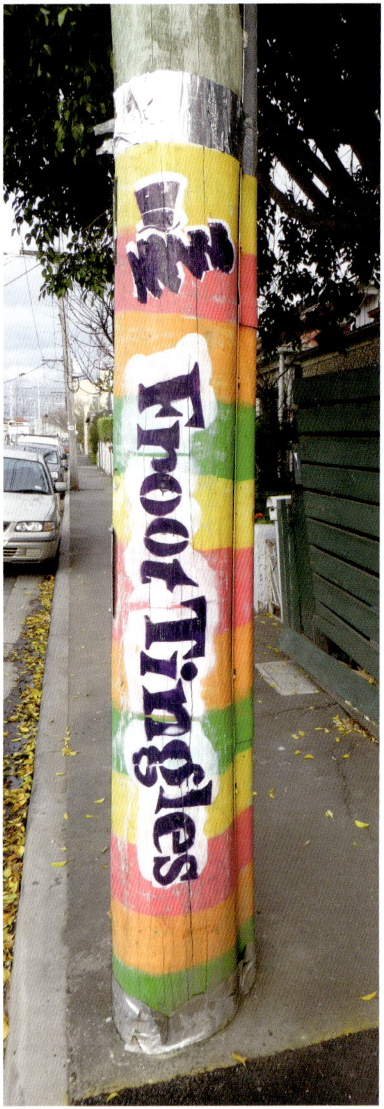

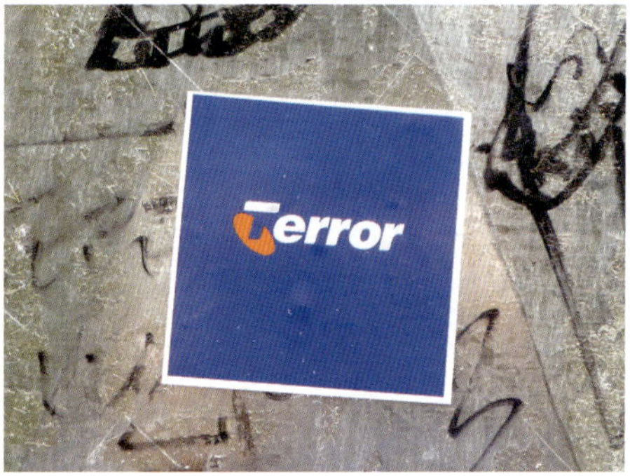

LEFT Unknown artist, Melbourne, Australia, 2014

TOP RIGHT Unknown artist, Melbourne, Australia, 2016

BOTTOM RIGHT Unknown artist, Bendigo, Australia, 2013

OPPOSITE Sarah Masson, Melbourne, Australia, 2016

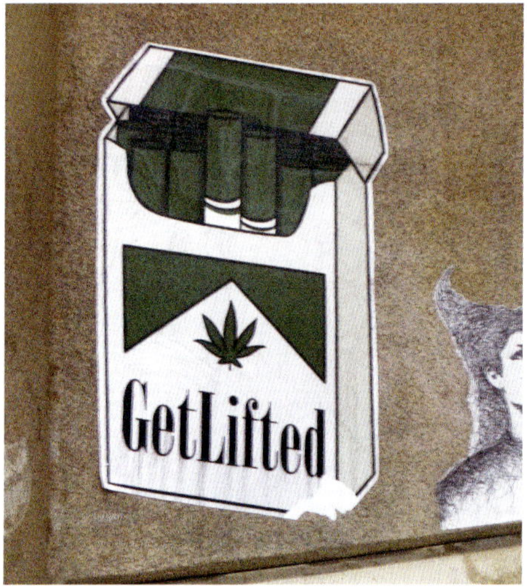

WHETHER or not we have lived in the right place and time to recognise a Fruit Tingles wrapper, the painted lamppost can make us smile because it's so out of place, but so apt at the same time. The *Terror* sticker that bears a striking resemblance to a telecommunications carrier and the Marlboro-inspired cigarette packet, sporting a marijuana leaf and an exhortation to 'get lifted', both play on our recognition of familiar logos while simultaneously subverting their meaning.

Sarah Masson's painting opposite in Melbourne's Hosier Lane makes light of our seemingly insatiable need to be visible on social media, using irony to modify the message.

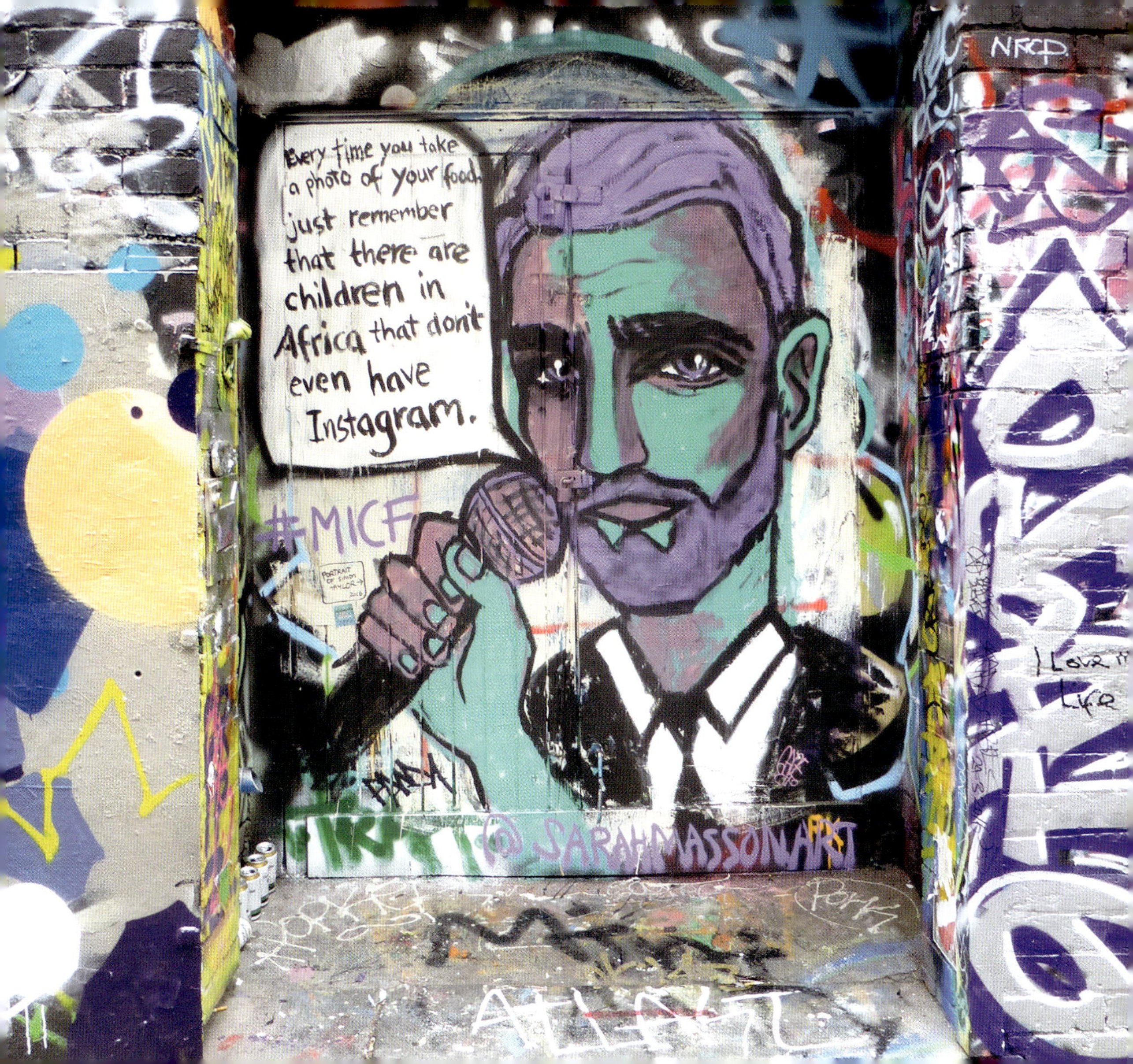
Every time you take a photo of your food just remember that there are children in Africa that don't even have Instagram.
#MICF
@SARAHMASSONART
I Love Life

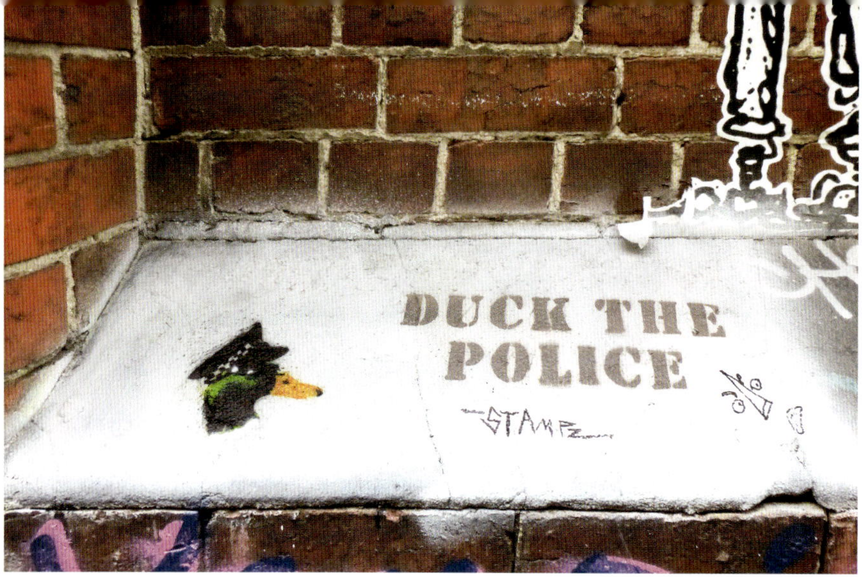
DUCK THE
POLICE
STAMPZ

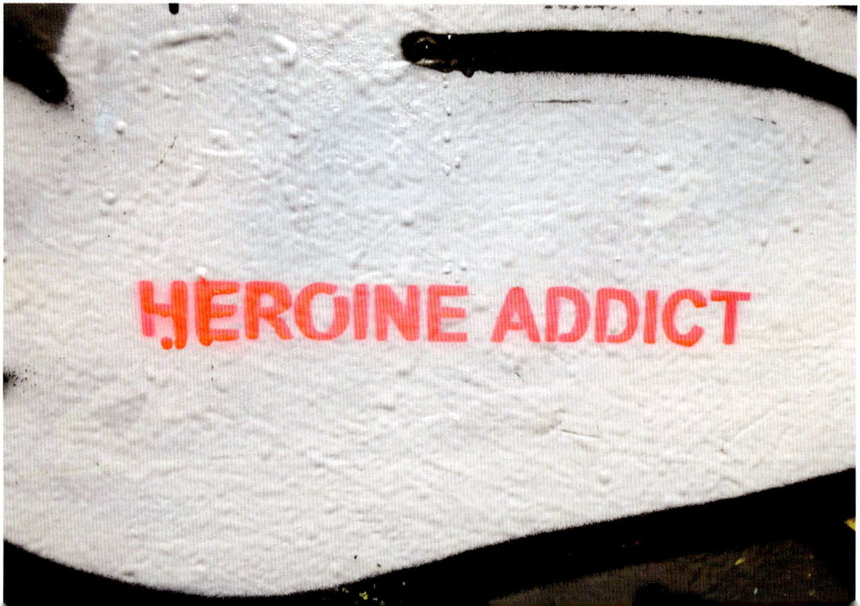
HEROINE ADDICT

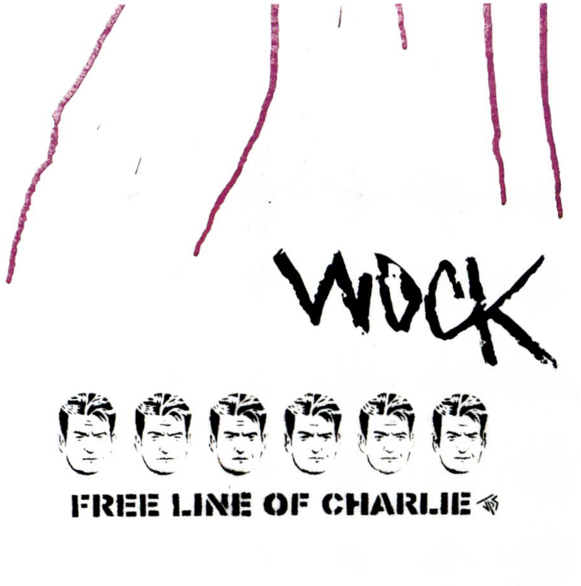

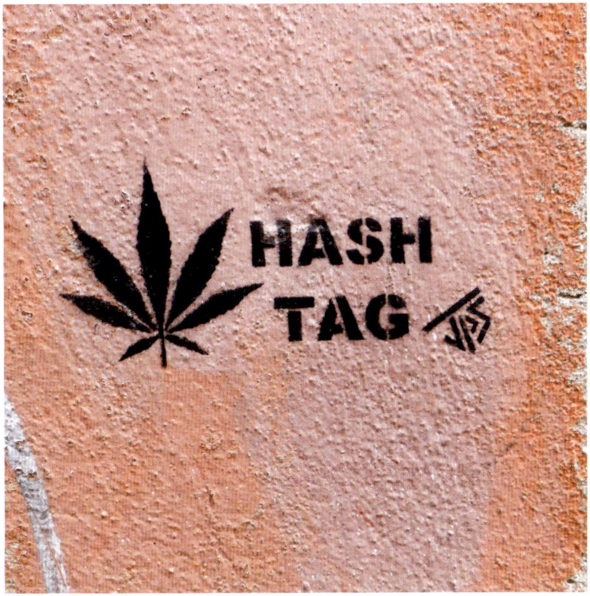

THESE four examples of stencil art, from cities half a world apart, remind us of the ambiguity of language and how it changes over time to accommodate new directions and interests in society. Police officers have long been the target of dissatisfaction to one degree or another. It's interesting that the puns in the other three images refer to illegal drugs. British artist JPS uses humour and entertaining word play in his stencils above and on pp. 40 and 55.

OPPOSITE TOP Stampz, Melbourne, Australia, 2015

OPPOSITE BOTTOM myheadsajungle, *Heroine Addict*, Melbourne, Australia, 2014

LEFT JPS, Stavanger, Norway, 2016

RIGHT JPS, Stavanger, Norway, 2016

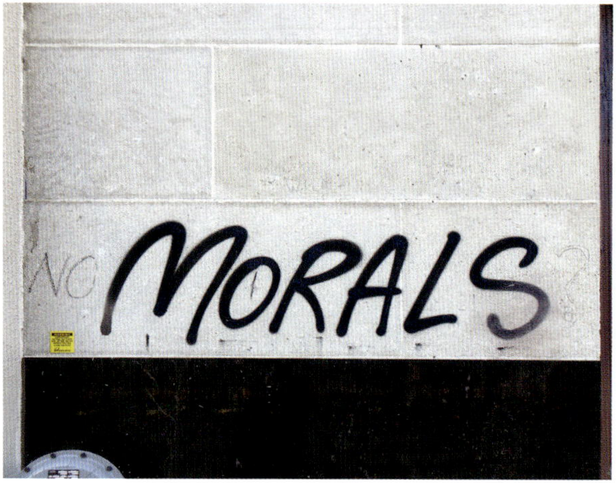

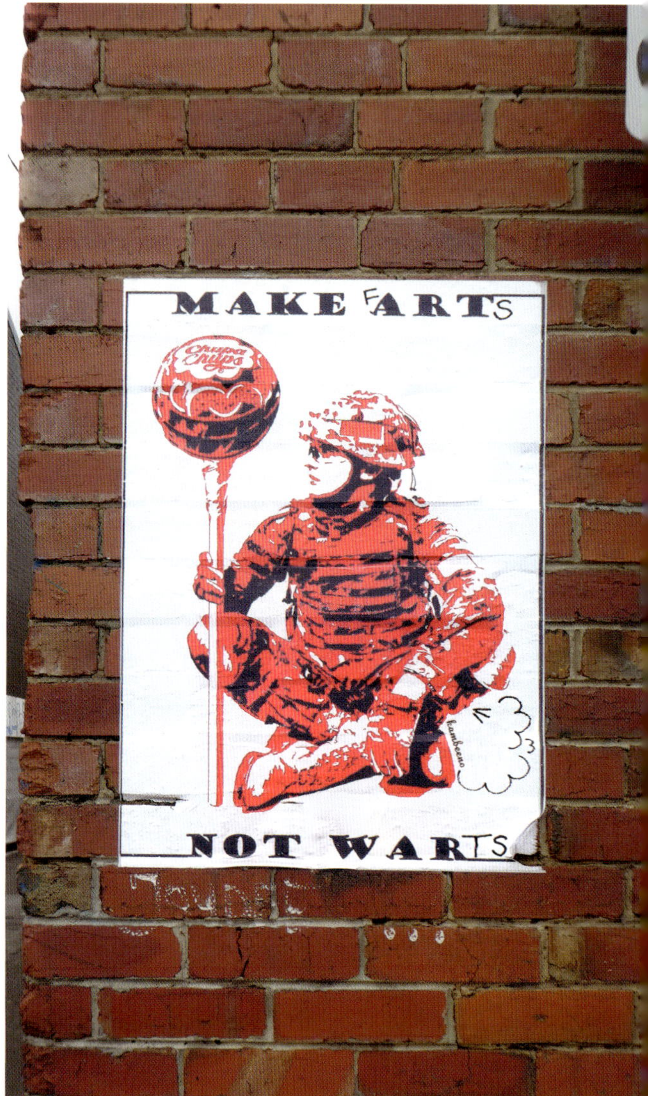

LEFT Unknown artist, Toronto, Canada, 2018

RIGHT Kambeeno, Melbourne, Australia, 2017

OPPOSITE TOP LEFT Unknown artist, Dublin, Ireland, 2015

OPPOSITE TOP RIGHT JPS, Stavanger, Norway, 2016

OPPOSITE BOTTOM LEFT Christian Palmer, *We Don't Need No Education*, Byron Bay, Australia, 2014

OPPOSITE BOTTOM RIGHT JPS, Stavanger, Norway, 2016

ON this page are two examples of art that show an unauthorised intervention by a passerby. Morals? Or NO morals? A clever wordsmith adjusted 'make art not war' to 'make farts not warts'. It's certainly irreverent, but the artist enjoyed the interaction.

On the opposite page, the skeleton in Dublin, with his ironic 'no worries', and the three wise monkeys in Australia's Byron Bay are examples of how text can subvert the visual references within an image. Street art is the theme of JPS's two small stencils in Stavanger and their amusing puns.

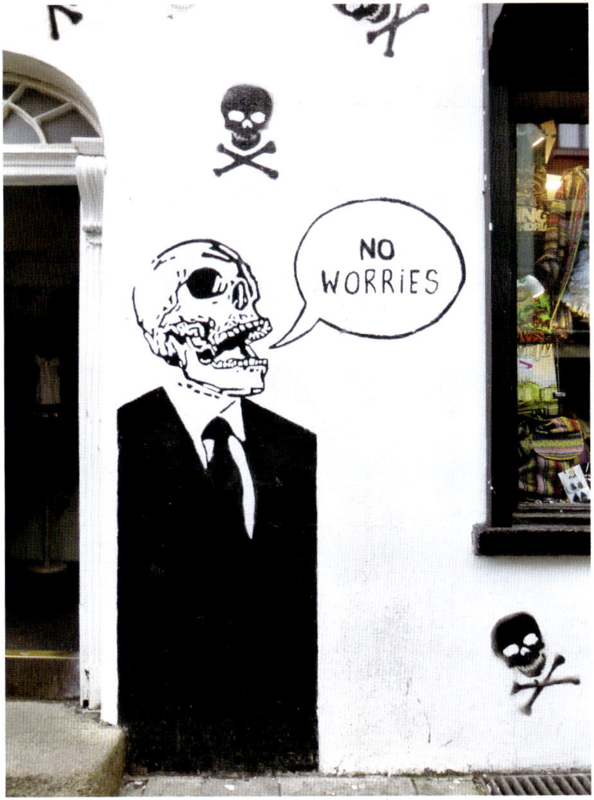
NO
WORRIES

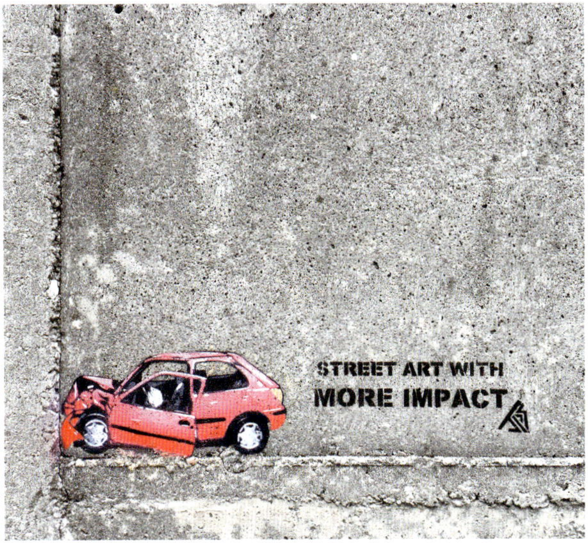
STREET ART WITH
MORE IMPACT

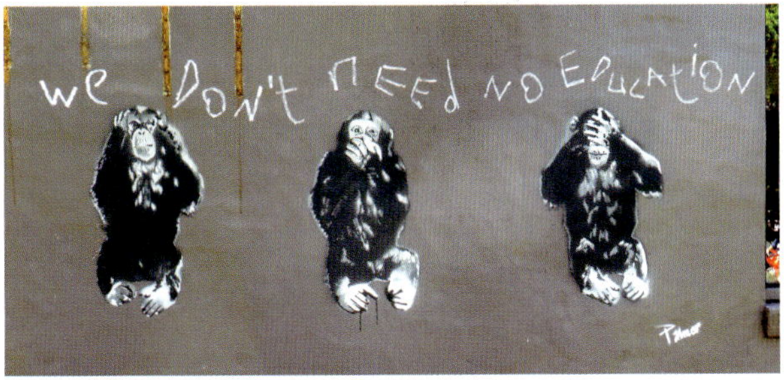
we Don't need no Education

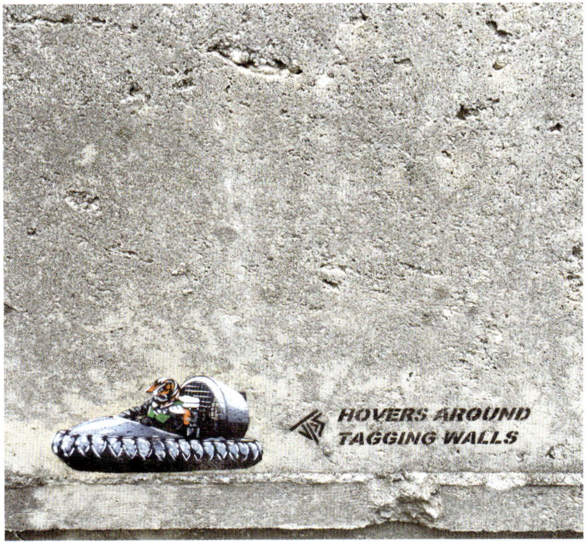
HOVERS AROUND
TAGGING WALLS

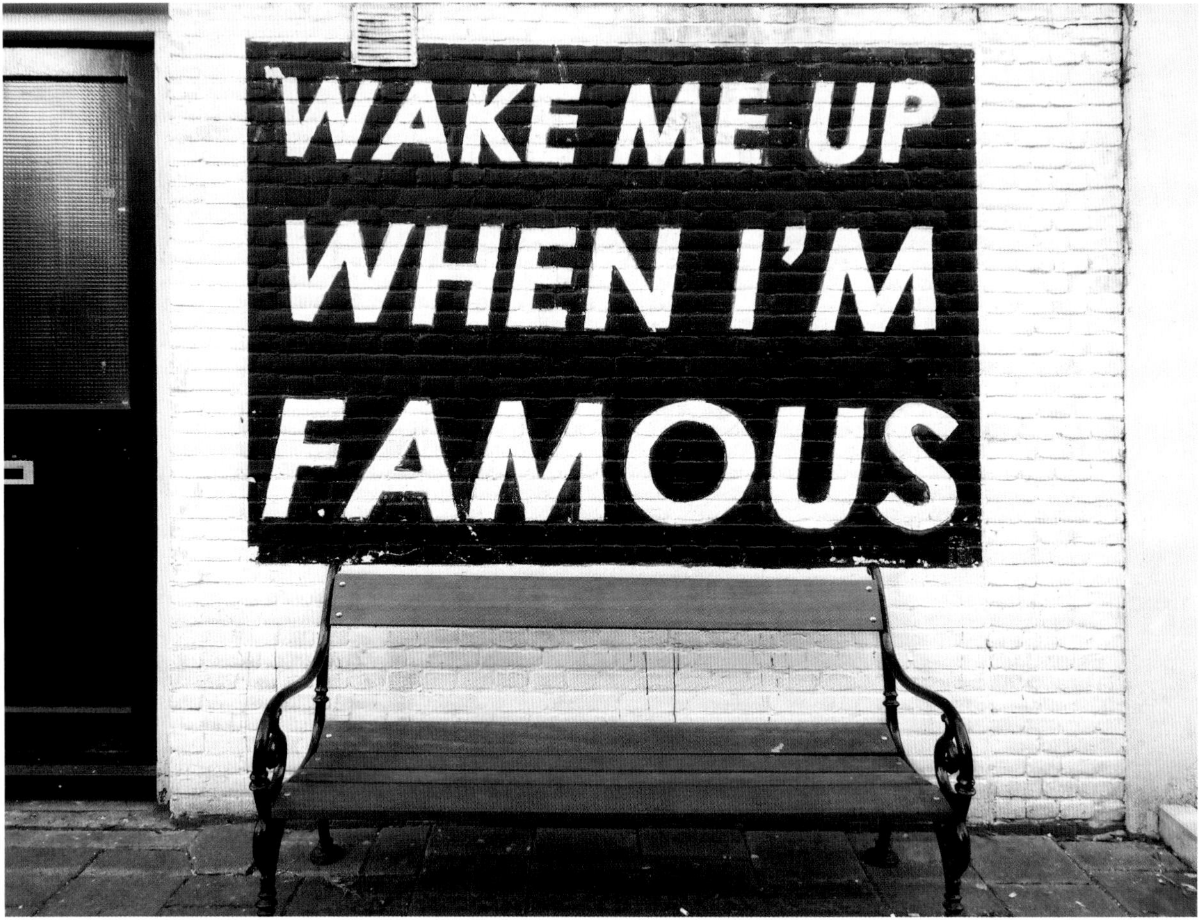
WAKE ME UP
WHEN I'M
FAMOUS

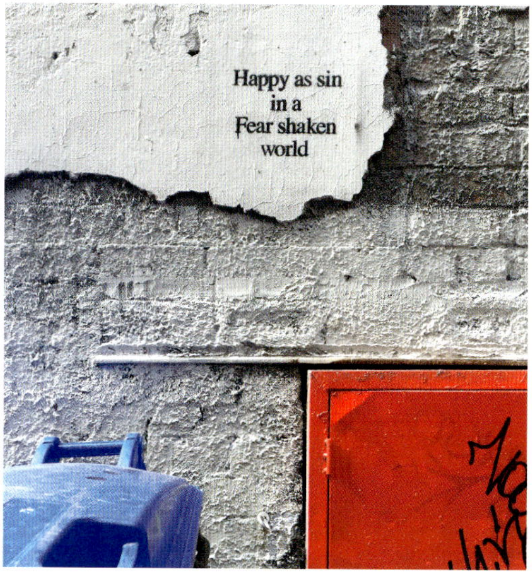

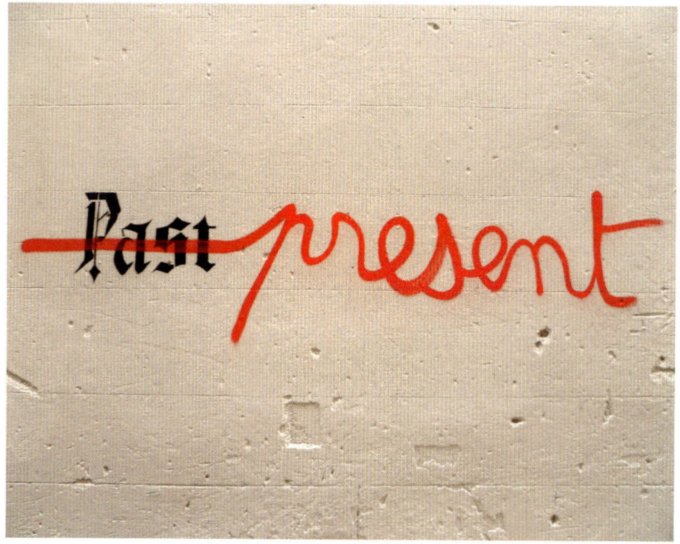

OPPOSITE Unknown artist, Amsterdam, Netherlands, 2018
LEFT Unknown artist, Melbourne, Australia, 2015
RIGHT Unknown artist, Melbourne, Australia, 2012

SONG lyrics have inspired two of the examples on these pages. The words 'wake me up when I'm famous' begin the chorus of the song 'Neurotic', recorded by Seaway in 2017. They have been painted in powerful and contrasting black and white on a wall behind a much photographed bench in Amsterdam.

Words from 'As Sure as I Am' by Crowded House inspired the unexpected phrase 'happy as sin in a fear shaken world', stencilled onto a laneway wall in Melbourne. The replacement of 'past' with 'present' is a wholly apt way to visually suggest this transition.

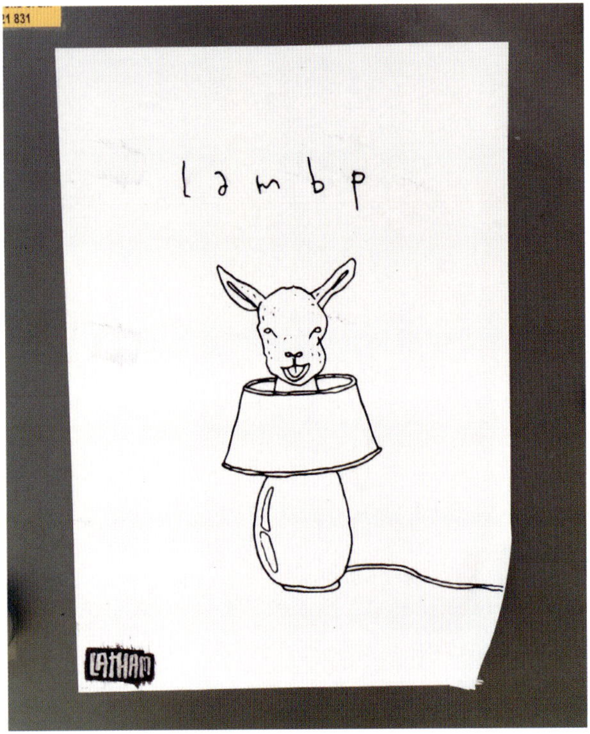

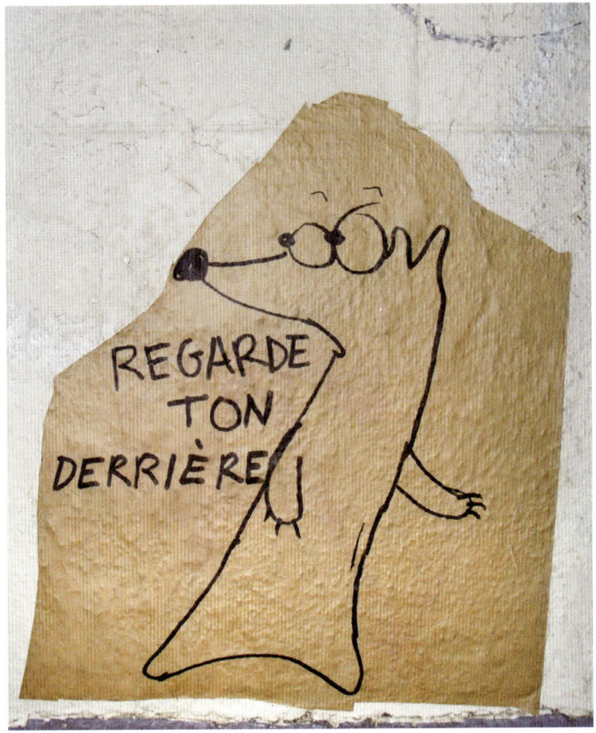

LEFT Latham, Sydney, Australia, 2015
RIGHT Unknown artist, Melbourne, Australia, 2006
OPPOSITE Hayley Welsh, Perth, Australia, 2017

WHIMSICAL images may not make us laugh-out-loud but the feeling of pleasure we gain from them can be just as strong. The simplicity and restraint of Latham's 'lambp' pun is enhanced by the joyful innocence of the creature's head, and the turning animal above IS definitely watching his back!

Hayley Welsh is a British artist who now makes her home in Perth, Australia while at the same time maintaining ties with the art community in her home town. Her gently surreal characters have a playful aura but the innocence is often undercut by an impression of self-doubt. The simple text on her painting – 'Together let us all combine' – heightens the sense of whimsy on this extravagantly pink wall.

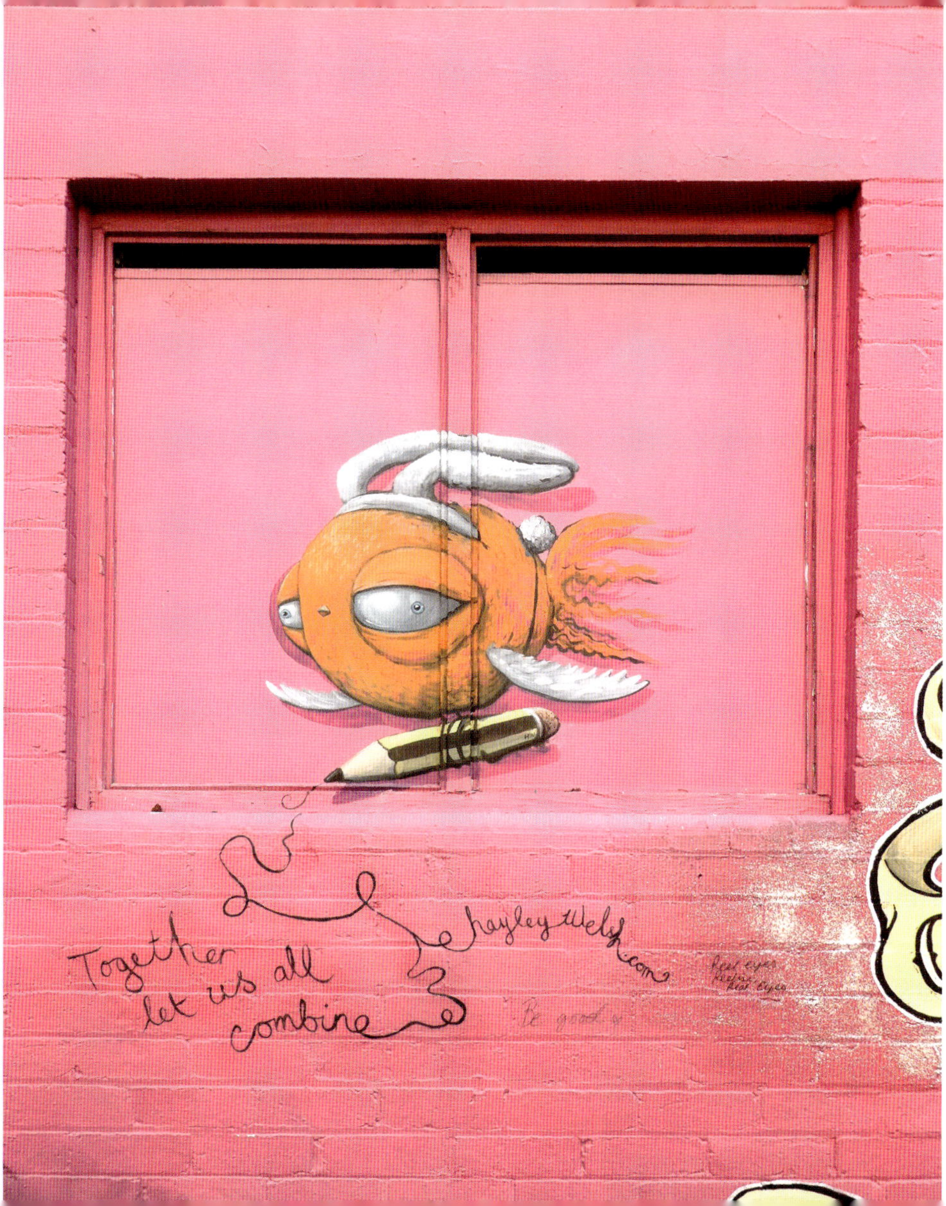
Together let us all combine
hayleywelsh.com

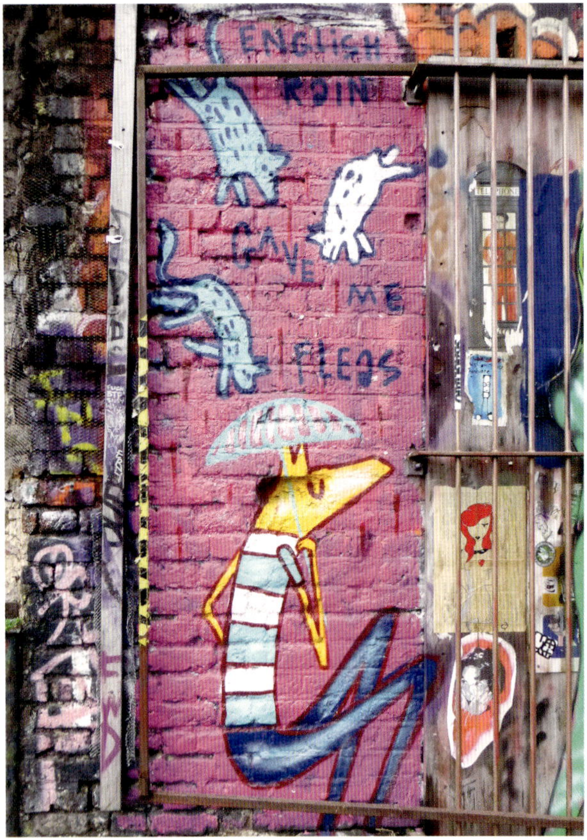

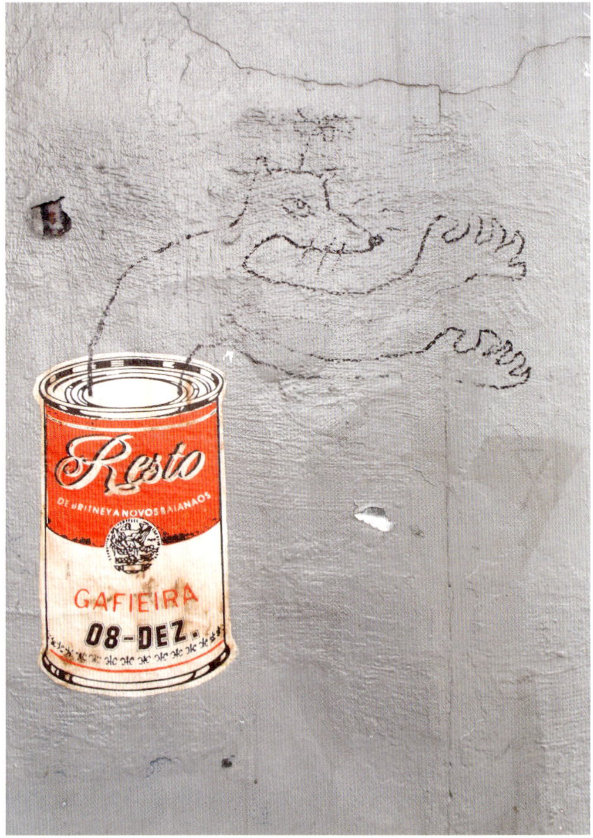

LEFT David Selor, London, UK, 2015
RIGHT Unknown artist, Rio de Janeiro, Brazil, 2012
OPPOSITE TOP Unknown artist, Bilbao, Spain, 2016
OPPOSITE BOTTOM Unknown artist, Bilbao, Spain, 2016

ANIMALS can be a wonderful source of inspiration, as these four images show. French artist David Selor's imaginary character in the striped top and jeans is called Mimil. He is half human–half animal, but what animal? Dog or fox or wolf? It doesn't matter – the interpretation is left to the viewer. Note that it's raining cats and dogs.

There is a childlike quality and a delightful energy in the rat escaping from the can in Rio de Janeiro (above) and the naïve line drawings (opposite), seen in the Basque town of Bilbao.

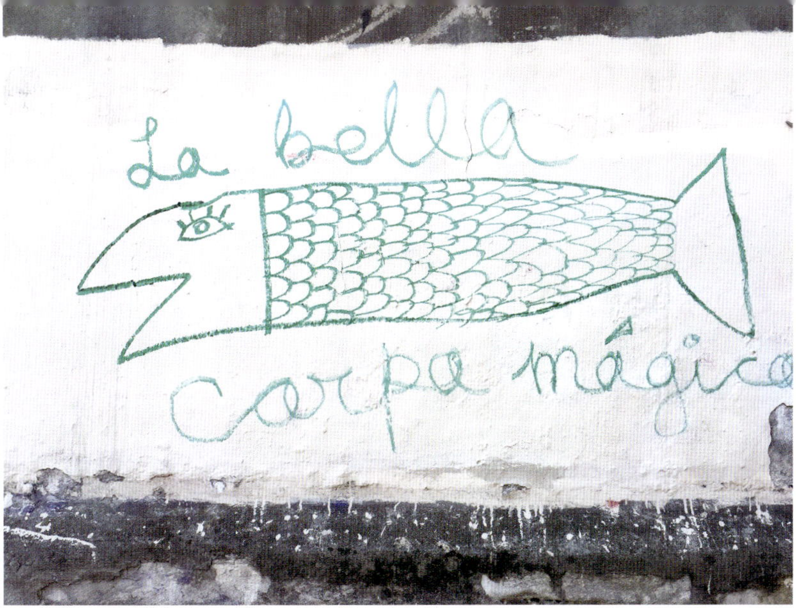
La bella
carpa mágica

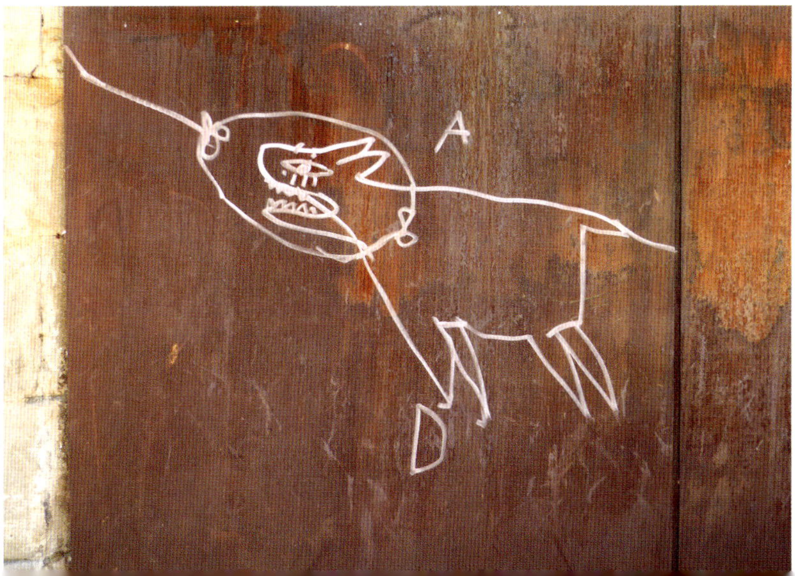

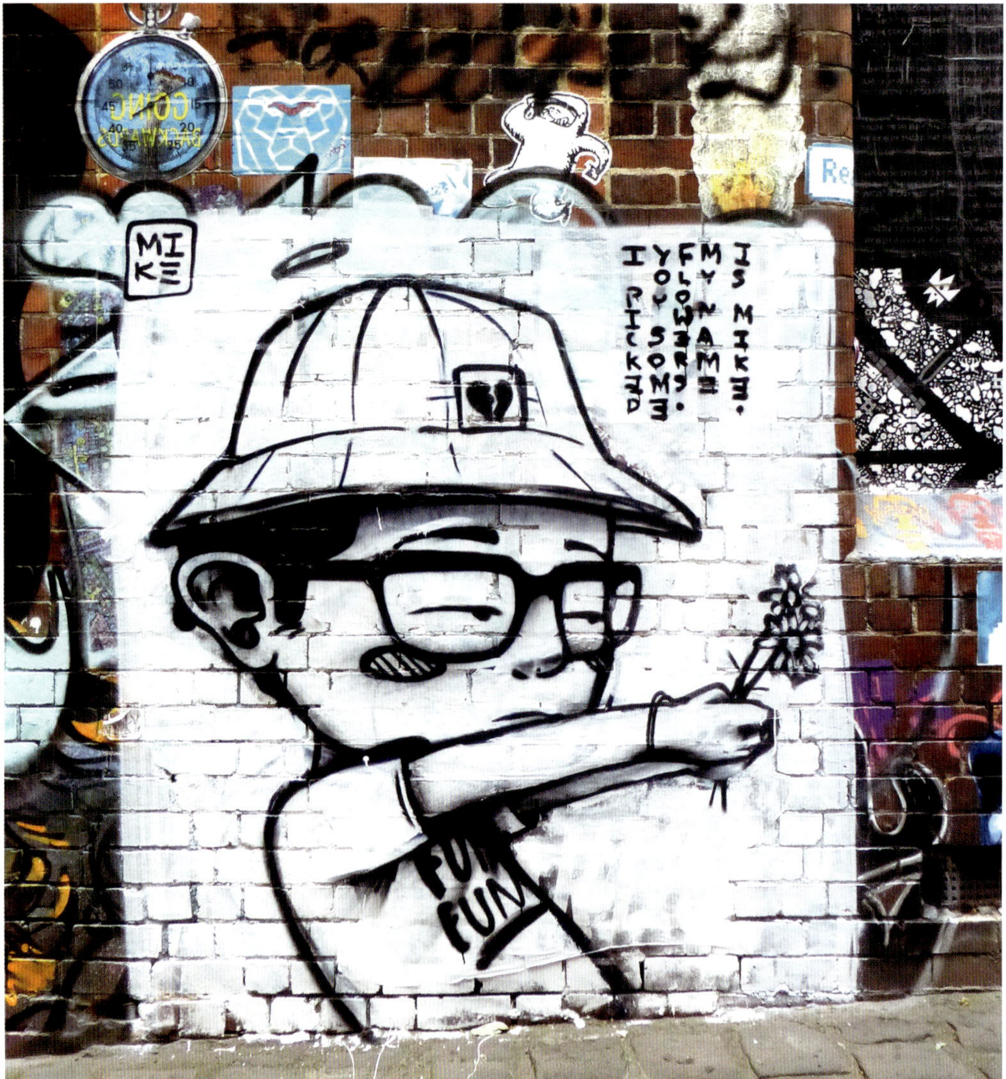
MIKE
I PICKED YOU SOME FLOWERS. MY NAME IS MIKE.
FUN FUN

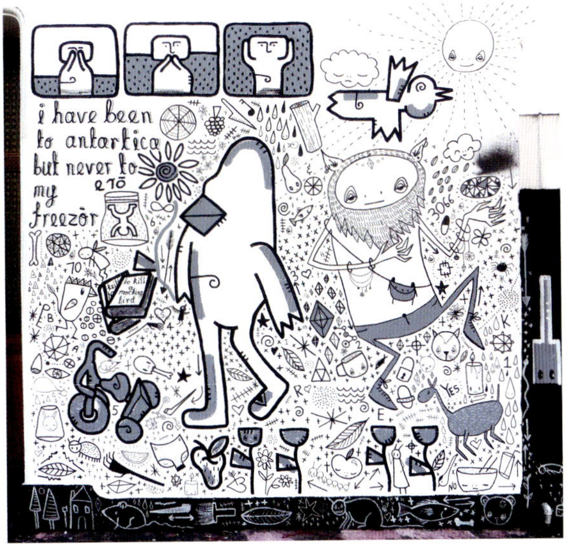

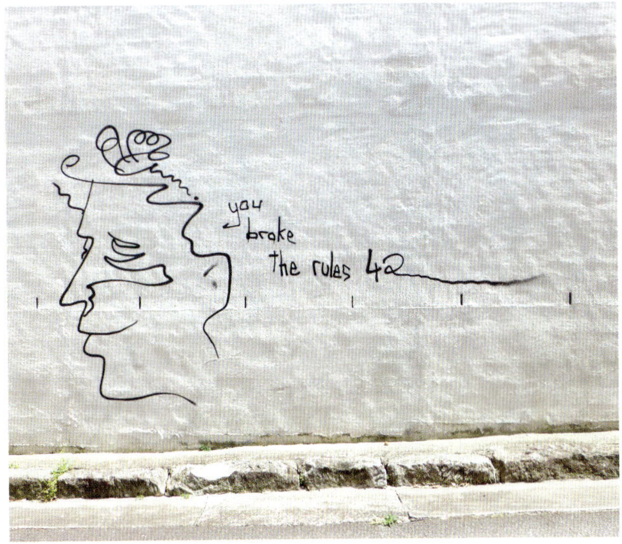

OPPOSITE Mike Eleven, Melbourne, Australia, 2015

LEFT Ero and Barek, Melbourne, Australia, 2015

RIGHT Unknown artist, Sydney, Australia, 2013

MIKE Eleven's whimsical self-portrait opposite makes us smile. Like the artists of the works above, he has omitted colour from his image, thus allowing the characters and details to speak for themselves without the emphasis added by the use of colour.

Ero and Barek's collaborative wall (above left) encourages us to take time to smell the roses as we scan the details – favourite books, three wise monkeys and a series of lazy-eyed characters. The simple line drawing above on a wall in Sydney leaves us wondering about the rules that were broken.

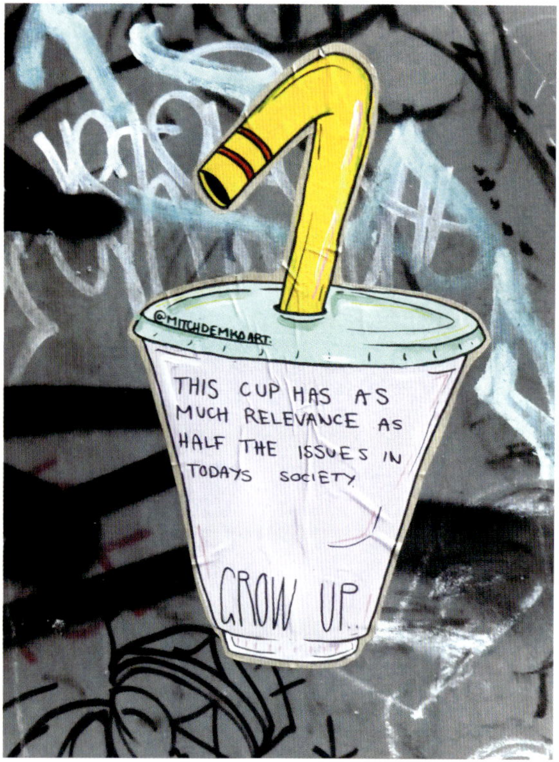

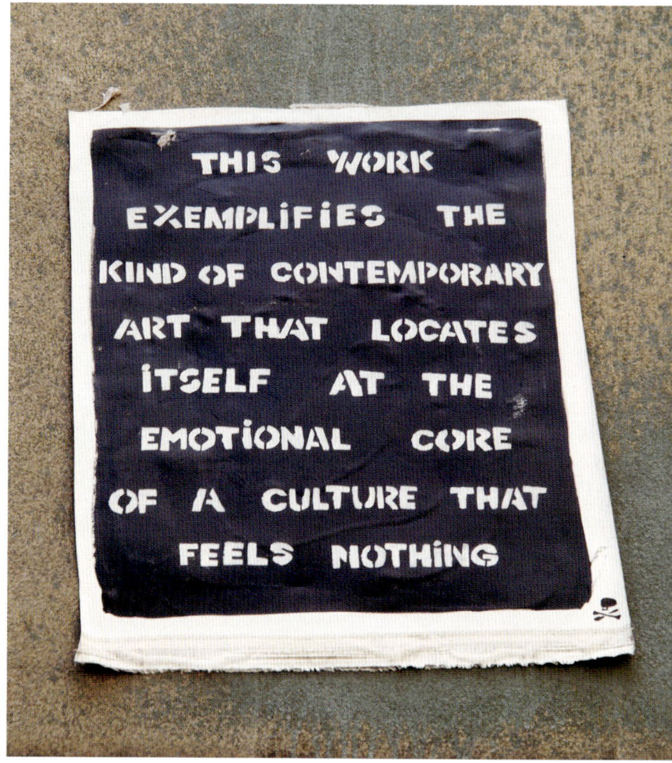

WHAT does it all mean? Culture? Media? Celebrities? Mitch Demko draws attention (above left) to the way we spend time and energy worrying about issues that have little importance, in much the same way that the paste-up (above right) queries our values and integrity. The anonymous writer in Geelong seems to have run out of puff before finishing that list opposite, but the scrawler in Warsaw found a simple way to add a smile to our day. It looks like a quick job though, possibly done at night, with a spotter watching the artist's back.

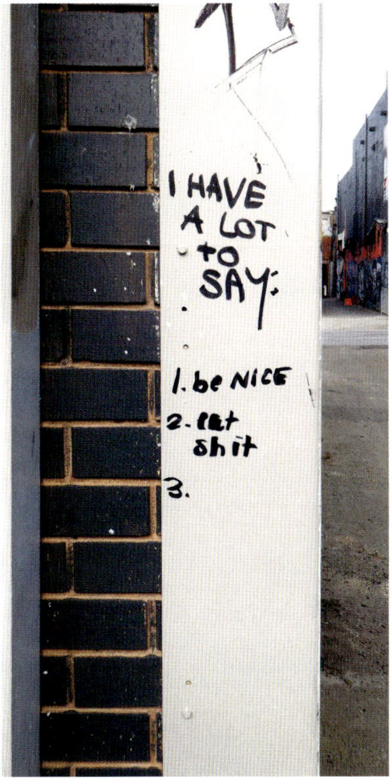

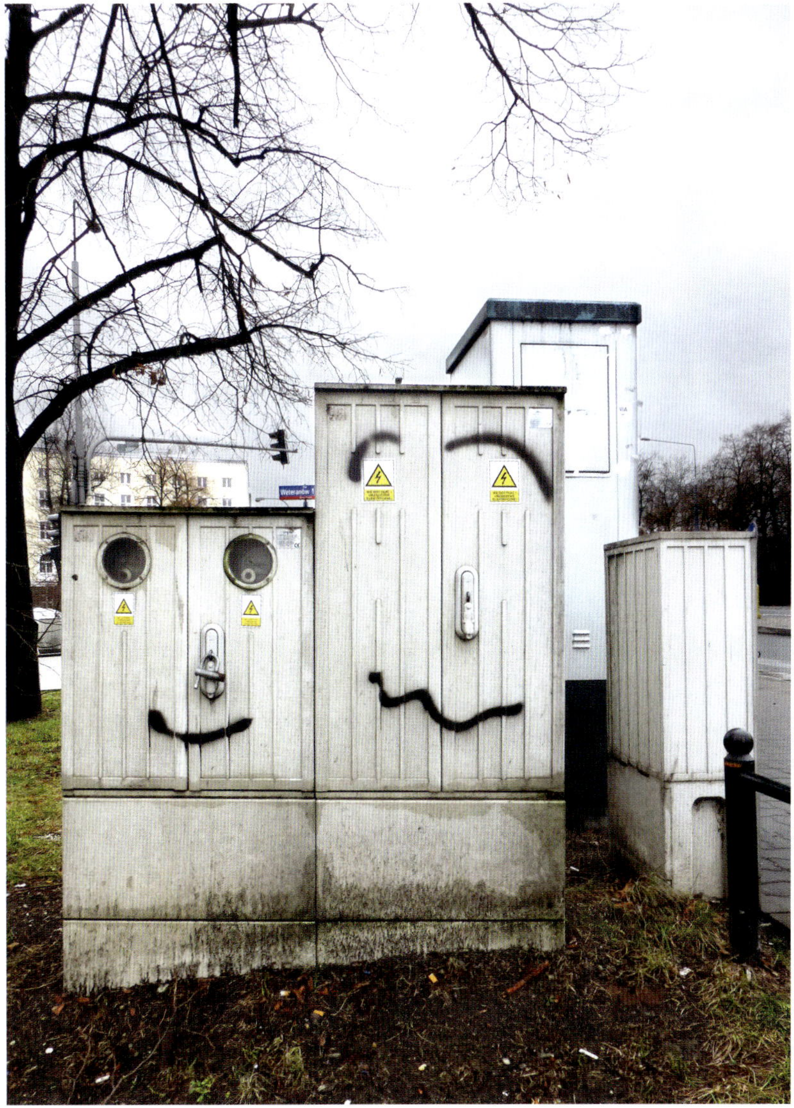

OPPOSITE LEFT Mitch Demko, Melbourne, Australia, 2017

OPPOSITE RIGHT Unknown artist, Melbourne, Australia, 2012

LEFT Unknown artist, Geelong, Australia, 2017

RIGHT Unknown artist, Warsaw, Poland, 2015

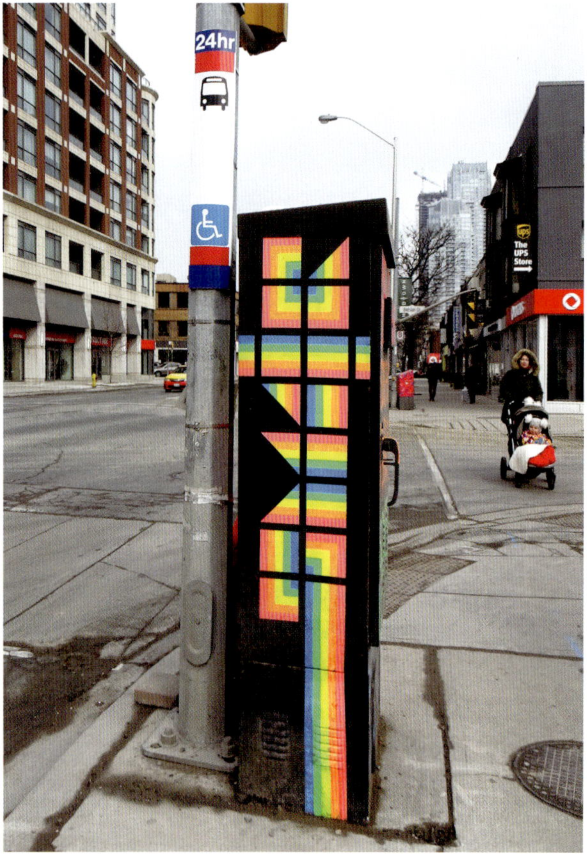

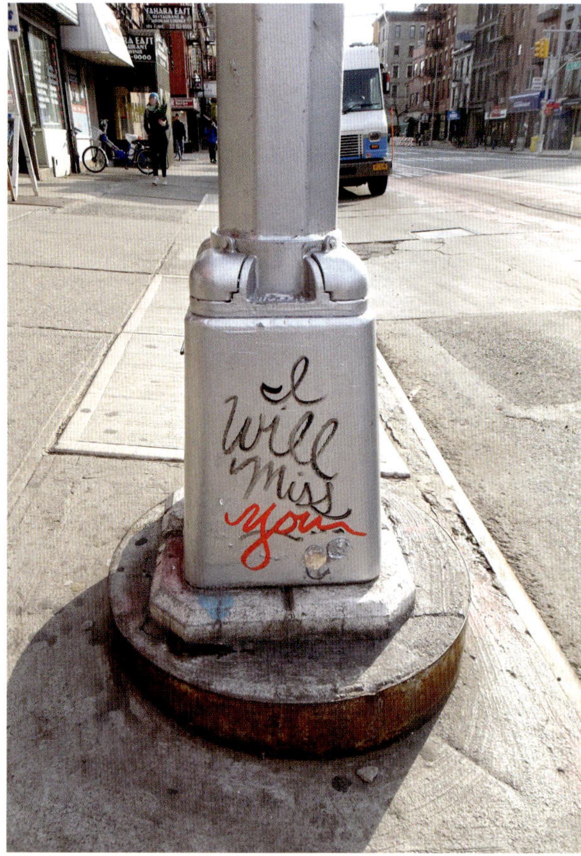

MESSAGES drawn on functional street furniture can take us by surprise. In recent years Toronto-based artist Bareket Kezwer has been painting and drawing *SMILE* on surfaces large and small as part of her #365daysofsmile project. By using bright colours and eye-catching designs like those in the work above left, she wants to spread joy and remind us to live in the moment. The passerby can't be sure, though, whether the message scribbled on the base of a lamppost in Manhattan (above right) has a specific someone in mind, or if they can take heart from it.

What could be more refreshing than the look of absolute delight on the faces of Zabou's Thelma and Louise characters? That 'Yeah bitches!' on the cap says it all.

LEFT Bareket Kezwer, Toronto, Canada, 2018

RIGHT Unknown artist, New York City, USA, 2018

OPPOSITE Zabou, London, UK, 2015

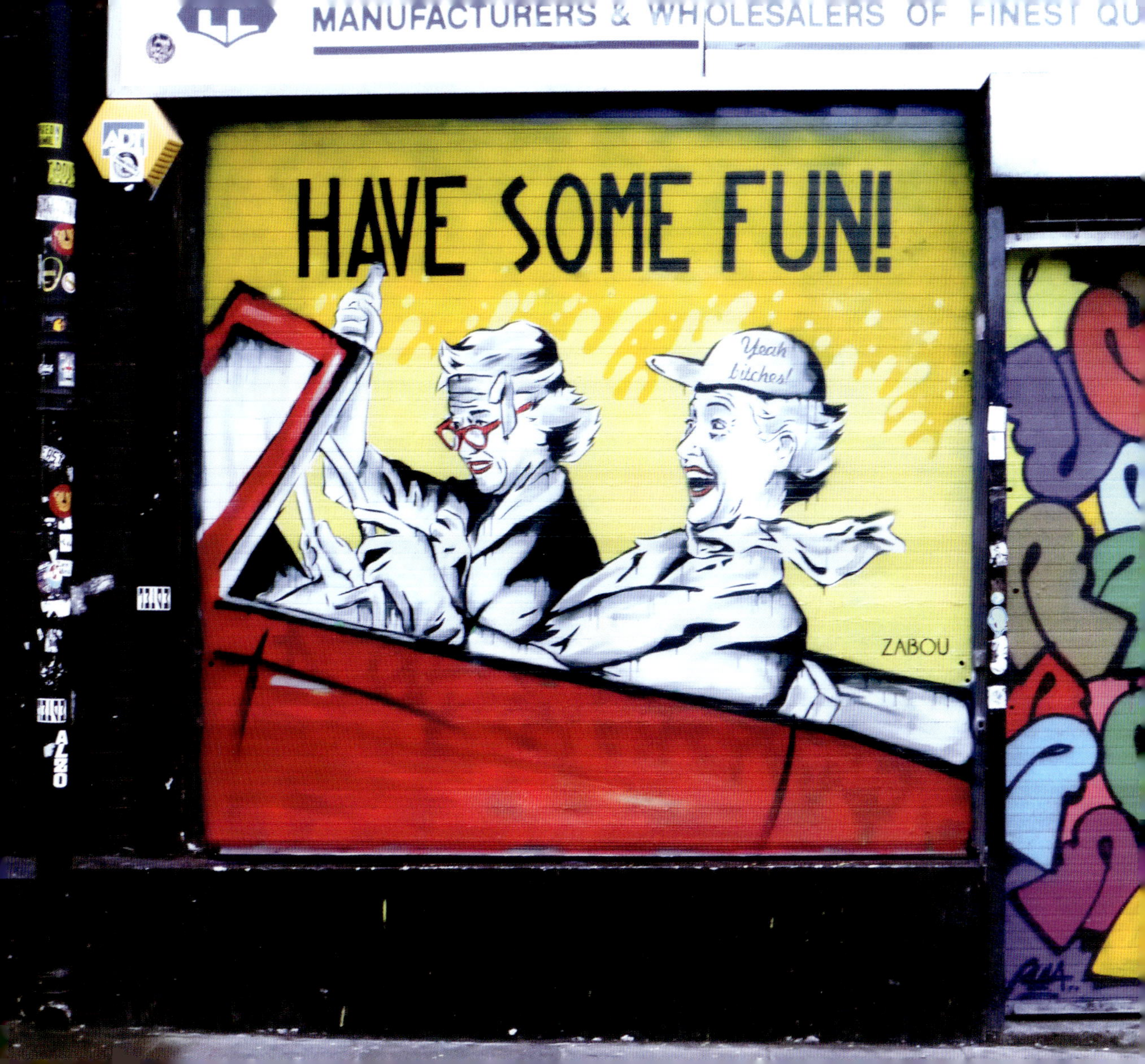
MANUFACTURERS & WHOLESALERS OF FINEST QU
HAVE SOME FUN!
Yeah bitches!
ZABOU

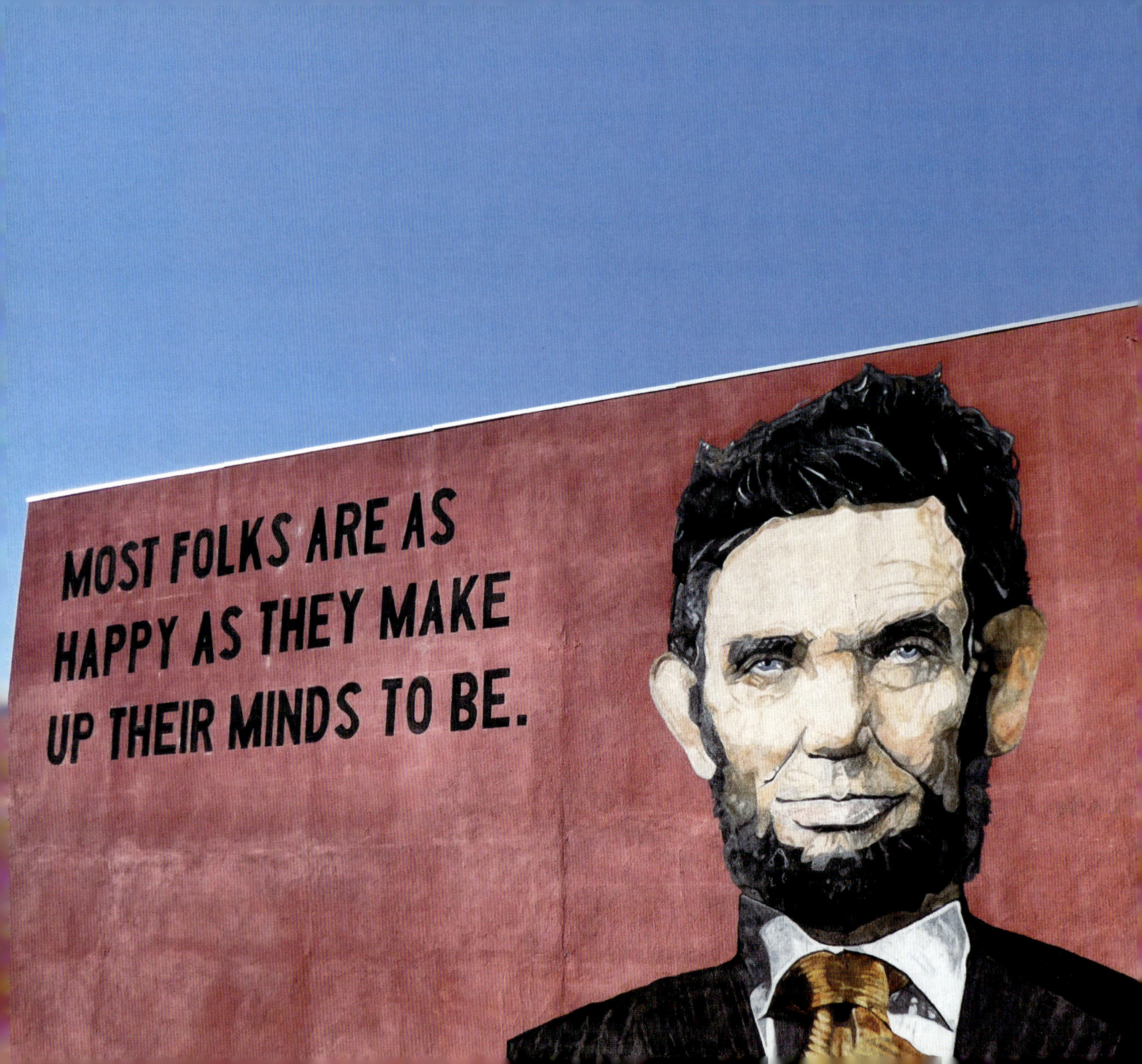
MOST FOLKS ARE AS
HAPPY AS THEY MAKE
UP THEIR MINDS TO BE.

Words of Wisdom

Street art offers the perfect vehicle to fulfil the human desire to give advice to others. And sometimes, just sometimes, 'words of wisdom' are shared. We might look up and see Abraham Lincoln suggesting that it's our own attitudes that create our sense of wellbeing and happiness. Or we might glimpse out of the corner of our eye a tiny sticker that reminds us that life is full of bumps. Both are true.

Such words of wisdom can often be found in unexpected places – at the beach, on rooftops, even scrawled on fire hydrants and bridge stanchions. The message can be gentle and heartfelt, flippant or profound. It might give hope and encouragement or advice and caution. It might encourage us to give thanks for what we have or inspire us to think bigger.

You will read quotations from scholars and celebrities on the following pages. You will also see misquotations – these are often as engaging as the quotes of respected figures. Sometimes they are inadvertent but when they are done with humorous intent, they can make us laugh out loud or, like the poignant stencils of ±MaisMenos±, encourage us to ponder the difficult things in life.

Both the imposing statement and the humble message have the ability to reward the observant passerby. While we might not agree with the comments or their sentiments, they do give us pause for thought, and may even warm our hearts and make us smile. Isn't that enough?

OPPOSITE Trek Thunder Kelly, Los Angeles, USA, 2017
RIGHT Unknown artist, Los Angeles, USA, 2018

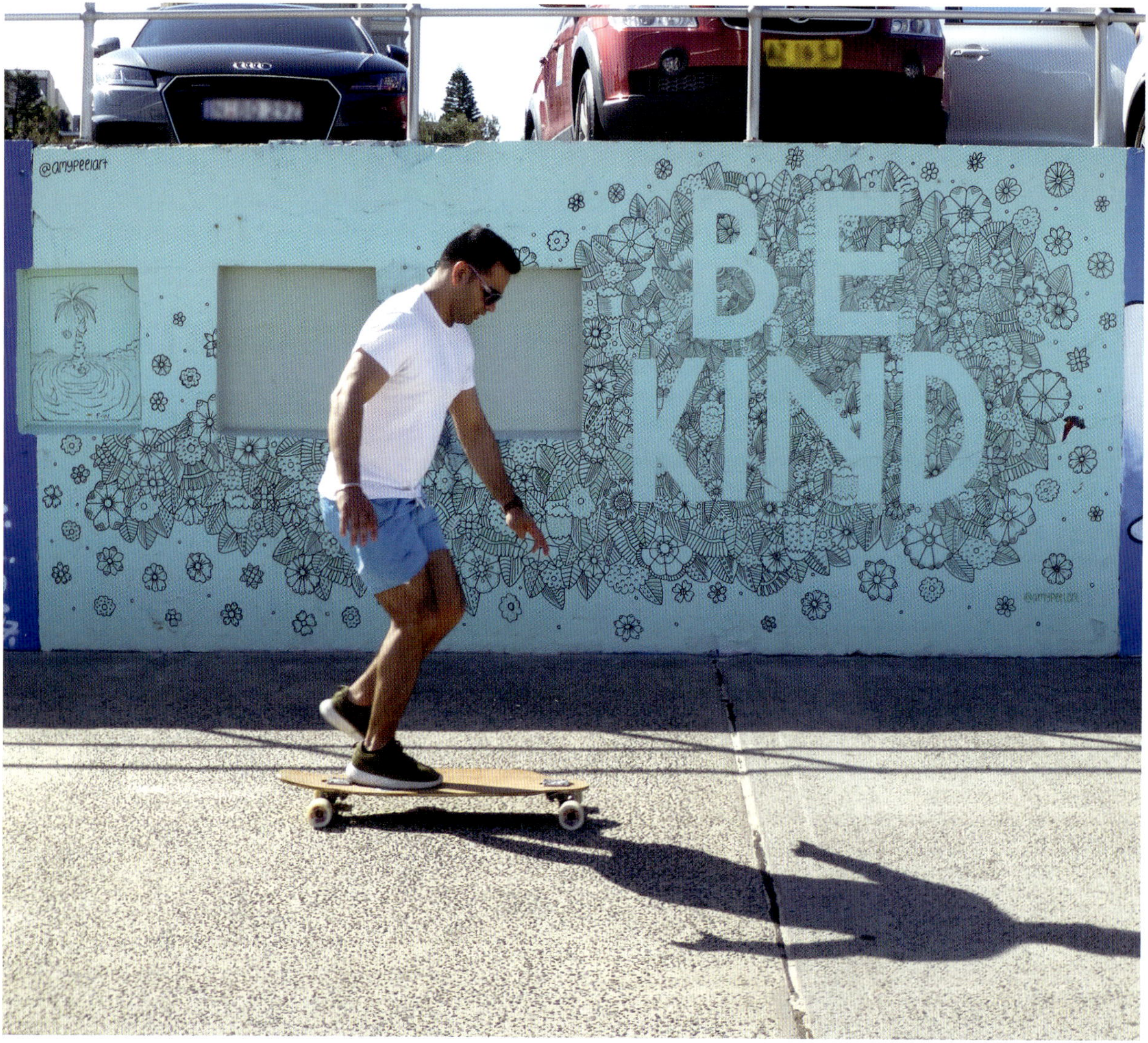
@amypeelart
BE
KIND

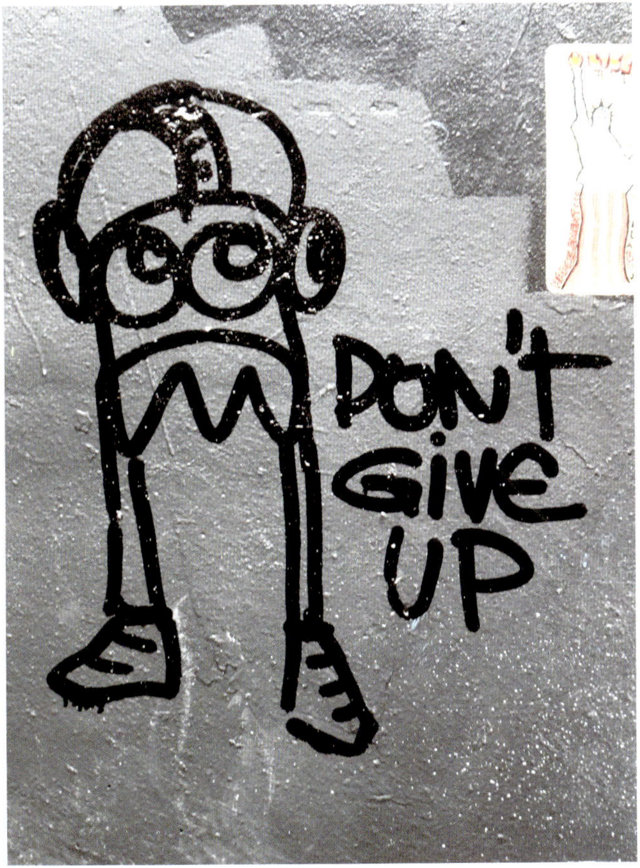

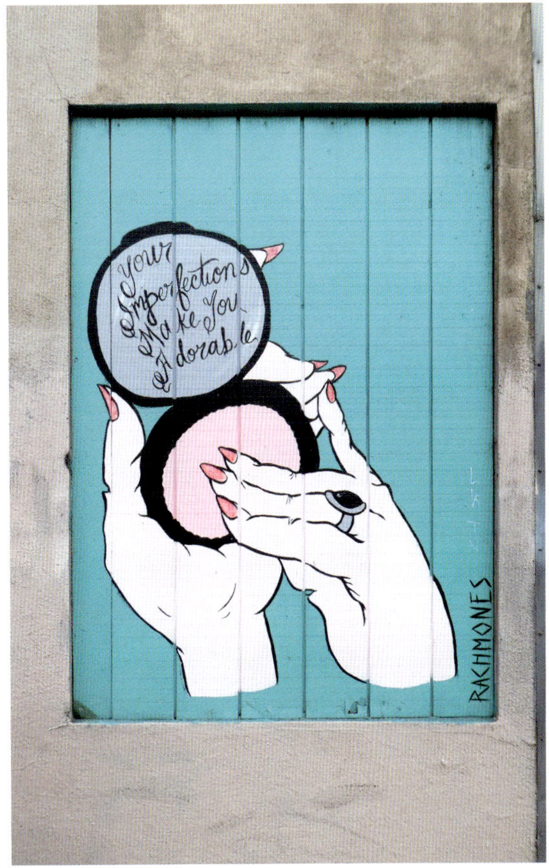

OPPOSITE Amy Peel, *Be Kind*, Sydney, Australia, 2017
LEFT Unknown artist, Paris, France, 2018
RIGHT Jaclyn Rose, San Francisco, USA, 2017

THE words of encouragement on these pages are inspirational. *Be Kind*, by Amy Peel, sits in a bouquet of floral detail in a seafront environment on the graffiti wall at Sydney's Bondi Beach. The quirky character telling us not to give up was photographed in Paris, the city said to be the most romantic in the world.

Jaclyn Rose's acceptance of our imperfections appeared on a wall in San Francisco's South of Market district (aka SoMa) – a hub for nightclubs and museums. Her words of wisdom about the big and little things in life, including our 'connectedness' via social media, are more often stitched on a small scale.

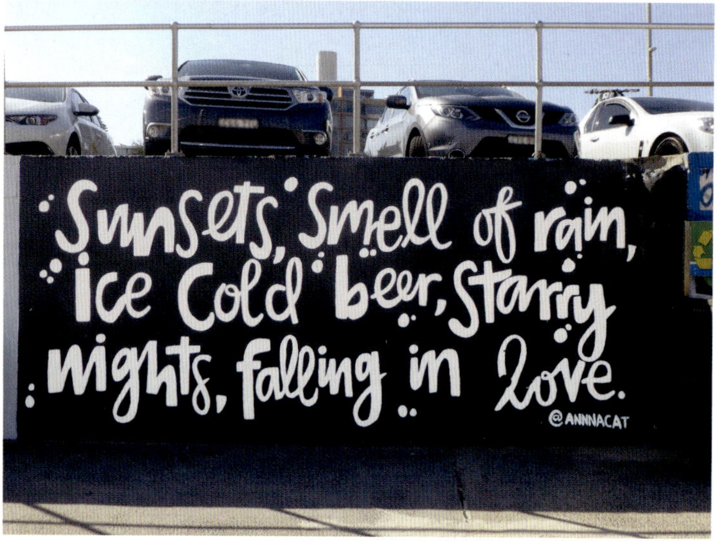

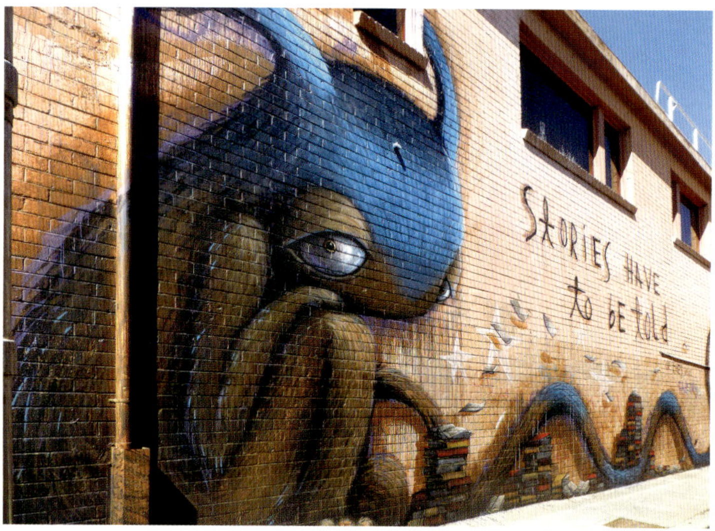

TOP Anna Elizabeth, *Simple Things*, Sydney, Australia, 2017
BOTTOM Hayley Welsh, Melbourne, Australia, 2015
OPPOSITE Zenith, Ostend, Belgium, 2018

LIKE Amy Peel's mural on the previous spread, Brisbane-based Anna Elizabeth's poetic offering at top was painted on the Bondi Beach Graffiti Wall. Created over three sunny days, it reminds us to appreciate those things that are so easily overlooked in the hustle and bustle of life. The text accompanying Hayley Welsh's timid character says 'Stories have to be told or they will fade away'. The sense of nostalgia is matched by a sense that this is part of a larger narrative.

Zenith (aka Matthias Schoenarts) is far more well known for his day job than as the artist of such extravagant walls as *Think Outside the Box*. He is the actor who has had starring roles in *Far from the Madding Crowd* and *Red Sparrow*. With fellow artists Bué and Chase he formed the collective Buck in the 1990s. They reunited in 2017 to paint walls, including this one opposite, for The Crystal Ship Festival in Ostend.

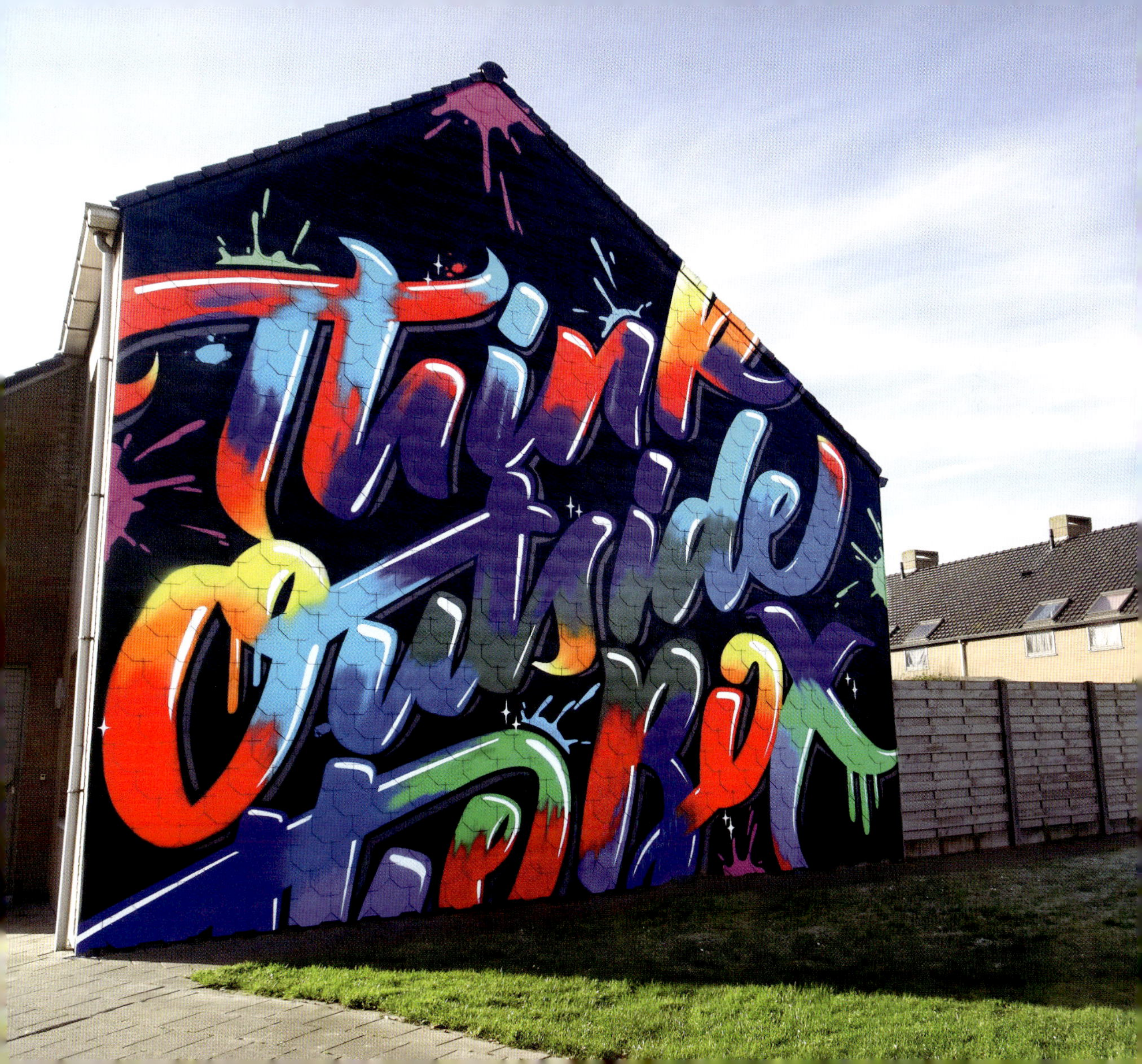

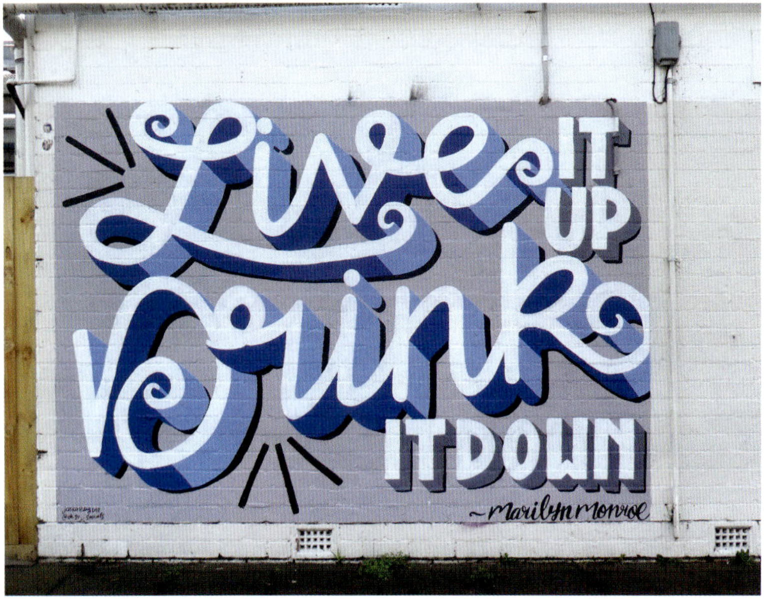

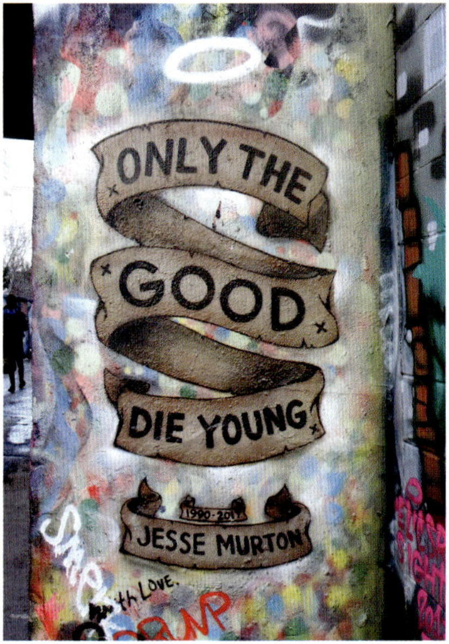

THE frivolous quotations from Hollywood stars Marilyn Monroe and Hedy Lamarr about enjoying life, above, and how to be glamorous, opposite right, may make us smile, but in these politically correct times they may also raise eyebrows. It's encouraging to see that the superficial statement at opposite left so typical of our look-good age, 'happiness is a flat tummy', has been contradicted by the added scribble.

'Only the Good Die Young' is a song from Billy Joel's 1977 album *The Stranger*. It's a poetic sentiment but an ambiguous one with multiple interpretations.

LEFT Jessica Riley, Melbourne, Australia, 2017

RIGHT Unknown artist, Toronto, Canada, 2018

OPPOSITE LEFT Leah Grant, *Happiness Is*, Adelaide, Australia, 2016

OPPOSITE RIGHT TeneT, Melbourne, Australia, 2016

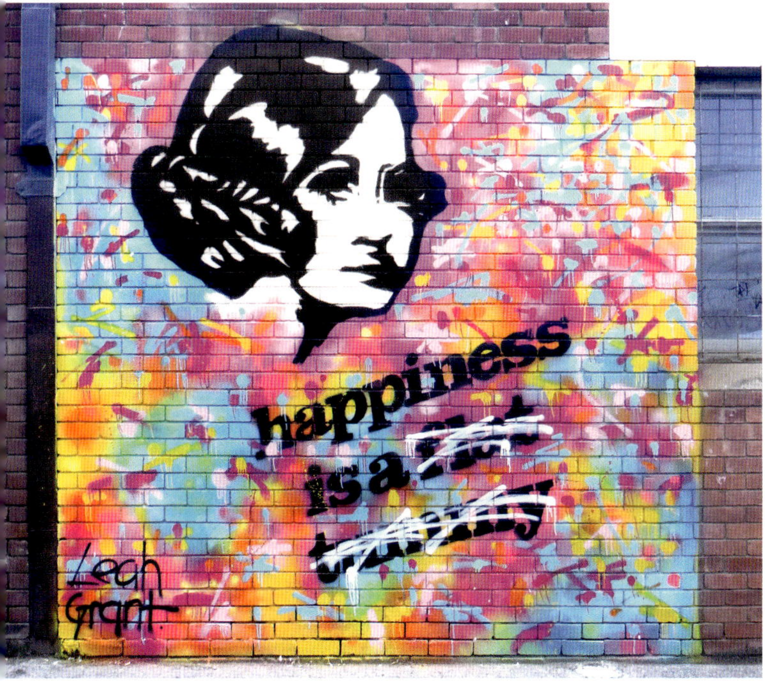
happiness
is a
Leah
Grant

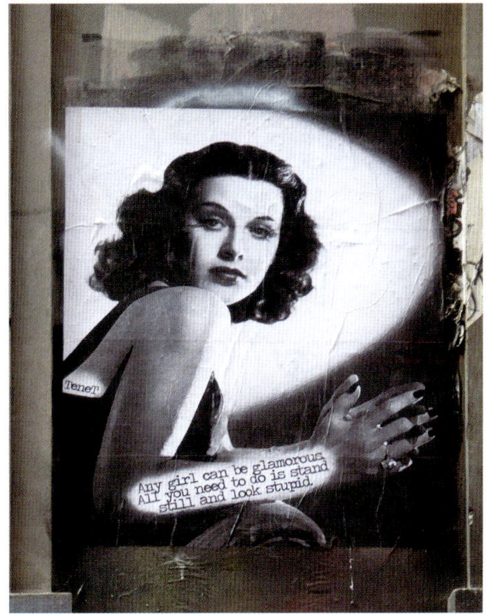
TeneT
Any girl can be glamorous.
All you need to do is stand
still and look stupid.

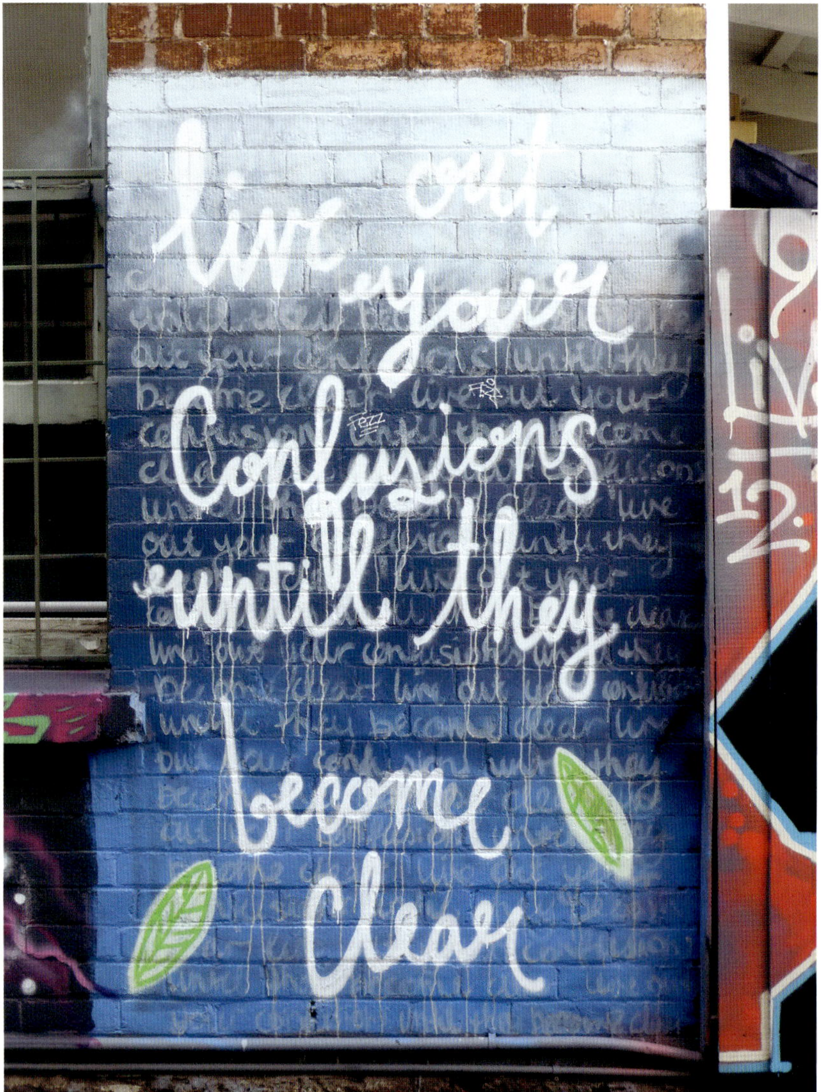
live out your
Confusions
until they
become
Clear

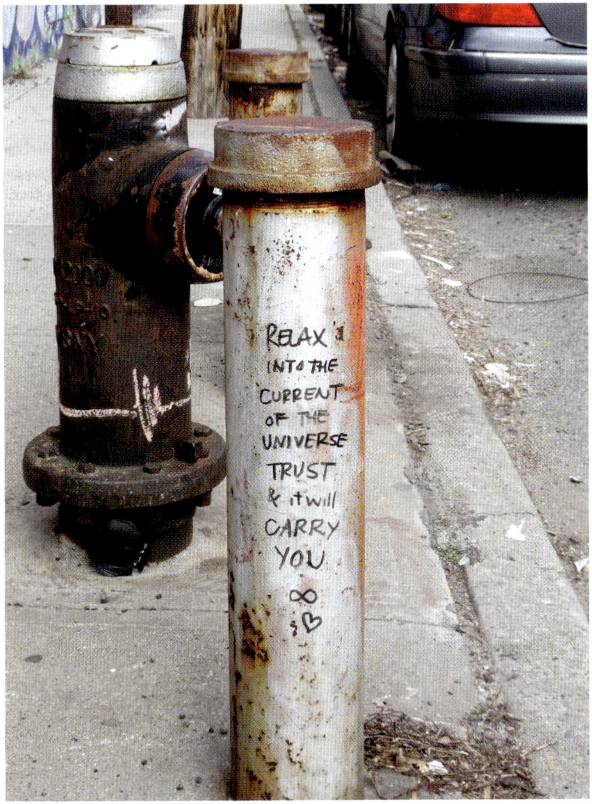

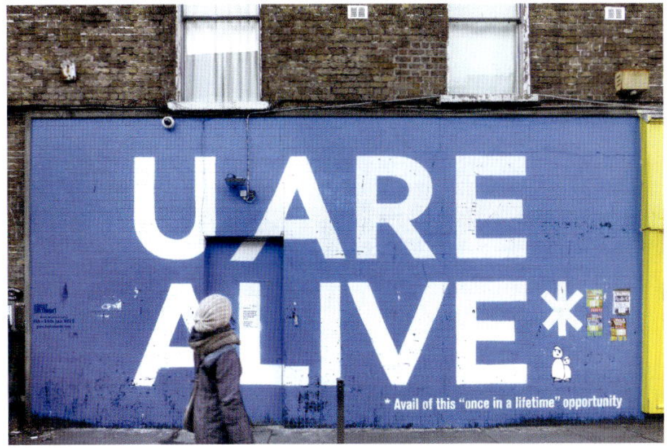

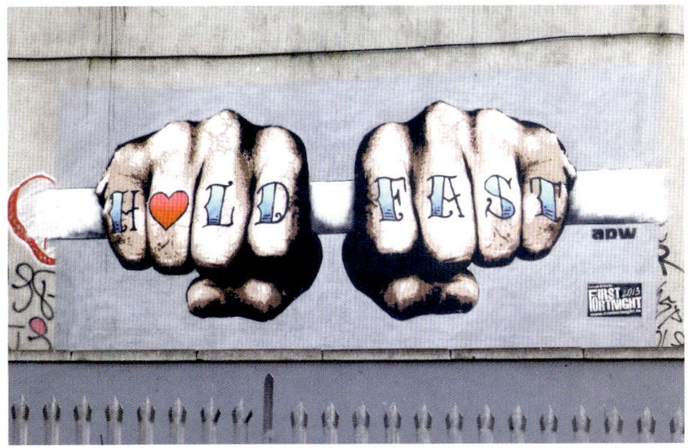

OPPOSITE Georgia Frances King and Katie Marie Clarke, *Saturn Return*, Melbourne, Australia, 2014

LEFT Unknown artist, New York City, USA, 2018

TOP RIGHT Maser, *U Are Alive*, Dublin, Ireland, 2015

BOTTOM RIGHT ADW, *Hold Fast*, Dublin, Ireland, 2015

'**LIVE** out your confusions until they become clear' is a quote from the diary of the 20th-century author Anaïs Nin. The pale repetition of the quote across the background of the visual version opposite subtly reinforces the handwritten message.

U Are Alive by Maser at top right is a powerful statement about appreciating the here and now. 'Hold fast' is a traditional sailor's tattoo which refers to holding tight to the rigging. Its second, more politically charged meaning is to never give up in the face of an obstacle. The version above was painted by stencil artist ADW.

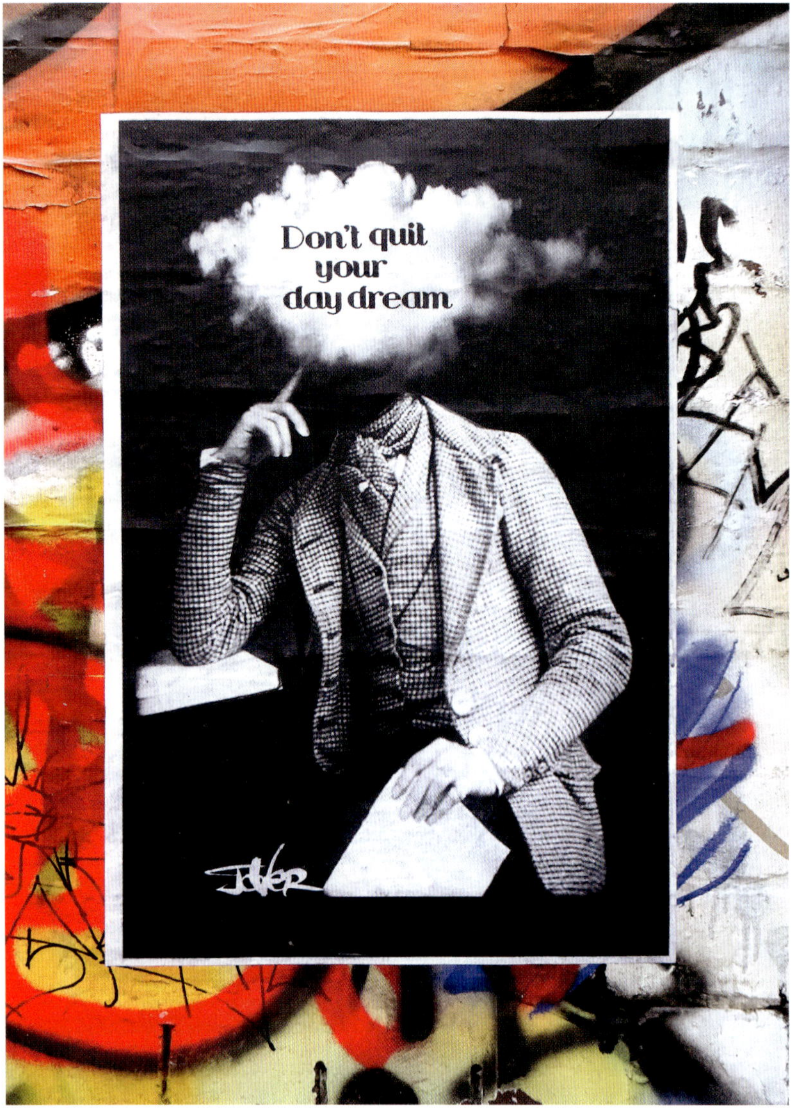

LEFT Loui Jover, *Daydream*, Melbourne, Australia, 2018

OPPOSITE TOP LEFT Unknown artist, Melbourne, Australia, 2016

OPPOSITE TOP RIGHT Escif, Valencia, Spain, 2013

OPPOSITE BOTTOM Lana Hughes and Rory Elphick, Animaux Circus, *The Time Is Now!*, Melbourne, Australia, 2018

THESE artworks, large and small, reinforce a positive approach to life. Queensland artist Loui Jover's combination of classic imagery and word play at left creates an engaging picture for contemplation by the passerby. Based on the humorous saying 'don't give up your day job', the work subverts the meaning by encouraging a temporary escape from reality.

The three works on the opposite page have used time as their inspiration. At top left an anonymous artist has added their version of 'seize the day' to a wall that already displays a visual conversation. Escif's simple, subtle painting of a cassette at top right is inscribed with a deeper and more complex message – 'today is the future' – a reminder that we shouldn't procrastinate. The same thought is at the core of design studio Animaux Circus' brightly coloured rooftop declaration.

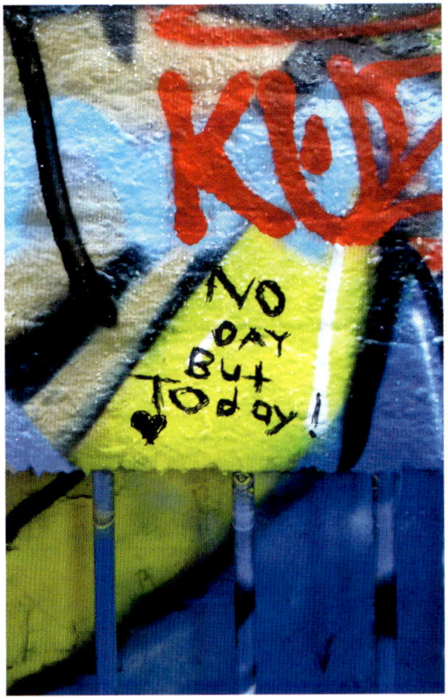
NO DAY But Today!

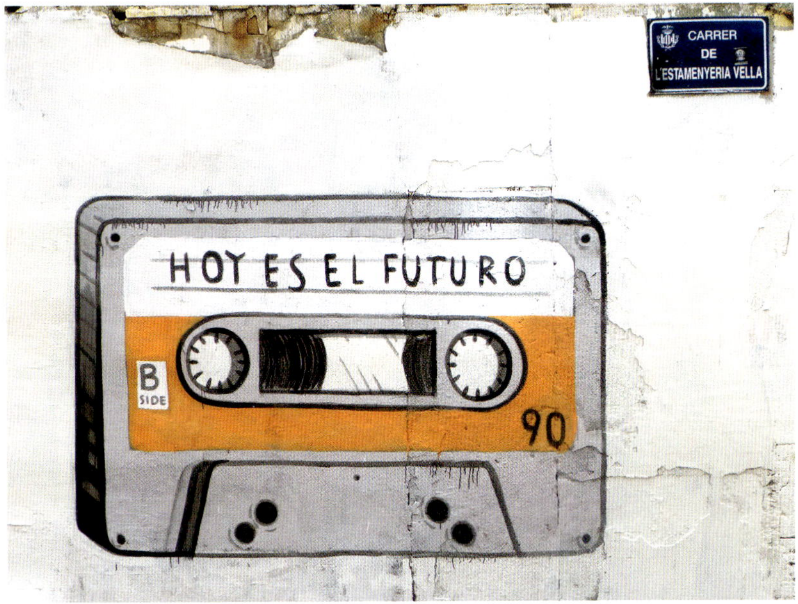
CARRER DE L'ESTAMENYERIA VELLA
HOY ES EL FUTURO
B SIDE
90

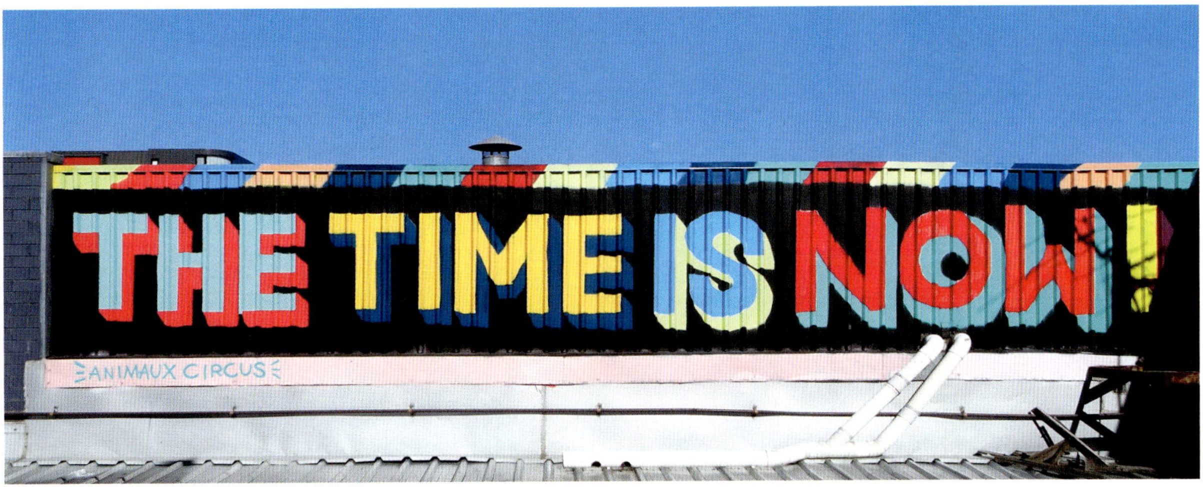
THE TIME IS NOW!
ANIMAUX CIRCUS

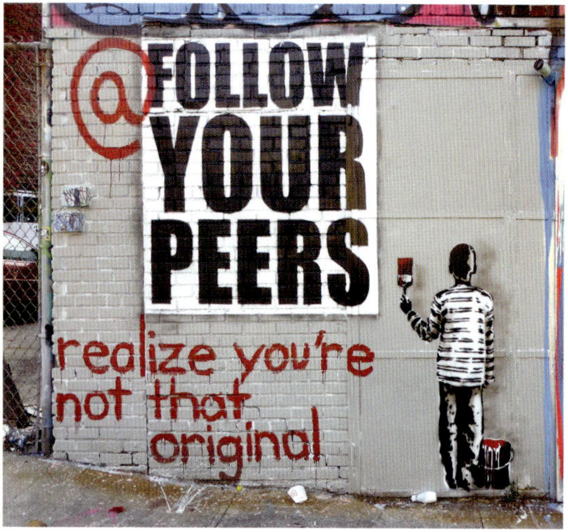

TOP Rene Gagnon, *Follow Your Peers*, New York City, USA, 2018

BOTTOM ±MaisMenos±, *Goods*, Lisbon, Portugal, 2016

OPPOSITE ±MaisMenos±, *Debt*, Lisbon, Portugal, 2016

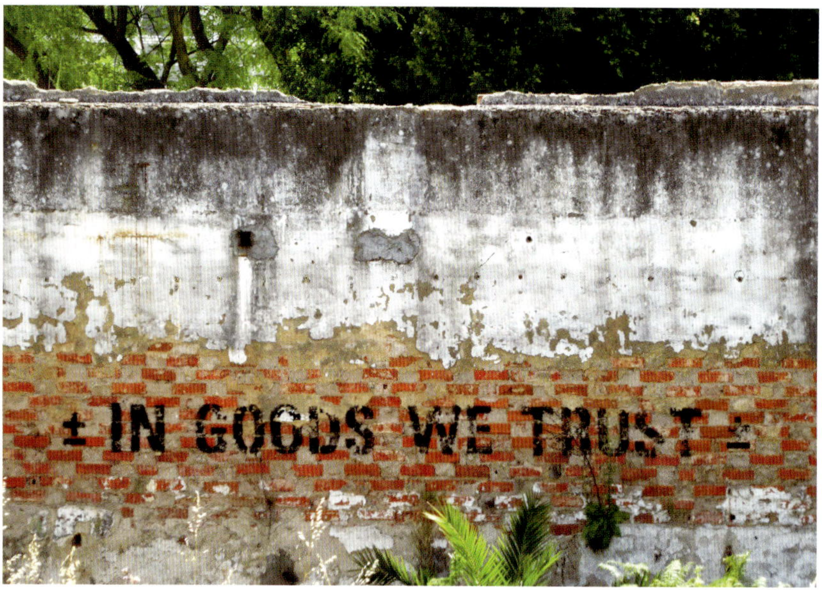

STENCILLED images maintain their simplicity, allowing the message to speak with few distractions. Rene Gagnon's advice to 'follow your peers' captures the observer's attention, successfully drawing it to the sad truism of the handwritten coda.

The strength inherent in the simplicity of a stencil is nowhere more effective than in the work of ±MaisMenos±. With his name translating to ±MoreLess±, ±MaisMenos± is undertaking an ongoing project of visual intervention in the urban environment. The artist offers direct, incisive statements that use clever word play to encourage the viewer to think about the dominant social and economic systems.

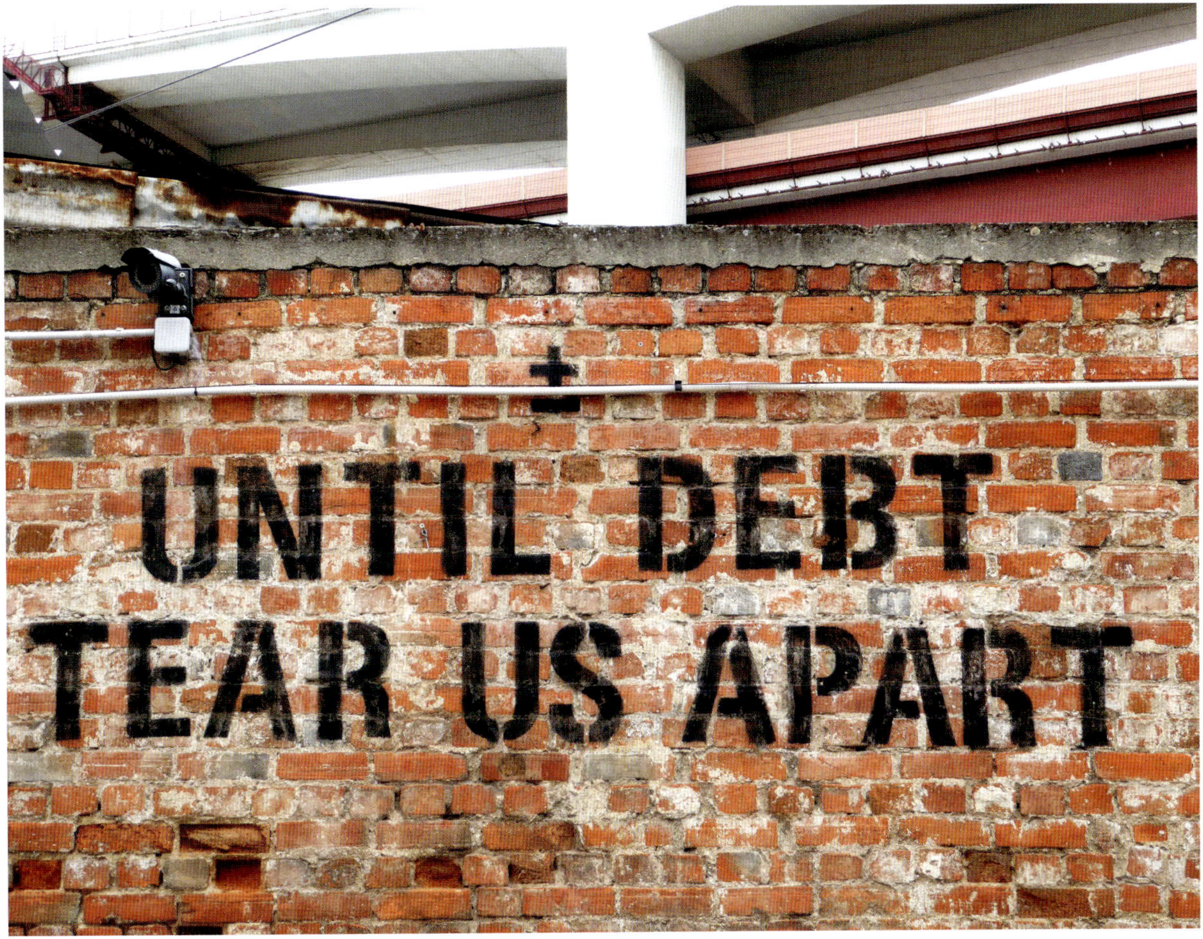
UNTIL DEBT
TEAR US APART

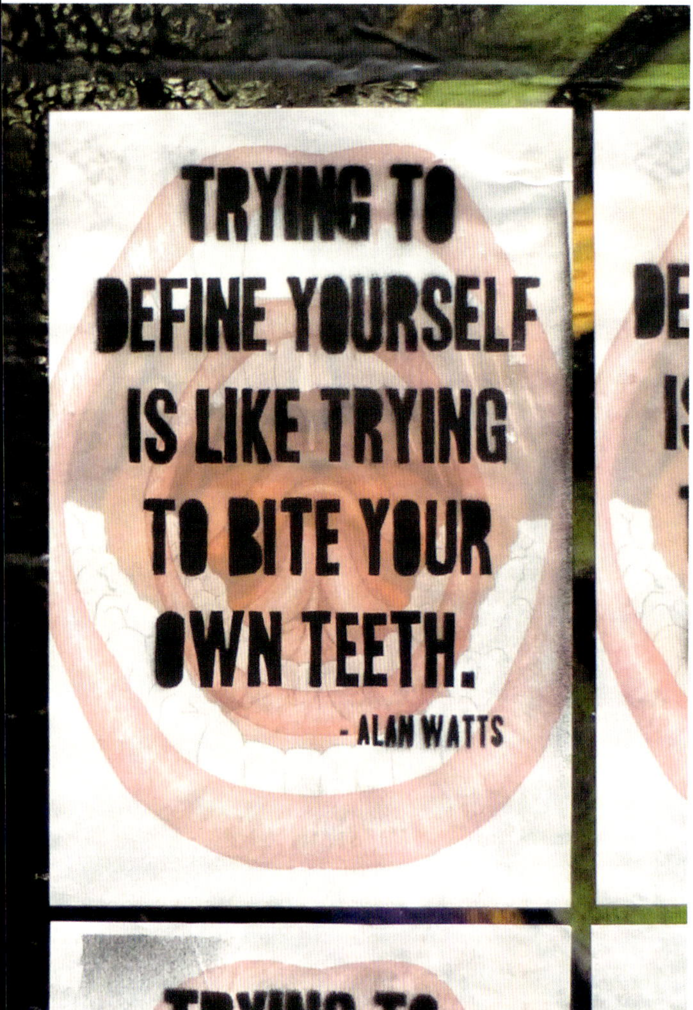
TRYING TO
DEFINE YOURSELF
IS LIKE TRYING
TO BITE YOUR
OWN TEETH.
- ALAN WATTS

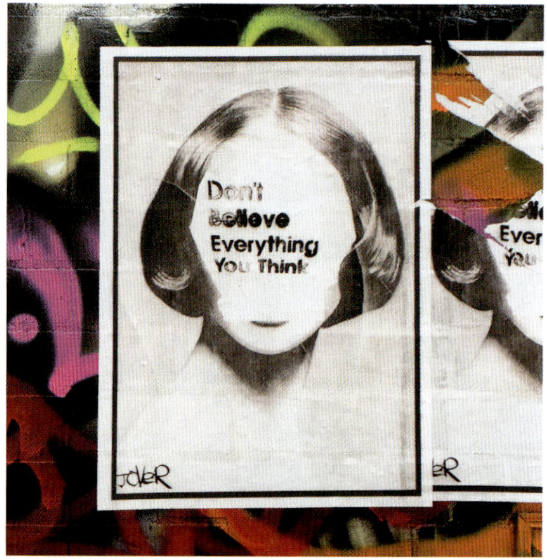
Don't
Believe
Everything
You Think

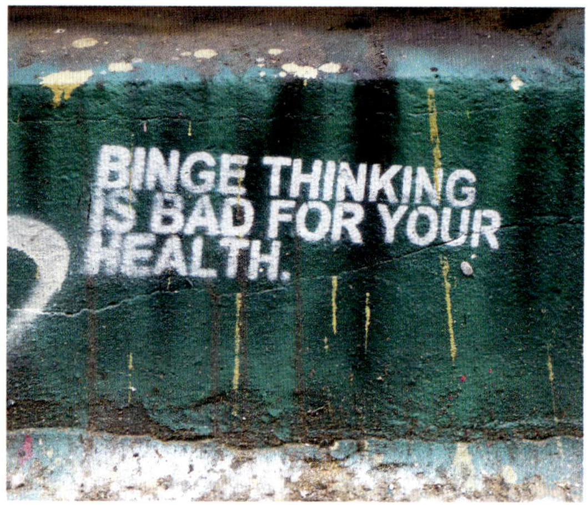
BINGE THINKING
IS BAD FOR YOUR
HEALTH.

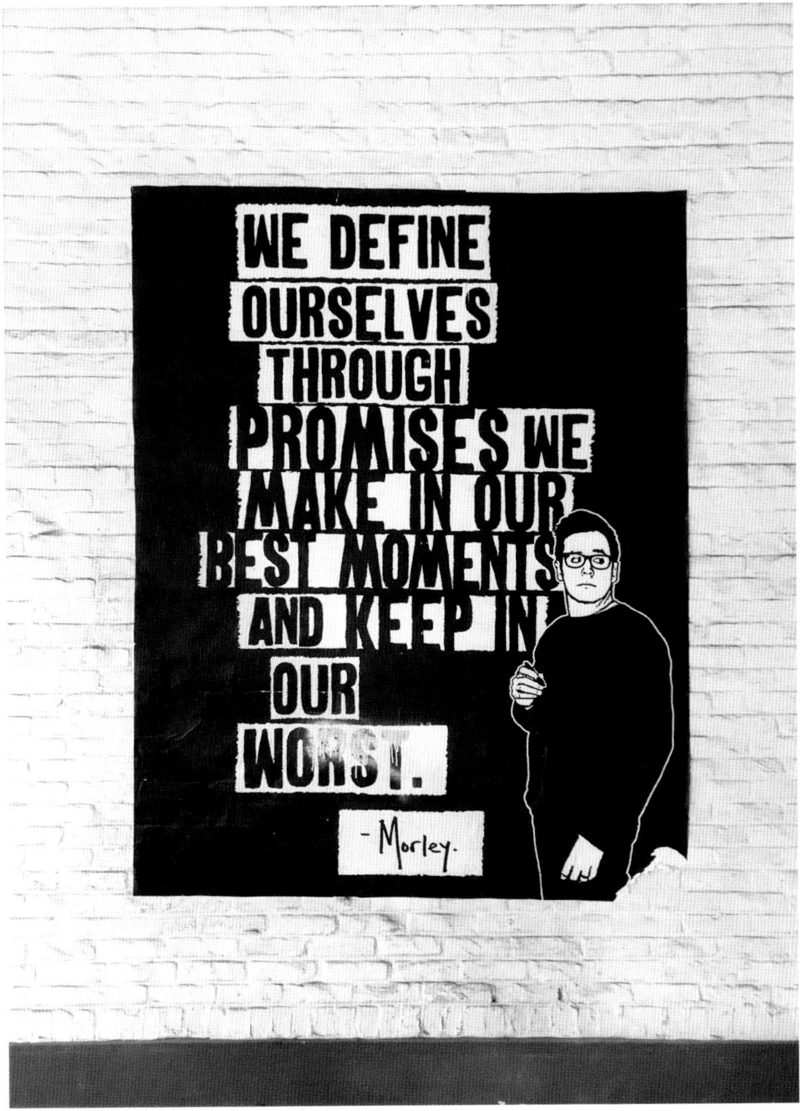

OPPOSITE LEFT Unknown artist, Melbourne, Australia, 2013

OPPOSITE TOP RIGHT Loui Jover, *Believe*, Melbourne, Australia, 2017

OPPOSITE BOTTOM RIGHT myheadsajungle, *Binge Thinking Is Bad for Your Health*, Melbourne, Australia, 2014

LEFT Morley, *Promises*, Ghent, Belgium, 2018

YES, thinking CAN do our heads in. Queensland artist Loui Jover warns us against overthinking in his small paste-up at opposite top right, while myheadsajungle's humorous message below it reminds us that binge thinking can have a deleterious effect on our mental well-being.

How DO we define ourselves? Morley's serious response at left is quite different to the pithy statement by British philosopher and author Alan Watts, opposite, pasted up by an anonymous artist. Morley's posters can be seen as war cries, offerings of encouragement and hope. They are pasted up illegally, so he works quickly and efficiently. He includes a self-portrait in each poster so that passersby feel that they are being addressed personally.

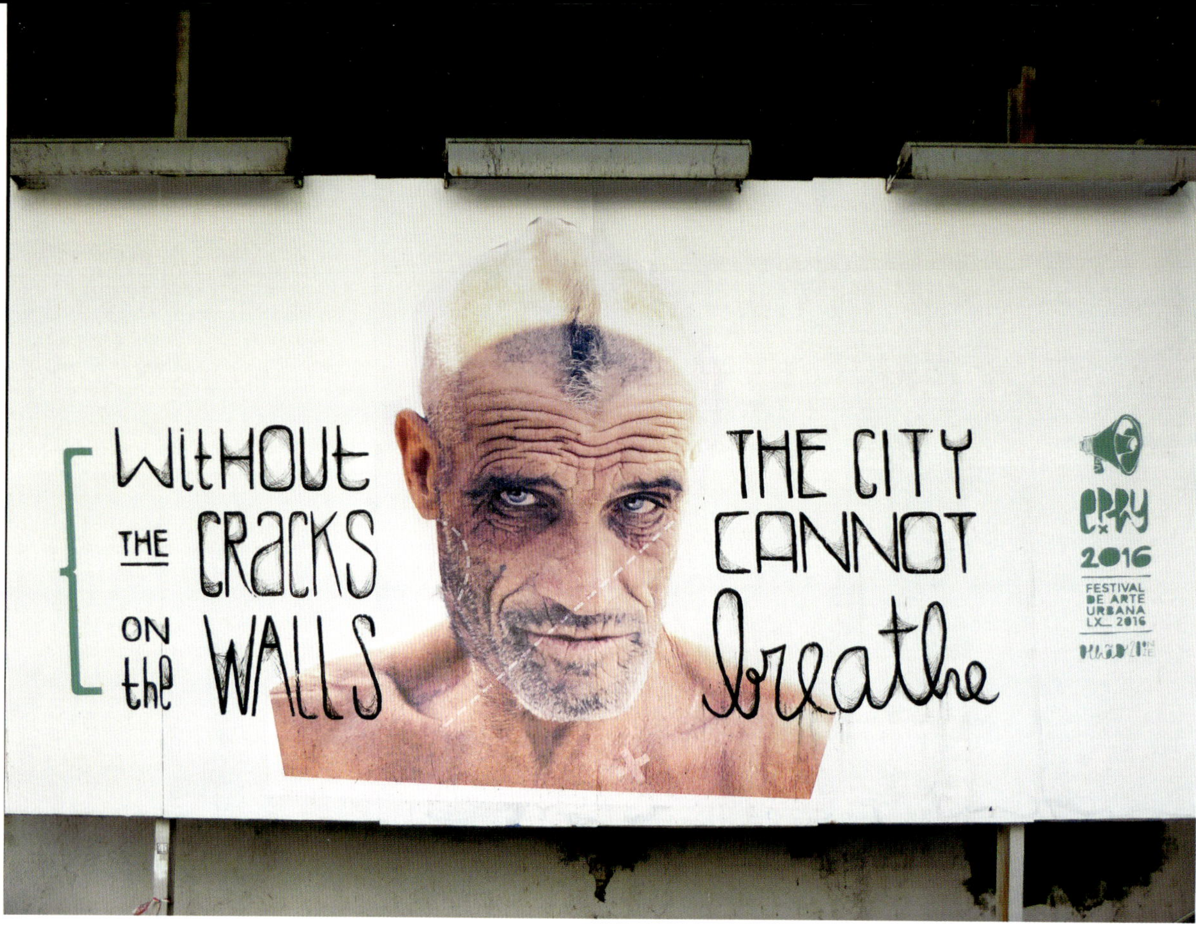

ABOVE Ephy, Lisbon, Portugal, 2016

OPPOSITE LEFT Morley, *Someday*, Los Angeles, USA, 2016

OPPOSITE TOP RIGHT WRDSMTH, Melbourne, Australia, 2015

OPPOSITE BOTTOM RIGHT WRDSMTH, Melbourne, Australia, 2015

THE observations and messages on these pages are sensitive and thought-provoking. The humorous image on Ephy's wall above adds another layer of meaning to the handwritten text.

On the opposite page Morley again encourages us to think about our own lives. He says that the size of the text is the volume at which the words are communicated, so small text is a hushed whisper while large text is a shout to anyone within eyeshot. At far right Los Angeles–based WRDSMTH spreads his motivational messages by pasting a page of text above his trademark stencil of an old-school typewriter. Working prolifically but remaining anonymous, he is inspired by life as he sees it being lived out around him.

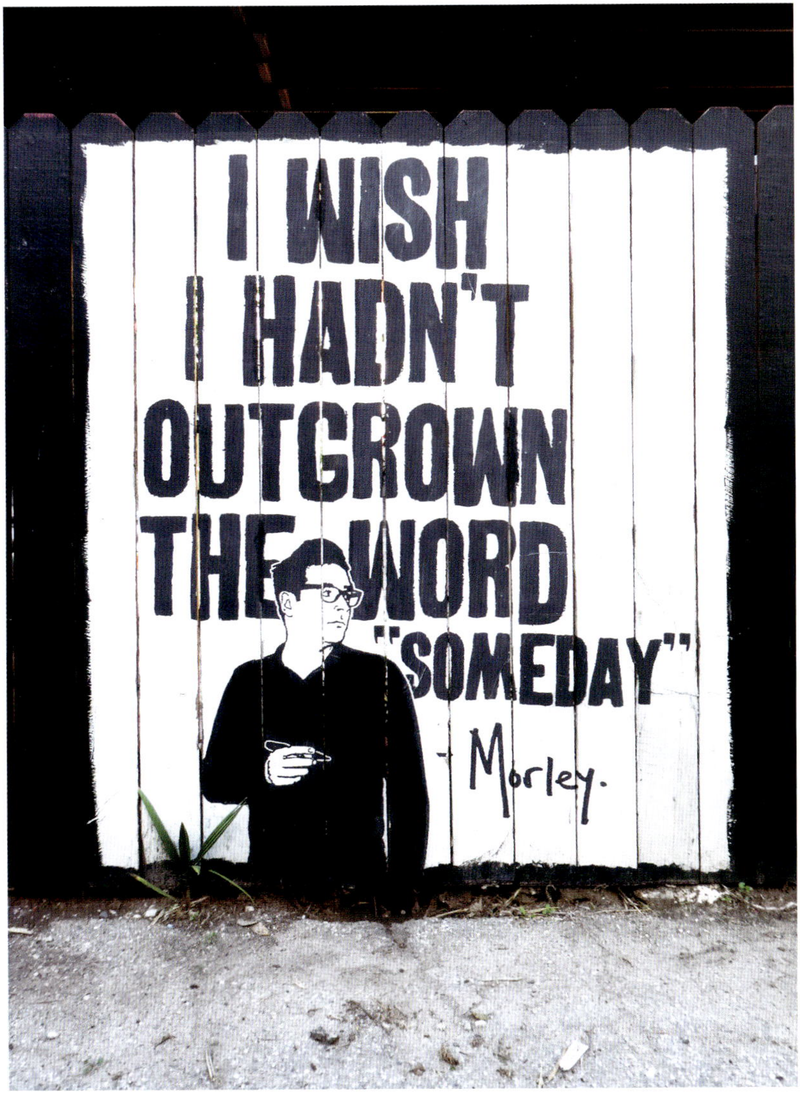
I WISH
I HADN'T
OUTGROWN
THE WORD
"SOMEDAY"
- Morley.

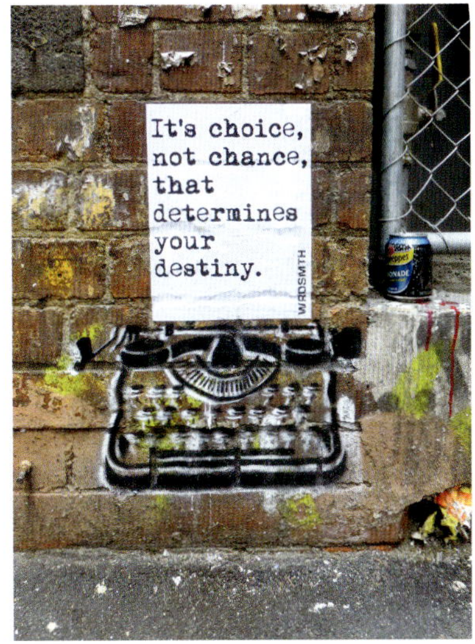
It's choice,
not chance,
that
determines
your
destiny.
WRDSMTH

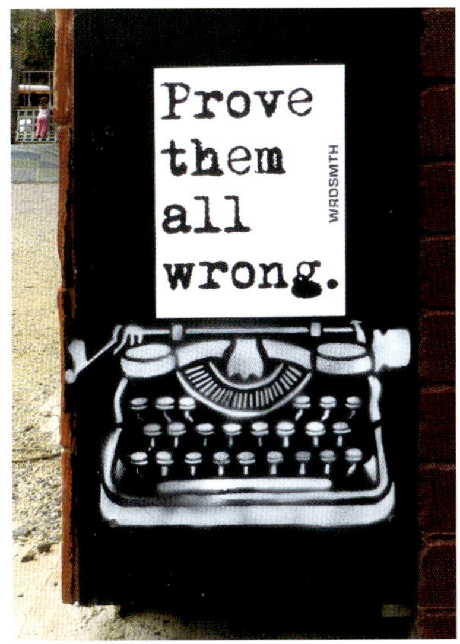
Prove
them
all
wrong.
WRDSMTH

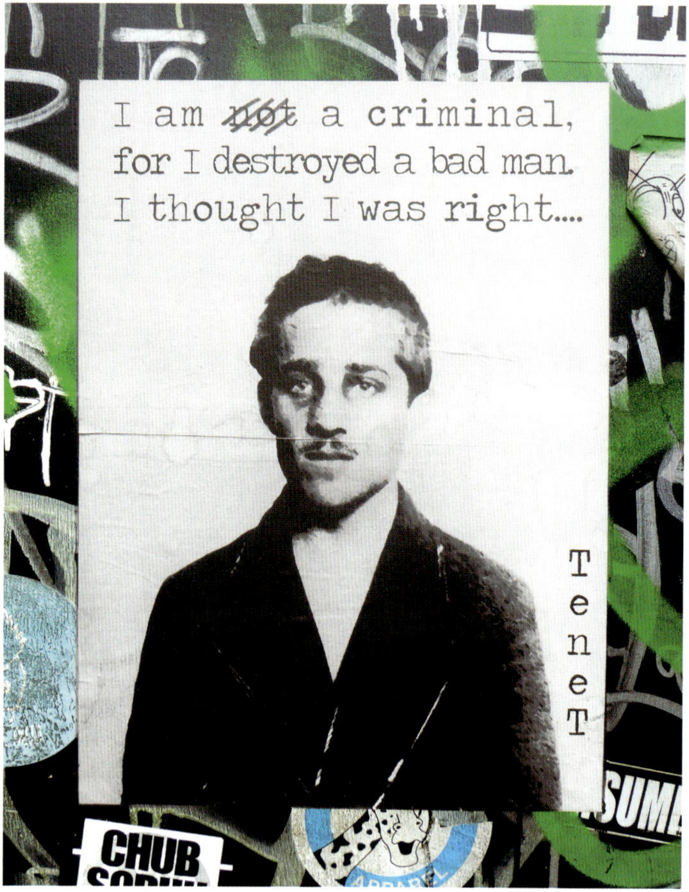
I am ~~not~~ a criminal,
for I destroyed a bad man.
I thought I was right....
TeneT
CHUB

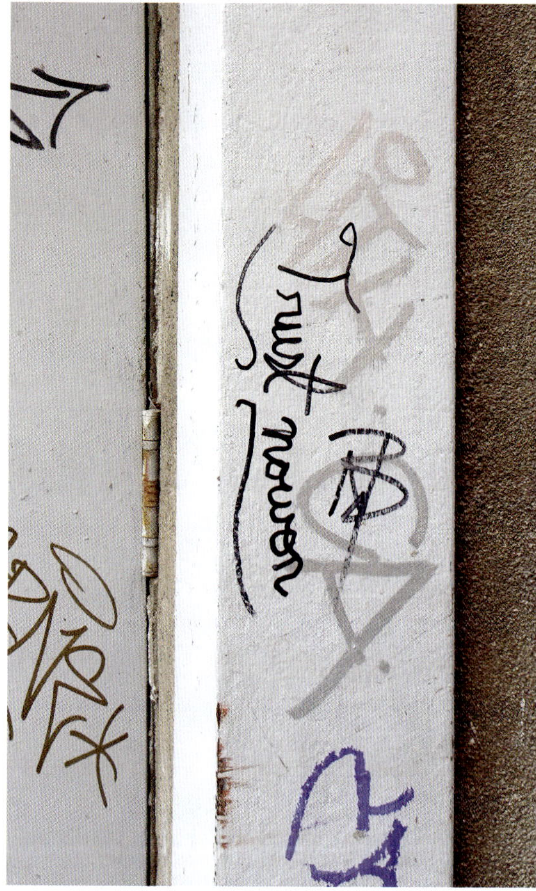

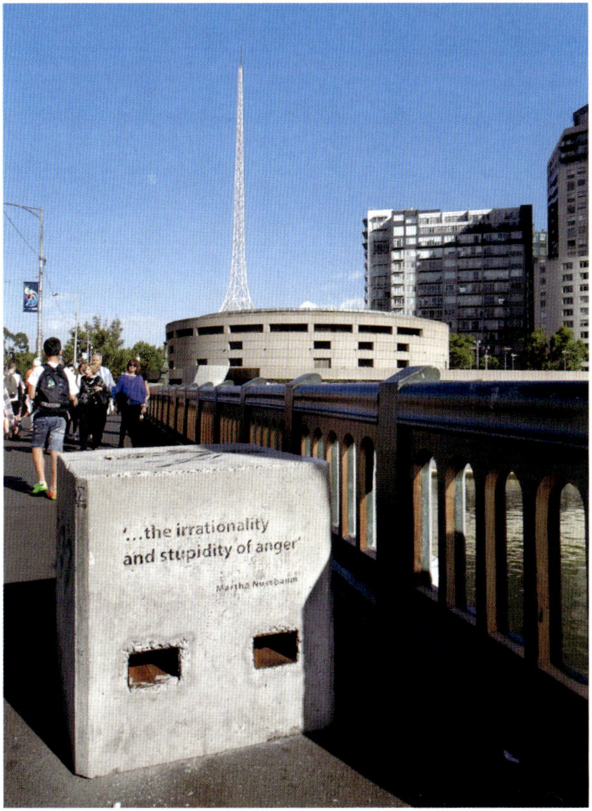

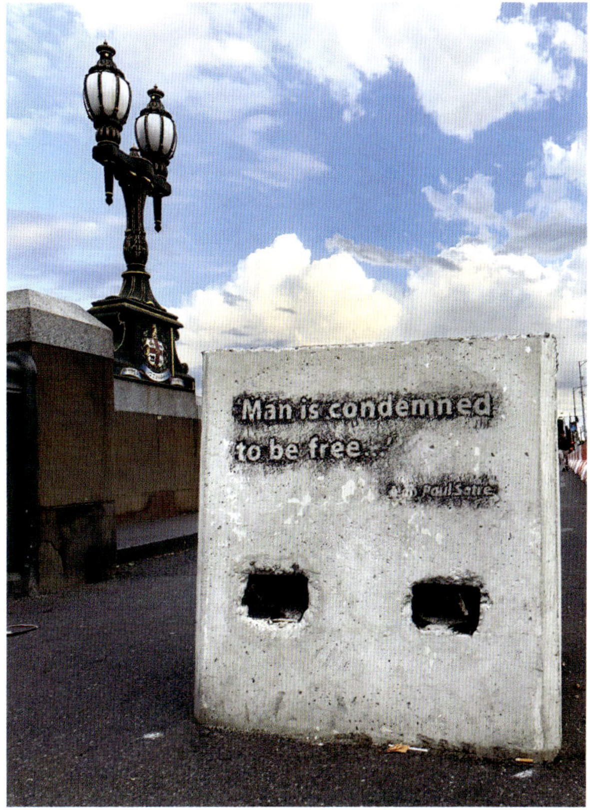

OPPOSITE LEFT TeneT, Melbourne, Australia, 2017

OPPOSITE RIGHT Unknown artist, Toronto, Canada, 2018

LEFT and **RIGHT** Nina Sanadze and Julie Shiels, *Concrete Knowledge*, Melbourne, Australia, 2018

TENET'S paste-ups speak of beliefs, philosophies and principles. Gavrilo Princip, the subject of the paste-up opposite, assassinated Franz Ferdinand, the Archduke of Austria, thus precipitating World War I. Interestingly, 'not' was scribbled out by a passerby after the work was installed. The spelling mistake in the scribbled message 'Trust nowon' makes it all the more heartfelt.

While concrete bollards have been installed in big cities the world over as counterterrorist devices, they can also be seen as a threat to freedom. In many places artists have made them a canvas on which to express their frustration and their refusal to submit to fear. Nina Sanadze and Julie Shiels added quotes by renowned writers and thinkers to a series of bollards in Melbourne, a collection they've called *Concrete Knowledge*.

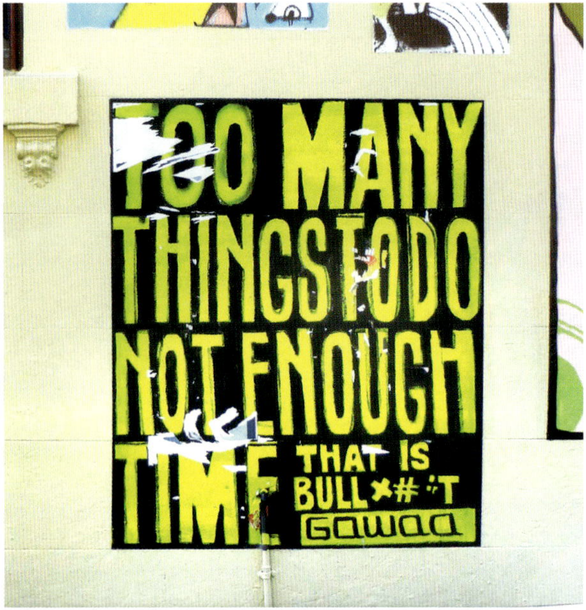

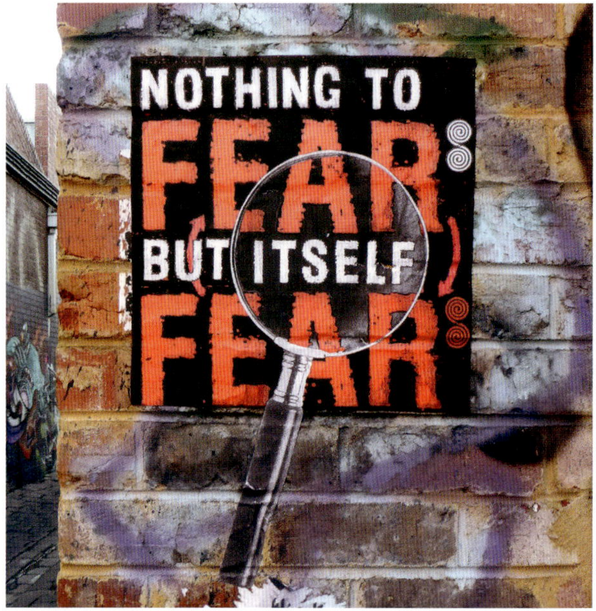

OPPOSITE Rob Sharp, New York City, USA, 2018
LEFT Gawaa, *No Bullshit*, Sydney, Australia, 2015
RIGHT Phoenix, Melbourne, Australia, 2014

EACH of these walls delivers a personal call to arms. They charge us to fear complacency and warn us not to waste time procrastinating. Above left, Gawaa, a Mongolian artist living and working in Sydney, tells us not to make excuses. Above right, Phoenix used the well-known phrase 'nothing to fear but fear itself' as the motif of his series *The Mathematics of Fear* to draw attention to the Australian government's reaction to the drownings at sea of asylum seekers arriving by boat.

Rob Sharp reminds us of Yoda's advice opposite in a classic *Star Wars* moment from *The Empire Strikes Back* – put 100 percent into what you do, or don't bother. This is sage council from the Jedi Master.

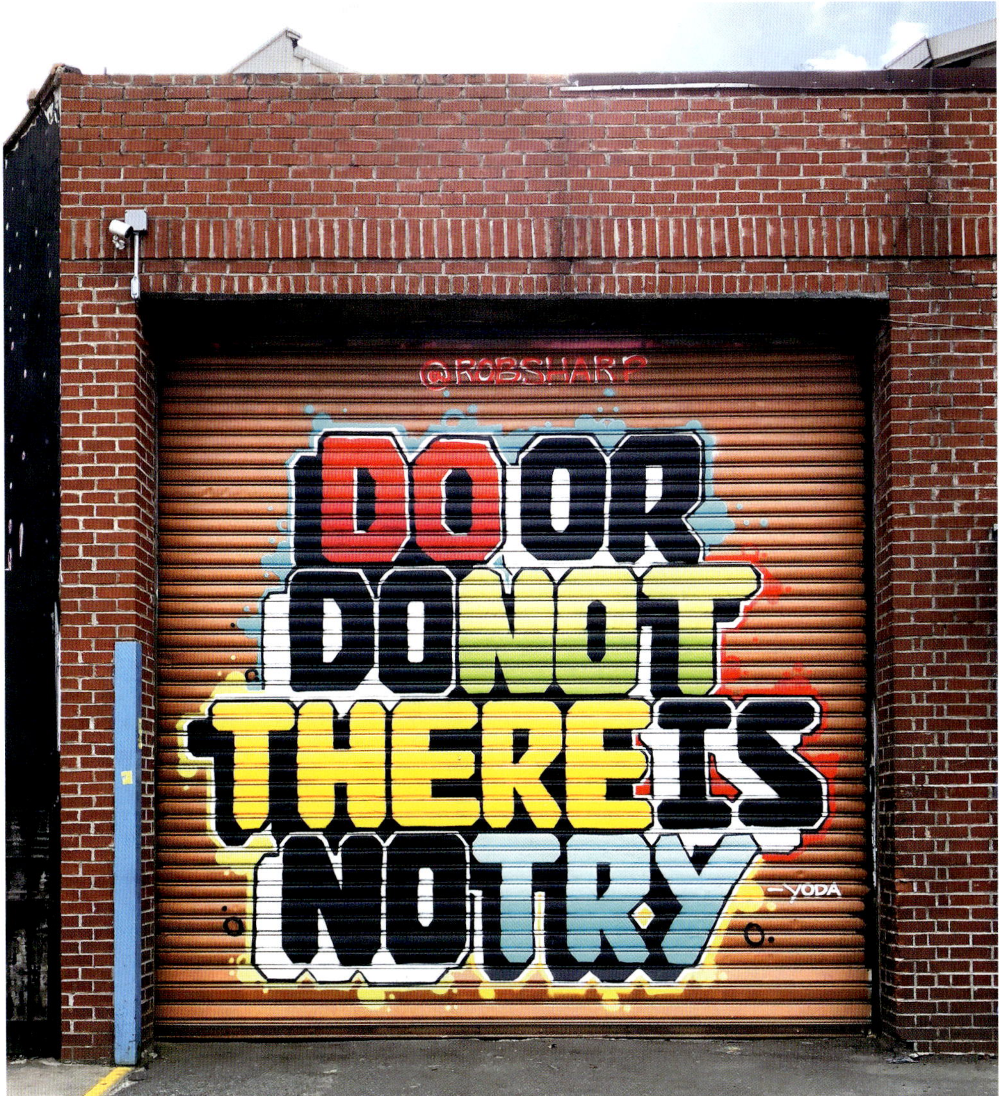
@ROBSHARP
DO OR
DO NOT
THERE IS
NO TRY
—YODA

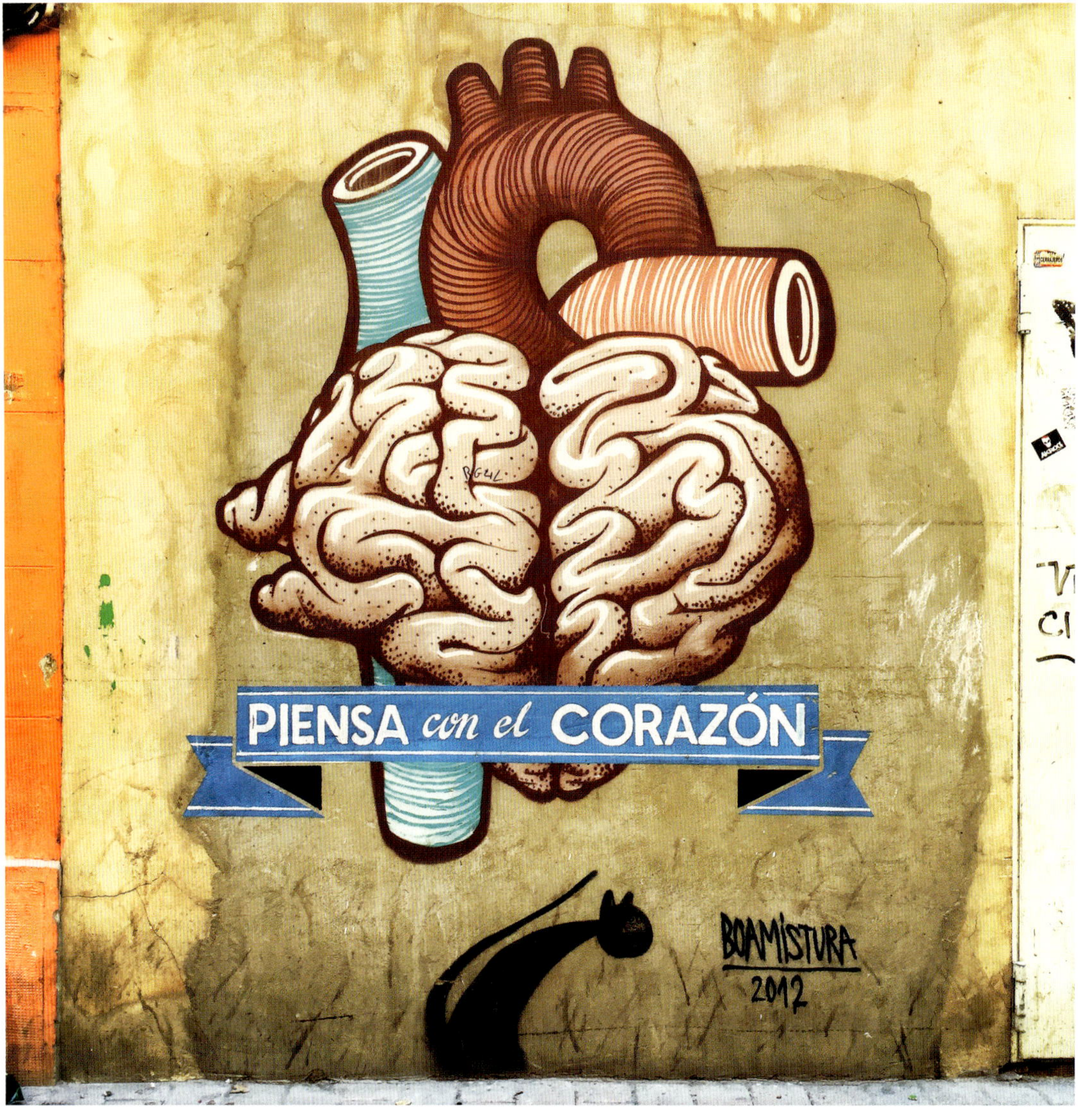
PIENSA con el CORAZÓN
BOAMISTURA
2012

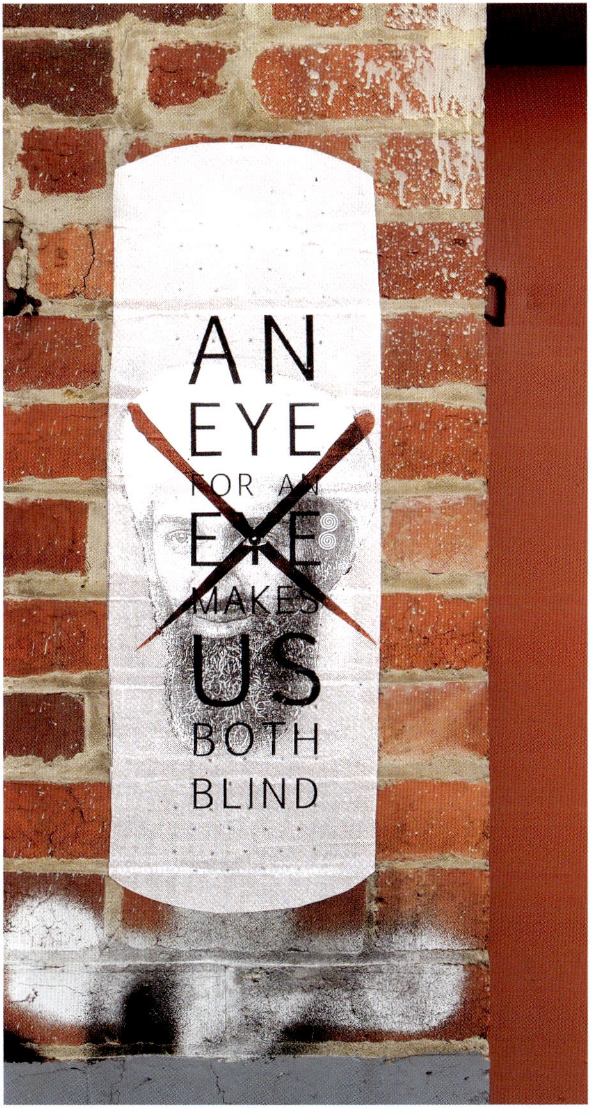

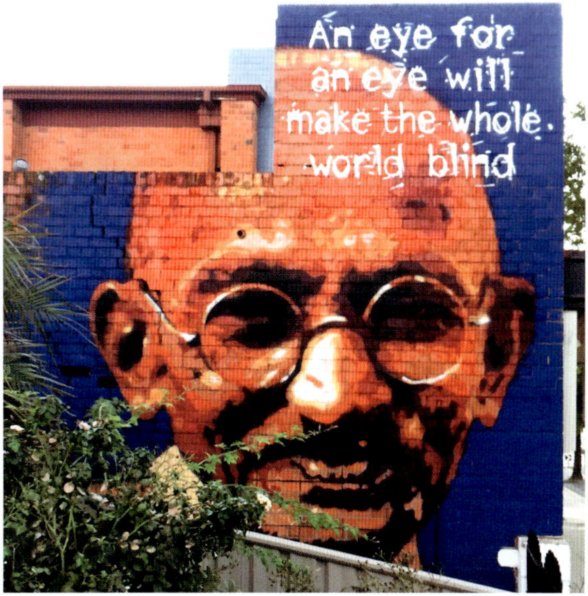

OPPOSITE Boa Mistura, *Piensa con el Corazón*, Zaragoza, Spain, 2016
LEFT Phoenix, Melbourne, Australia, 2013
RIGHT Tim Bowtell, *Eye for an Eye*, Benalla, Australia, 2016

BOA Mistura is a multidisciplinary team of urban artists headquartered in Madrid. Their name means 'good mixture' in Portuguese. The conflated image of the heart and the brain on the opposite page matches the text scrolled across the bottom – 'think with the heart'.

The ancient saying 'an eye for an eye' is known as the law of retaliation. By adding Osama bin Laden into the mix at left, Phoenix brings the adage into the 21st century. The extension of the saying with the phrase 'will make the whole world blind', above, is attributed to Gandhi and reflects his policy of tolerance and non-violent civil disobedience.

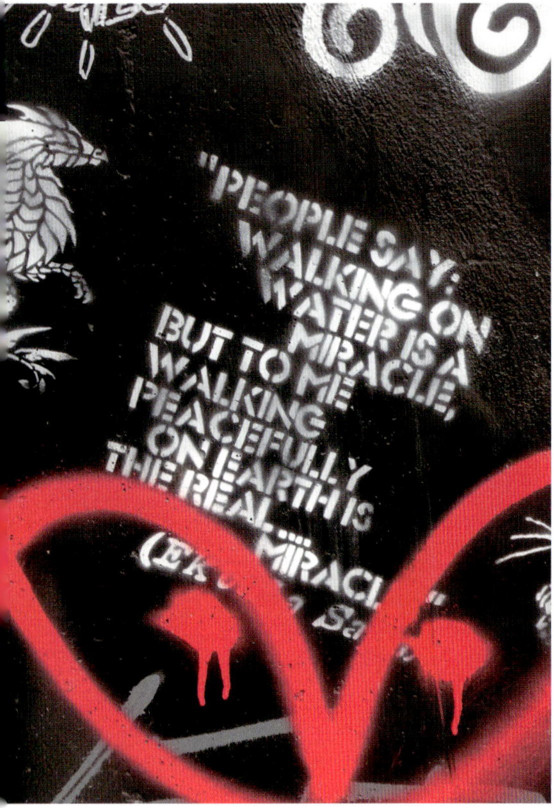
"PEOPLE SAY:
WALKING ON
WATER IS A
MIRACLE,
BUT TO ME
WALKING
PEACEFULLY
ON EARTH IS
THE REAL...
MIRACLE

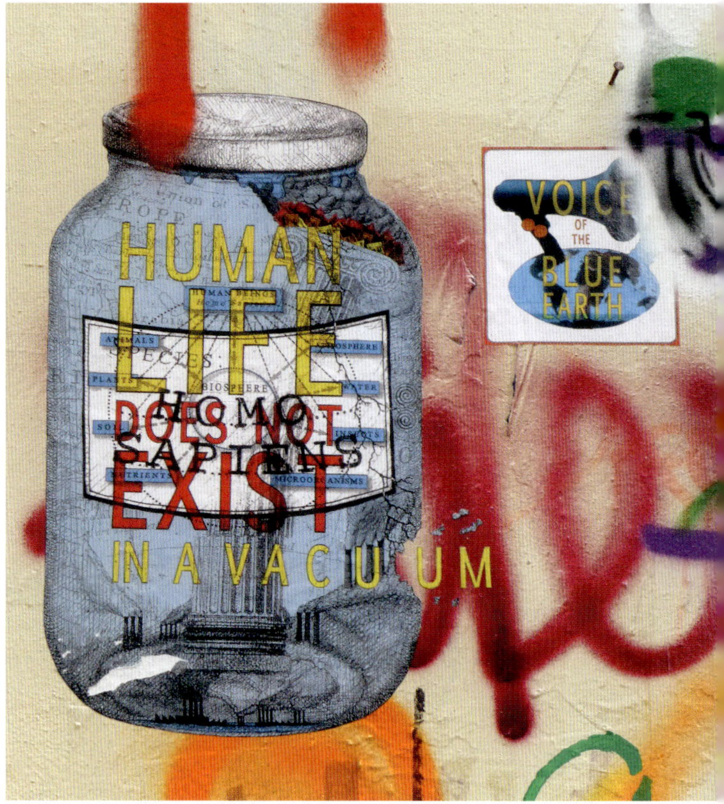
HUMAN
LIFE
DOES NOT
EXIST
IN A VACUUM
HOMO
SAPIENS
VOICE
OF
THE
BLUE
EARTH

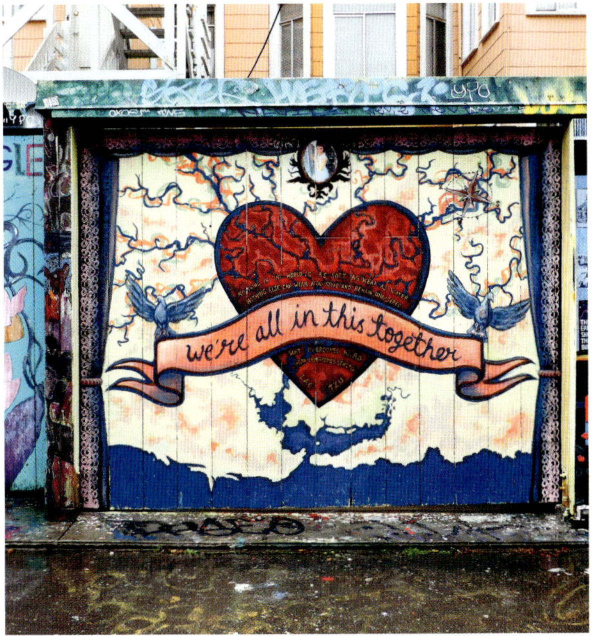

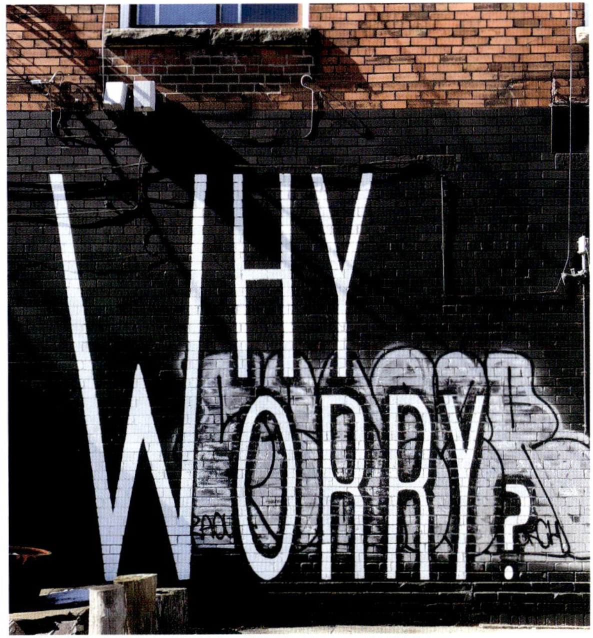

OPPOSITE LEFT SST Division, Paris, France, 2018

OPPOSITE RIGHT Phoenix, Melbourne, Australia, 2013

LEFT Unknown artist, Clarion Alley Mural Project, San Francisco, USA, 2017

RIGHT Unknown artist, Toronto, Canada, 2018

THESE four text-based works vary enormously in their presentation – stencil, paste-up and paint – and their messages. Quotes from the ancients, references to our treatment of the planet and a shrug sit here side by side.

The message with the heart above left was painted in Clarion Alley, well-known in San Francisco as a site where the arts are used as a voice for social activism. An inspirational quote from the 6th century BCE Chinese philosopher Lao Tzu has been included in the fine print, although it's too small to read in this image. At right on the opposite page Phoenix reminds us that human life does not exist in a vacuum – we really ARE in this together. *Why Worry?* shrugs off our concern for the planet and each other in the interests of complacency.

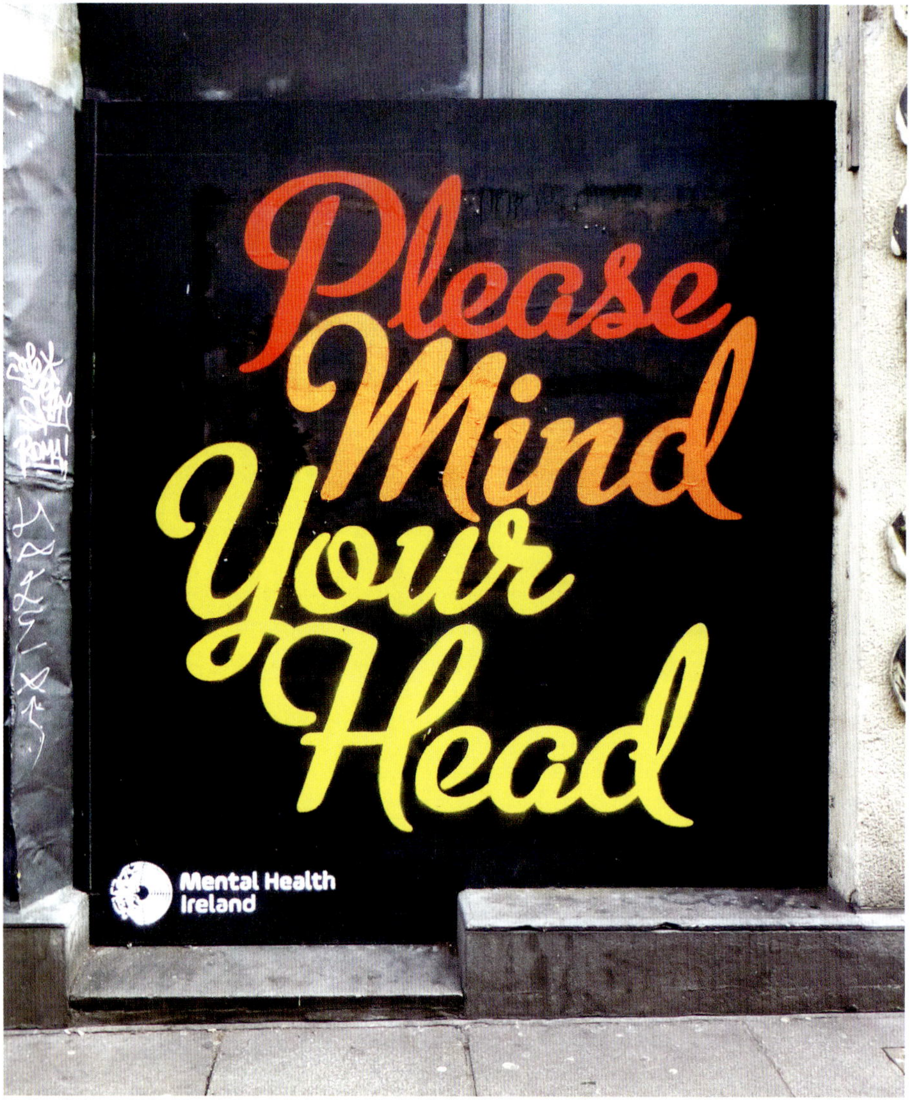
Please
Mind
Your
Head
Mental Health
Ireland

OUR psychological wellbeing is an issue for each of us as individuals but also as members of a community. It's good to be aware, to laugh and to accept that life can be difficult at times. Mental Health Ireland commissioned *Please Mind Your Head* as part of their ongoing campaign promoting mental health and well-being.

Stress Less is an amusing street-side intervention, made simply by applying adhesive tape to the surface. A similar message, accompanied by a relaxed dude, is written on a wall in London at right. Loui Jover's tongue-in-cheek comment below is superimposed on vintage imagery. It reminds us that we all have our quirks and foibles below the surface. And what is 'normal' anyway?

OPPOSITE Morgan, *Please Mind Your Head*, Dublin, Ireland, 2015

LEFT Loui Jover, *Normal*, Melbourne, Australia, 2018

TOP RIGHT Unknown artist, London, UK, 2015

BOTTOM RIGHT Unknown artist, Stavanger, Norway, 2016

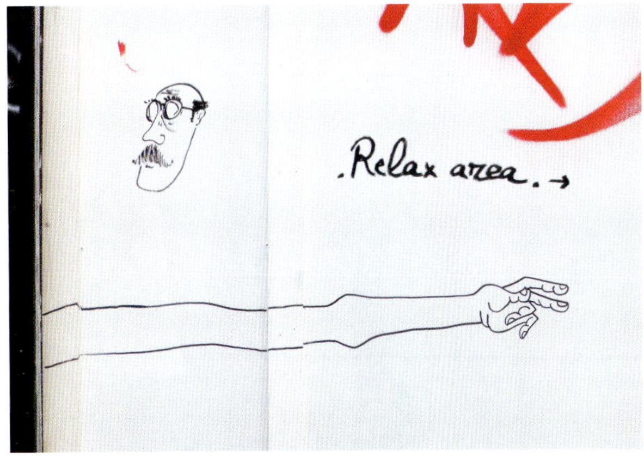

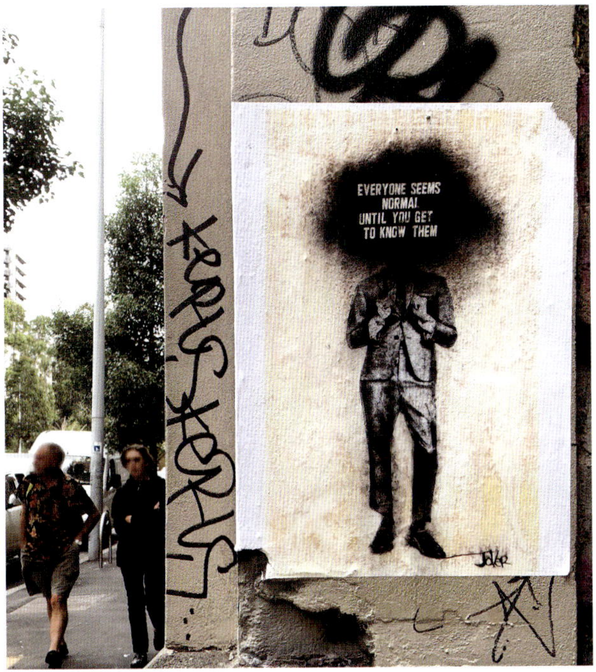

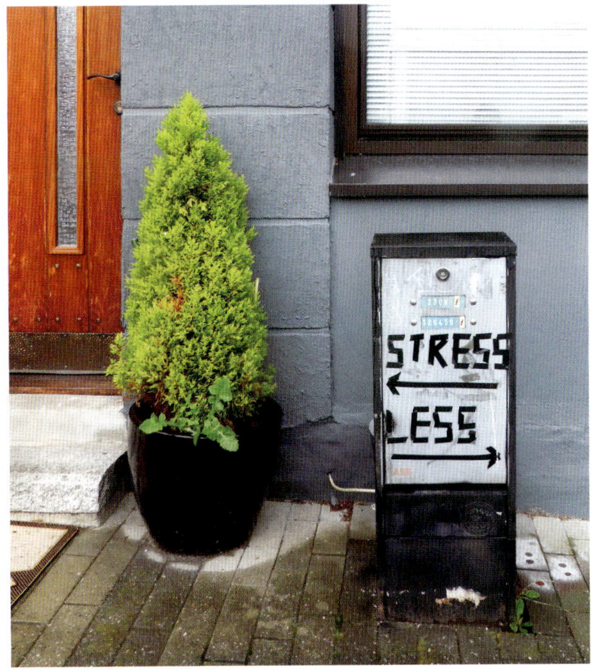

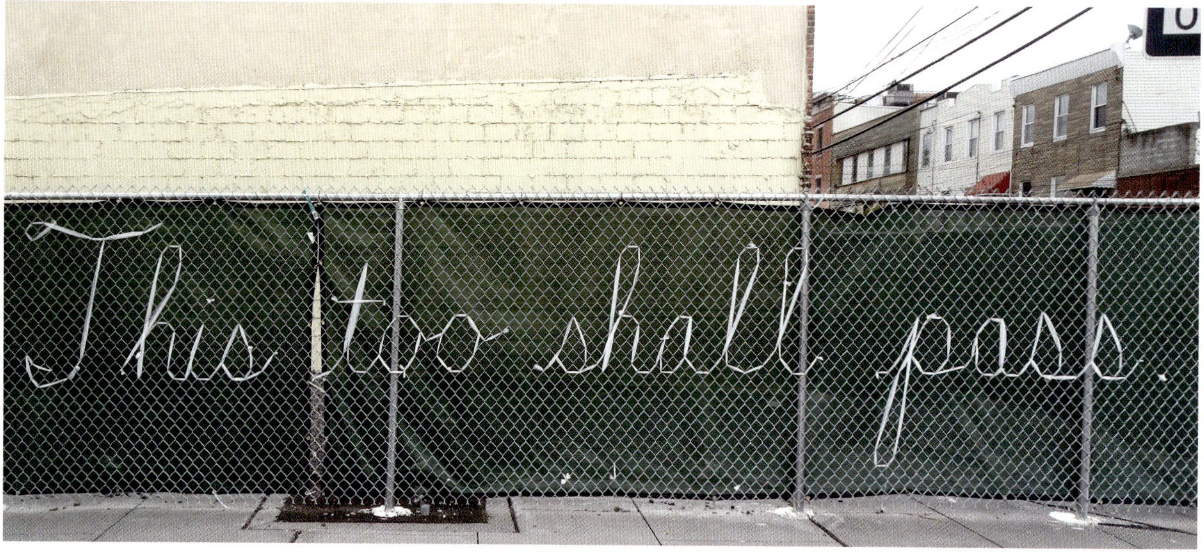
This too shall pass.

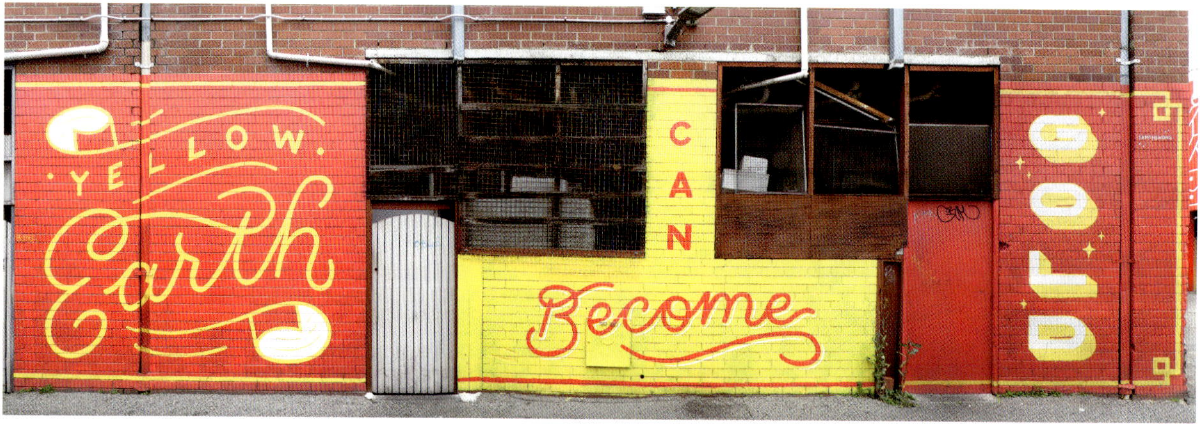
YELLOW
Earth
CAN
Become
GOLD

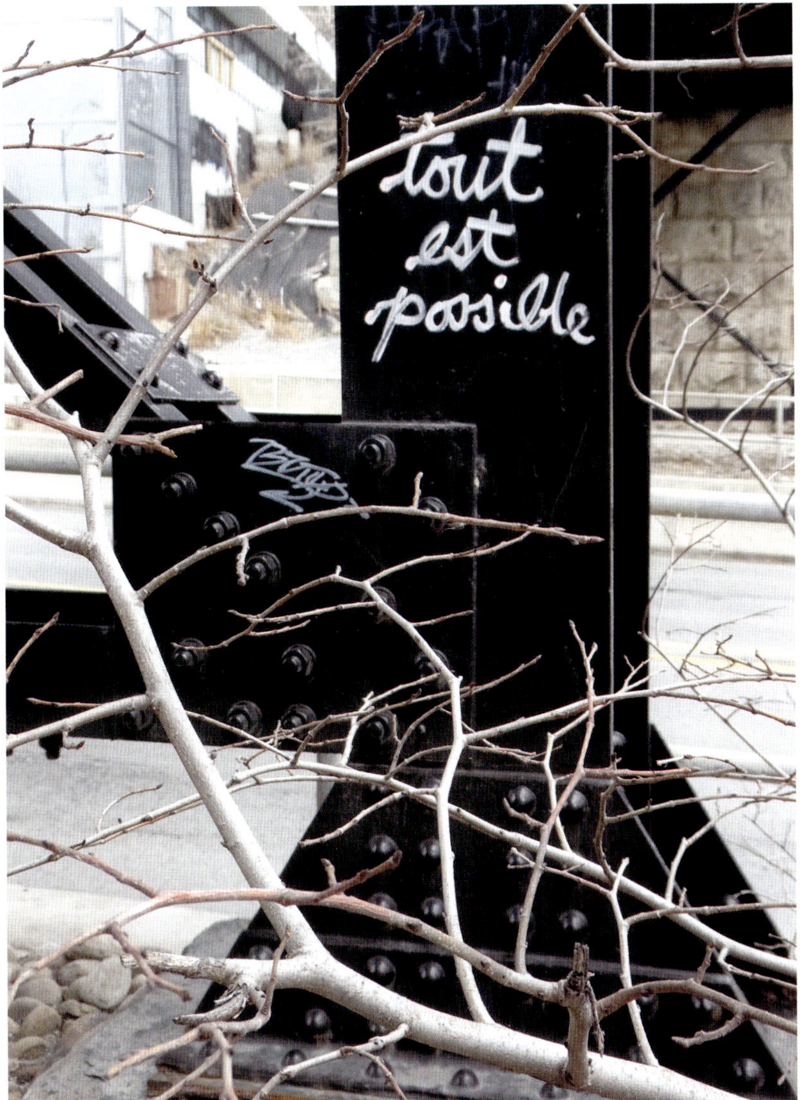

OPPOSITE TOP Norm Kirby, *This Too Shall Pass*, Jersey City, USA, 2018

OPPOSITE BOTTOM Matthew Wong, *Yellow Earth*, Perth, Australia, 2017

LEFT Unknown artist, Toronto, Canada, 2018

THE earliest version of the philosophical statement 'this too shall pass' has been found in the writings of medieval Persian Sufi poets. The artist Norm Kirby created the ephemeral version at opposite top in Jersey City using fabric strips woven into a chain link fence. Pictured at bottom is the second half of a wall painted by Matthew Wong in Perth's Chinatown; the full wall reads: 'If people are of one heart, even the yellow earth can become gold.' The work carries a double meaning, referring both to the fact that the Chinese laboured on the nearby goldfields and that through their sense of community they created a new space in the growing city.

'Tout est possible' reminds us that everything is possible.

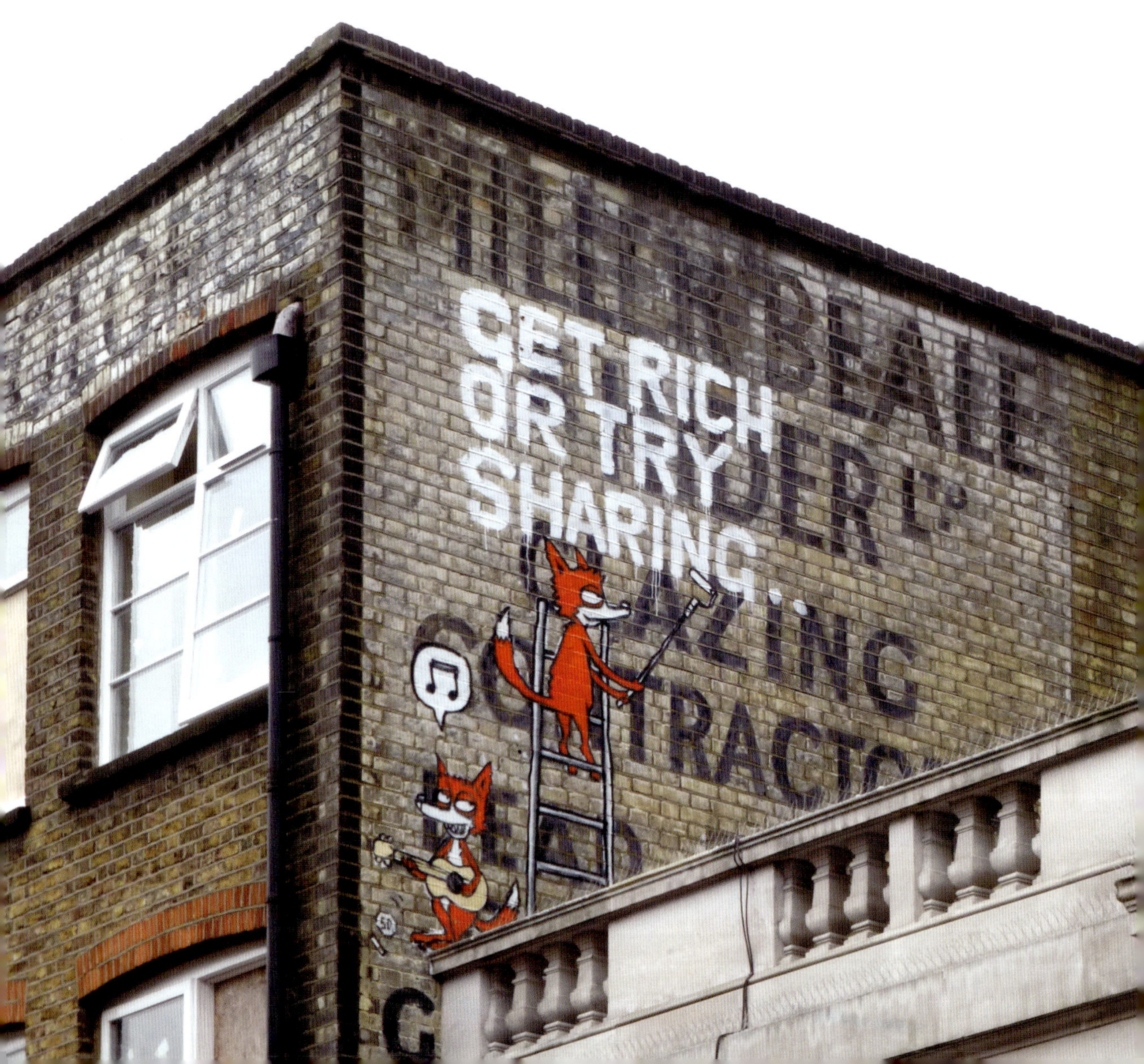
GET RICH
OR TRY
SHARING.

Dissent and Defiance

Words can be weapons. They can speak for the disenfranchised and be a dynamic voice for social change, especially in times of crisis or conflict. Writing on the wall can remind us of basic social inequalities – of poverty, homelessness, violence and gender disparity. As elections draw near, street art becomes an instrument for both sides of the political divide. Then content becomes more controversial and images of politicians appear with slogans that are often provocative, if not downright inflammatory.

Street art can tell uncomfortable truths in a way that the spoken word can't. By placing a work where a viewer would least expect to see it, an artist can add layers of meaning to a comment that we have heard so many times before that it has become virtually inaudible. So can humour. The text on Mau Mau's wall opposite, painted over a ghost sign in London's Camden, is a playful parody of the film title *Get Rich or Die Tryin'*.

Art that demands revolution is usually simple and raw. If it's sanctioned it loses much of its power to disturb and challenge. This is a significant area of difference between the art of Western nations and the remainder of the world. The issues vary too – in Brazil and South Africa visual acts of defiance and calls to revolution are common themes, expressed in protest stencils such as 'they must fall/we must rise' (p. 117). In contrast, art that explores issues arising from social media are far more common in Europe, the United States and Australia.

The art of visual protest has been refined by artists such as Shepard Fairey, who paints huge murals that support peace and justice, and walden, whose small stickers remind us of the vulnerable animal species we are pushing, or have already pushed, towards extinction.

OPPOSITE Mau Mau, *Get Rich or Try Sharing*, London, UK, 2015
RIGHT Unknown artist, Melbourne, Australia, 2013

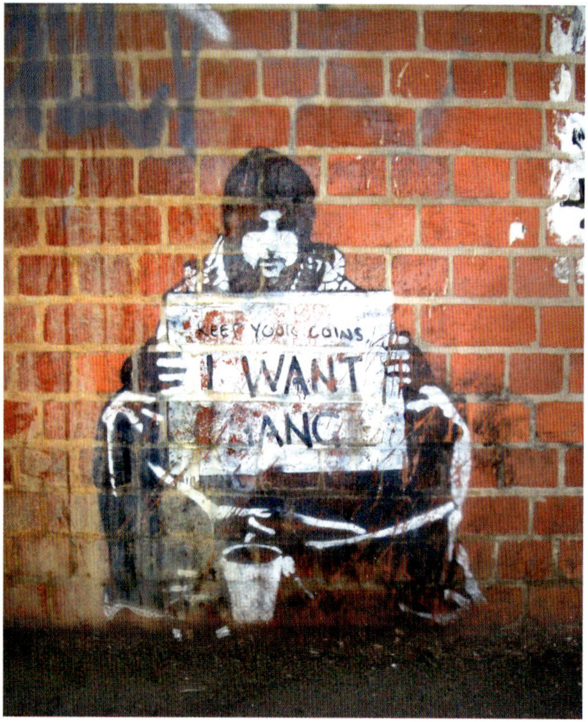

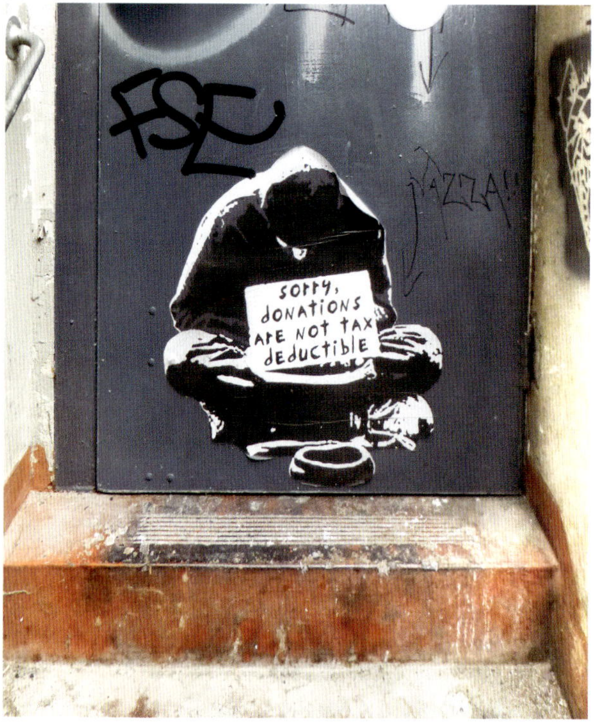

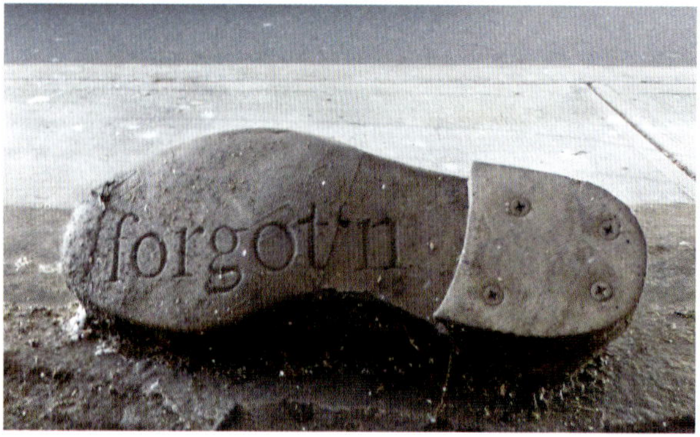

POVERTY, homelessness and dystopia have inspired the works on these pages. The life-sized figure of a man at top left, stencilled on a wall near a suburban Melbourne train station, holds a placard that subverts the expected request with 'keep your coins – I want change'. In the same vein, cel out's statement above highlights the need for a fundamental shift in thinking. Will Coles' concrete cast of a shoe has been inscribed with the word 'forgot'n' and placed so that it almost disappears into the everyday grime of the roadside.

Brooklyn-based British artist David Hollier's portrait of American journalist and author Hunter S. Thompson opposite is part of a series of works called *Imago Verbosa*. He created it by painting text around the contours and features of the face, using an extended quote from *Generation of Swine*, a compilation of articles written by Thompson for the *San Francisco Examiner*.

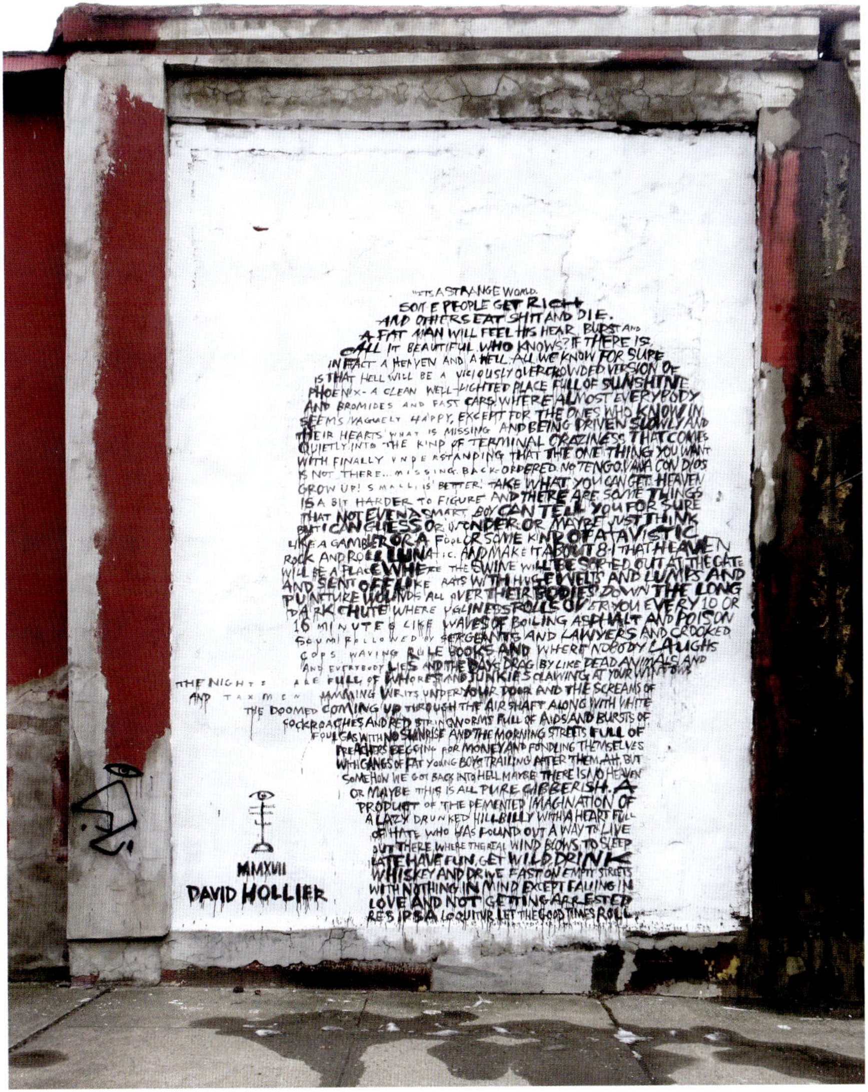

OPPOSITE TOP LEFT Meek, *Begging for Change*, Melbourne, Australia, 2006

OPPOSITE BOTTOM LEFT Will Coles, Sydney, Australia, 2015

OPPOSITE RIGHT cel out, *Not a Deduction*, Melbourne, Australia, 2013

LEFT David Hollier, *Hunter S. Thompson*, Jersey City, USA, 2018

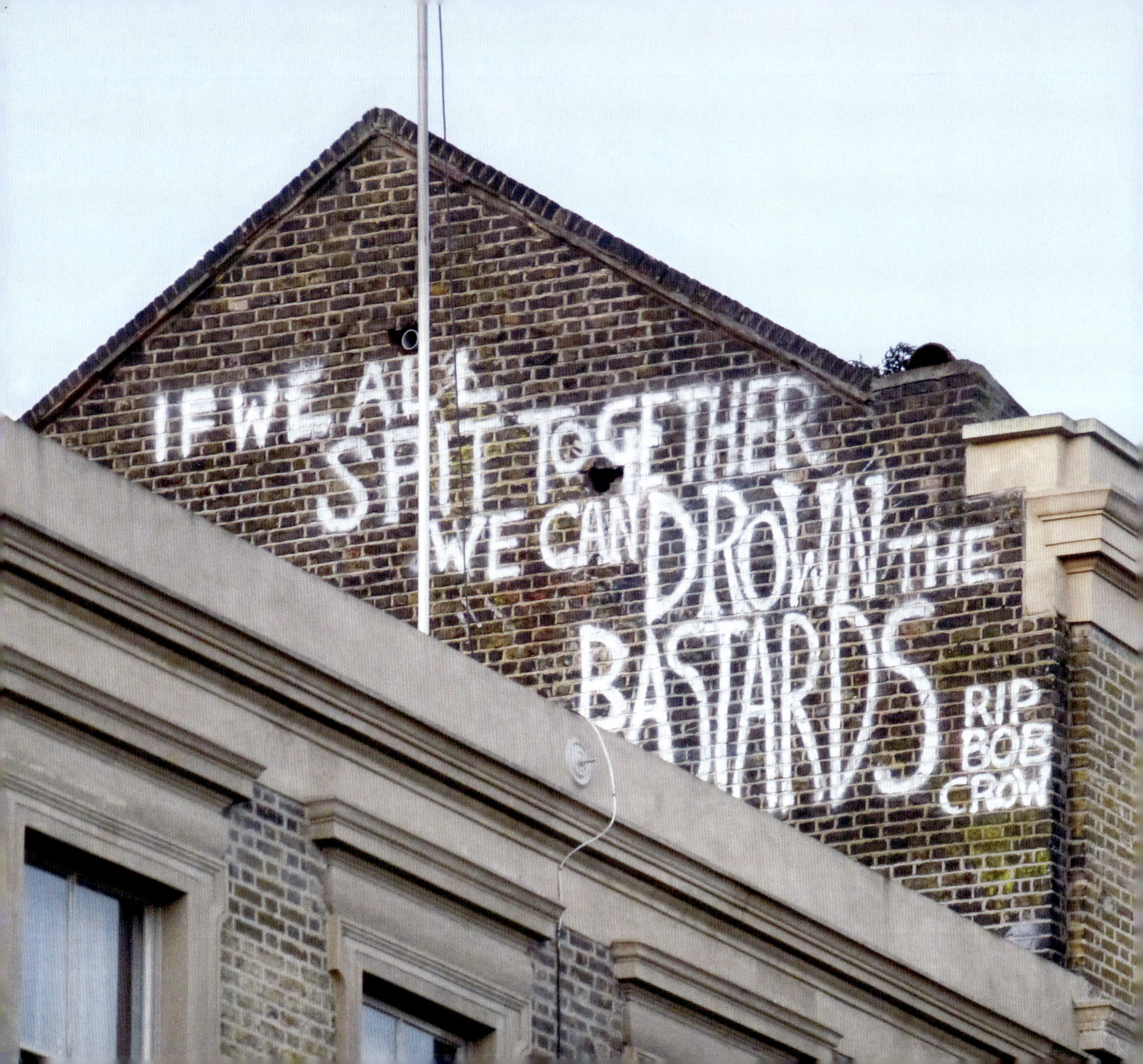
IF WE ALL SPIT TOGETHER WE CAN DROWN THE BASTARDS
RIP BOB CROW

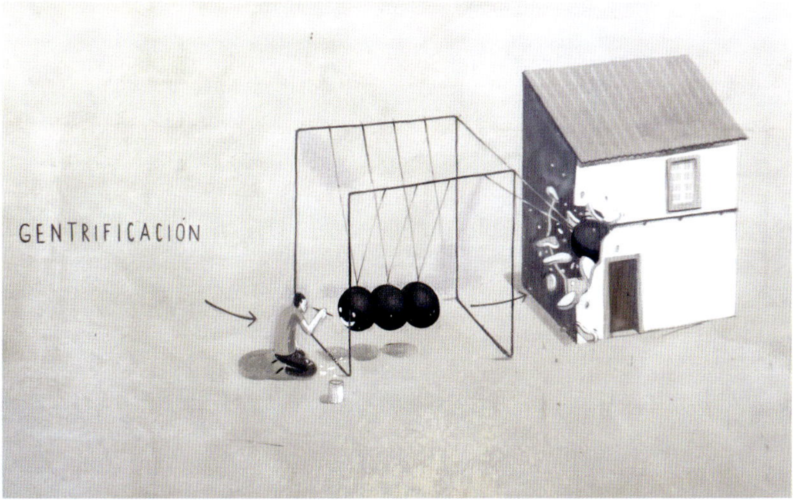

OPPOSITE Unknown artist, London, UK, 2015

TOP Escif, Valencia, Spain, 2013

BOTTOM LEFT Megan Wilson and Christopher Statton, *Housing Is a Human Right*, San Francisco, USA, 2017

BOTTOM RIGHT Oscar Low, *Common Wealth*, Auckland, New Zealand, 2015

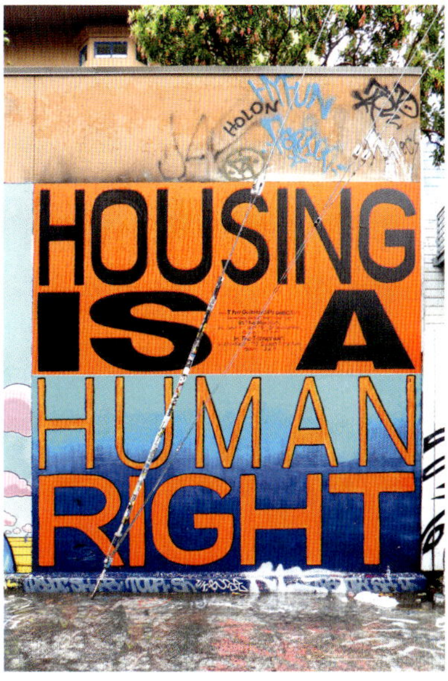

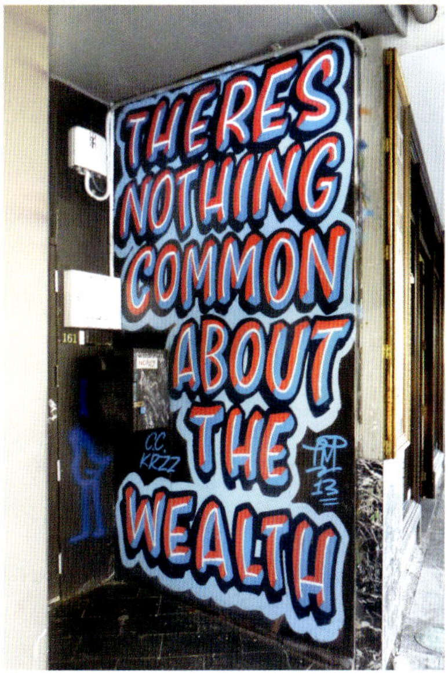

THE statement opposite, quoting the late British trade union leader Bob Crow, is an example of how a terse declaration can inspire social activism through an unexpected location (and humour).

Inequities of wealth and the reality of housing shortages and homelessness are issues in today's world. Spanish artist Escif's image about gentrification at top is subdued and elegant – a pithy observation about contemporary life. The message painted by Megan Wilson and Christopher Statton in San Francisco's Clarion Alley at bottom left draws attention to the Gubbio Project – a local initiative that provides safe sleeping spaces for the homeless in two churches in the city's most affected neighbourhoods. There is a sense of nostalgia in Oscar Low's lettering, but the sentiment is contemporary.

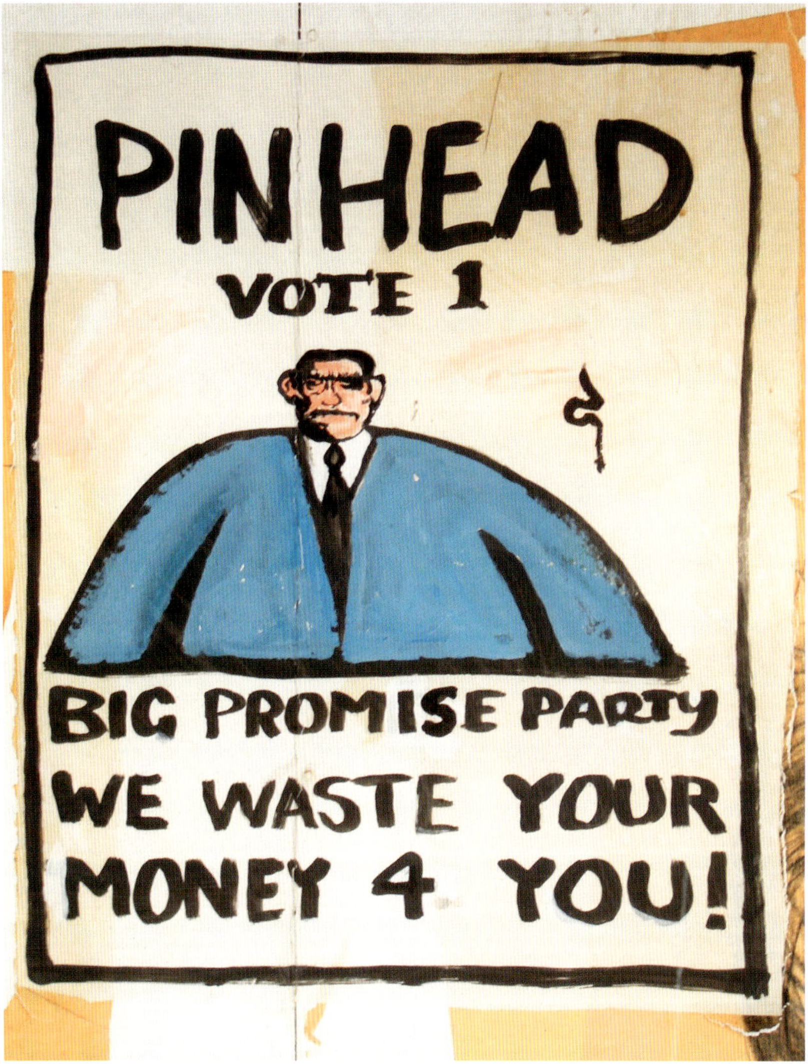
PIN HEAD
VOTE 1
BIG PROMISE PARTY
WE WASTE YOUR
MONEY 4 YOU!

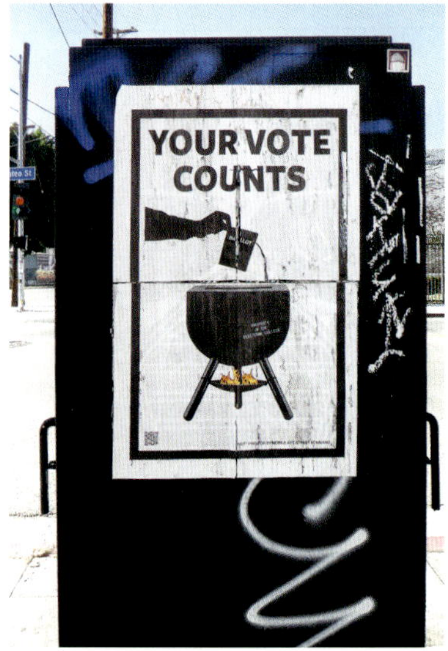
YOUR VOTE
COUNTS

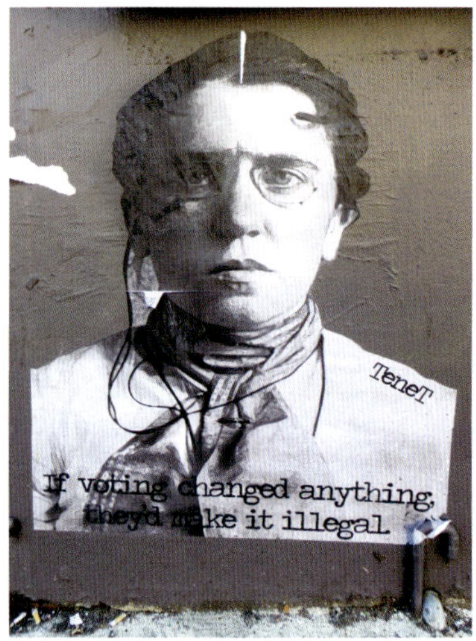
TeneT
If voting changed anything,
they'd make it illegal.

OPPOSITE LEFT Unknown artist, Darwin, Australia, 2008

OPPOSITE TOP RIGHT Unknown artist, Los Angeles, USA, 2016

OPPOSITE BOTTOM RIGHT TeneT, Melbourne, Australia, 2016

LEFT Unknown artist, Melbourne, Australia, 2012

RIGHT K-GUY, *Gimme Some Truth*, London, UK, 2015

POLITICS is a favourite subject of street artists, especially those who work under the cloak of anonymity. Sarcasm, wit and irony can be powerful tools of resistance, defiance and protest. Such work can make us laugh or cause us to question our thinking. The integrity of the voting system is questioned in two of the works opposite. 'If voting changed anything, they'd make it illegal' is a statement attributed to the Russian-American feminist and anarchist Emma Goldman.

K-GUY's eye chart at right uses lyrics from John Lennon's 'Gimme Some Truth' to make a statement about politics in this post-truth world.

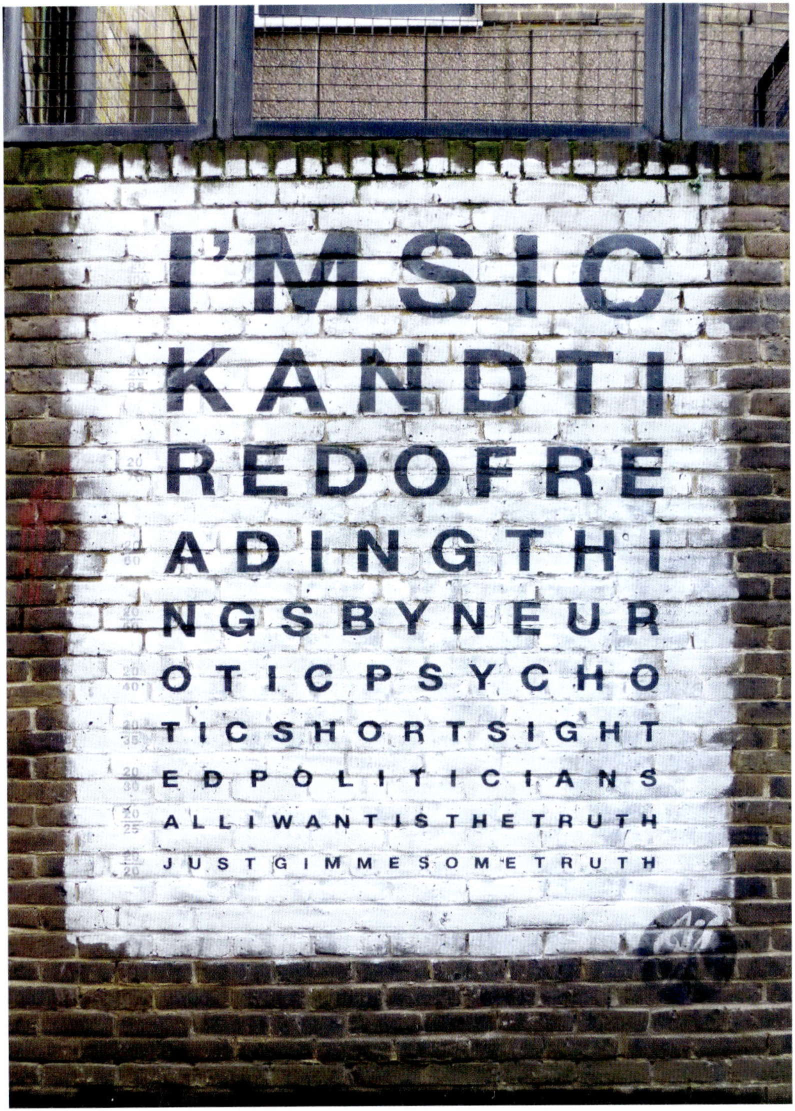

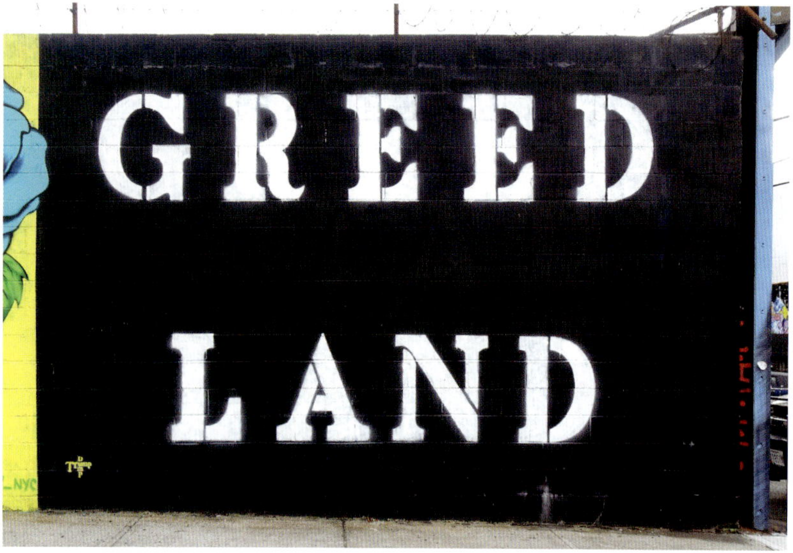

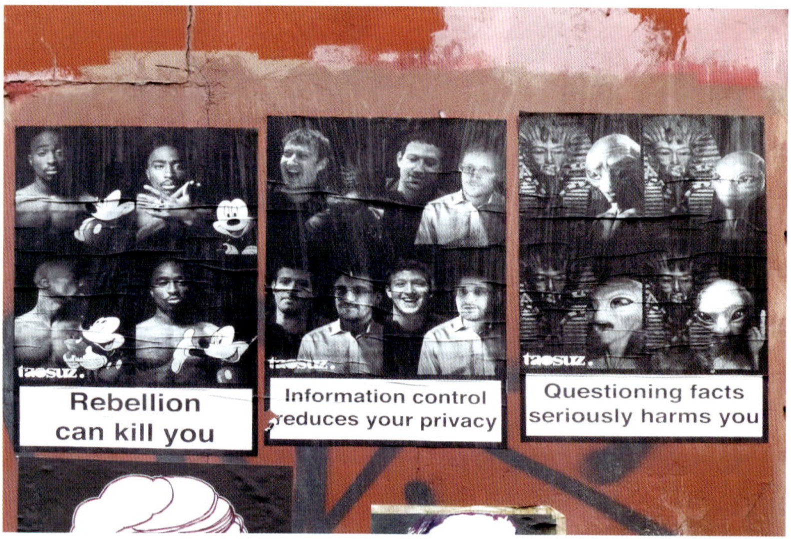

TOP John Fekner, *Greed Land*, New York City, USA, 2018

BOTTOM Taosuz, London, UK, 2015

OPPOSITE Adam Fujita and Dirty Bandits, *Everything is NOT OK*, New York City, USA, 2018

JOHN Fekner's name has long been associated with street art. Active in New York since the 1970s, he sprays stencils, such as the one at top, that highlight social and environmental concerns specific to a community, issues such as greed, consumption and instant gratification. The works of Berlin-based artist Taosuz are photo-booth spoofs which explore the values of contemporary society through humour and the unexpected juxtaposition of characters, left.

Everything is NOT OK is a commentary on the state of American politics today, with special reference to gun violence. The neon-style font, typical of the work of Adam Fujita (aka Adam Fu), acts as a metaphor for 'keeping the lights on' the government.

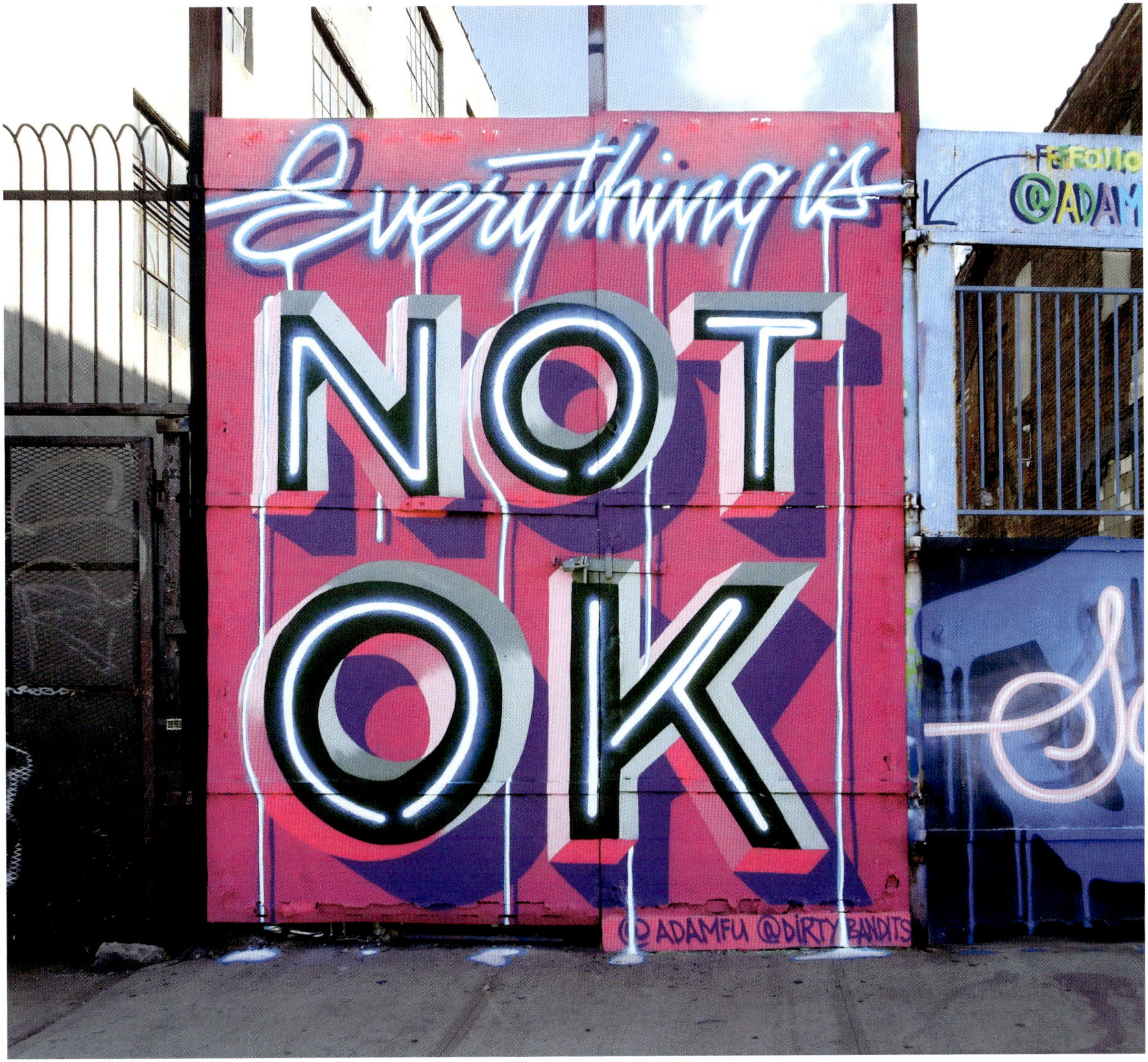
Everything is
NOT
OK
@ADAMFU @DIRTYBANDITS
@ADAM

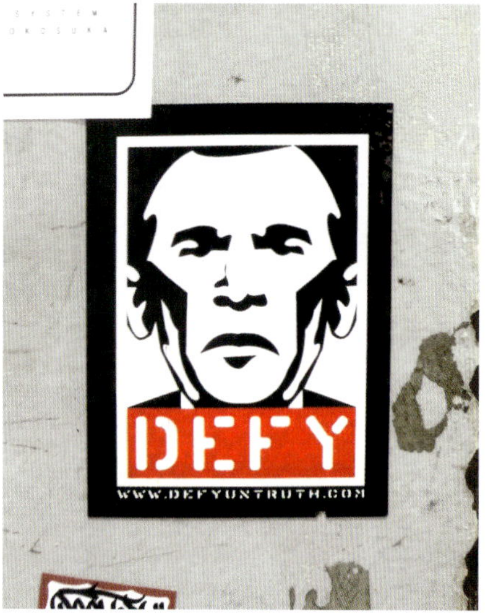
DEFY
WWW.DEFYUNTRUTH.COM

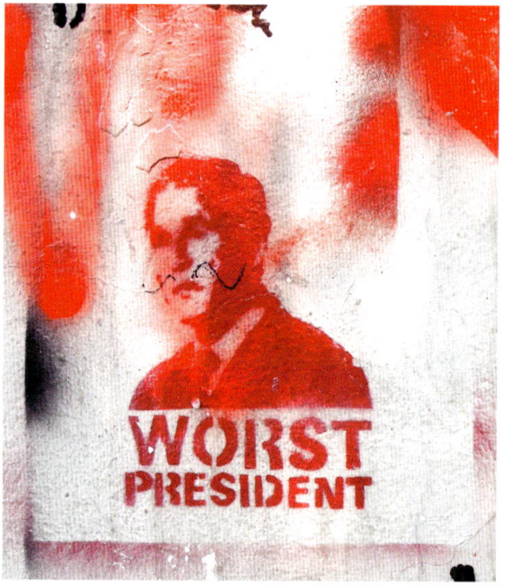
WORST
PRESIDENT

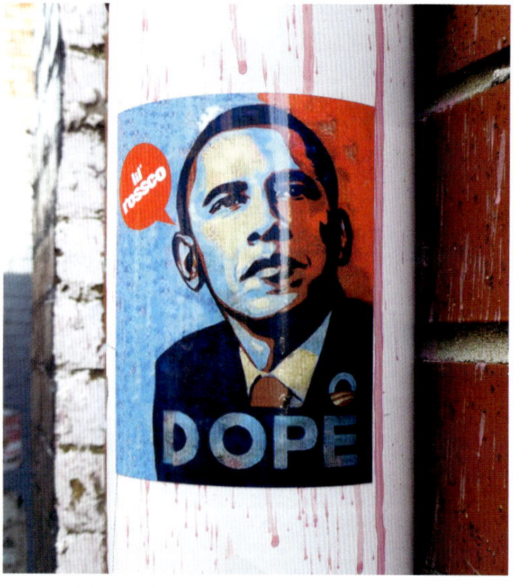
lil'
rossco
DOPE

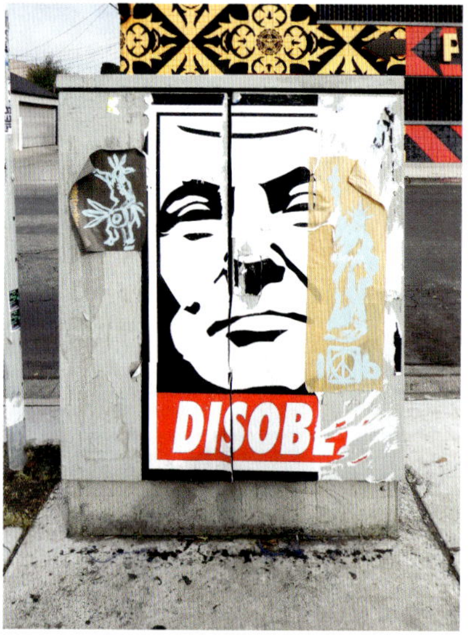
DISOB

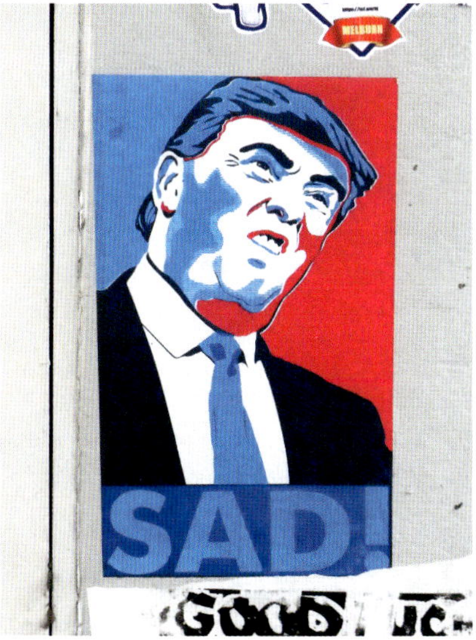

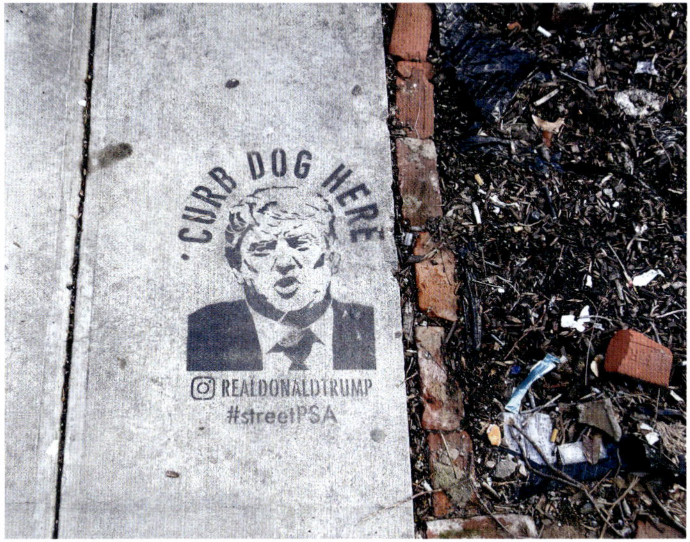

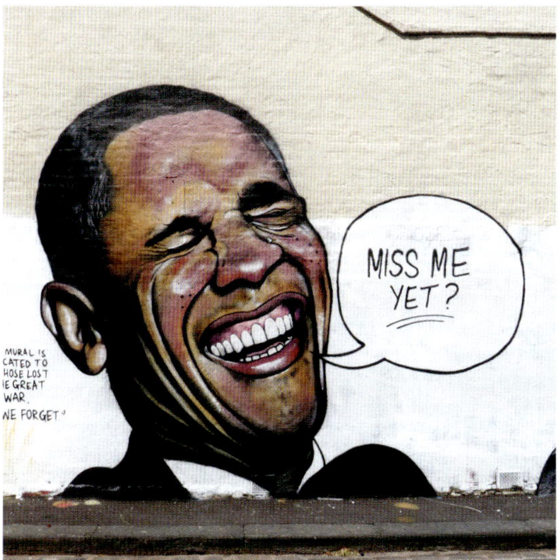

OPPOSITE TOP LEFT DefyUntruth, Tokyo, Japan, 2014
OPPOSITE TOP RIGHT Unknown artist, Santiago, Chile, 2013
OPPOSITE BOTTOM LEFT Unknown artist, Melbourne, Australia, 2014
OPPOSITE BOTTOM RIGHT Unknown artist, Los Angeles, USA, 2016
TOP LEFT Unknown artist, Melbourne, Australia, 2017
TOP RIGHT streetPSA, New York City, USA, 2018
BOTTOM Lushsux, Melbourne, Australia, 2017

ARTISTS are in an excellent position to contribute to, and in fact provoke, political debate by drawing the public's attention to issues of trust and integrity. These pages put the spotlight on the three most recent presidents of the United States of America, although the art was photographed in a range of countries such as Japan, Chile and Australia. None are flattering, either because of the image or its text and what it suggests. Two of them are parodies of the tricolour *Hope* poster designed by Shepard Fairey for Barack Obama's presidential campaign in 2008.

Miss Me Yet? is courtesy of Melbourne provocateur Lushsux, whose work offers a focal point for people and issues which are currently trending on social media. This image of Barack Obama was added to the streetscape two weeks after President Trump's inauguration on the other side of the world.

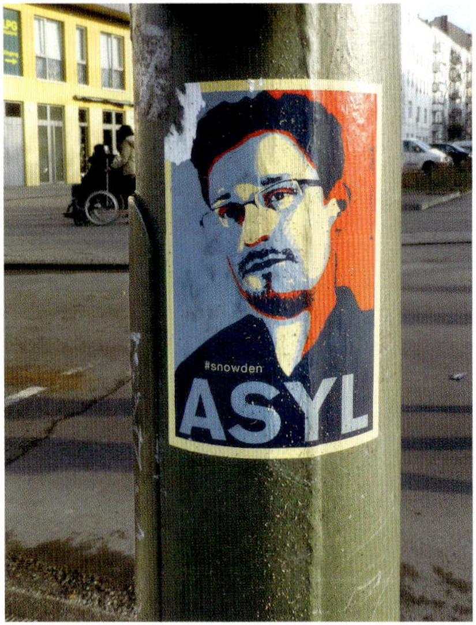

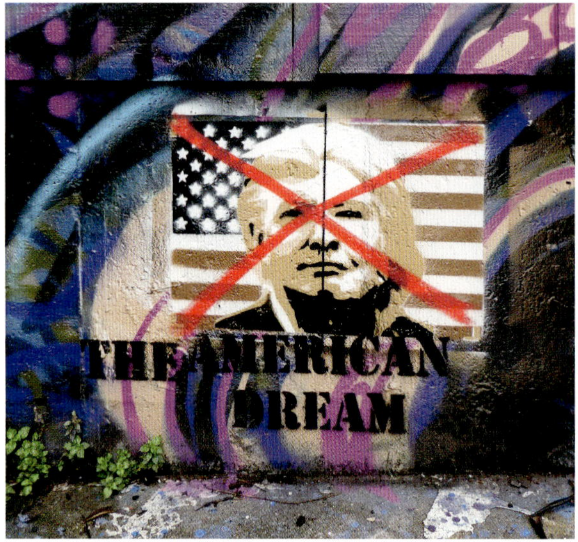

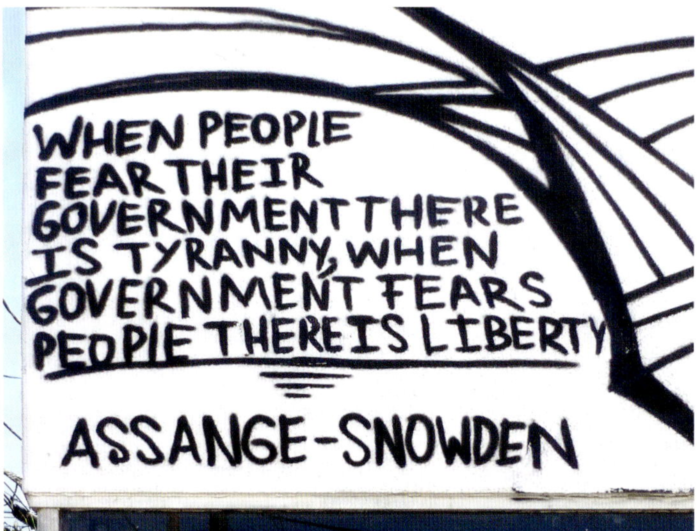

TOP LEFT Unknown artist, Berlin, Germany, 2015
TOP RIGHT Unknown artist, San Francisco, USA, 2017
BOTTOM Unknown artist, Houston, USA, 2013
OPPOSITE STRA, *Don't Panic!*, Melbourne, Australia, 2016

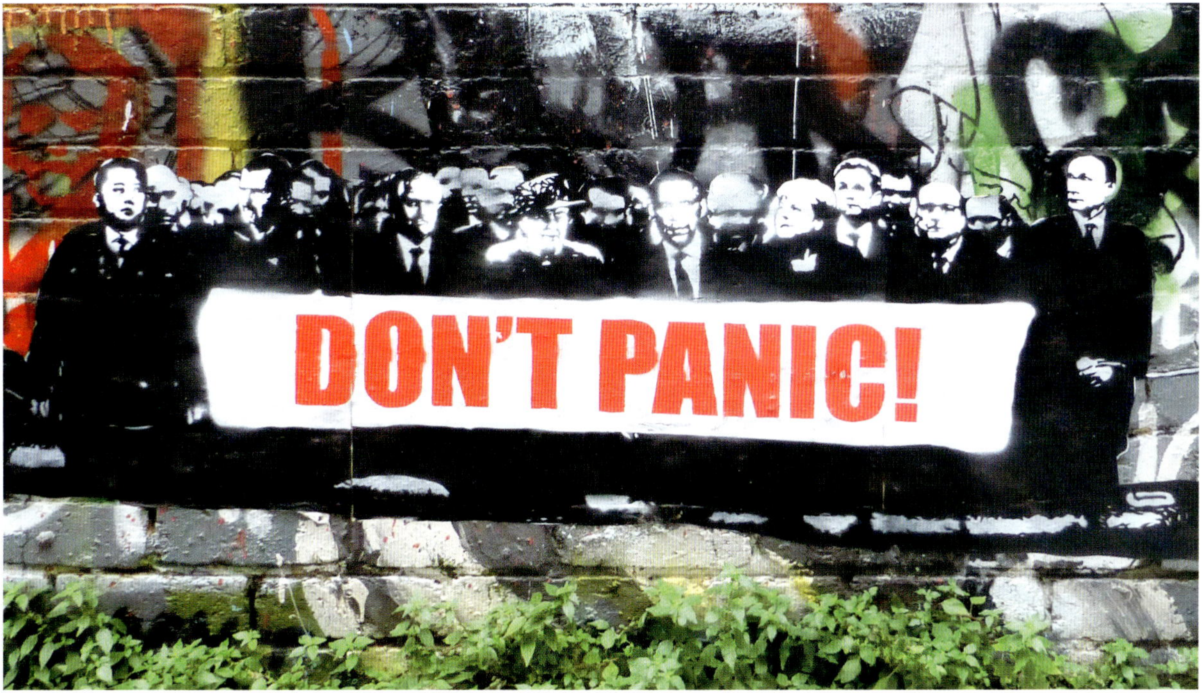

THE quotation at opposite bottom, often attributed to Thomas Jefferson, has been used by an unknown artist in reference to American Edward Snowden and Australian-born Julian Assange, who have each blown the whistle on official government wrongdoing. Top left is a sticker for a campaign to grant Snowden asylum in Germany. Controversy runs high – similar posters carried the words 'patriot' and 'traitor' as well as 'ASYL'.

The small stencil above, by French stencil artist STRA, shows recognisable world leaders and is an injunction to us, the public, not to panic. Or is it?

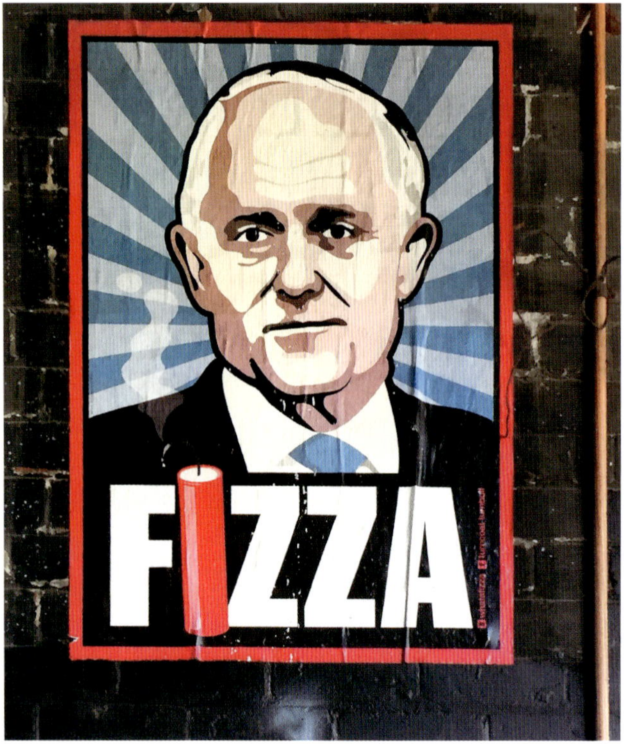

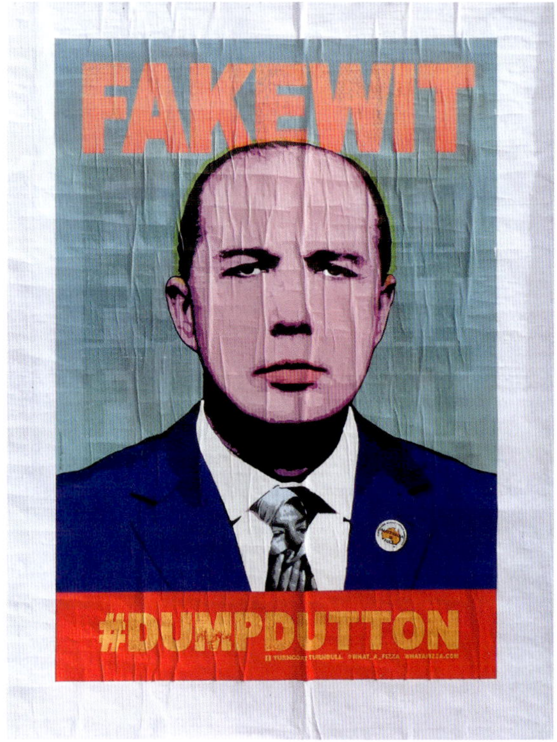

LEFT and **RIGHT** Michael Agzarian, Melbourne, Australia, 2017
OPPOSITE Sittoula Sitlakone, *Abbott FKD*, Melbourne, Australia, 2013

MICHAEL Agzarian used humour when selecting the tagline for the poster above left of Australia's former Prime Minister Malcolm Turnbull. A fizza is another name for a penny bunger – a firecracker that goes off with a fizz rather than the expected bang. On the right is a portrait of Peter Dutton, the federal Minister for Immigration and Border Security, wearing his 'Australia is full' badge. Unsurprisingly, such posters are often torn by disgruntled voters.

Sittoula Sitlakone designed the *Abbott FKD* poster in the lead-up to the 2013 Australian federal election. Tony Abbott, the then incumbent prime minister, has here been conflated with the well-known image of Colonel Sanders of KFC. The adjusted acronym speaks for itself.

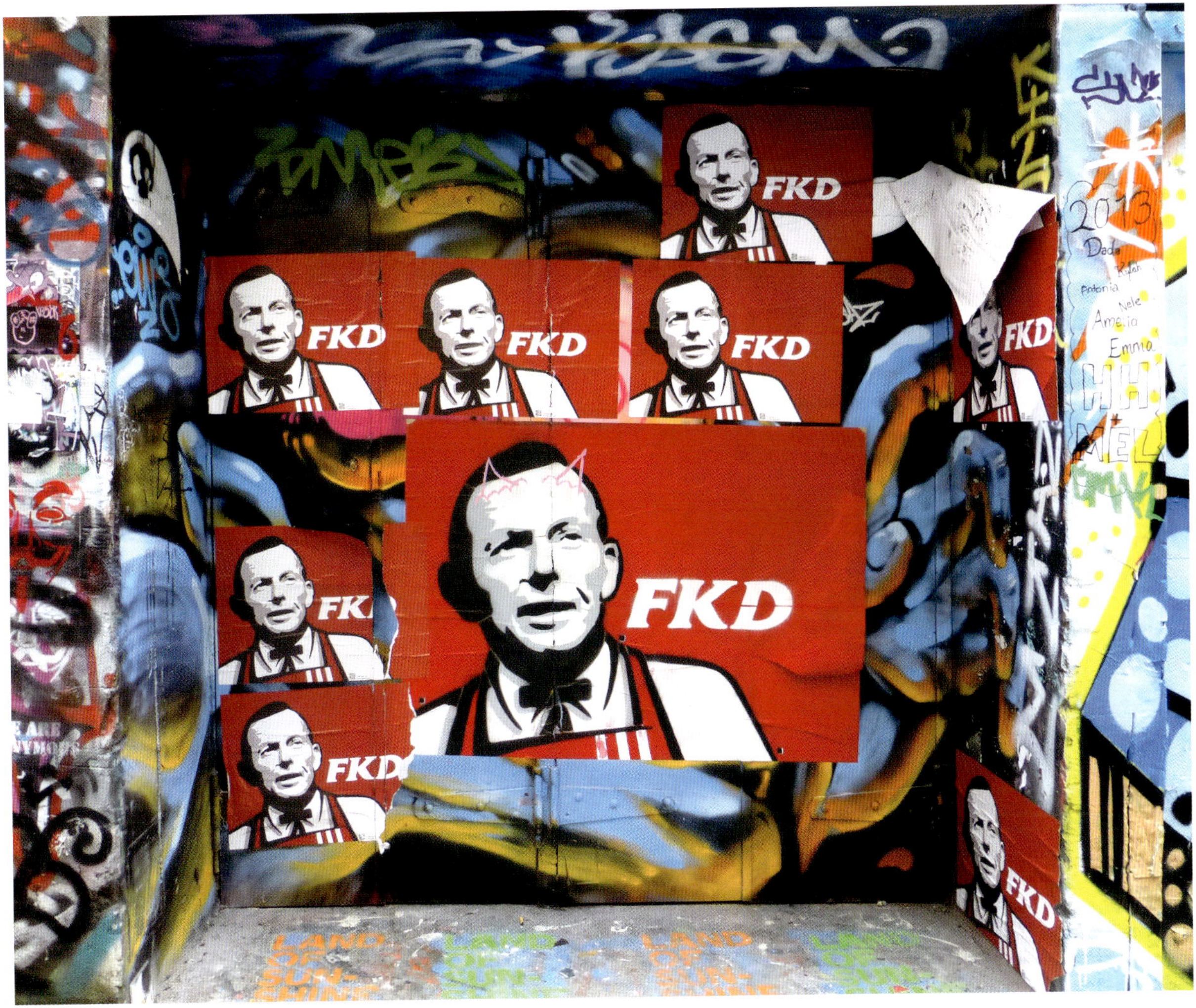
FKD
FKD
FKD
FKD
FKD
FKD
FKD
FKD
LAND OF SUN-SHINE

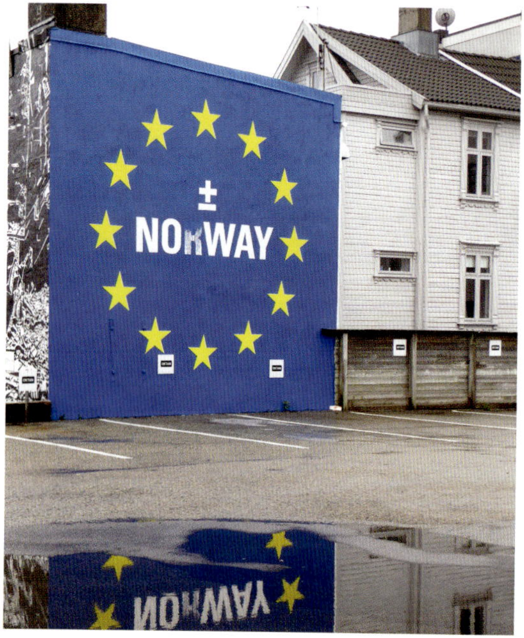
±
NORWAY

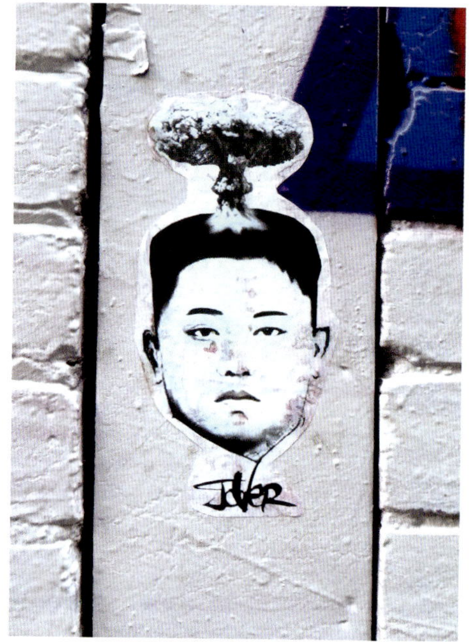

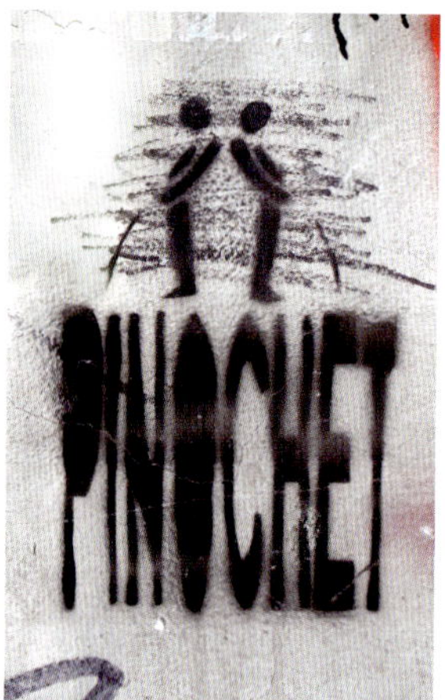
PINOCHET

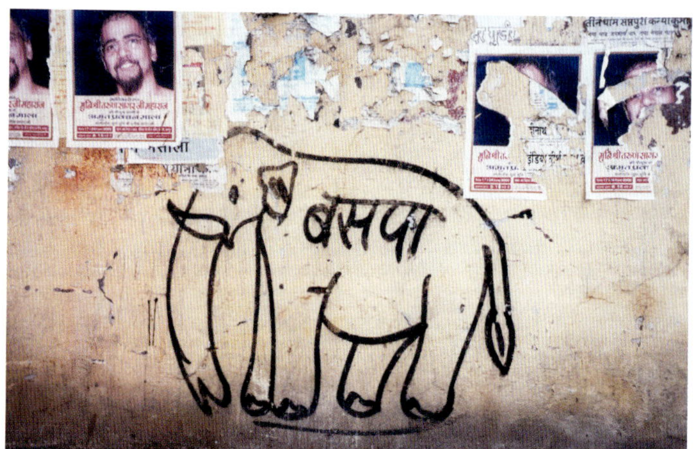
बसपा

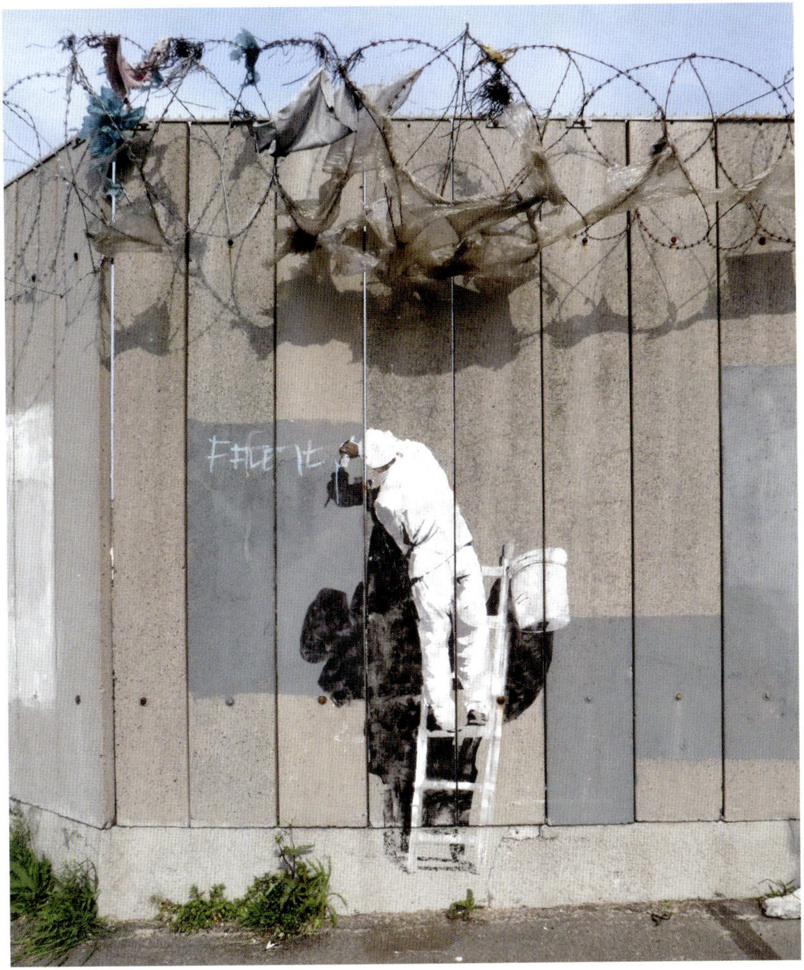

OPPOSITE TOP LEFT ±MaisMenos±, *No Way*, Stavanger, Norway, 2016

OPPOSITE TOP RIGHT Loui Jover, *Mind Blown*, Melbourne, Australia, 2017

OPPOSITE BOTTOM LEFT Unknown artist, Santiago, Chile, 2013

OPPOSITE BOTTOM RIGHT Unknown artist, Jaipur, India, 2001

LEFT Unknown artist, Cape Town, South Africa, 2017

BY dissolving the 'r' in Norway on the European Union flag opposite, ±MaisMenos± has drawn attention to the fact that Norway has twice voted in national referenda to reject membership of the EU. The Pinochet stencil from Santiago at bottom left reflects both sides of the political divide: one person sprayed and another disagreed. The elephant at bottom right is the earliest street art photograph in this book. The work was painted on a wall in Jaipur as part of an election campaign in India at the dawn of the 21st century.

Emphasised by the barbed wire along the top, the wall in Cape Town at left draws attention to division and separation. *Face It* can be interpreted as questioning the absurdity of segregation, apt in a country where apartheid was the national policy until the 1990s.

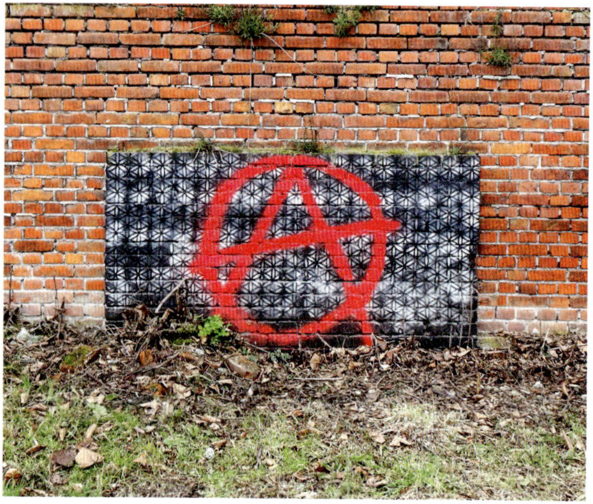

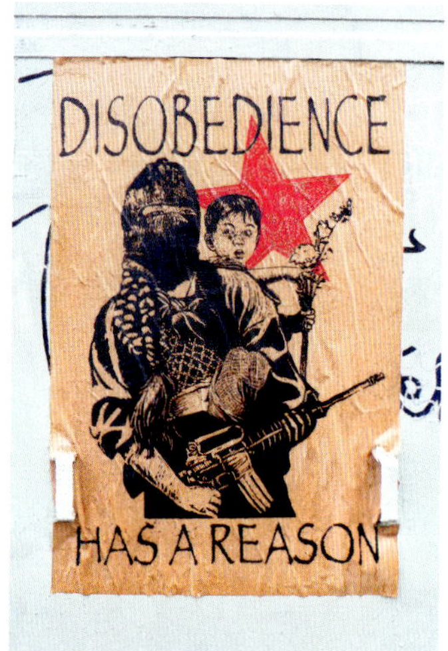
DISOBEDIENCE
HAS A REASON

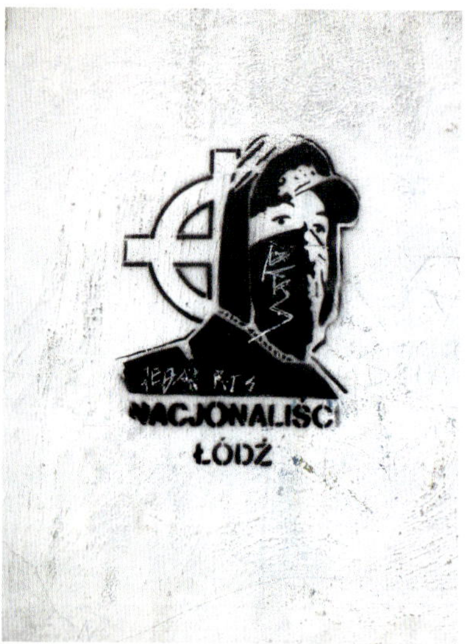
NACJONALIŚCI
ŁÓDŹ

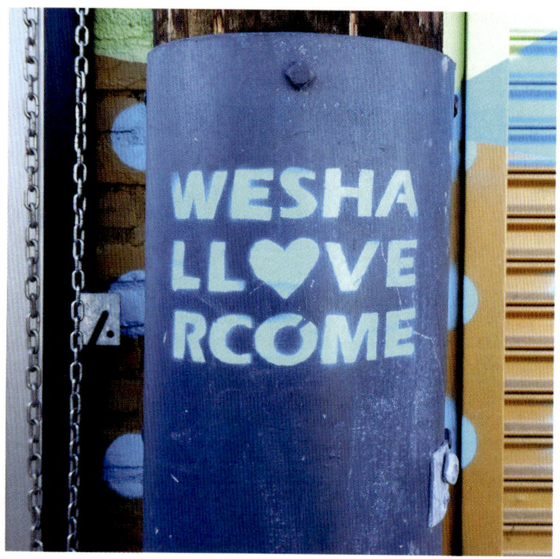
WESHA
LLOVE
RCOME

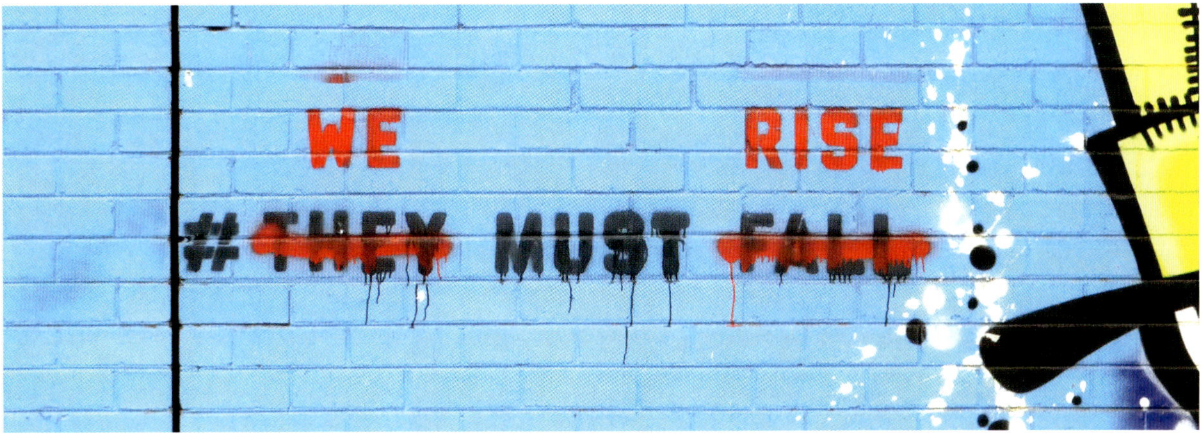

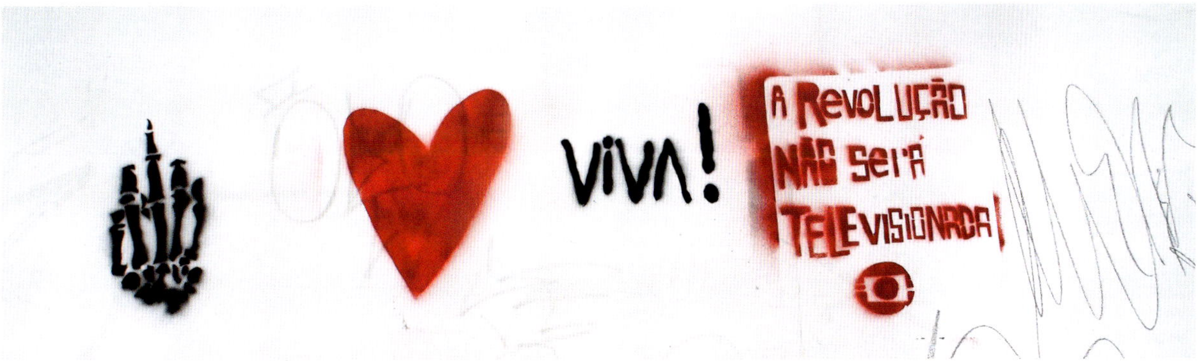

OPPOSITE TOP LEFT Unknown artist, Ghent, Belgium, 2018
OPPOSITE TOP RIGHT Unknown artist, San Francisco, USA, 2017
OPPOSITE BOTTOM LEFT Unknown artist, Łódź, Poland, 2014
OPPOSITE BOTTOM RIGHT Unknown artist, Los Angeles, USA, 2017
TOP Unknown artist, Johannesburg, South Africa, 2017
BOTTOM Unknown artist, Rio de Janeiro, Brazil, 2012

REBELLION and anarchy are the stuff of much visual political protest. From the anarchy wall in Ghent to the *Disobedience* paste-up in San Francisco and the masked figure in Poland, rebellion is an integral part of the message from urban scrawlers who want to see social and political change. *We Shall Overcome* strikes a more positive note, especially with the replacement of the 'o' with the heart symbol.

The two sets of stencils above are calls to action. The revolution won't be televised, passive entertainment: the change will be achieved through action rather than passive resistance. 'We must rise' is a more active and positive approach than 'they must fall'.

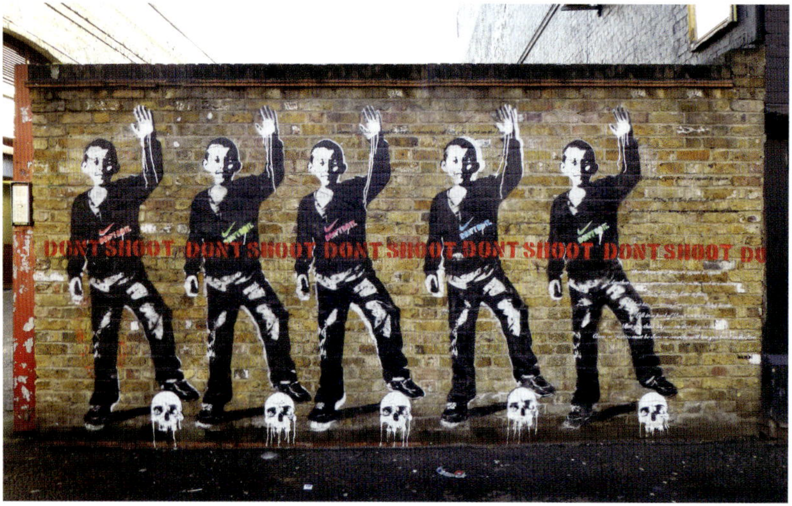
DONT SHOOT DONT SHOOT DONT SHOOT DONT SHOOT DONT SHOOT

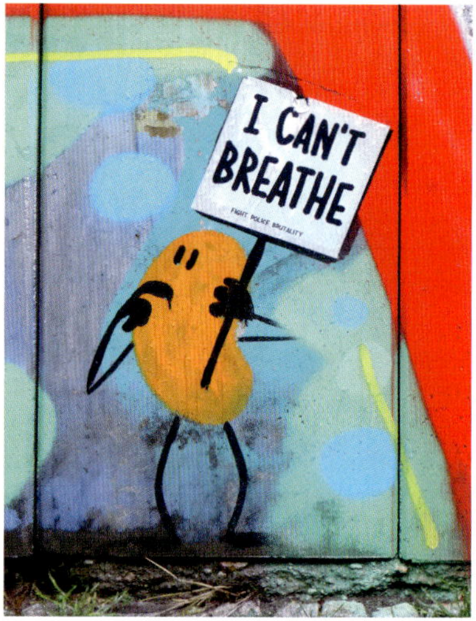
I CAN'T BREATHE

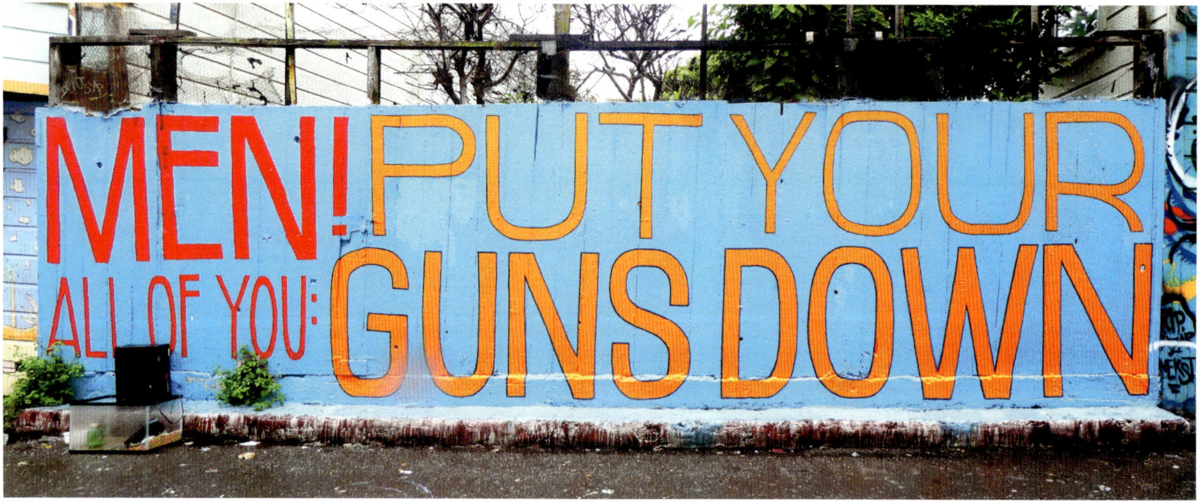
MEN! PUT YOUR
ALL OF YOU: GUNS DOWN

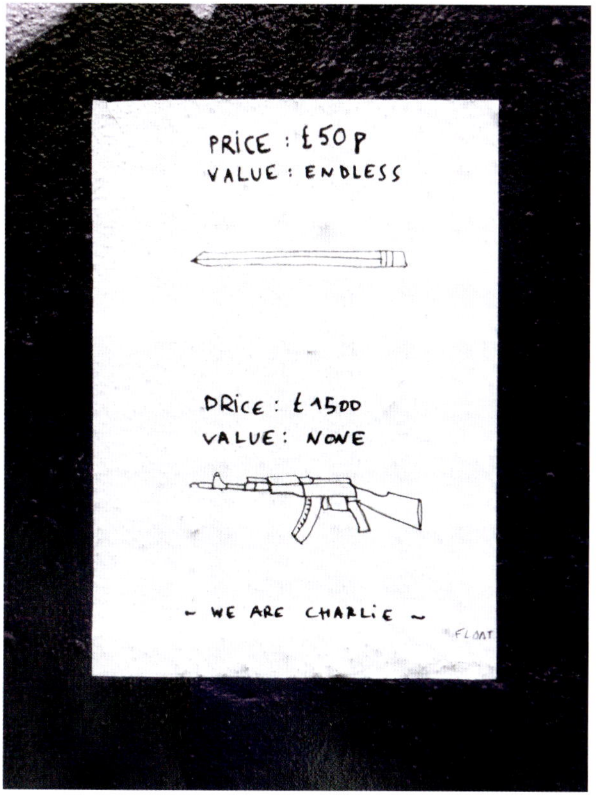

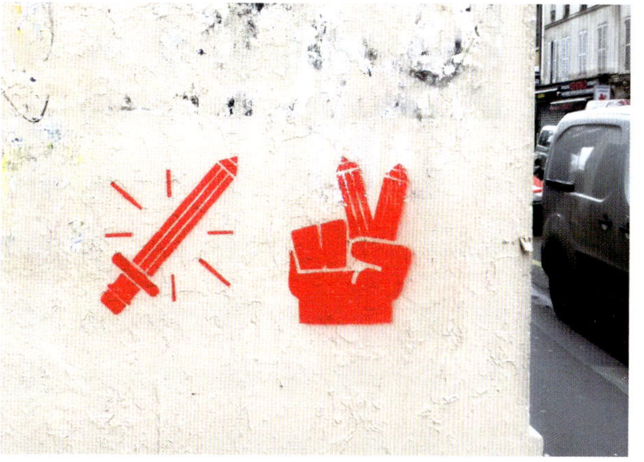

OPPOSITE TOP LEFT Bambi, *Don't Shoot*, London, UK, 2015

OPPOSITE TOP RIGHT Unknown artist, Berlin, Germany, 2015

OPPOSITE BOTTOM Erin Feller (Airy Waters), *MEN! ALL OF YOU: Put Your Guns Down*, San Francisco, USA, 2017

LEFT Unknown artist, London, UK, 2015

RIGHT Unknown artist, Paris, France, 2015

POWERFUL visual statements in London and Berlin against police brutality, and in San Francisco about firearm control, all pictured opposite, reflect community concern about gun violence across the globe. *Don't Shoot*, painted in London's Shoreditch, and *I Can't Breathe*, painted in Berlin, are rallying cries against the excessive use of force by police in the cases of Michael Brown and Eric Garner, two African American men who died in the United States in 2014.

The power of the written word is the concept behind the overwhelming response to the 2015 killing of 12 journalists working on the satirical weekly newspaper *Charlie Hebdo* in Paris. 'Je suis Charlie' became a slogan of solidarity in support of freedom of expression.

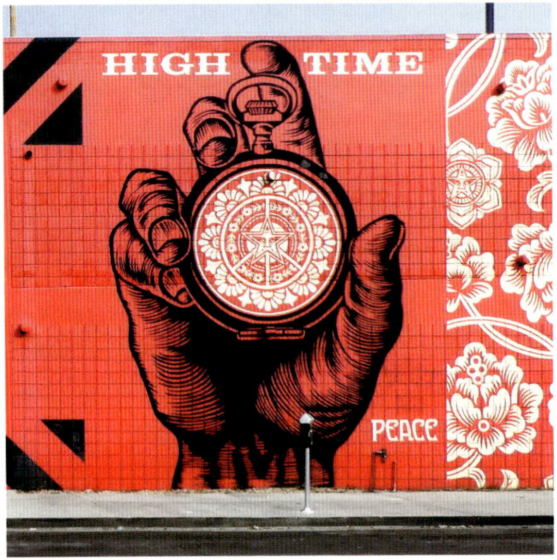

TOP Shepard Fairey/obeygiant.com, Los Angeles, USA, 2016

BOTTOM Shepard Fairey/obeygiant.com and Kelly RISK Graval, *Peace and Justice*, Miami, USA, 2017

OPPOSITE Shepard Fairey/obeygiant.com, *Make Art Not War*, Berlin, Germany, 2014

PEACE features in these three murals created by American artist Shepard Fairey, the work in Miami below made in collaboration with Kelly RISK Graval. The clean lines, strong colours and bold contrasts create powerful images that speak of order and harmony. Using his distinctive visual style, Fairey often raises awareness of human rights issues and controversial political topics.

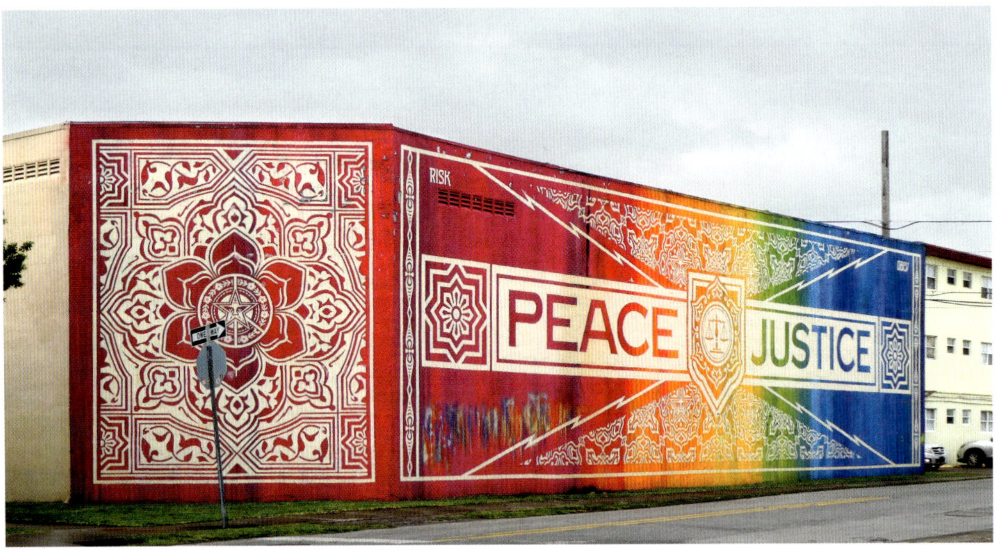

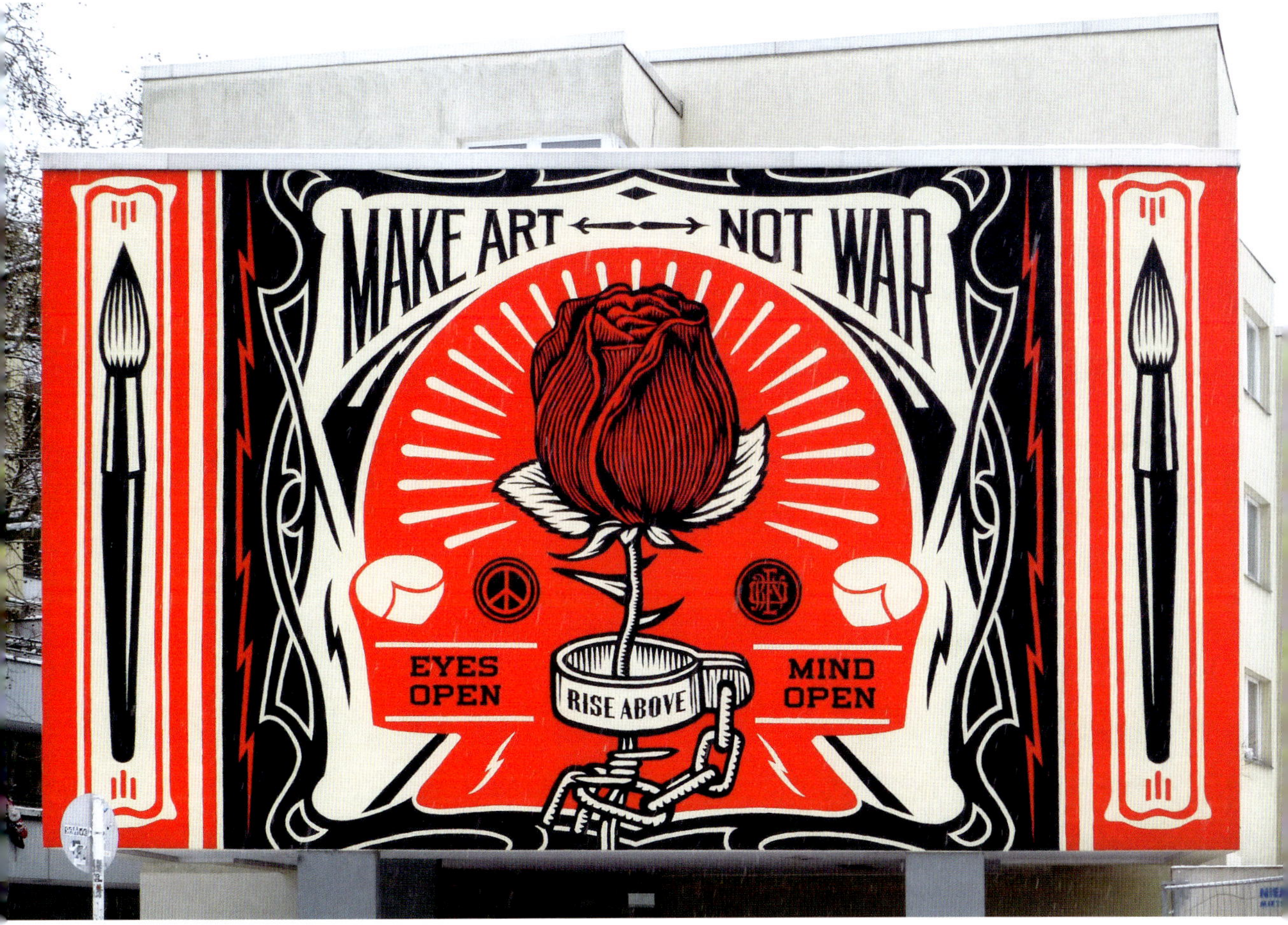
MAKE ART
NOT WAR
EYES
OPEN
RISE ABOVE
MIND
OPEN

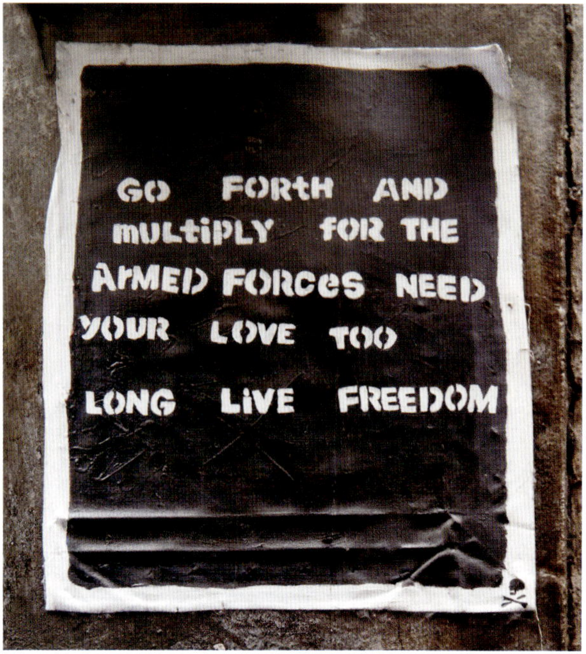

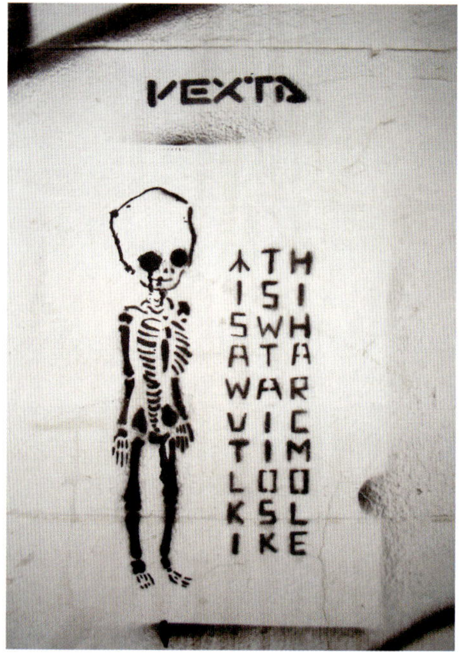

BLACK on white, white on black, and perhaps a little red for contrast – each of these combinations creates a powerful visual background for a message commenting on hate, violence, war and power. Text is an integral element of each one. Australian artist Vexta, now based in New York, often uses her voice to protest about injustice – here the victims of war, above right.

Yipi Yipi Yeah's street sign intervention (opposite top left) uses simple images to represent religion and culture standing shoulder to shoulder as a sign of brotherhood. The *Power of Love* mural in Toronto echoes words attributed to Jimi Hendrix, although he probably paraphrased a quote by the Indian spiritual teacher Sri Chinmoy. The text stencilled in French by SST Division translates as 'There are no holy wars, there are no just wars, there are only dirty wars and surgical strikes'.

LEFT Unknown artist, Melbourne, Australia, 2012

RIGHT Vexta, Melbourne, Australia, 2006

OPPOSITE TOP LEFT Yipi Yipi Yeah, Madrid, Spain, 2016

OPPOSITE TOP RIGHT Murals by Marg, *Power of Love*, Toronto, Canada, 2018

OPPOSITE BOTTOM SST Division, Paris, France, 2018

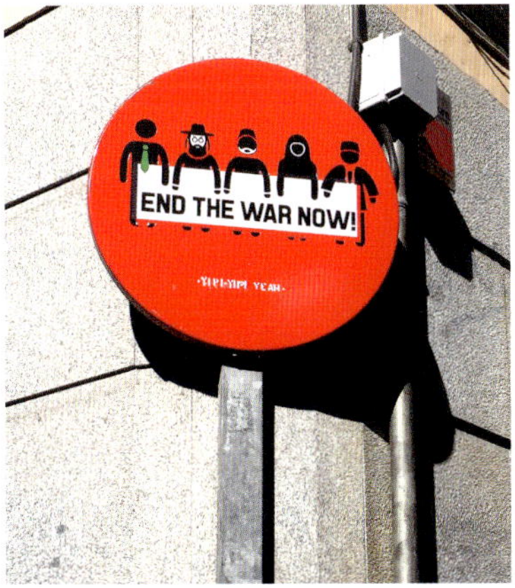
END THE WAR NOW!

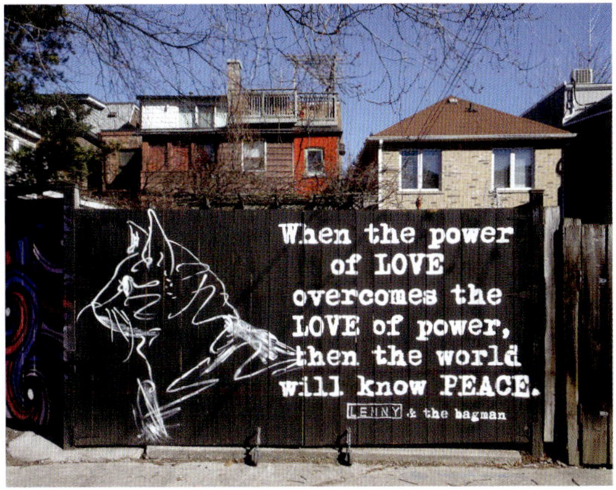
When the power
of LOVE
overcomes the
LOVE of power,
then the world
will know PEACE.
LENNY & the bagman

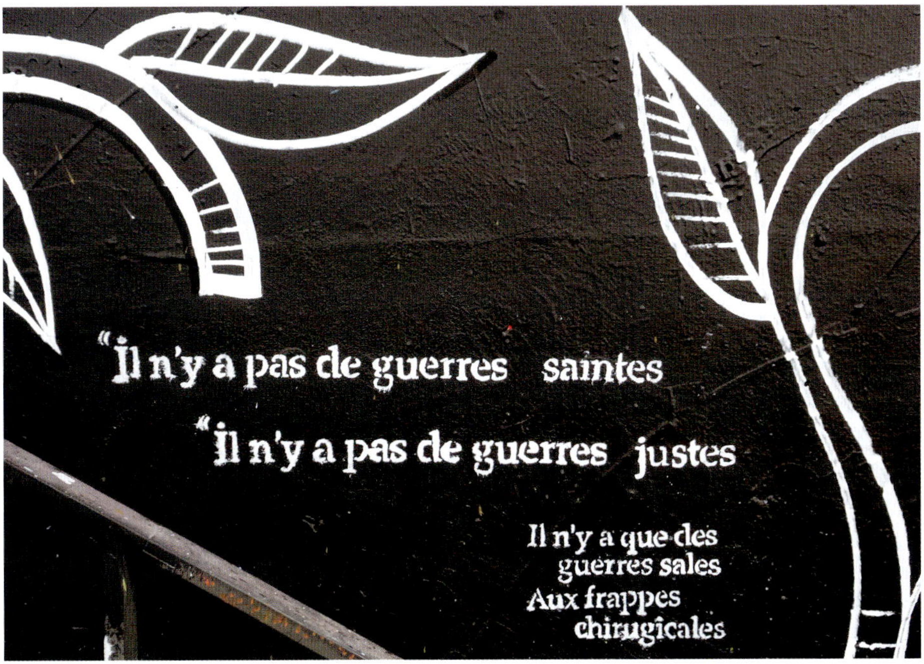
"Il n'y a pas de guerres saintes
"Il n'y a pas de guerres justes
Il n'y a que des
guerres sales
Aux frappes
chirugicales

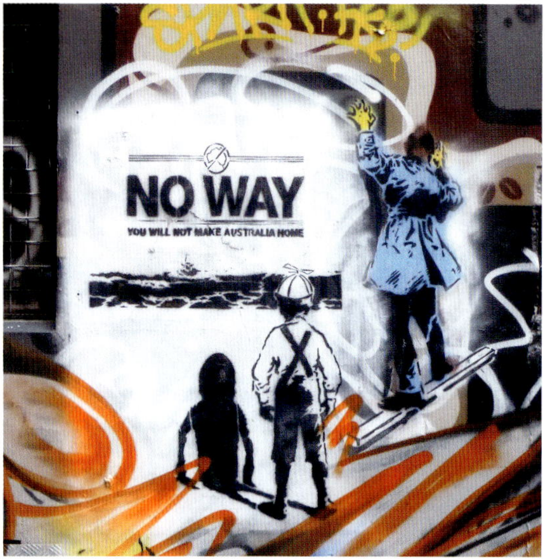

TOP Drasko, Melbourne, Australia, 2016

BOTTOM Unknown artist, New York City, USA, 2018

OPPOSITE TOP LEFT Unknown artist, Melbourne, Australia, 2017

OPPOSITE BOTTOM LEFT Unknown artist, Sydney, Australia, 2016

OPPOSITE RIGHT Unknown artist, Melbourne, Australia, 2017

MUCH resistance art is anonymous, for obvious reasons. This holds true for four of the five images on these pages, all of which react to the international human rights issue of the treatment of refugees and asylum seekers. Melbourne artist Drasko's multi-layered stencil at left was sprayed in response to the Australian government's stance on non-acceptance of asylum seekers arriving by sea.

The *No Borders* poster is recognisable as a message from the international No Border network, which advocates the abolition of international borders. The other two works opposite are simple statements in support of asylum seekers.

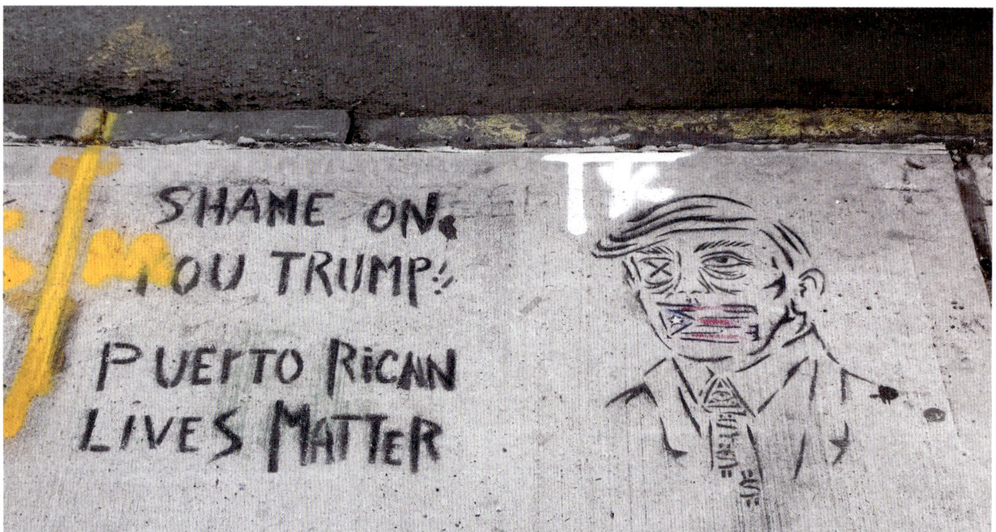

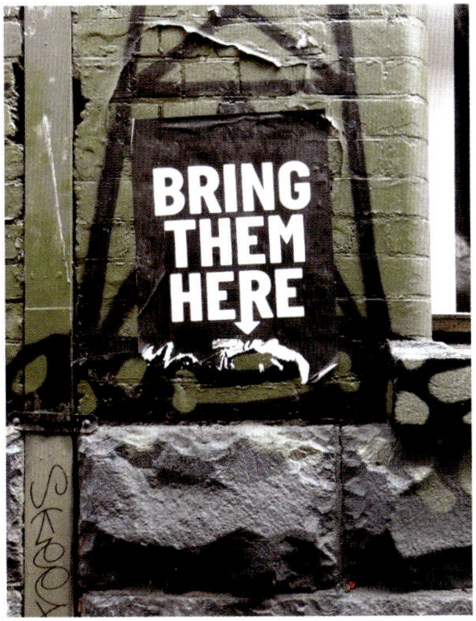
BRING
THEM
HERE

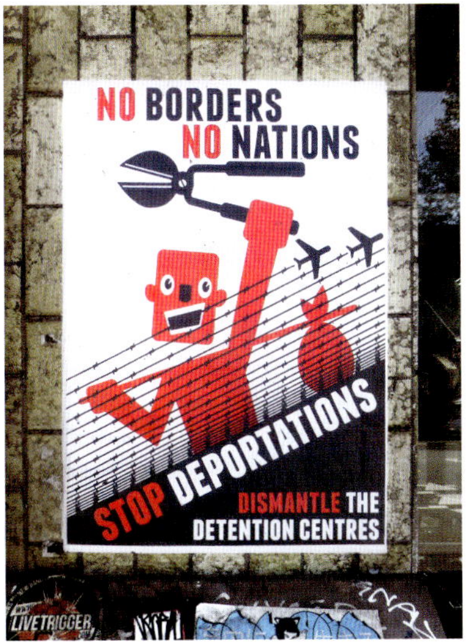
NO BORDERS
NO NATIONS
STOP DEPORTATIONS
DISMANTLE THE
DETENTION CENTRES
LIVETRIGGER

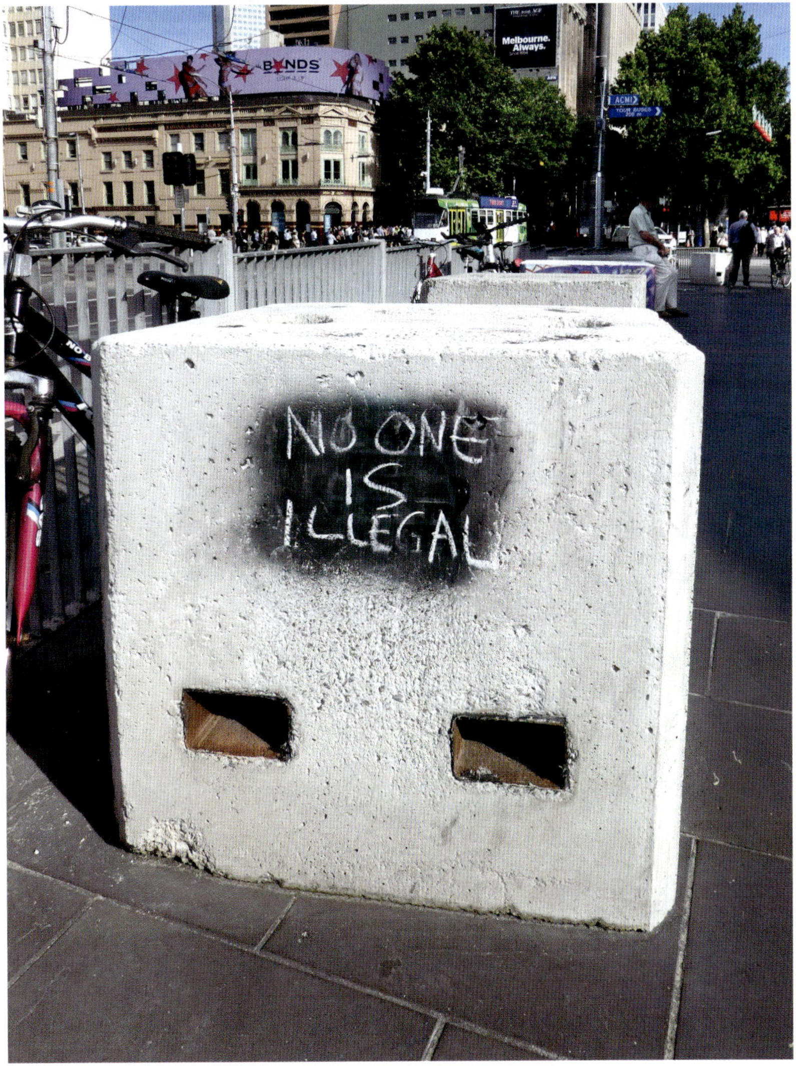
Melbourne. Always.
ACMI
NO ONE
IS
ILLEGAL

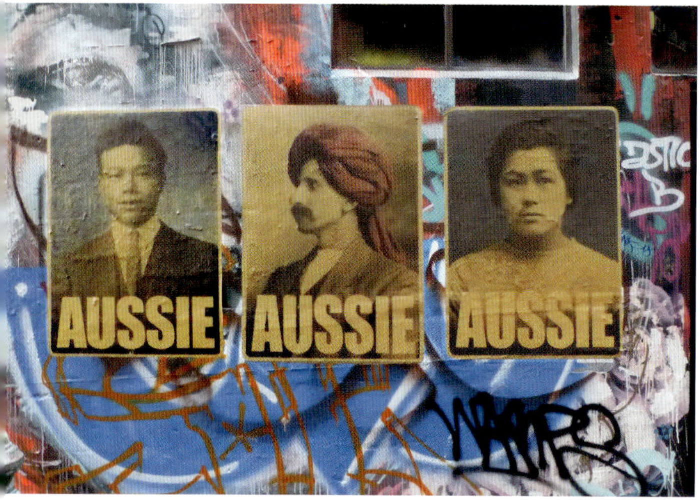

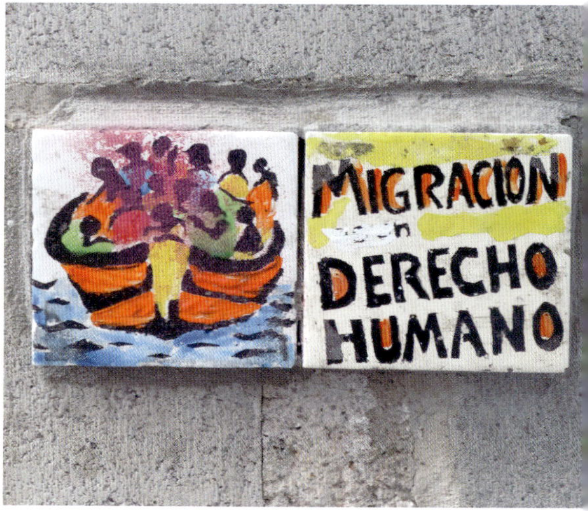

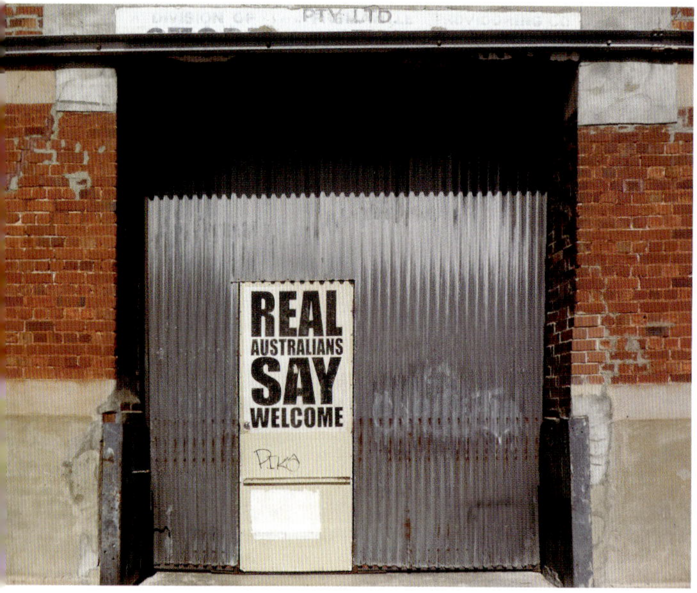

TOP LEFT Peter Drew, Melbourne, Australia, 2016

BOTTOM LEFT Peter Drew, Fremantle, Australia, 2017

RIGHT Unknown artist, Barcelona, Spain, 2016

OPPOSITE LEFT Peter Drew, Melbourne, Australia, 2016

OPPOSITE RIGHT Unknown artist, Geelong, Australia, 2014

ARTISTS like Adelaide-based Peter Drew believe that street art is well placed to tell the stories of refugees and asylum seekers. As a result of a crowd-funding campaign, Drew travelled widely around Australia pasting up posters that celebrate multiculturalism and welcome those who seek asylum. The small ceramic tiles above, attached to a wall in Barcelona's Ciutat Vella, translates as 'migration is a human right'.

The droll *Public Announcement* poster at opposite right shows signs of weathering as well as the efforts of those who disagree with the sentiment it expresses.

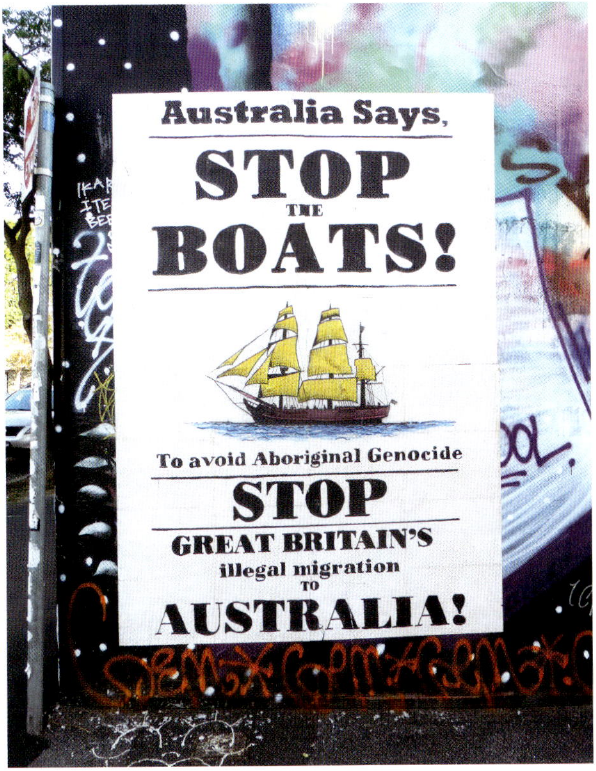
Australia Says,
STOP
THE
BOATS!
To avoid Aboriginal Genocide
STOP
GREAT BRITAIN'S
illegal migration
TO
AUSTRALIA!

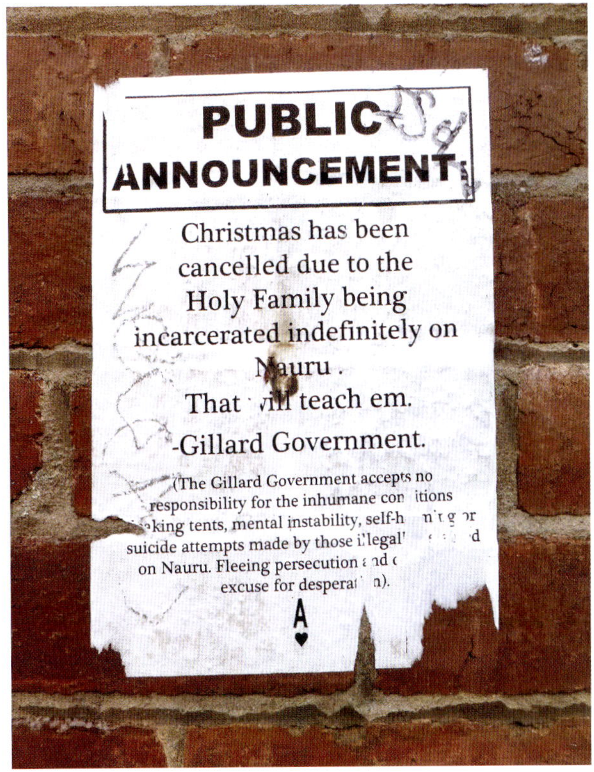
PUBLIC
ANNOUNCEMENT
Christmas has been
cancelled due to the
Holy Family being
incarcerated indefinitely on
Nauru .
-Gillard Government.
(The Gillard Government accepts no
responsibility for the inhumane
suicide attempts made by those
on Nauru. Fleeing persecution
excuse for
A

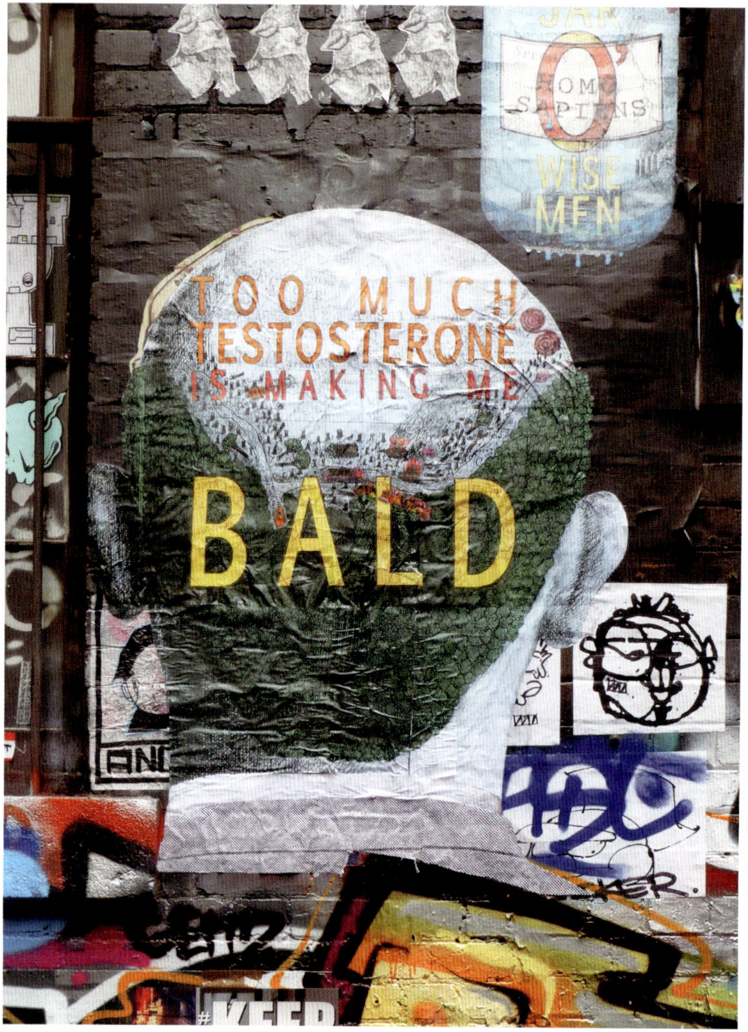
WISE
MEN
TOO MUCH
TESTOSTERONE
IS MAKING ME
BALD

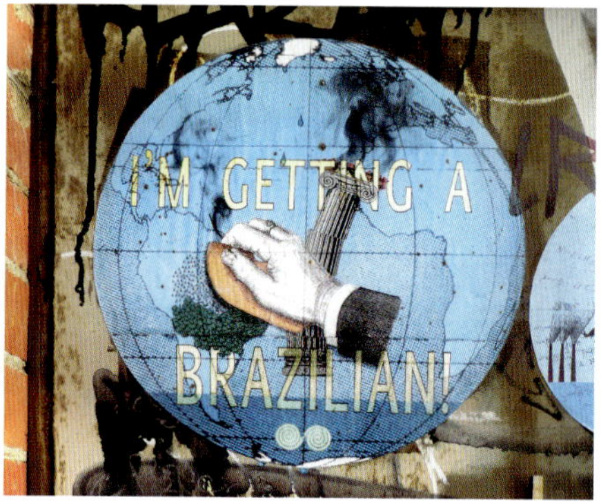
I'M GETTING A
BRAZILIAN!

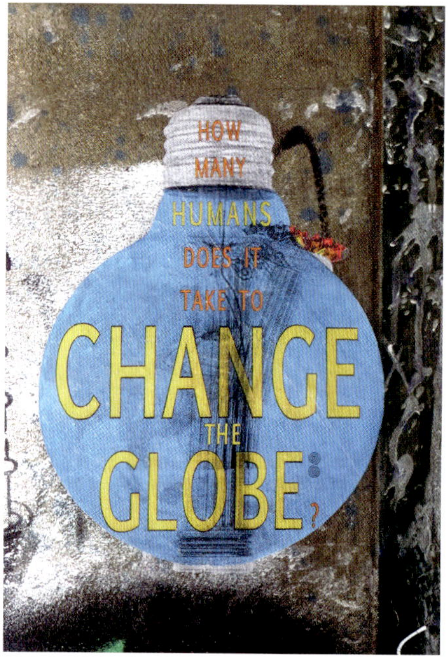
HOW
MANY
HUMANS
DOES IT
TAKE TO
CHANGE
THE
GLOBE?

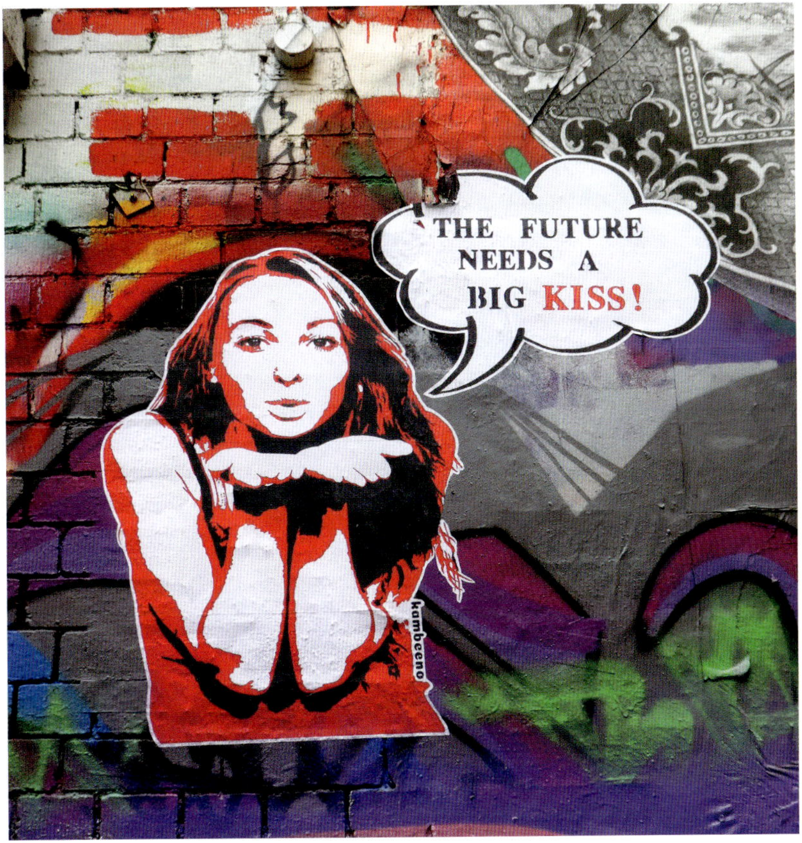

OPPOSITE, ALL Phoenix, Melbourne, Australia, 2014

LEFT Kambeeno, Melbourne, Australia, 2017

PHOENIX is a Melbourne art activist who contributes to the public forum by pasting up collages that draw attention to issues that he believes are important. The three paste-ups opposite reflect on environmental concerns and form part of his *Voice of the Blue Earth* series. Each composition is multilayered and placed on a surface ripe with pre-existing imagery. His witty tag lines challenge the passerby to think and to act.

The Future Needs a Big Kiss, by stencil artist Kambeeno, counterbalances these images with a cheerful message in one of his signature red, black and white paste-ups.

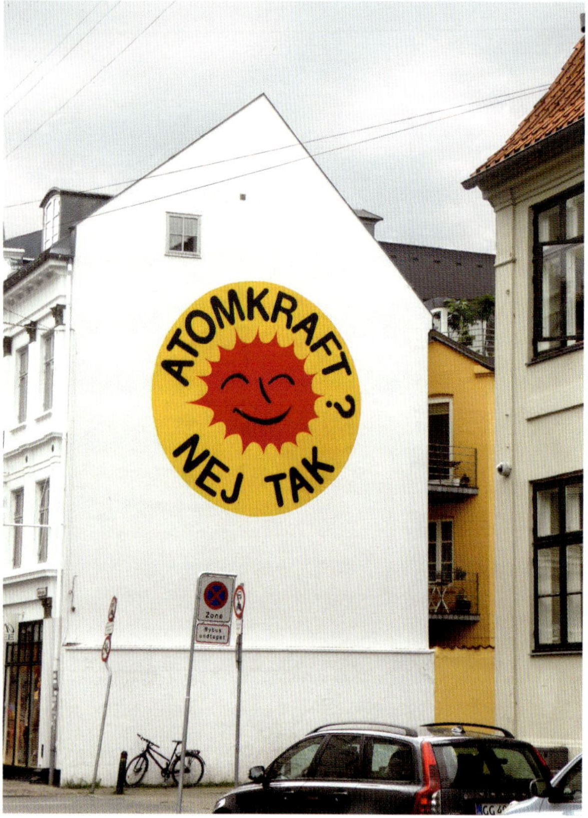

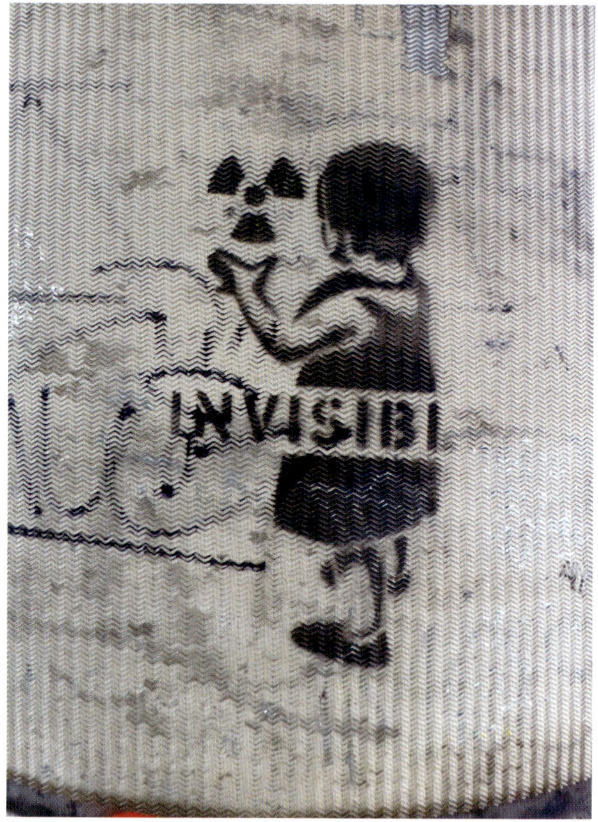

LEFT Anne Lund and Søren Lisberg, Aarhus, Denmark, 2016

RIGHT 281_Anti Nuke, Tokyo, Japan, 2014

OPPOSITE Therese Refvik, *What to Do with Broken Hearts*, Stavanger, Norway, 2016

THE so-called Smiling Sun design above left was devised in 1975 by 21-year-old Danish activists Anne Lund and Søren Lisberg. The accompanying text has been translated into 45 national and regional languages and has become an internationally recognised symbol for opposition to nuclear power. The simple one-colour *Invisible* stencil by 281_Anti Nuke was sprayed on surfaces in Tokyo's Shibuya district in the wake of the Fukushima nuclear disaster in 2011. The juxtaposition of the child and the toy-shaped nuclear symbol is powerful.

Norwegian stencil artist Therese Refvik (aka Tref) creates images with a strong sense of nostalgia. The happiness of the boy opposite, painted on a German World War II bunker on Sola Strand near Stavanger, belies the poignancy of the work's message, with its tank for recycling broken hearts.

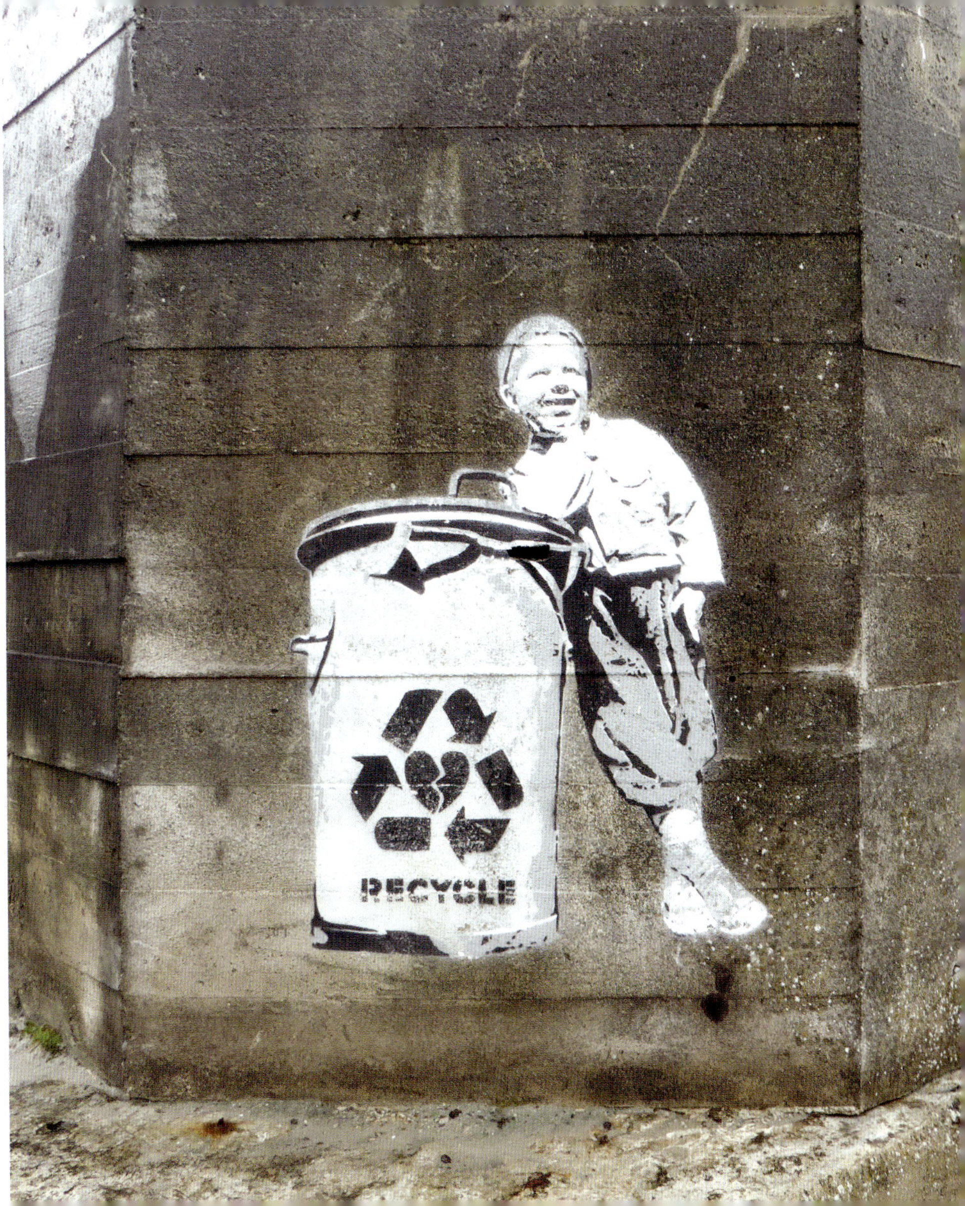
RECYCLE

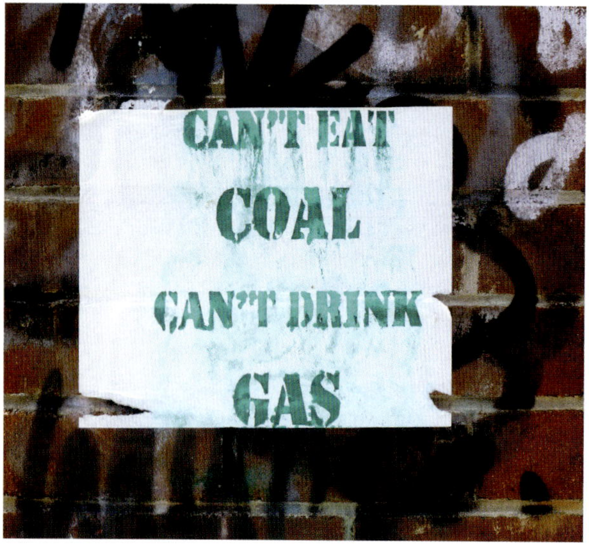

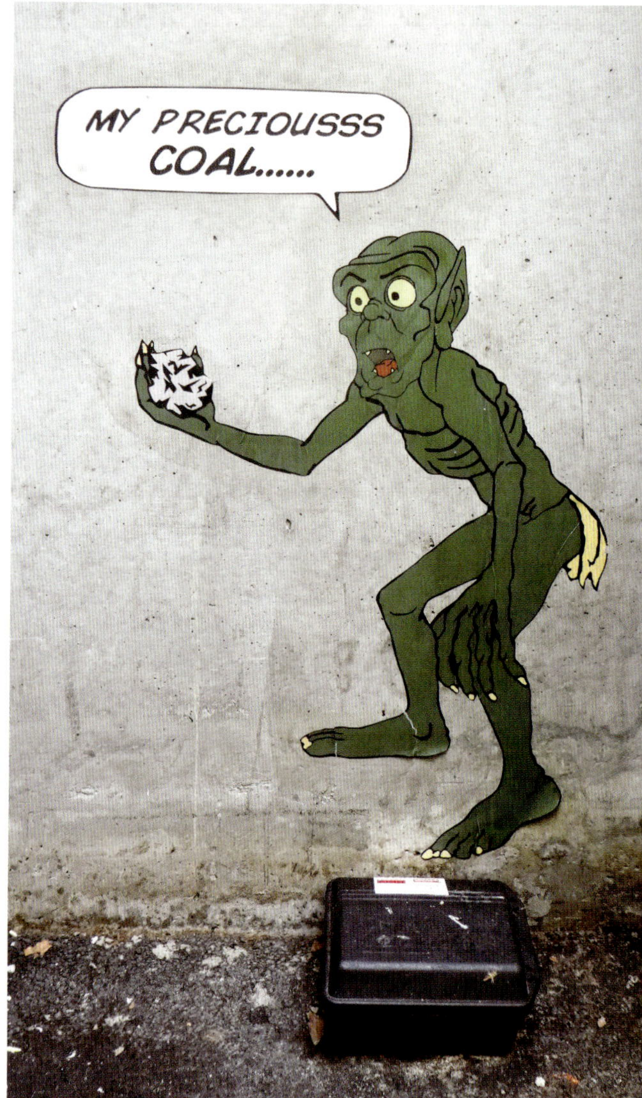

LEFT Unknown artist, Sydney, Australia, 2013
RIGHT cel out, *One Lie to Rule Them All*, Melbourne, Australia, 2017
OPPOSITE LEFT Unknown artist, Toronto, Canada, 2018
OPPOSITE TOP RIGHT Calm, *Monsanto Monsters*, Melbourne, Australia, 2017
OPPOSITE BOTTOM RIGHT Unknown artist, Bergen, Norway, 2016

THE effect of using non-renewable resources is changing ecosystems and having a profound effect on biodiversity around the globe. Greed is often at the core of this exploitation of finite reserves. cel out's satirical *Lord of the Rings* spoof at right, showing Gollum with his 'preciousss' coal, reflects this abuse of the land. The simple stencil above reminds us that mineral resources won't feed us.

A number of artists draw our attention to the worldwide plight of the honeybee. We rely on bees to pollinate much of the food we eat, and without healthy colonies, the continued production of some crops is at risk. Monsanto is one of the huge companies that peddles pesticides that are thought to be one of the major causes of bee population decline.

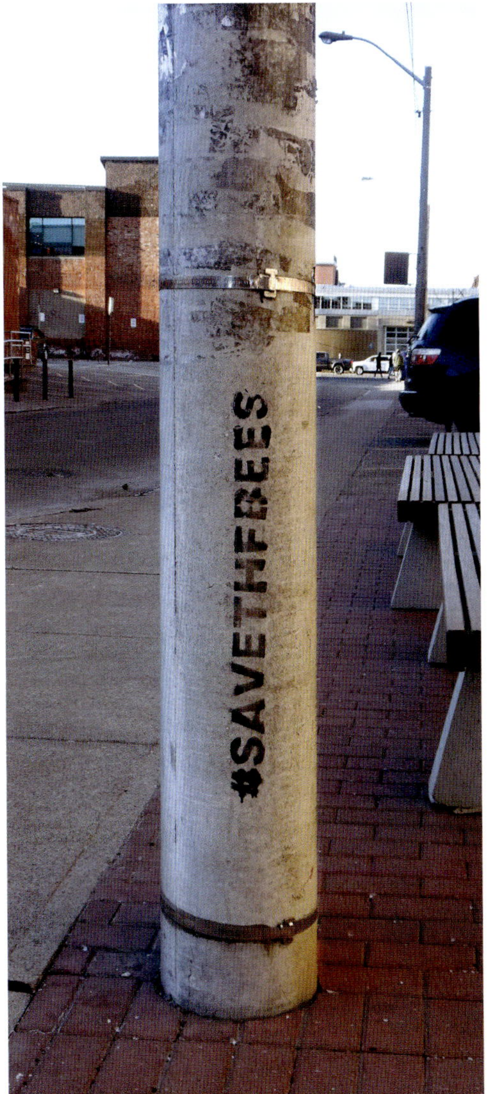
#SAVETHEBEES

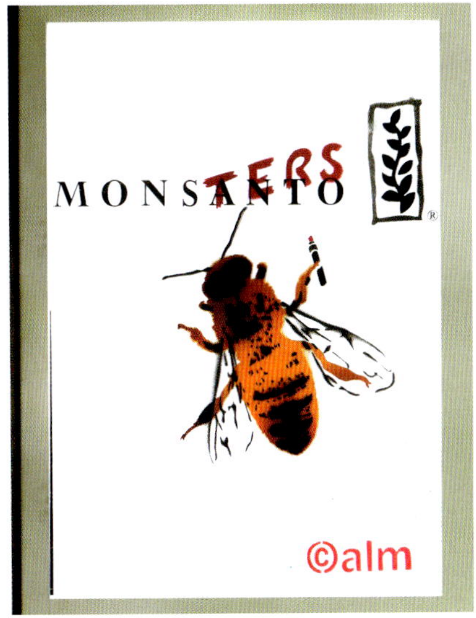
MONSANTO
TERS
©alm

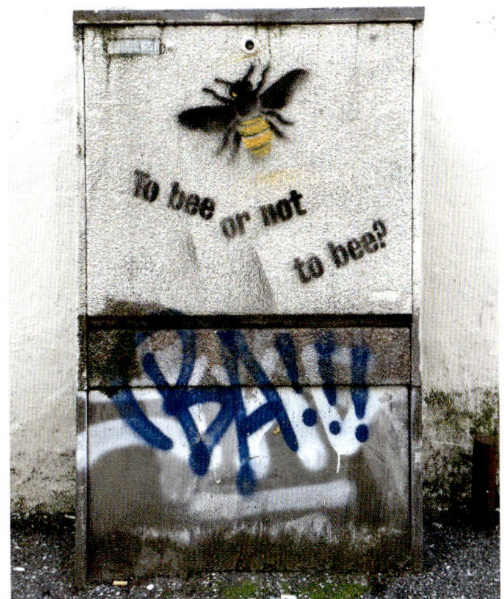
To bee or not to bee?

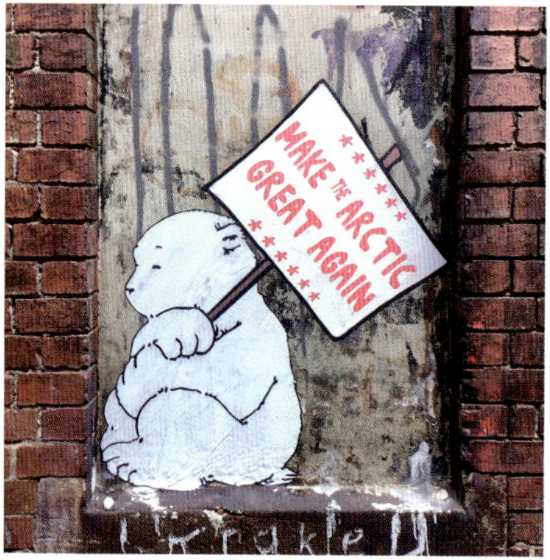
MAKE THE ARCTIC
GREAT AGAIN

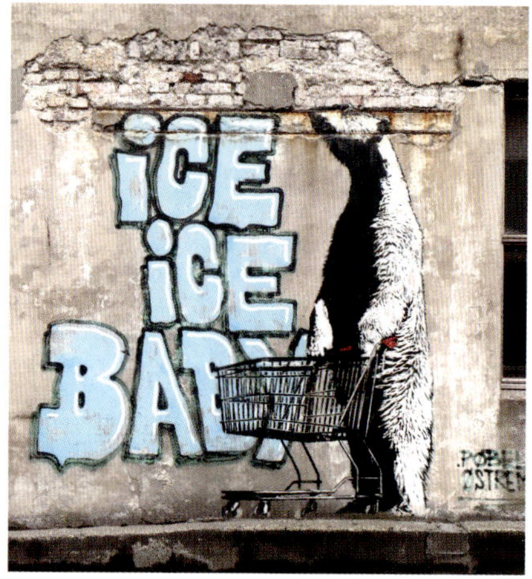
ICE
ICE

WANTED
BY INTERPOL
PAUL WATSON
NEEDED
BY
HUMANITY
THANK YOU
SEA SHEPHERD
LOVE YOUR WORK PAUL!
*A TRUE HERO... THANKS PAUL...

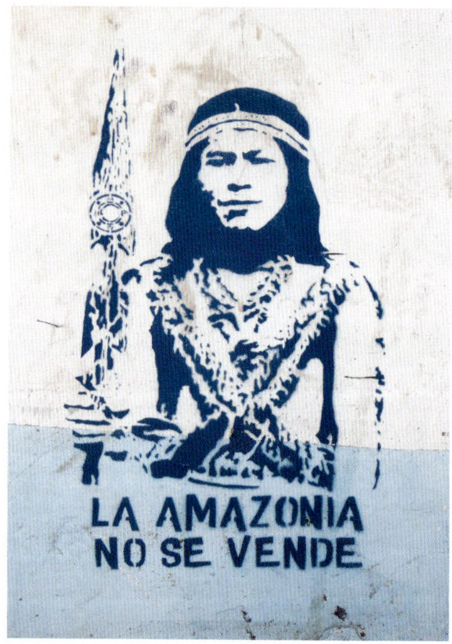
LA AMAZONIA
NO SE VENDE

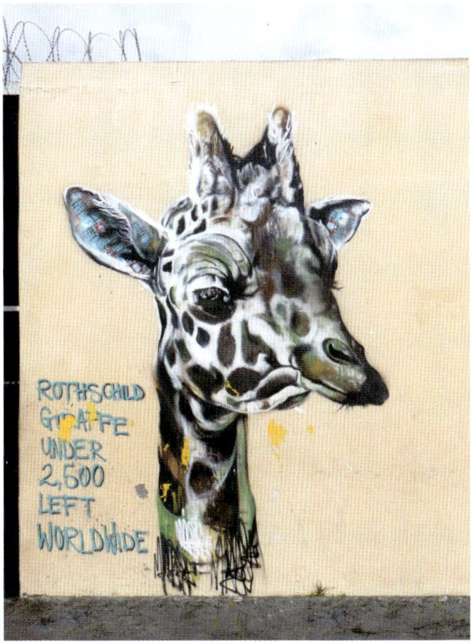

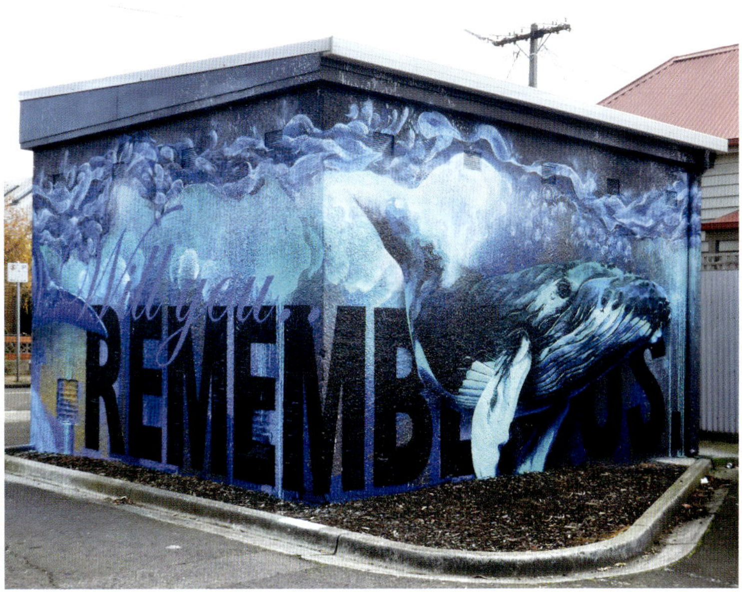

OPPOSITE TOP LEFT cel out, *Make the Arctic Great Again*, Melbourne, Australia, 2017

OPPOSITE TOP RIGHT Pøbel and Atle Østrem, Stavanger, Norway, 2016

OPPOSITE BOTTOM LEFT Calm, Melbourne, Australia, 2014

OPPOSITE BOTTOM RIGHT Unknown artist, Madrid, Spain, 2016

LEFT Louis Masai, Cape Town, South Africa, 2017

RIGHT Andrew J. Bourke, *Will You Remember Us?*, Melbourne, Australia, 2017

THE works we see on these pages draw attention to the fight against climate change by addressing issues such as the deforestation of the Amazon Basin and the conservation status of the polar bear, the humpback whale and Rothschild's giraffe, which range from vulnerable to endangered. *cel out* misquotes a famous politician in the text on the placard held by his bear (opposite top left) while Pøbel's bear, looking for ice at the supermarket, is accompanied by the words, painted by Atle Østrem, of a hip hop song released by rapper Vanilla Ice in 1989. Calm's poster celebrates wildlife conservationist and environmental activist Paul Watson of Greenpeace and the *Sea Shepherd*. It is significant that it has been scribbled on by supporters.

Louis Masai's Rothschild's giraffe and Andrew J. Bourke's humpback whale were painted in public spaces to remind us of the importance of these animals. Bourke asks the provocative question, 'Will you remember us?'

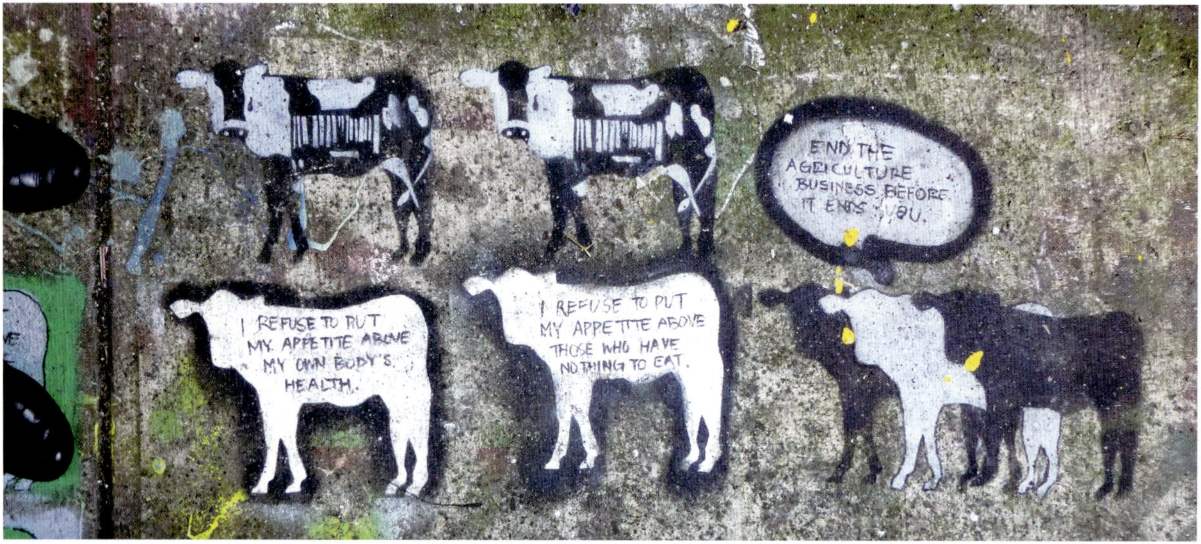

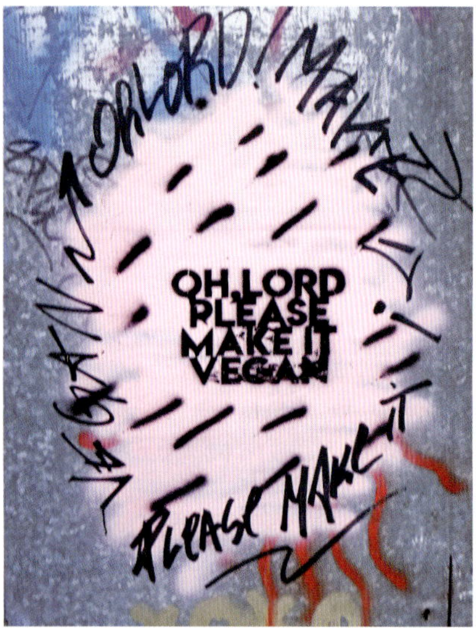

TOP Unknown artist, Melbourne, Australia, 2016

BOTTOM Unknown artist, Doel, Belgium, 2018

OPPOSITE, ALL walden, London, UK, 2015

THEY say that a picture is worth a thousand words. The images on these pages reflect the voices of artists who are speaking on behalf of animals, who have no voice. The use of the barcodes in the stencilled and handwritten work above on a laneway path emphasises the commodity status of animals.

Examples from walden's *Extinction Project*, opposite, are sensitively drawn miniatures pasted on walls, especially in London's Shoreditch. Each of the extinct animals is accompanied by a taxonomic label and extinction dates and can be read as a eulogy to the animal itself.

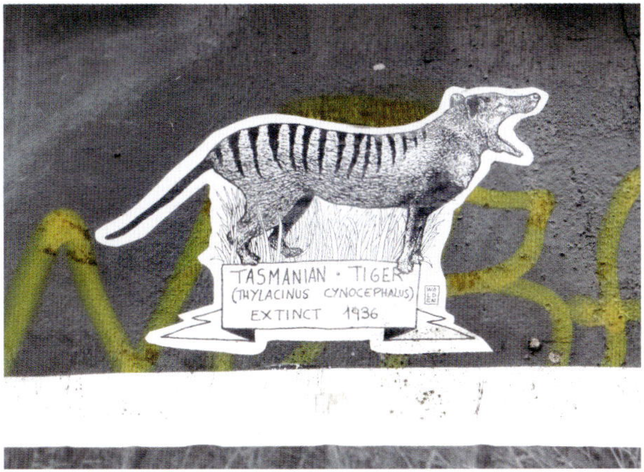
TASMANIAN · TIGER
(THYLACINUS CYNOCEPHALUS)
EXTINCT 1936
WALDEN

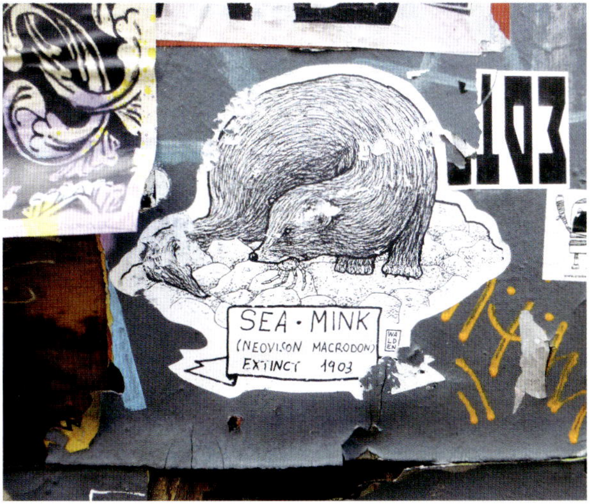
SEA · MINK
(NEOVISON MACRODON)
EXTINCT 1903
WALDEN

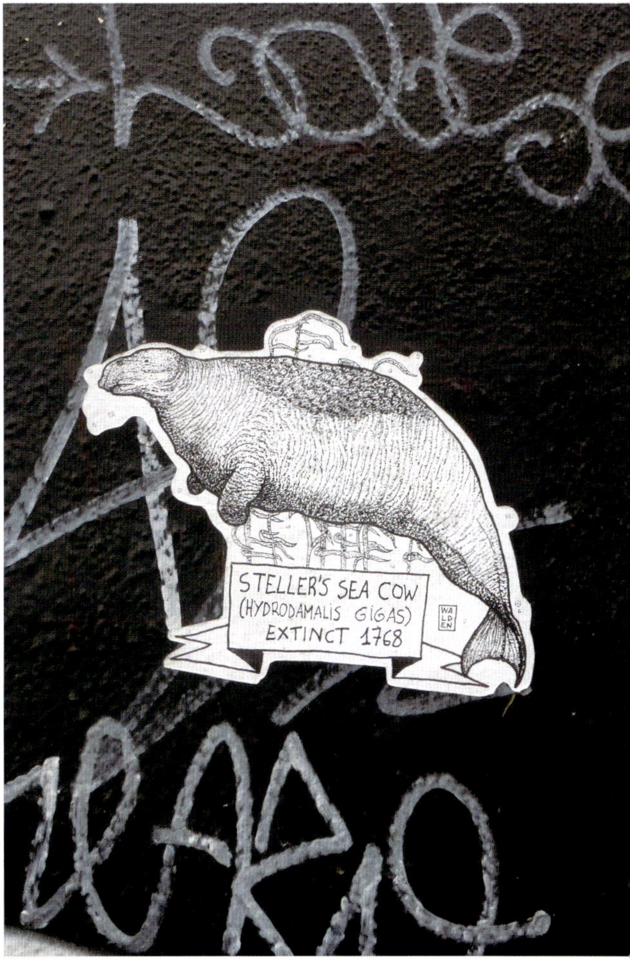
STELLER'S SEA COW
(HYDRODAMALIS GIGAS)
EXTINCT 1768
WALDEN

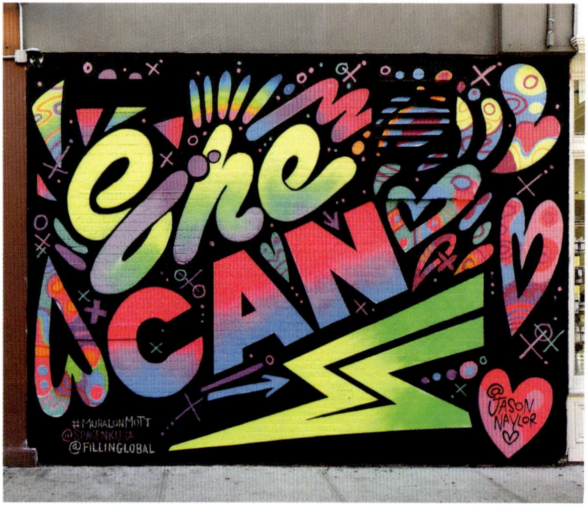

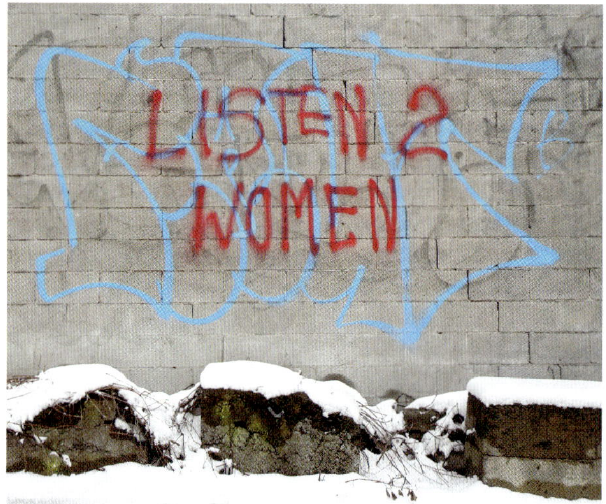

LEFT Jason Naylor, New York City, USA, 2018
RIGHT Unknown artist, Montreal, Canada, 2018
OPPOSITE Lucy Lucy, *Voice Choice Power*, Melbourne, Australia, 2017

WOMEN have great power and these three artists recognise it, whether it be the neon exclamation that 'she can' by Jason Naylor or the humble 'listen 2 women' statement sprayed onto a wall in wintry Montreal.

Melbourne-based French artist Lucy Lucy painted two figures with the superimposed text – 'voice', 'choice' and 'power' – on the wall of a women's refuge in Melbourne's inner north. Dressed in glorious colour and pattern, so typical of the artist's work, and surrounded by a field of flowers, their voices echo powerfully as they speak out against violence to women.

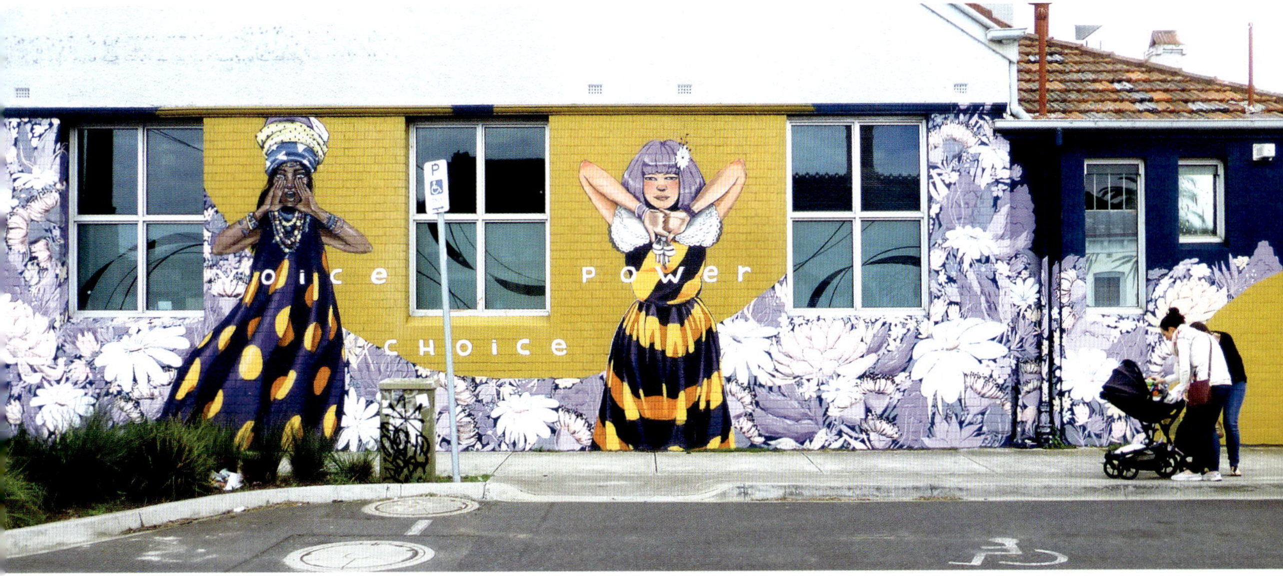
oice
power
choice

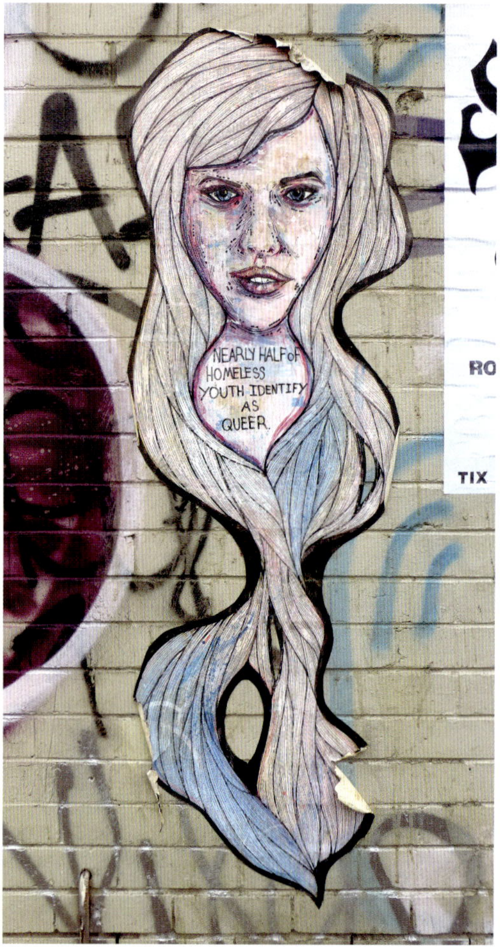

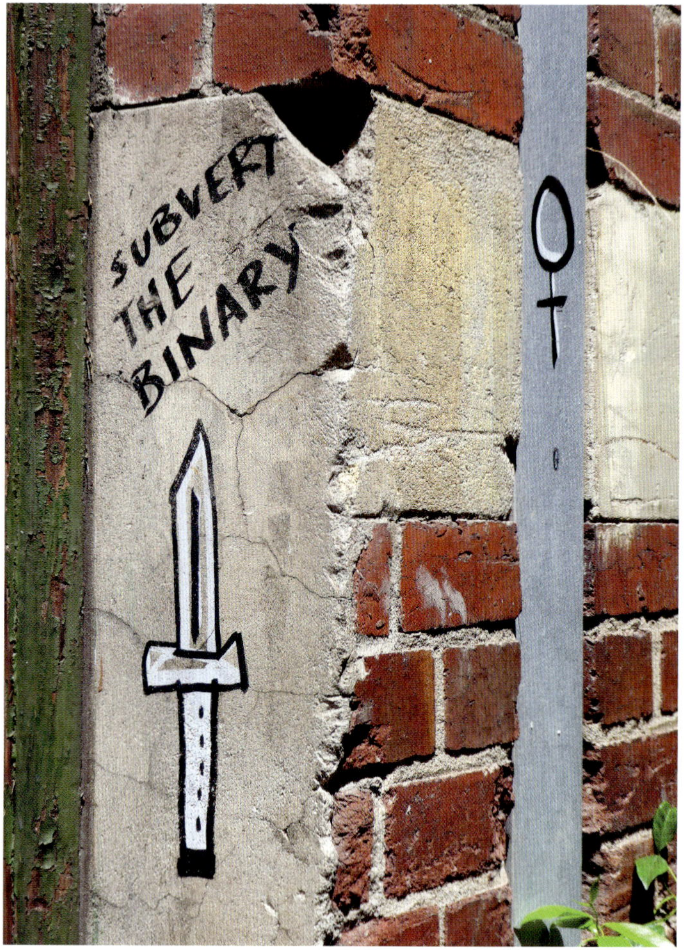

LEFT Astrotwitch, Melbourne, Australia, 2016
RIGHT Unknown artist, Melbourne, Australia, 2017
OPPOSITE Lana Milburn, Melbourne, Australia, 2017

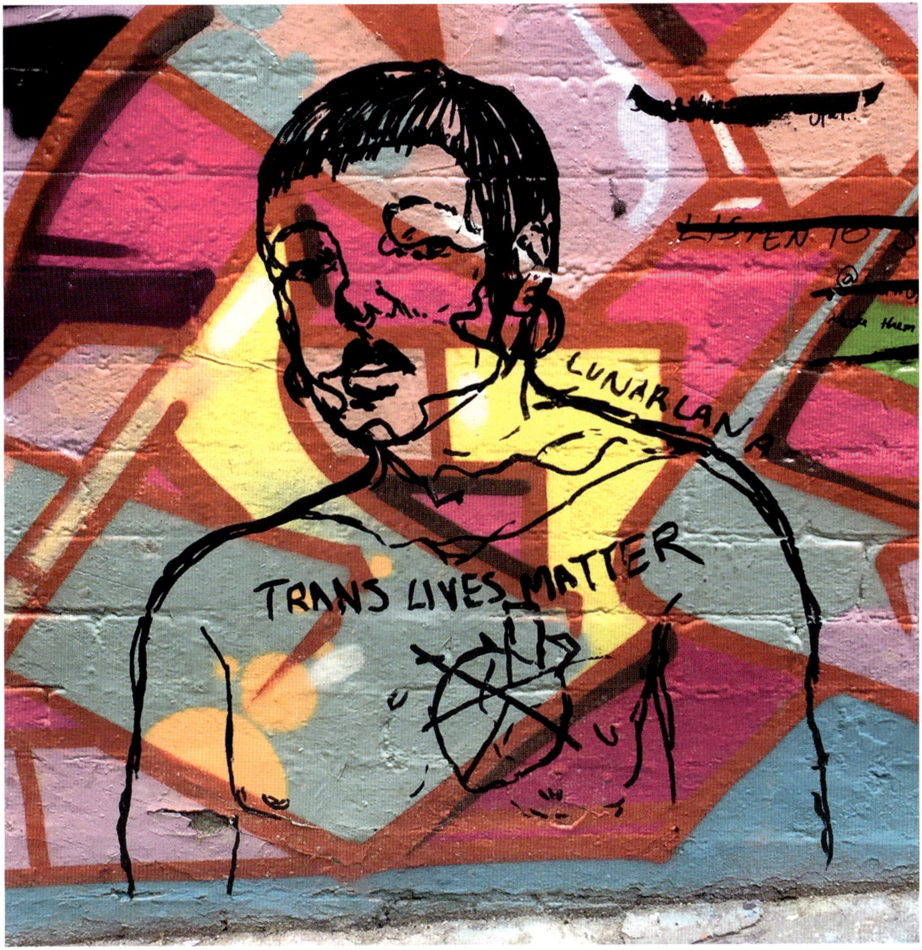

GENDER is a cultural construct and in most societies the gender binary classifies us into distinct and opposite gender roles and identities. This is slowly changing in today's world. The text included on the sensitive drawing by Astrotwitch opposite left – 'nearly half of homeless youth identify as queer' – reminds us that the struggle for understanding and acceptance is far from over.

The fact that Lana Milburn feels the need to state that 'trans lives matter' underlines the need for a broader understanding of the way that gender and gender expectations impact on individual lives.

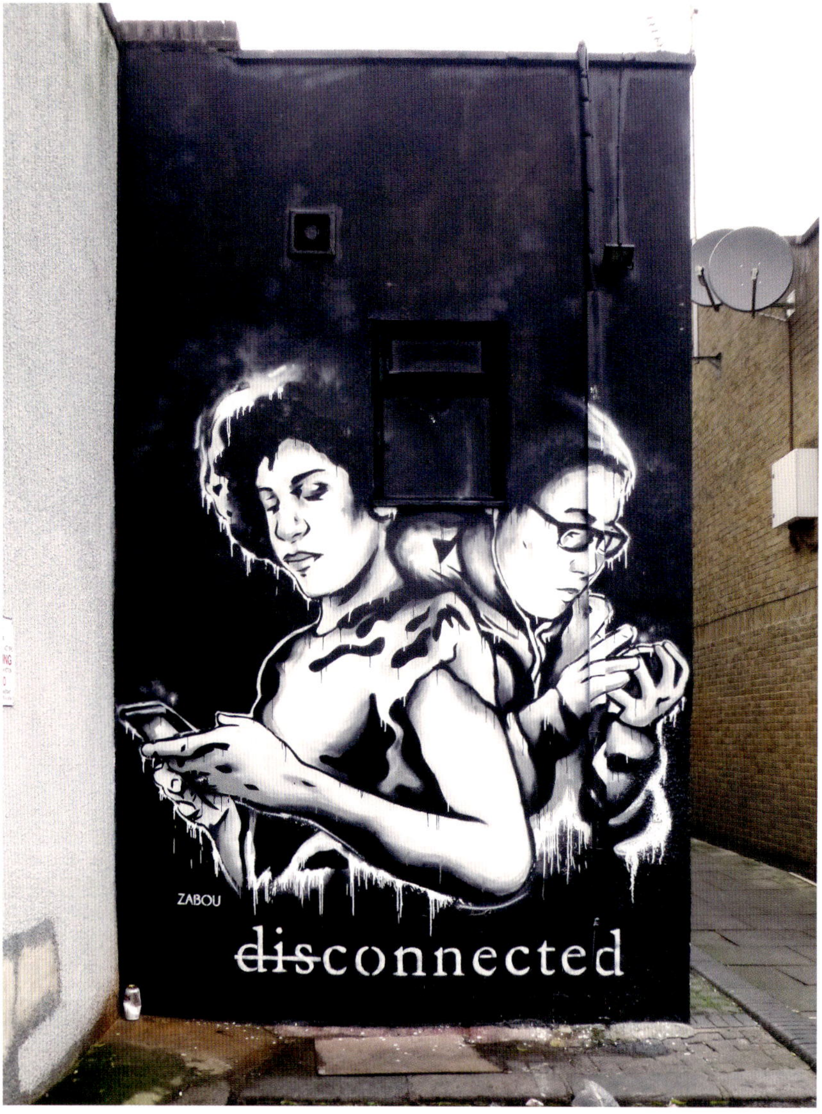
ZABOU
disconnected

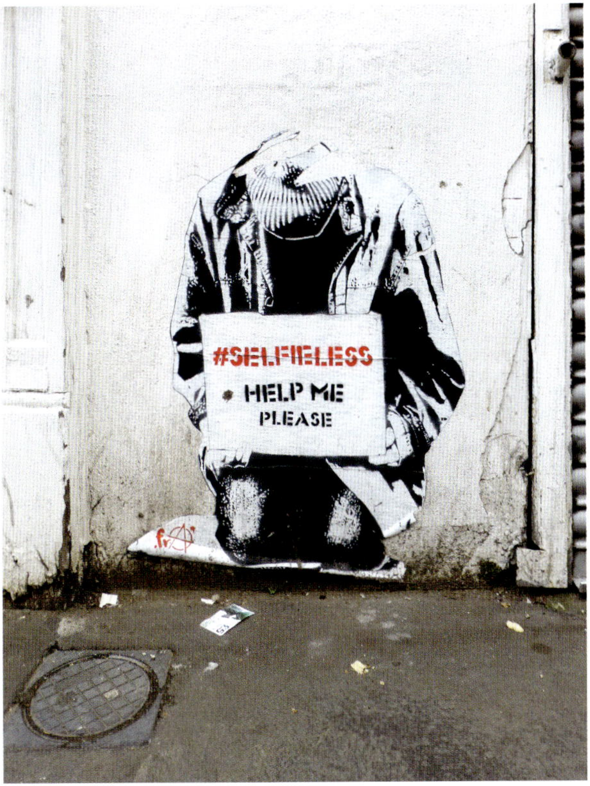

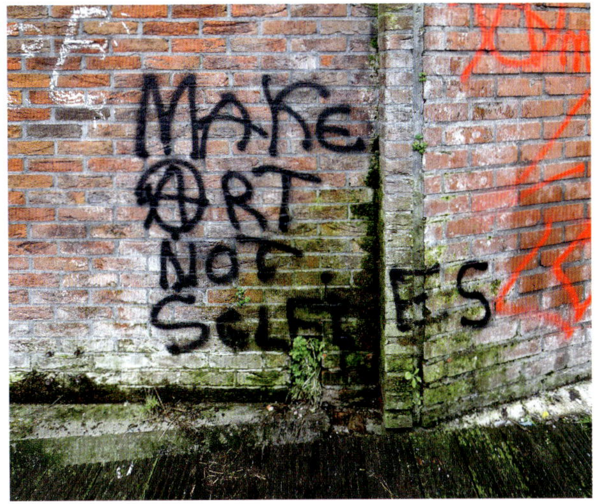

WE are consumed by the digital world. The fallout can be seen here in the work of three commentators. Zabou, a French artist who has been based in London since 2012, applies irony effectively in her art. Are we connected to others by our personal devices or, as she so wryly puts it opposite, disconnected, and increasingly unaware of the 'real' world around us?

Also working with the simplicity of strong black and white contrast in his stencilled paste-up, Swiss-based artist .frA* refers to the contemporary social trend of defining ourselves and our lives via selfies. A further sense of frustration with this trend is evident in the text above by the anonymous writer in Ghent.

OPPOSITE Zabou, London, UK, 2015
LEFT .frA*, *SELFIELESS*, London, UK, 2015
RIGHT Unknown artist, Ghent, Belgium, 2018

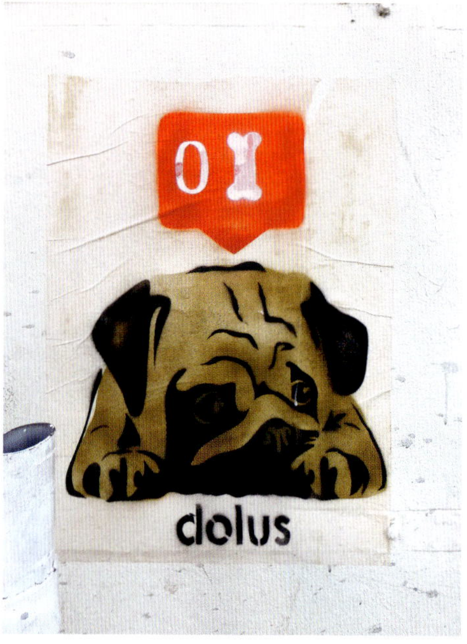
01
dolus

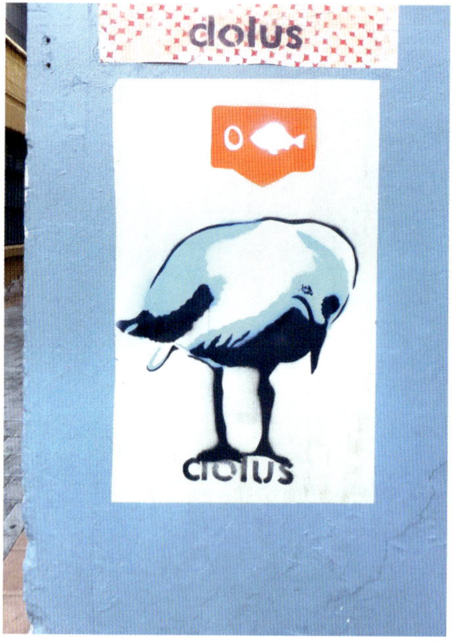
dolus
0
dolus

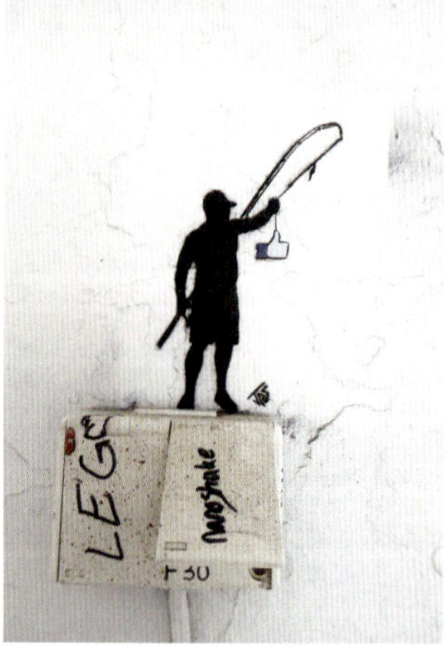

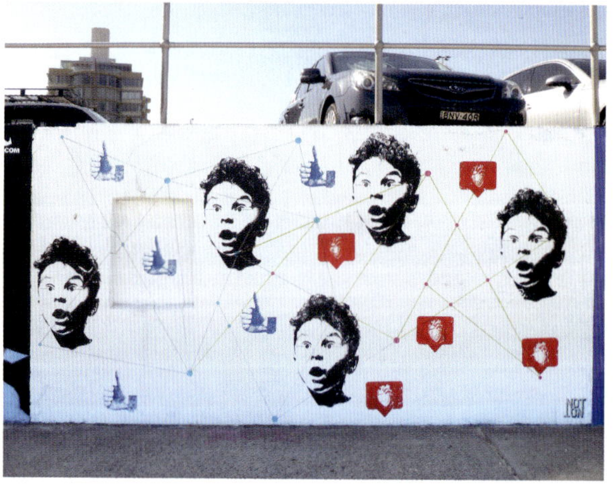

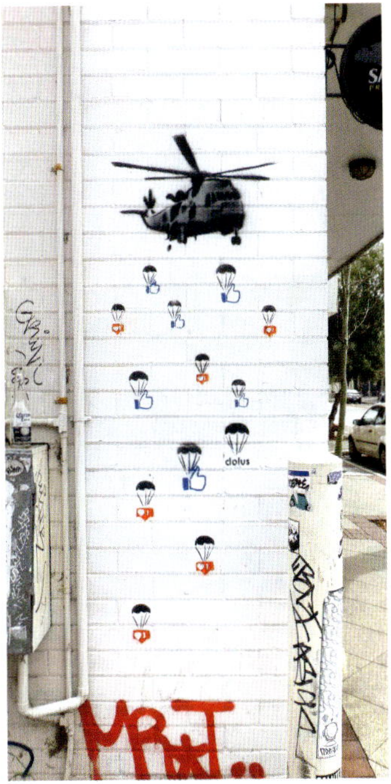

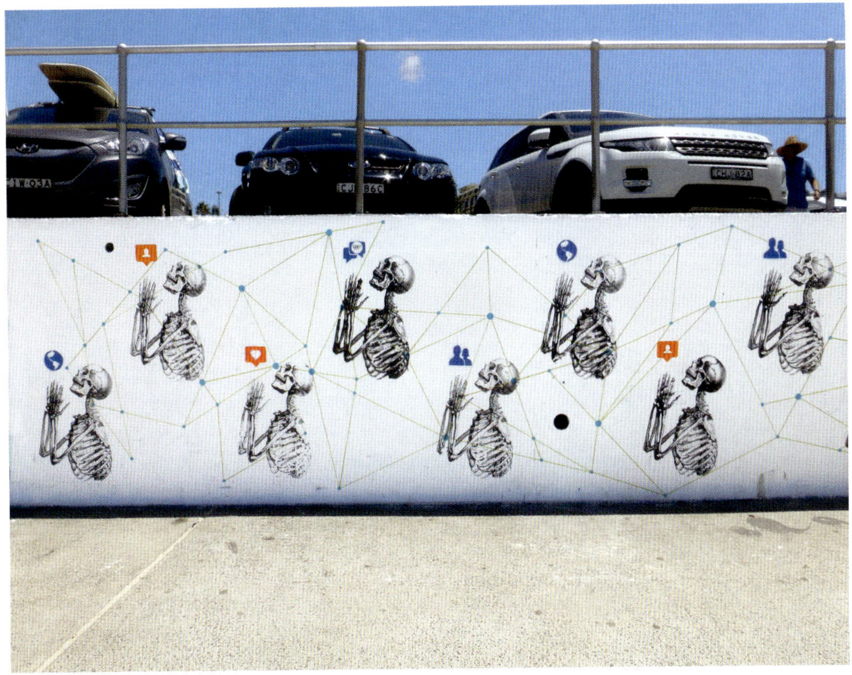

OPPOSITE TOP LEFT Dolus, *Zero Bones*, Perth, Australia, 2014

OPPOSITE TOP RIGHT Dolus, *Zero Fish*, Perth, Australia, 2014

OPPOSITE BOTTOM LEFT JPS, Stavanger, Norway, 2016

OPPOSITE BOTTOM RIGHT NOTNOT, Sydney, Australia, 2017

LEFT Dolus, *Social Media*, Perth, Australia, 2014

RIGHT NOTNOT, Sydney, Australia, 2017

IN today's world, emojis ARE text. They save time and energy and are a readily understood and efficient form of mobile communication. With our personal approval ratings quantifiable on social media, we are increasingly tempted to judge our success by the number of followers or likes we collect. Opposite, Perth-based artist Dolus uses animals (at top) to help us laugh at this while English stencil artist JPS creates a visual pun of fishing for likes at bottom left.

Stencil artist NOTNOT is based in Sydney. His satirical work echoes our need for acceptance and approval. On his wall at opposite bottom right, the statement 'switch to power off' has been subtly printed either side of the boy's eyes, highlighting the way that social media is constantly demanding our attention. His stencils, such as the skeletons above praying for likes, are applied to a vertical surface via silk screen and squeegee.

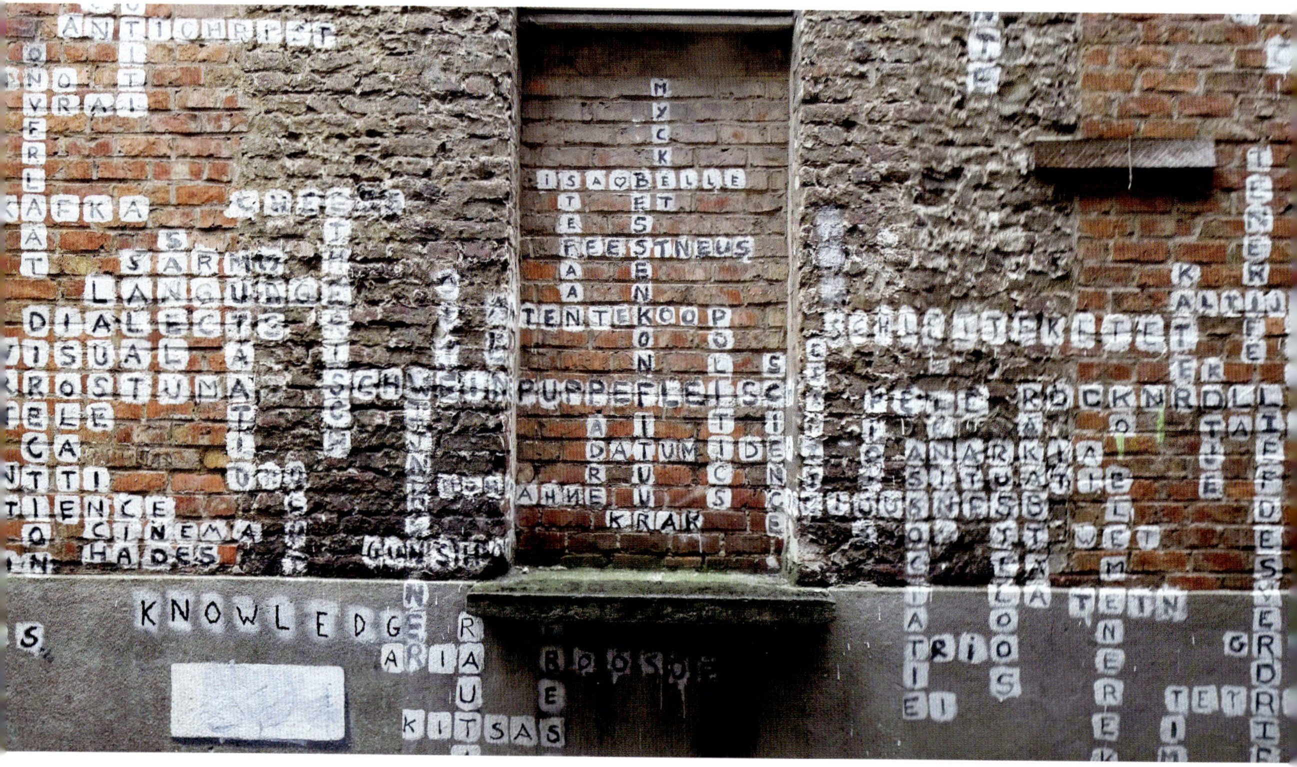

ABOVE Unknown collaboration, Ghent, Belgium, 2018
OPPOSITE Felipe Pantone, *#LargestQR*, Hasselt, Belgium, 2018

ON these pages we can see two diametrically opposed means of communication, one text-based and the other digital. The photograph above is a detail of a crossword puzzle painted on a long wall in the historical centre of the Belgian city of Ghent. It has been created over a period of time in a range of languages and includes words such as ‘Kafka’, ‘rocknroll’ and ‘knowledge’.

The QR (or Quick Response) code was invented in 1964 to allow high-speed scanning in the Japanese automotive industry. The enormous version opposite was painted by Argentinian-Spanish artist Felipe Pantone. Framed by his signature vivid colours and graphic patterns, it is probably the largest one on Earth. Today the QR code is used for mobile tagging on personal devices. Try hovering your smart phone over the page to read about the artwork.

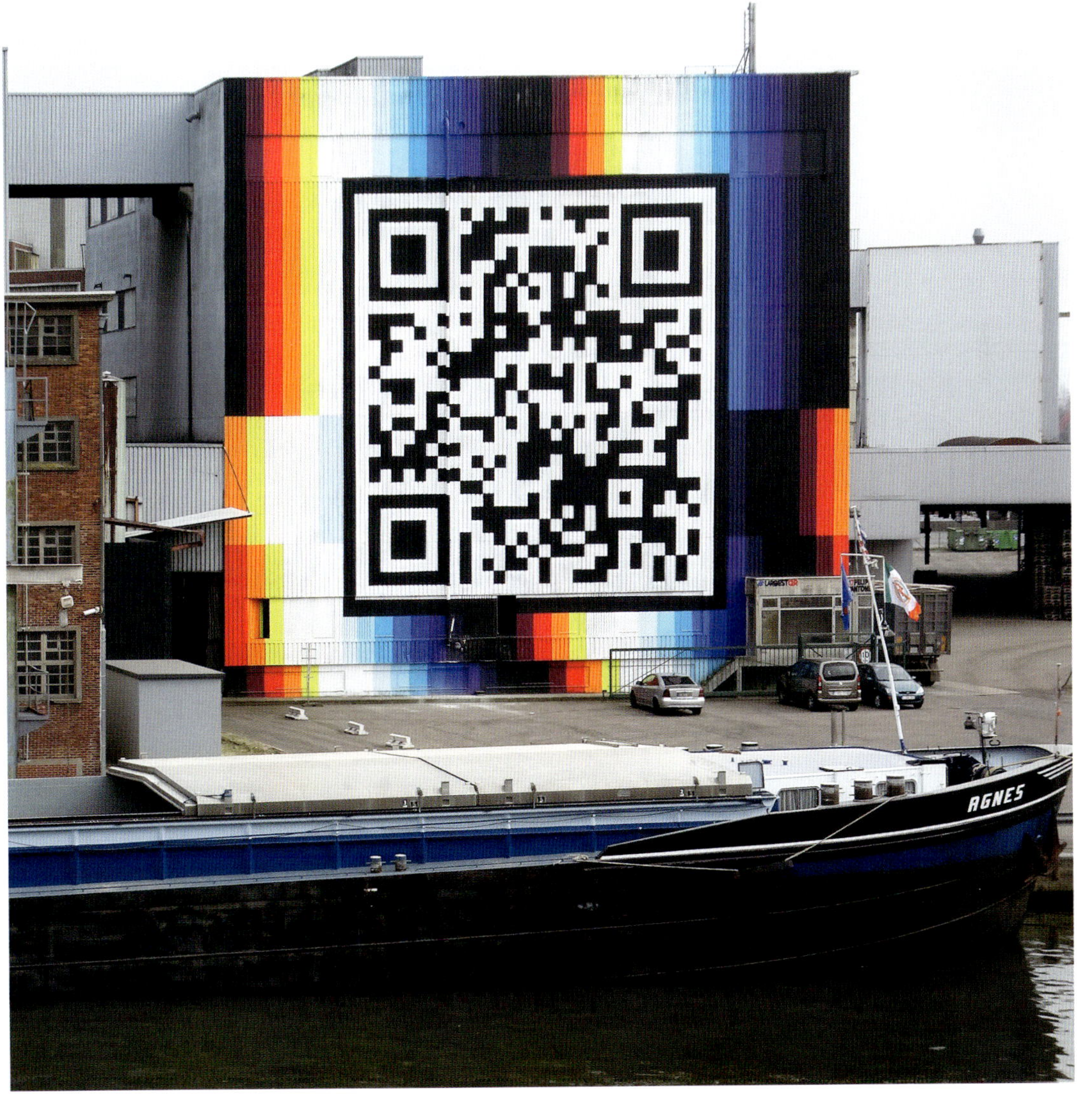
AGNES

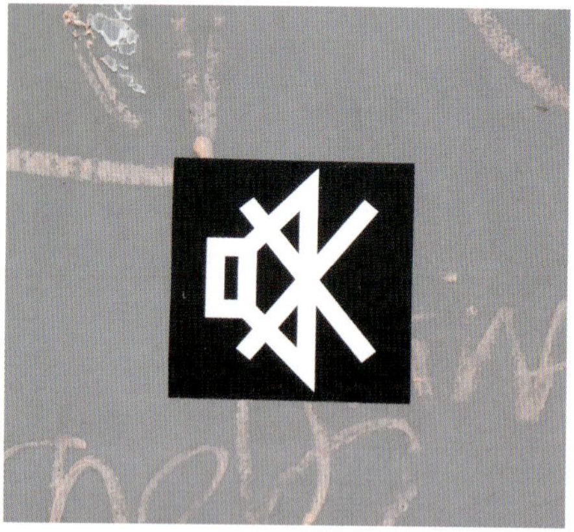

MUCH of what we know of the world around us reaches us via the media. From the middle of the 20th century that role was taken by TV but today the content on the internet and personal smart devices is more relevant and influential. Whether it's because TV is seen as outdated or because of other issues about content, an urban scrawler has written a cynical 'dont look' across the screens of two units left out for rubbish collection. Wouldn't it be refreshing if we COULD mute the input of the media on demand, as Pøbel suggests?

Will Coles wants his art to make people think; thus he has embedded the word 'obsolescence' in the screen of the concrete TV opposite that he installed on a busy street corner in the centre of Melbourne.

TOP Pøbel, Stavanger, Norway, 2016

BOTTOM Unknown artist, Melbourne, Australia, 2014

OPPOSITE Will Coles, Melbourne, Australia, 2014

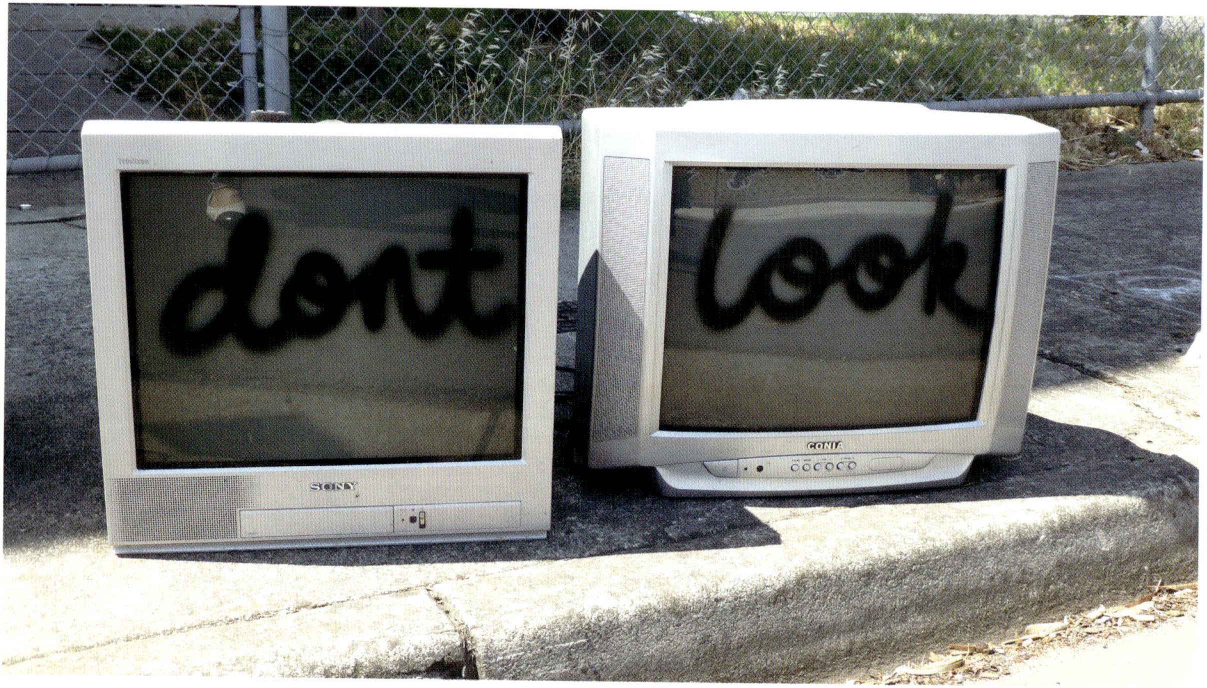

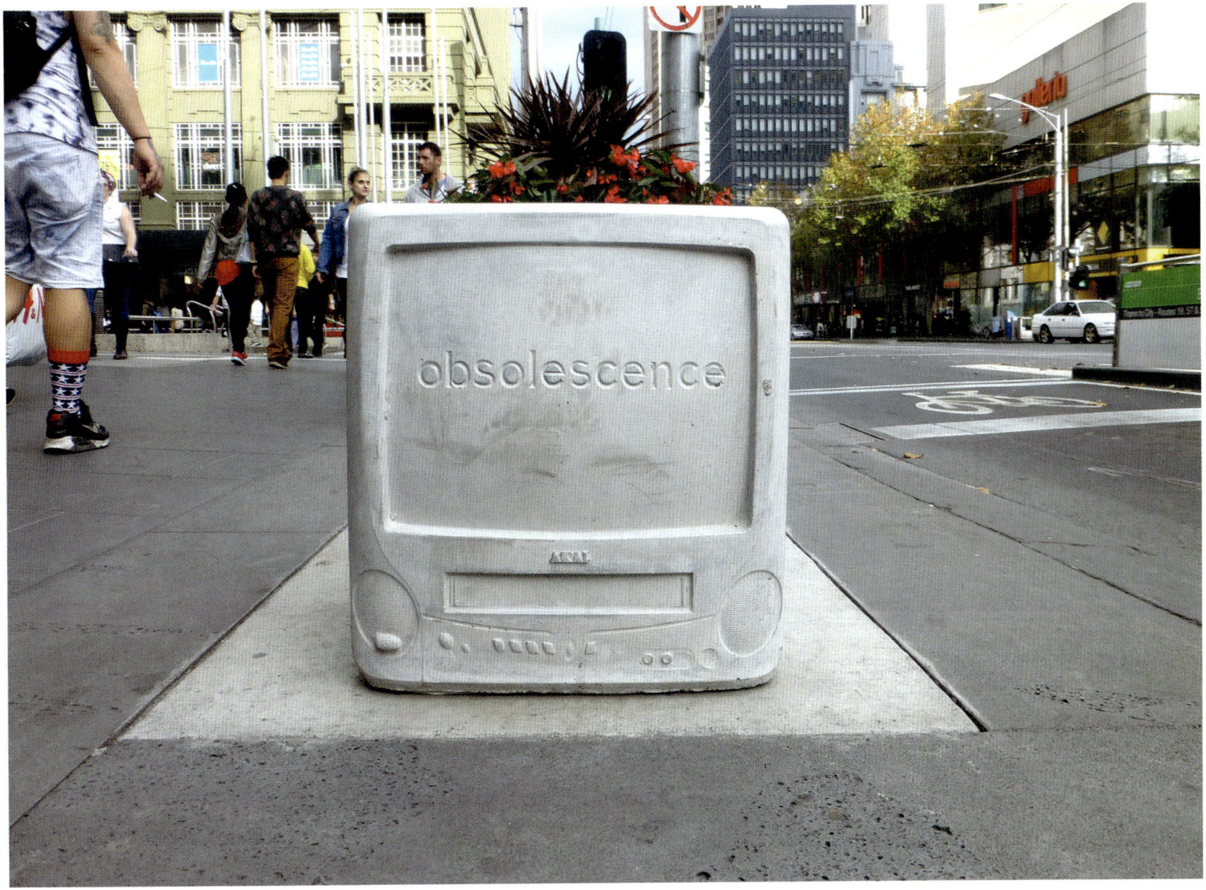
obsolescence
AKAI

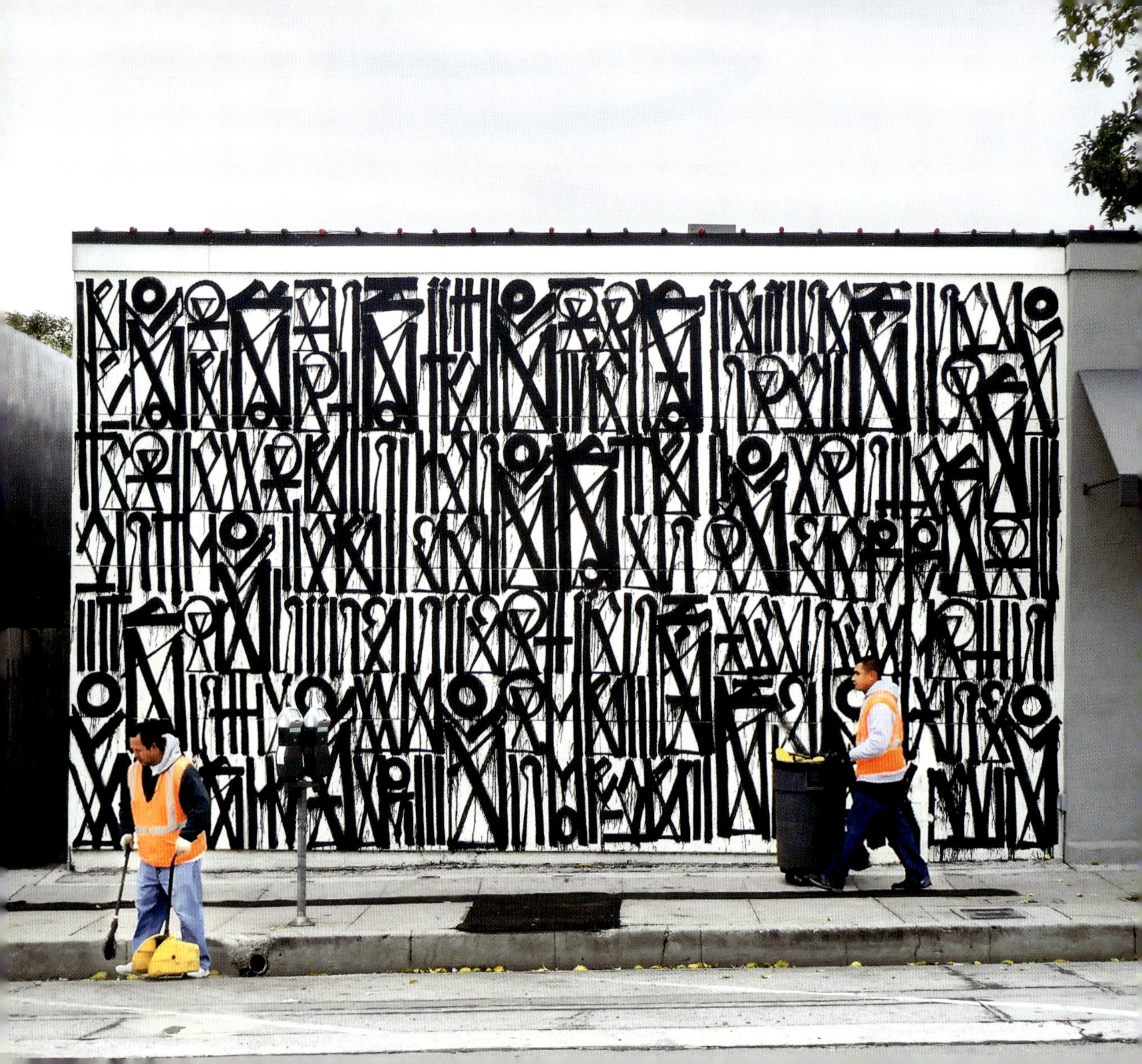

Calligraffiti and Glyphs

Calligraffiti is an art form that fuses the beauty of calligraphy with the scale and context of graffiti. Examples are visual compositions that value aesthetics over ease of communication. The word 'calligraphy' is derived from the ancient Greek 'kallos' (beauty) and 'graphein' (to write), which is incidentally the same root as the word 'graffiti'. Letters become symbols that form words and pictures at the same time.

The visual expressions of calligraffiti run the gamut from readable to abstract, and vary from culture to culture and artist to artist. Sometimes they reflect the cultural background of the artist, such as the influence of Arabic text on eL Seed and sometimes they are a personal invention of the artist, such as the rune-like marks of Retna, opposite. Every artist has their own style, technique and preferred tools. These range from aerosol to brush to wide broom. Like all street art, one of the beauties of this form is its freedom from rules.

The strokes that combine to create a composition may be simple or complex, spontaneous or abstracted. Basic lines and shapes and splats, such as the markings of Raul33, can become a language of their own within the form.

Some of the images on the following pages contain symbols that belong to different visual languages. There are hieroglyphics by Stampz, non-alphabet glyphs by Astral Nadir and the hand gestures of sign language by Owen Dippie.

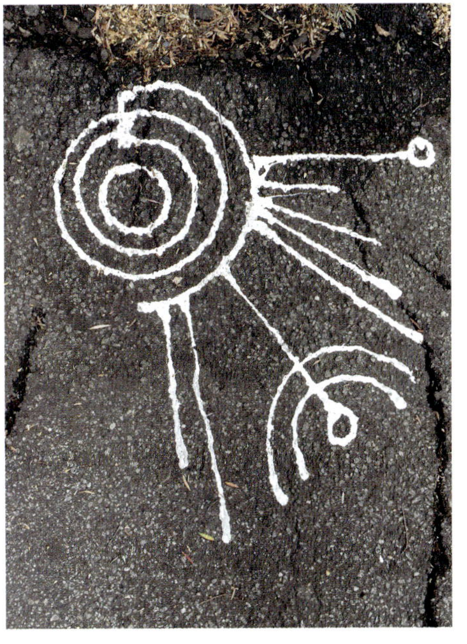

OPPOSITE Retna, Los Angeles, USA, 2016

RIGHT Astral Nadir, Melbourne, Australia, 2017

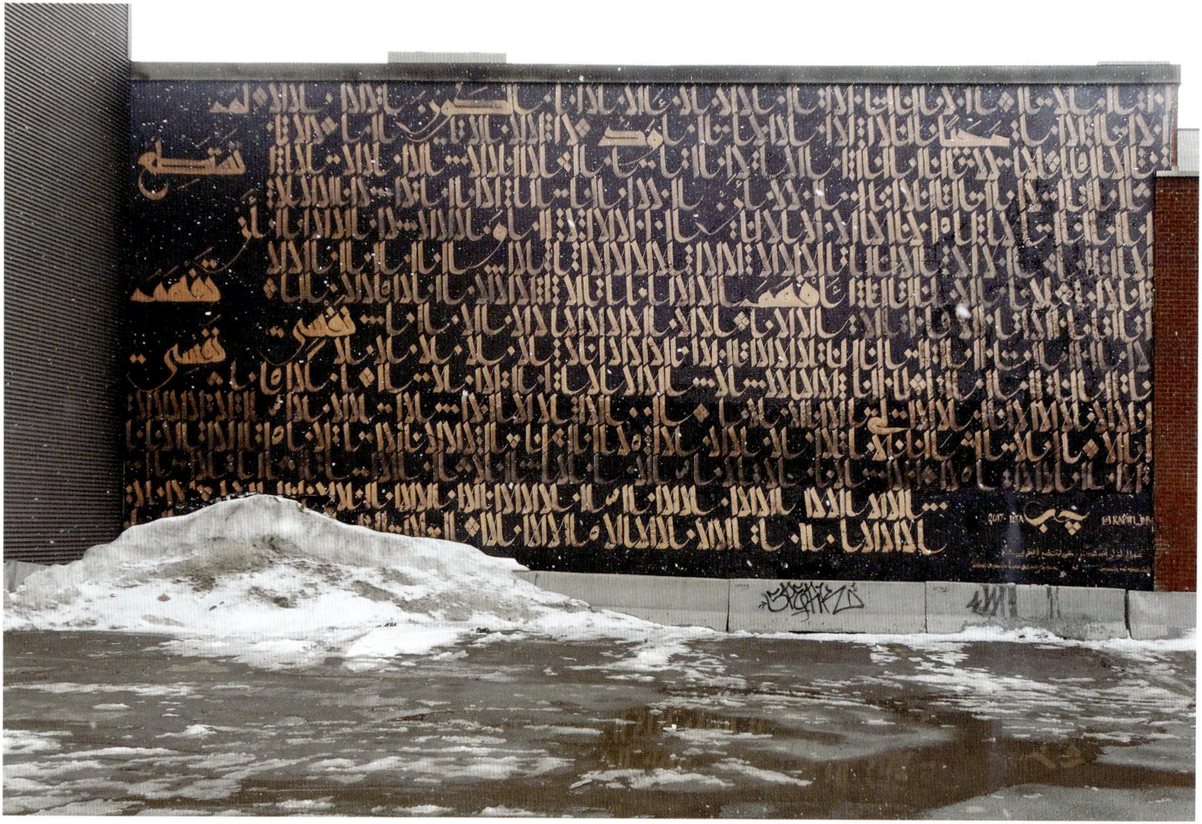

ABOVE Karim Jabbari, *I want to comprehend the Universe but I cannot understand myself*, Montreal, Canada, 2018

OPPOSITE TOP eL Seed, *our home, the most exotic place*, Melbourne, Australia, 2012

OPPOSITE BOTTOM KAB-101, Perth, Australia, 2017

BOTH eL Seed and Karim Jabbari reflect their Tunisian roots and the influence of Arabic calligraphy in their work. In Montreal Jabbari used copper-coloured metallic paint on the black side wall of the Al-Omah Al-Islamiah Mosque, seen here through falling snow. His elegant brushstrokes were influenced by the script in his father's books.

eL Seed's name was inspired by the medieval Spanish warrior El Cid. The artist believes that the viewer doesn't need to understand what is written to feel the peace embodied in works such as the one opposite top, that beauty is a universal language that doesn't need to be translated. The simplicity of the calligraphy painted by KAB-101 in Perth is emphasised by the intensity of the colour that sits behind it.

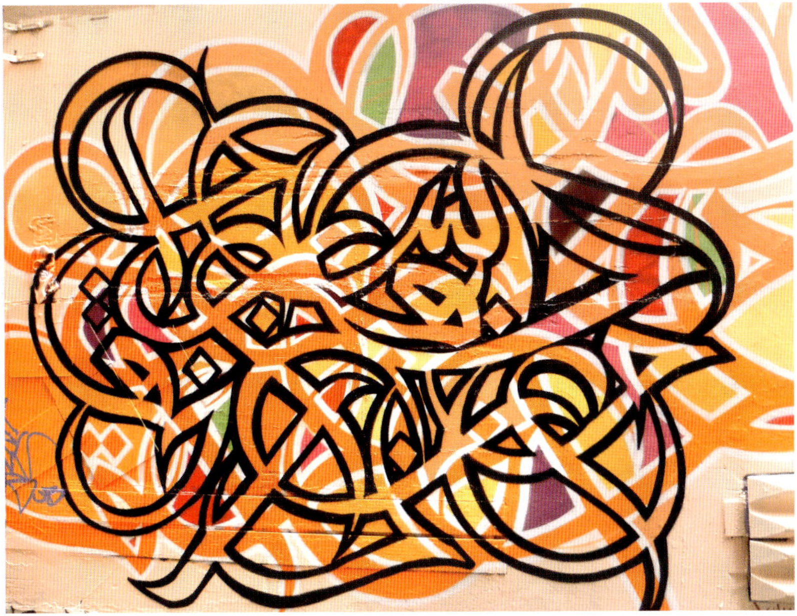

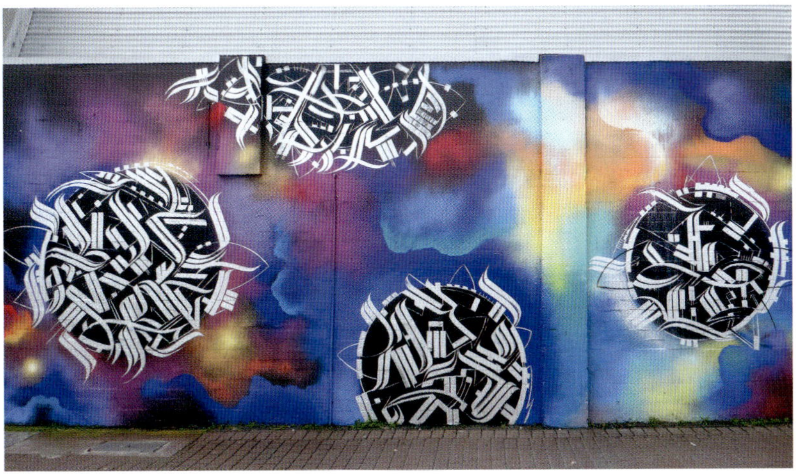

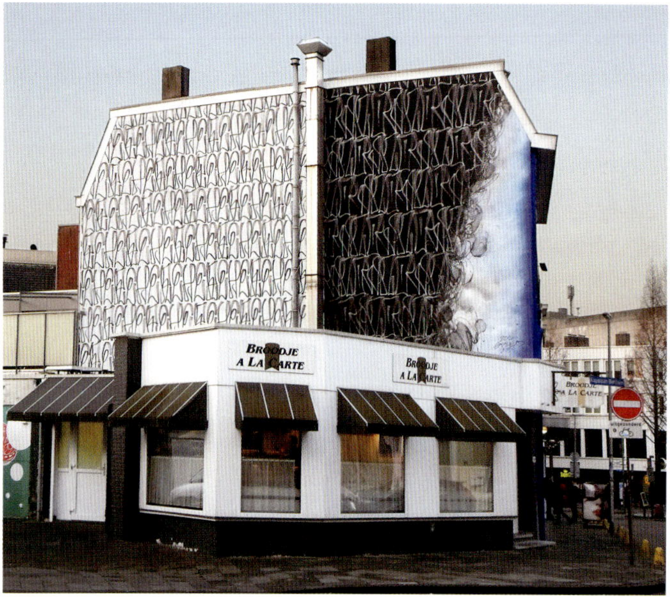

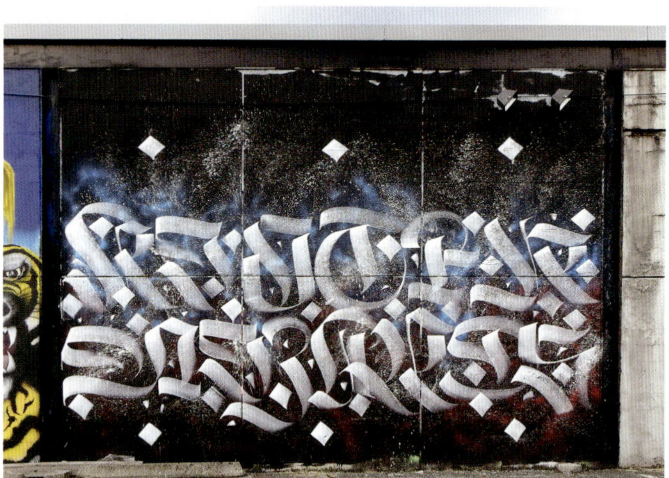

TOP Stohead, Heerlen, Netherlands, 2018
BOTTOM Andrea Riot, Jersey City, USA, 2018
OPPOSITE Retna, Miami, USA, 2018

THE three artists on these pages use very different visual languages, but all reflect a sense of energy, strength and harmony. At left German writer Stohead has written 'here' and 'now' endlessly across a wall in Heerlen, with the line work on the right dissolving into the haze of his well-known 'liquid smoke'. Andrea Riot is an Italian artist and designer based in London. His seemingly effortless script is created with subtle changes in line strength on the wall at bottom.

Based in Los Angeles, Retna has developed his own recognisable alphabet – a constructed script, sometimes called a glyphic style. With it he creates walls of singular power and beauty.

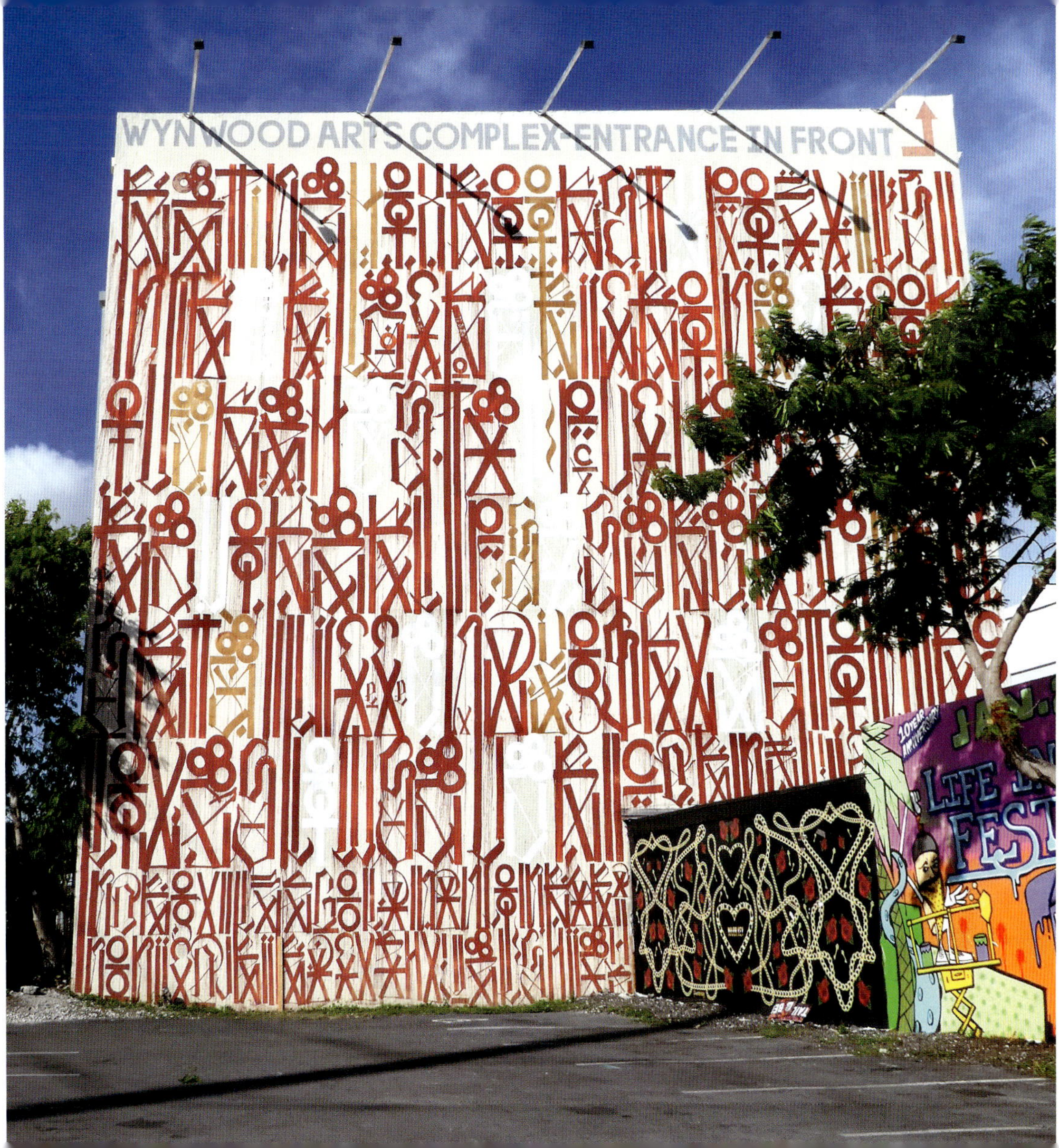
WYNWOOD ARTS COMPLEX-ENTRANCE IN FRONT
10 YEAR ANNIVERSARY

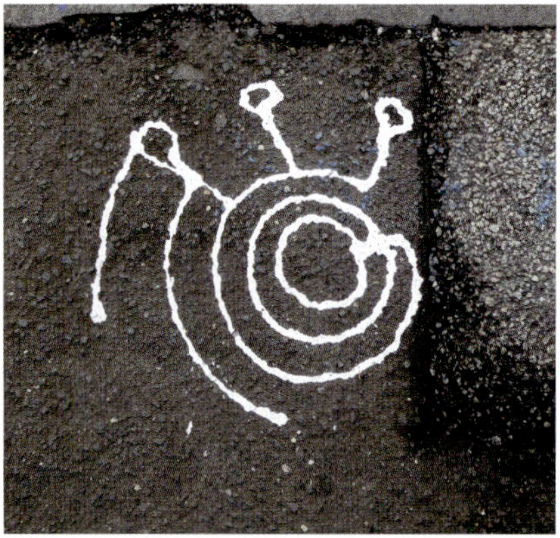
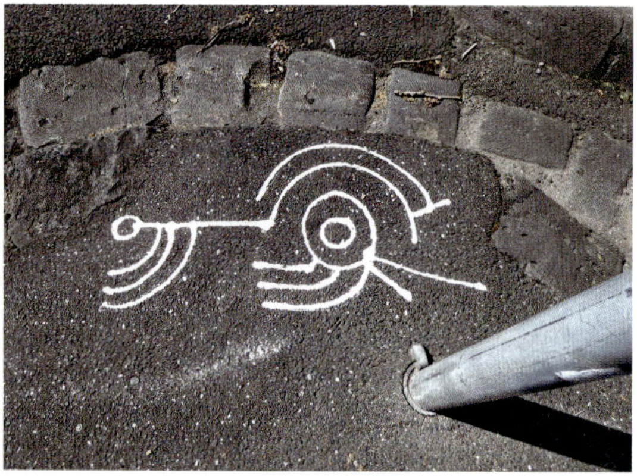
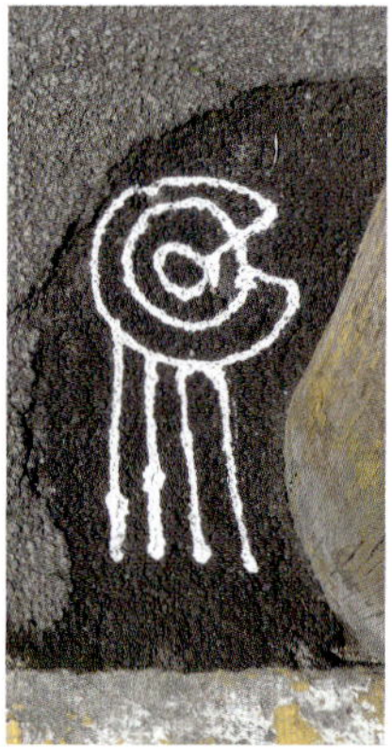
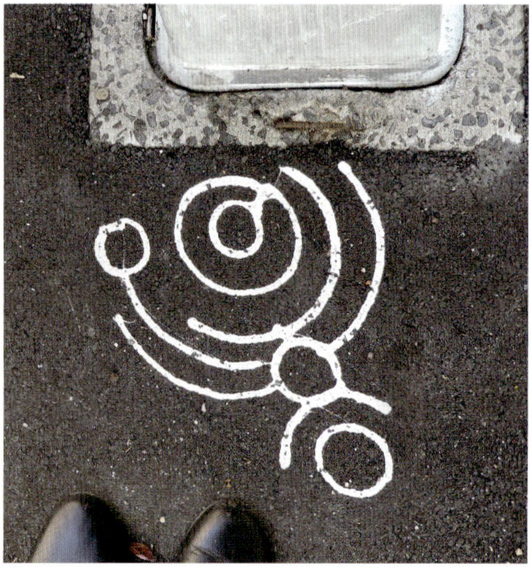
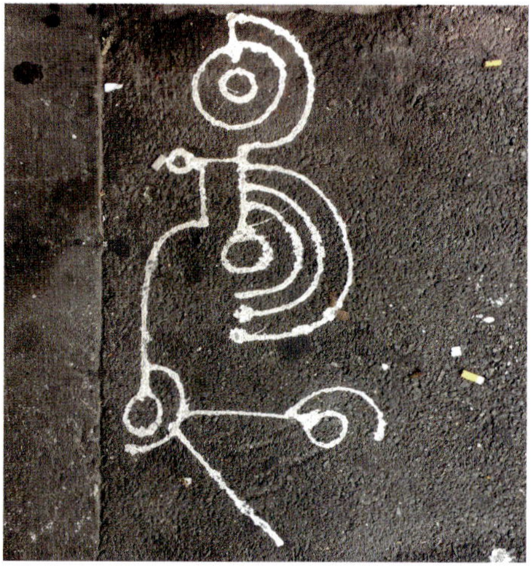
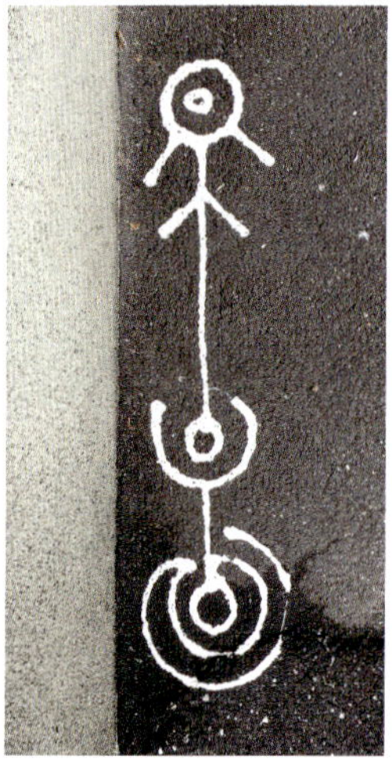

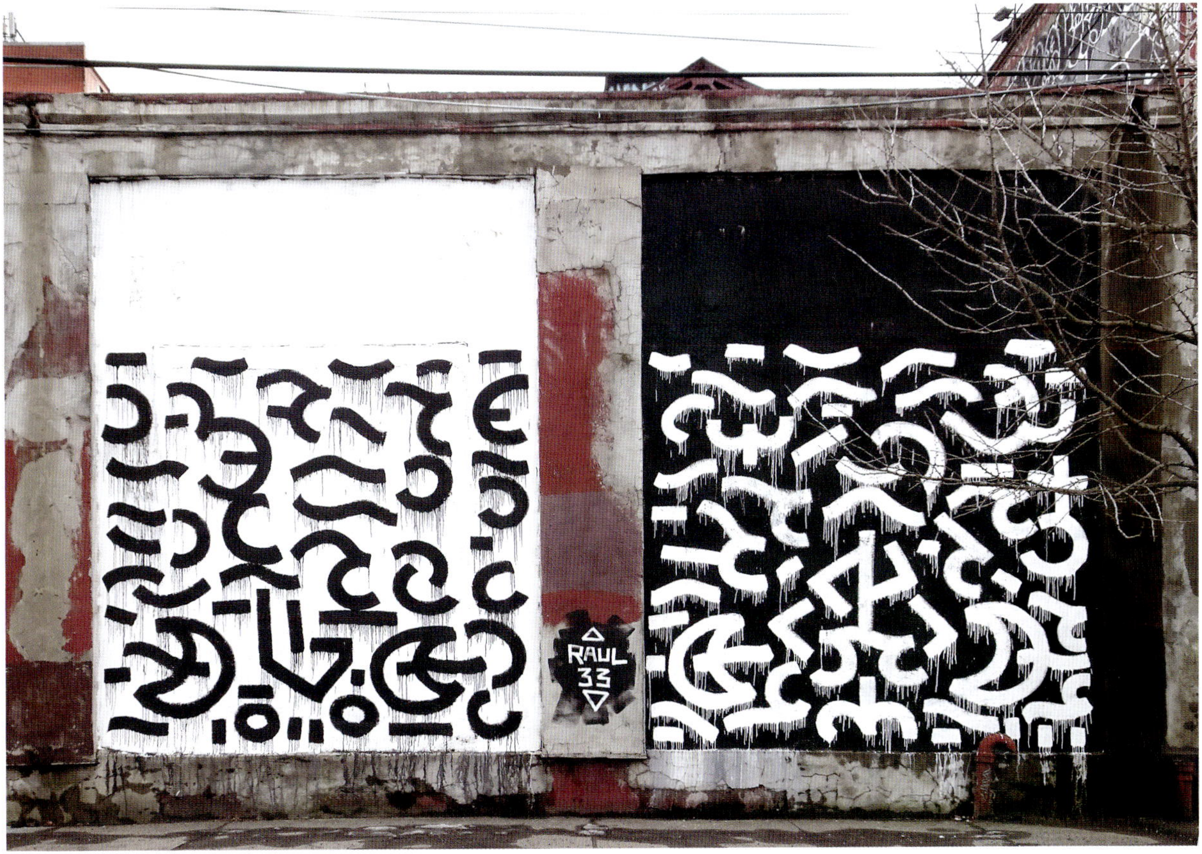

OPPOSITE, ALL Astral Nadir, Melbourne, Australia, 2017

ABOVE Raul33, Jersey City, USA, 2018

ASTRAL Nadir has left a trail of glyphs on the footpaths of the inner Melbourne neighbourhoods of Collingwood and Fitzroy. His mysterious runes, such as those opposite, are inspired by the psyche and created spontaneously rather than planned. They can be found abutting walls, following the line of the curb or wrapped around lampposts.

The language of Raul33's art is reduced to lines. Visible drips are an integral part of his work and suggest the immediacy of his process. The contrast of black on white beside white on black lends strength to the simplicity of the marks.

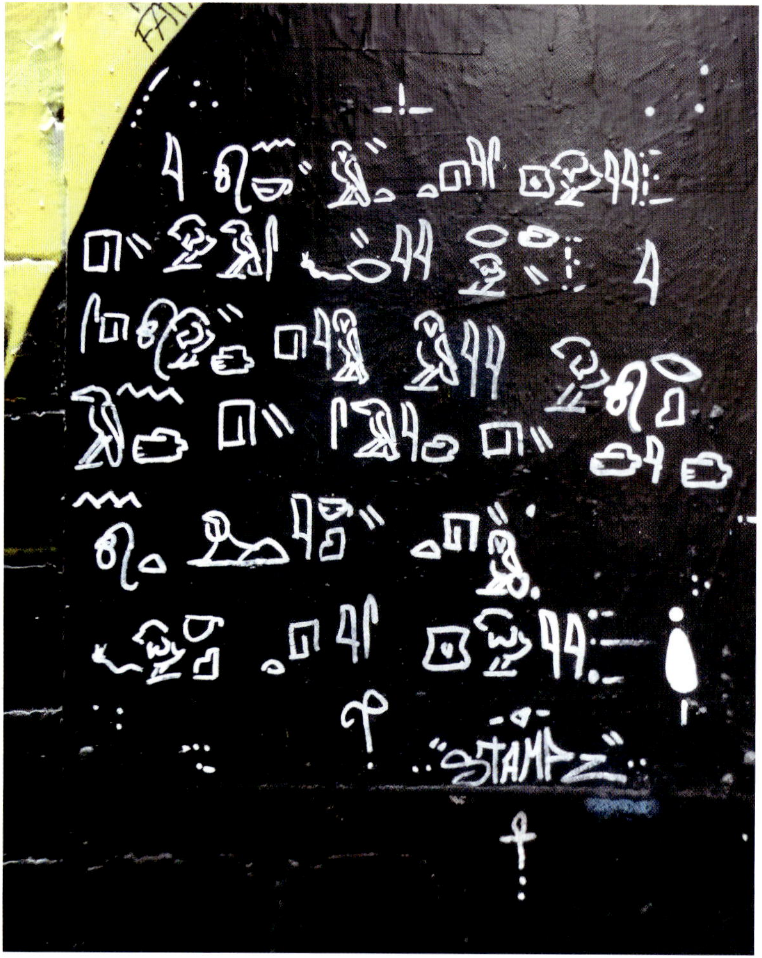
STAMPZ

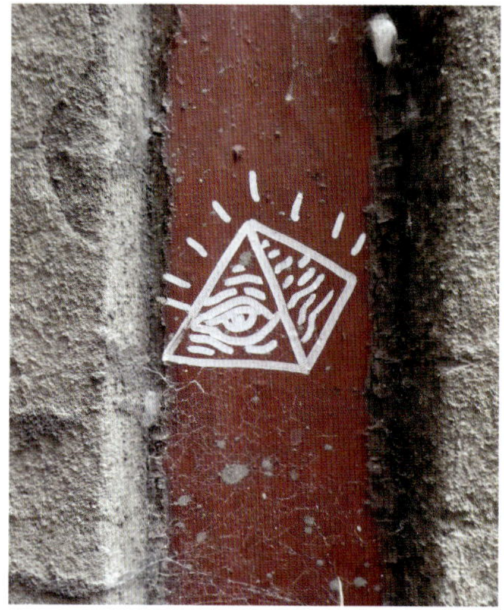

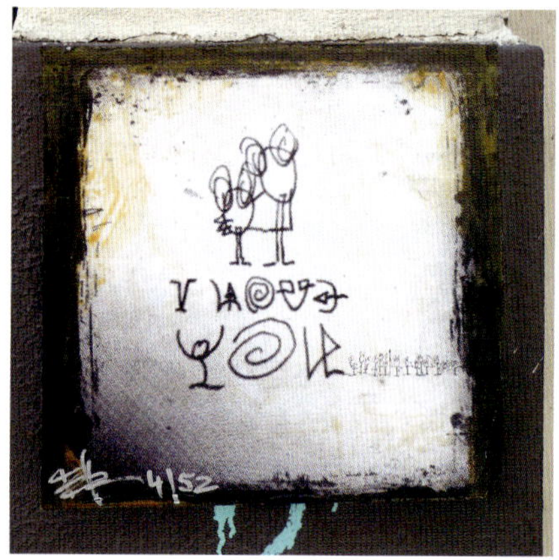
4/52

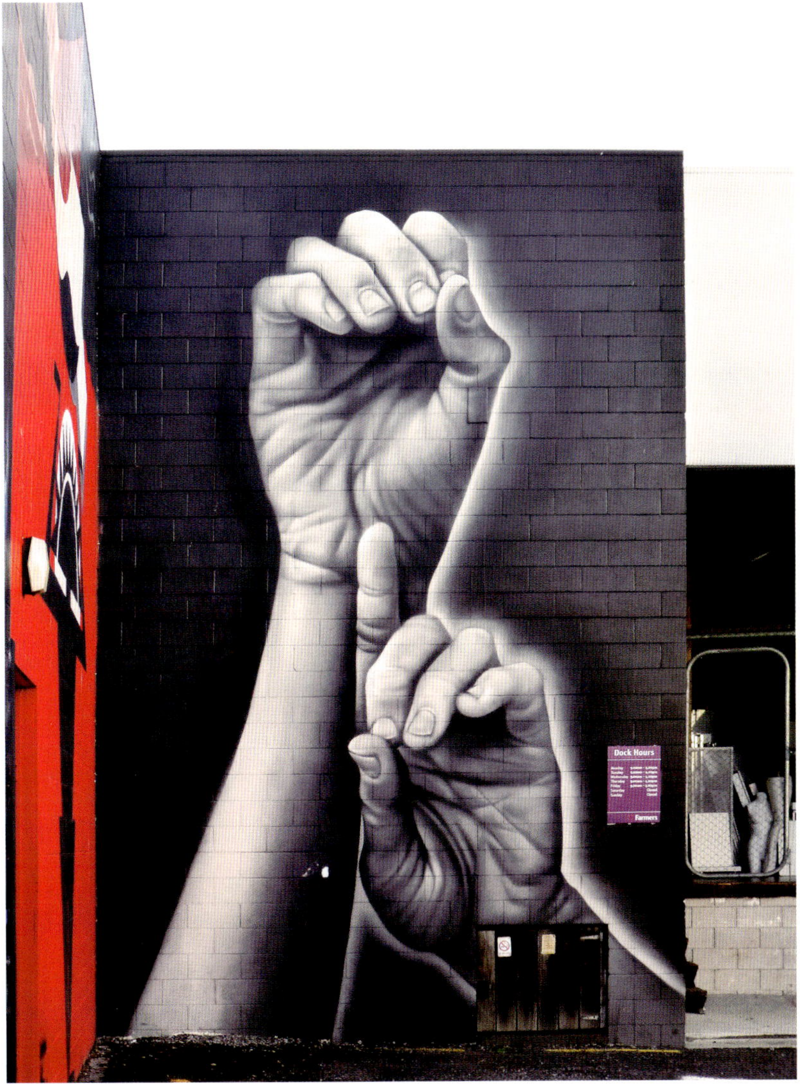

OPPOSITE LEFT Stampz, Melbourne, Australia, 2016

OPPOSITE TOP RIGHT Unknown artist, Melbourne, Australia, 2017

OPPOSITE BOTTOM RIGHT Unknown artist, New York City, USA, 2013

LEFT Owen Dippie, Taupo, New Zealand, 2013

THE hieroglyphic text at opposite left was written by a then 16-year-old artist who goes by the name of Stampz. He'd been taught to write basic hieroglyphics by a teacher and this example tells the story of an encounter he had with another artist who dissed him and his work. The punch line is quite rude! The two small ideograms beside it contain messages, simple and fun.

The image at left of two hands signing an 'o' and a 'd' is in fact the signature of New Zealand artist Owen Dippie. He has used sign language as the 'font'.

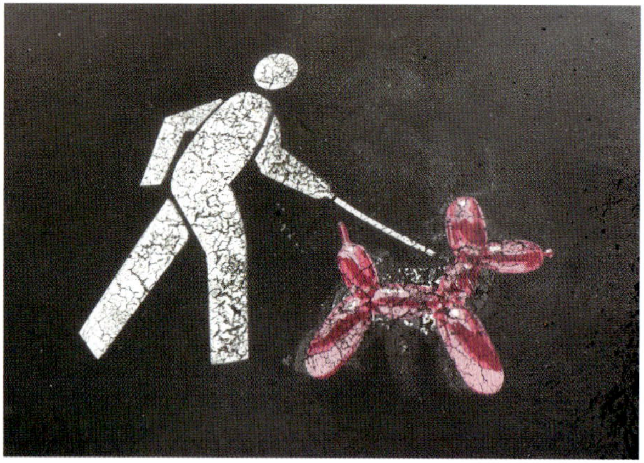
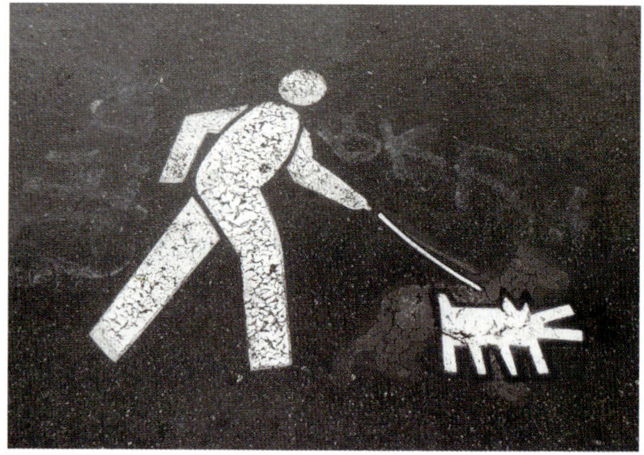
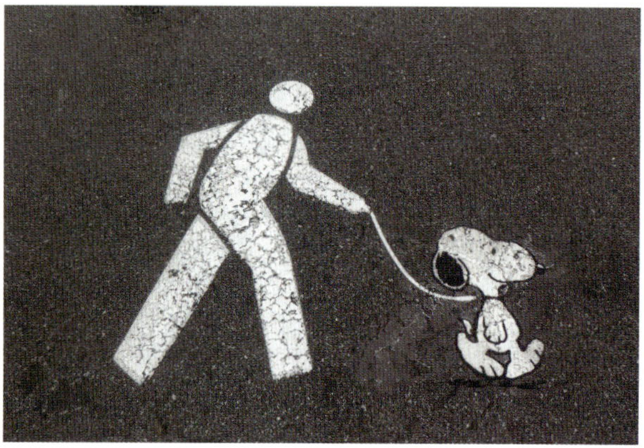
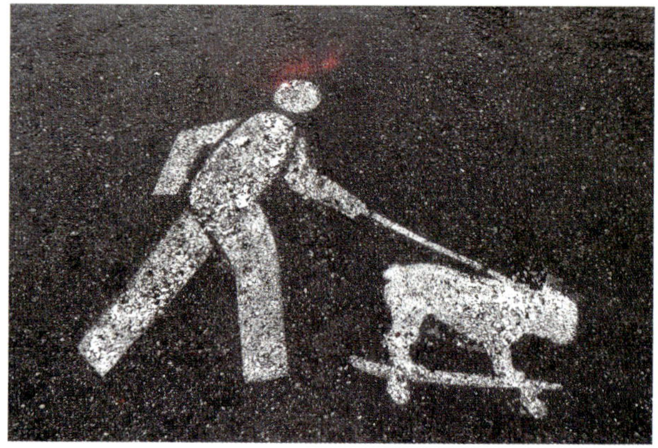

Underfoot

Let's face it, the footpath is generally not the most visually stimulating feature of our urban environment. But there are places where looking down past our feet rather than at our smart phones can have its delights. One of those special places is Duboce Park, a popular dog-walking site in San Francisco. Local artist fnnch painted out the simple dogs stencilled by council workers and replaced them with a variety of far more engaging canines. There's a Jeff Koons–style balloon dog, a Keith Haring version of the barking dog, Snoopy and a boxer on a skateboard. There's even an origami corgi and a cat on a lead.

Stencils are the most popular, but not the only, technique used to add text and images to concrete and asphalt. Stencil designs can be simple, quick to apply and easy to read, all of which suits a message in a place where the viewer is on the move. Often these messages are a form of social protest, a call to arms.

There are also artists who get down and dirty with a paintbrush. Feik Frasao paints mutant bugs and beetles and I'm The Boss paints the clothes on his splattered characters. More ephemeral still are messages written in charcoal and chalk. The tools inspire spontaneity but it's their fate to be scuffed quickly or washed away by rain. Such comments are usually gentle and more personal – 'you are beautiful', 'I love you', 'I believe in you'.

The *Rats Crossing* stencil, sighted at night while walking through Greenwich Village in New York City, was quite fitting as a couple of healthy-looking specimens had just crossed the road.

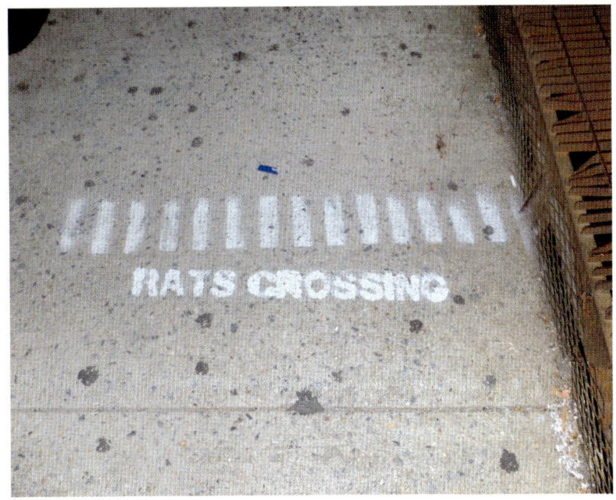

OPPOSITE, ALL fnnch, San Francisco, USA, 2017
RIGHT Unknown artist, New York City, USA, 2013

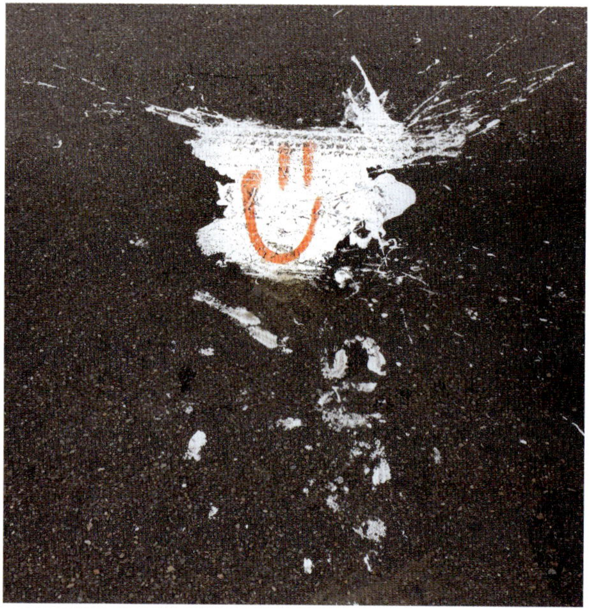

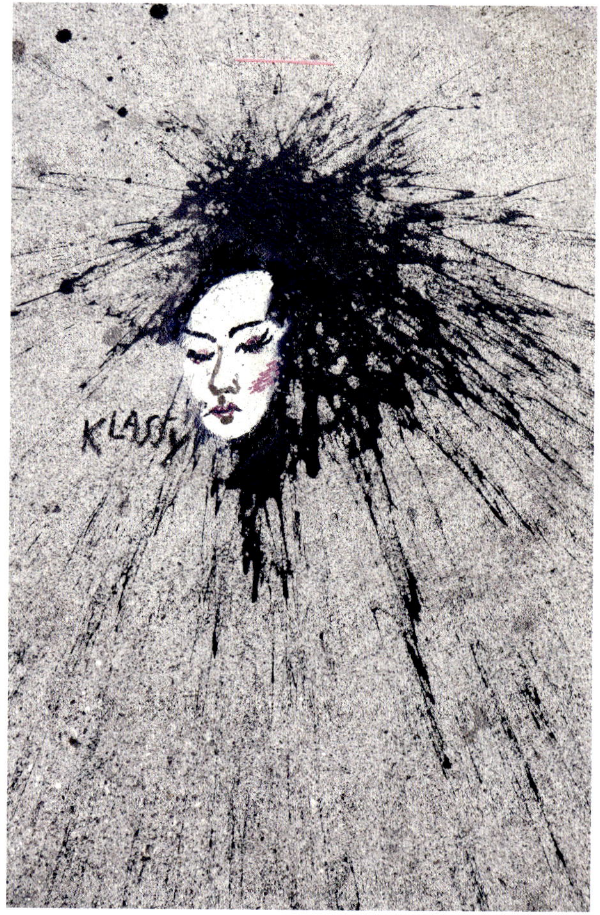

LEFT Unknown artist, Sydney, Australia, 2017

RIGHT Klassy, *Kabuki*, Los Angeles, USA, 2016

OPPOSITE LEFT I'm The Boss, *Spongebob splat pants*, Perth, Australia, 2017

OPPOSITE TOP RIGHT I'm The Boss, *Splatrick*, Perth, Australia, 2017

OPPOSITE BOTTOM RIGHT I'm The Boss, *Flopinn*, Perth, Australia, 2017

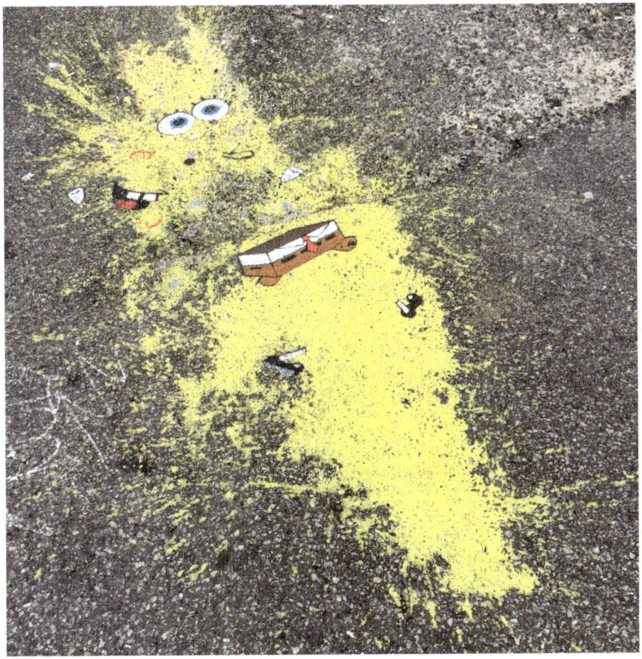

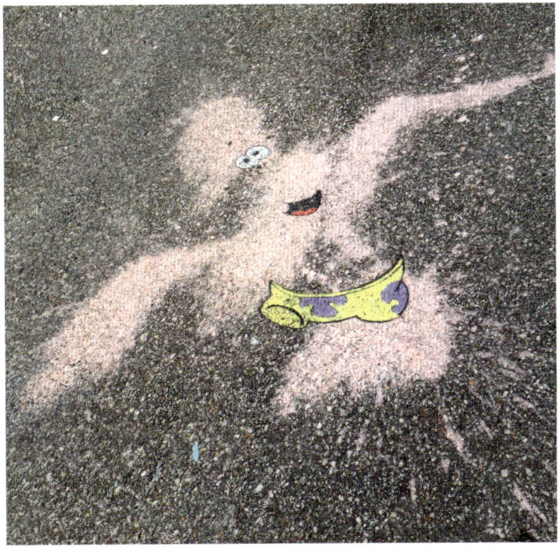

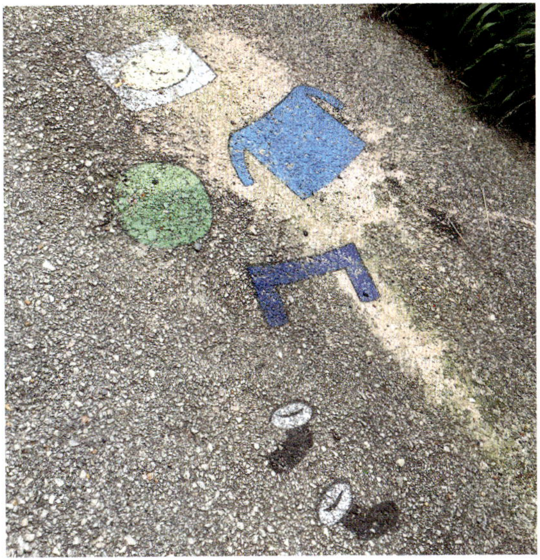

WHO would have thought that spills and splashes could create such a lively canvas underfoot? If we're lucky, every now and again we find an artist who has taken advantage of a splatter or splash on a horizontal surface. Klassy paints beguiling faces that emerge from spills and stains on the footpath. I'm The Boss creates cartoon-inspired characters that are humorously deconstructed roadkill, such as *Spongebob splat pants* and his friends on this page.

These are perfect examples of the pleasure that rewards looking down at where we step.

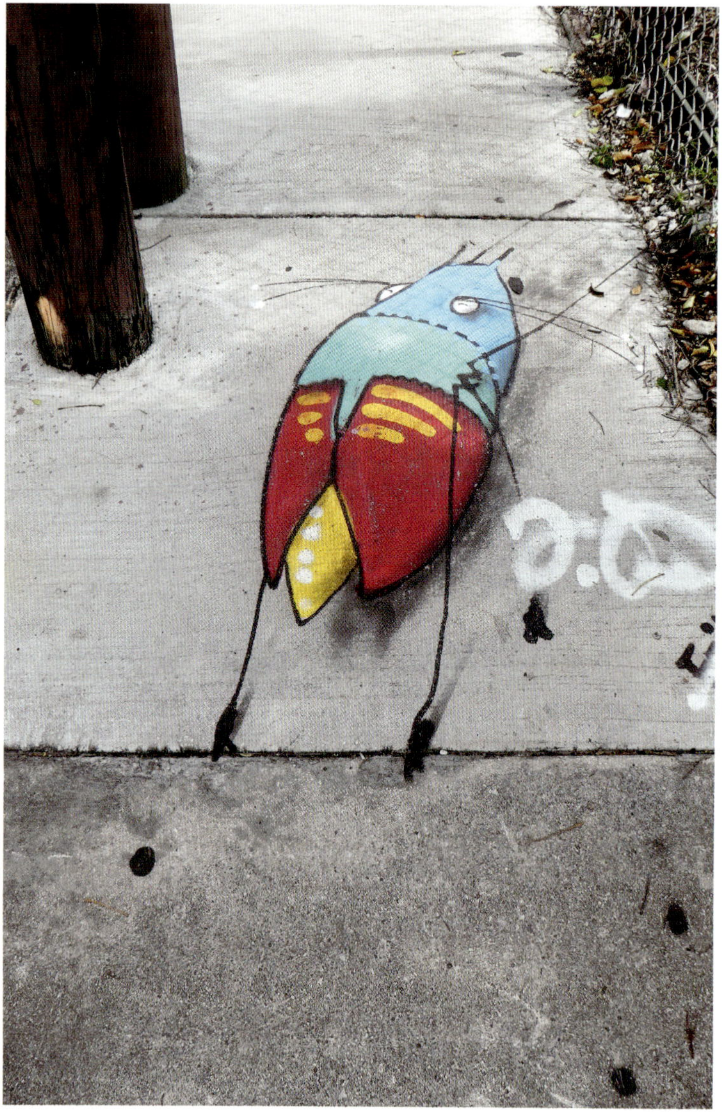

THIS PAGE, BOTH Feik Frasao, Miami, USA, 2017

OPPOSITE TOP LEFT Jeremy Novy, *Koi*, Los Angeles, USA, 2016

OPPOSITE CENTRE LEFT Jeremy Novy, *Koi*, Miami, USA, 2017

OPPOSITE BOTTOM LEFT Jeremy Novy, *Koi*, San Francisco, USA, 2017

OPPOSITE RIGHT Jeremy Novy, *Koi*, Miami, USA, 2017

WHIMSICAL species of playfully mutant insects painted in bright colours bring back memories of childhood play for Brazilian artist Feik Frasao. Look closely and you will see bugs resplendent in patterned armour and electric antennae.

Jeremy Novy uses stencils to create schools of black, orange and white koi that float sinuously beneath our feet. Particularly popular in Japan, koi symbolise qualities of courage, resilience and strength of character. The number of fish in an arrangement is also symbolic. Three is considered to be a lucky number, referring to the three stages of life – birth, marriage and death.

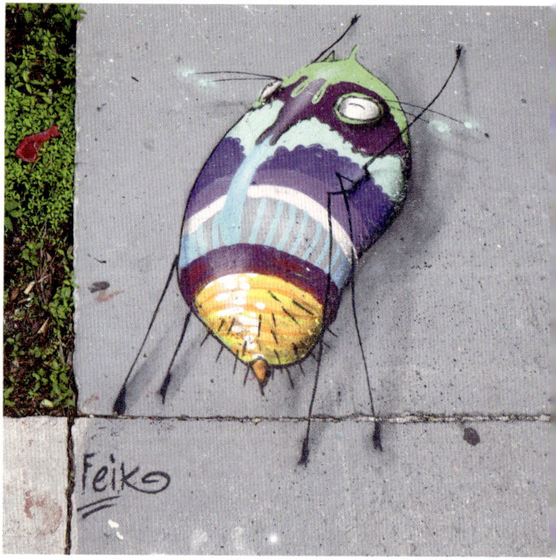

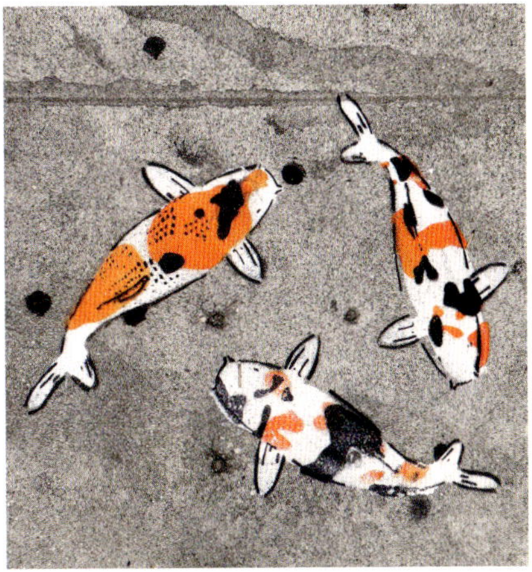

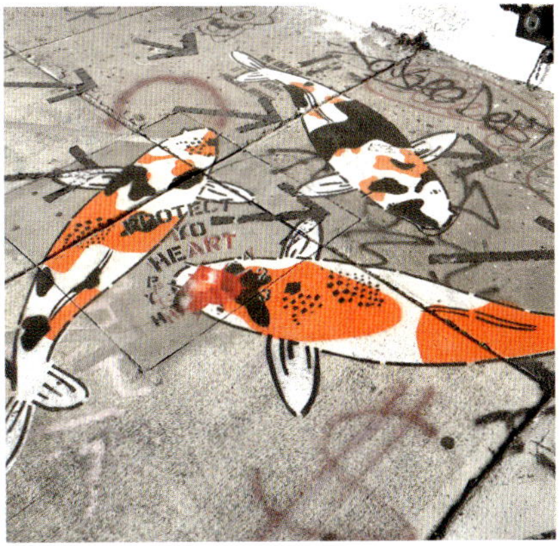

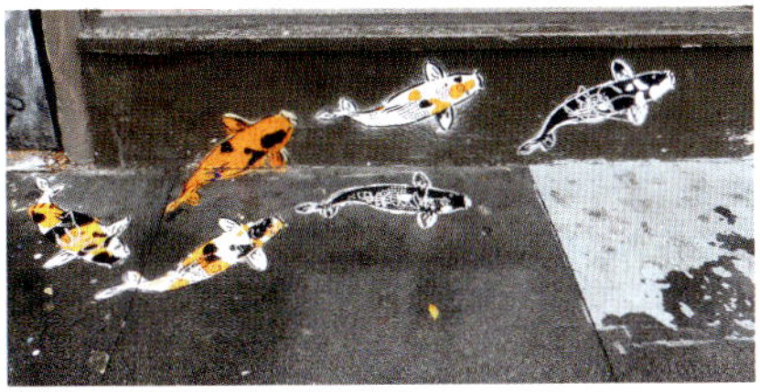

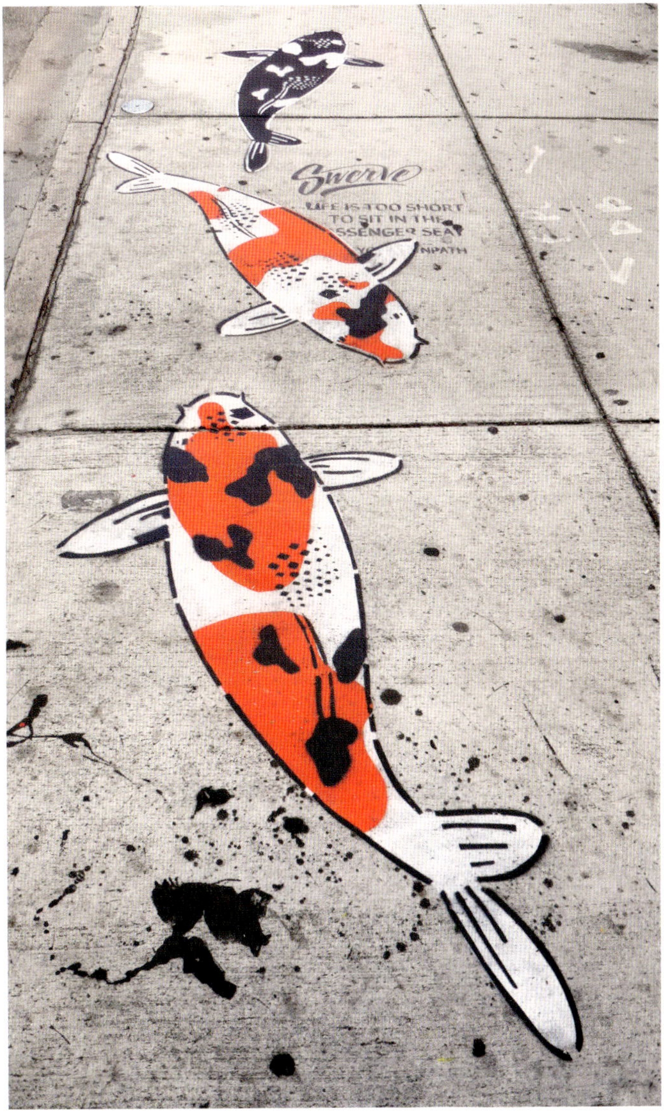
Swerve
LIFE IS TOO SHORT
TO SIT IN THE

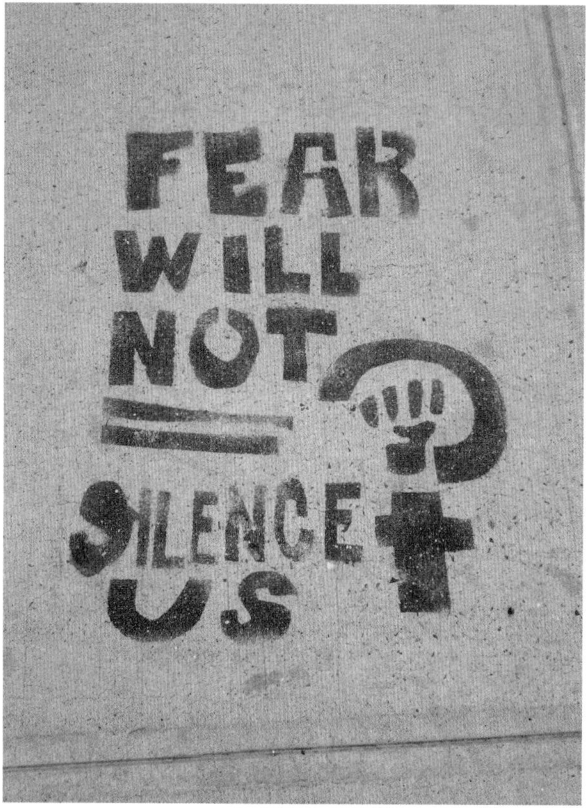

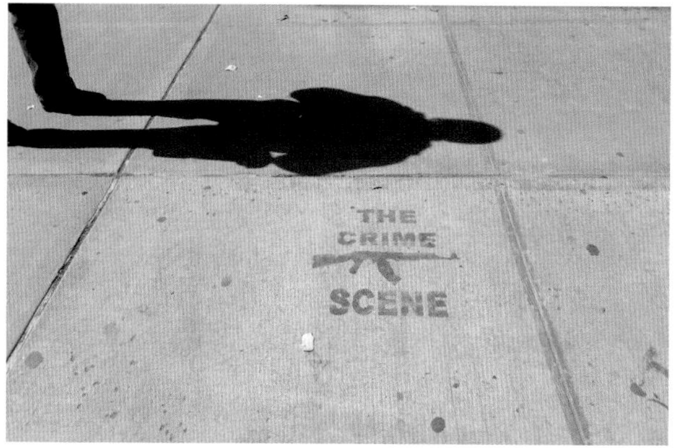

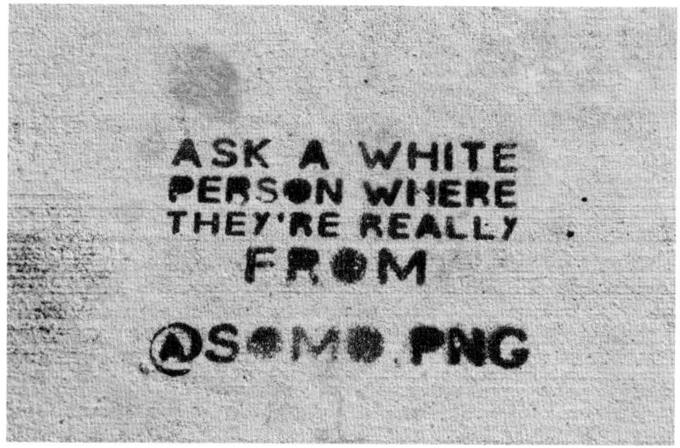

LEFT Unknown artist, New York City, USA, 2018

TOP RIGHT Unknown artist, New York City, USA, 2018

BOTTOM RIGHT SOMO.PNG, Miami, USA, 2017

OPPOSITE TOP LEFT and **RIGHT** CRISP, Melbourne, Australia, 2017

OPPOSITE BOTTOM LEFT and **RIGHT** CRISP, Los Angeles, USA, 2017

AS well as brightening our urban walks, artists can also use the footpath as a vehicle for thought-provoking social protest. The stencils above are reminders of issues such as inequity, crime and fear.

CRISP has travelled extensively making observations about big business and technology and stencil-bombing his corporate street fighters in cities as far flung as Miami, Sydney, Barcelona and Bogotá. Opposite we can see Facebook vs Instagram; Chevron vs Shell, in *The Oil Wars*; *Currency Fighters* Dollar vs Yuan; and *Fast Food Fighters* McDonalds vs KFC in *The Battle of Obesity*.

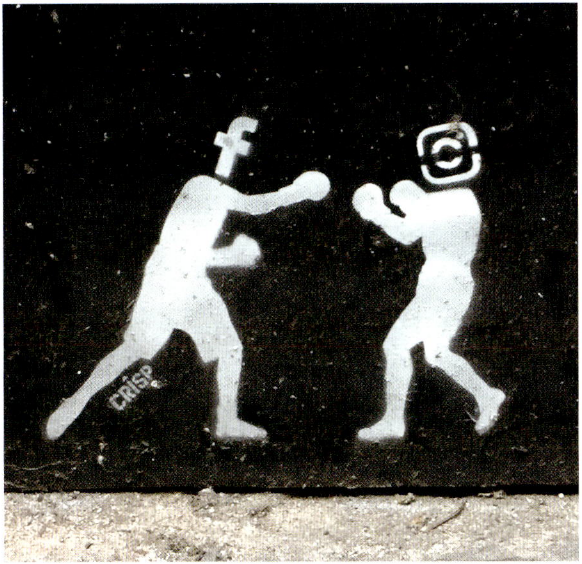
CRISP

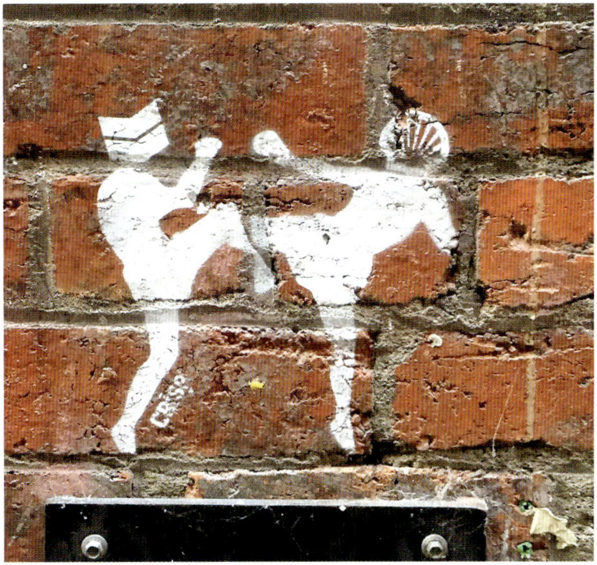
CRISP

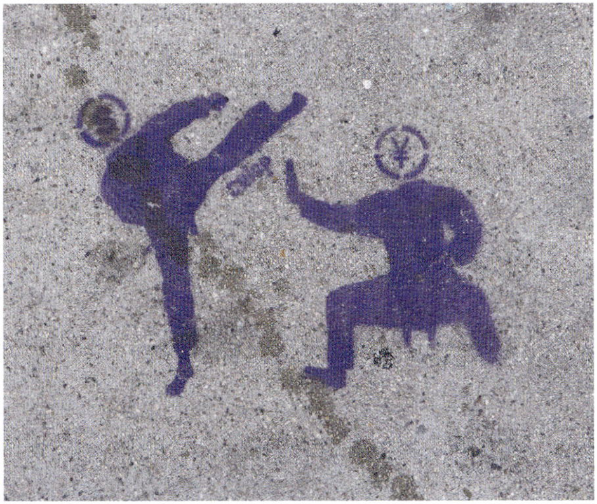
CRISP

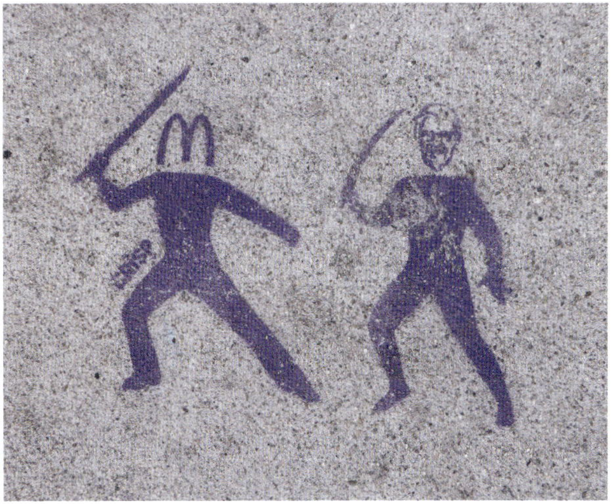
CRISP

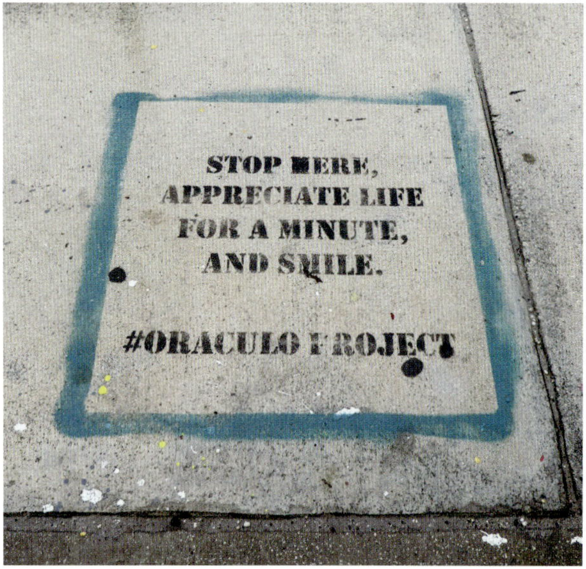

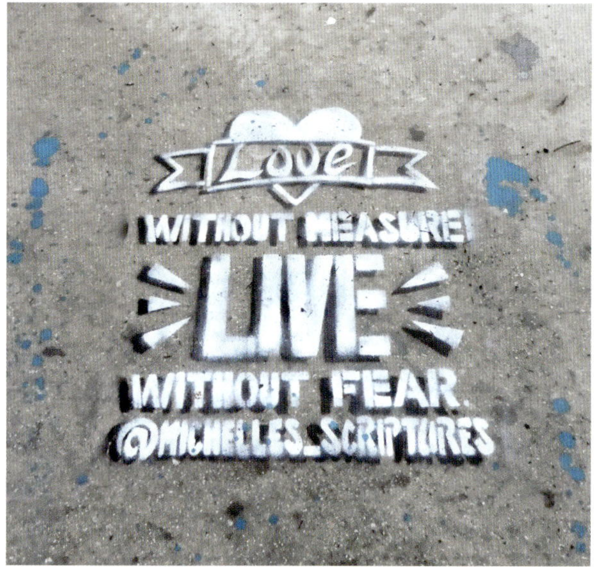

LEFT Oraculo Project, Miami, USA, 2017
RIGHT Michelle's Scriptures, Miami, USA, 2017
OPPOSITE TOP LEFT Unknown artist, Malmö, Sweden, 2016
OPPOSITE TOP RIGHT Unknown artist, Melbourne, Australia, 2017
OPPOSITE BOTTOM Unknown artist, Melbourne, Australia, 2018

THE anonymous Brazilian artist who goes by the name Oraculo Project leaves inspirational messages – stop and enjoy, appreciate what you have and be grateful. Michelle of Michelle's Scriptures writes street poetry and is well known in Miami for her sidewalk quotes.

Positive messages can be created and shared by any one of us. All we need is a piece of chalk or charcoal and we can share a message of love or belief.

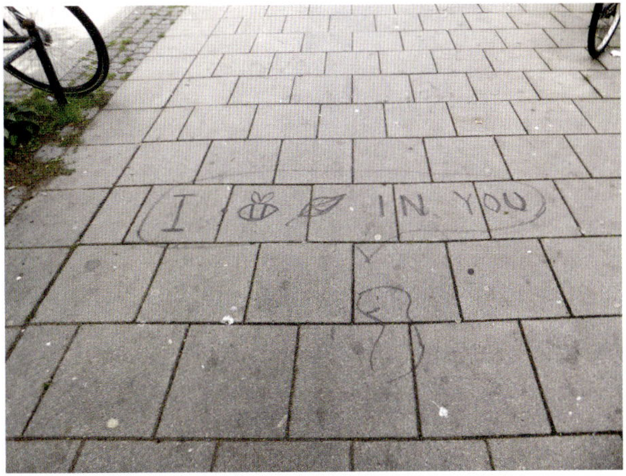
I
IN YOU

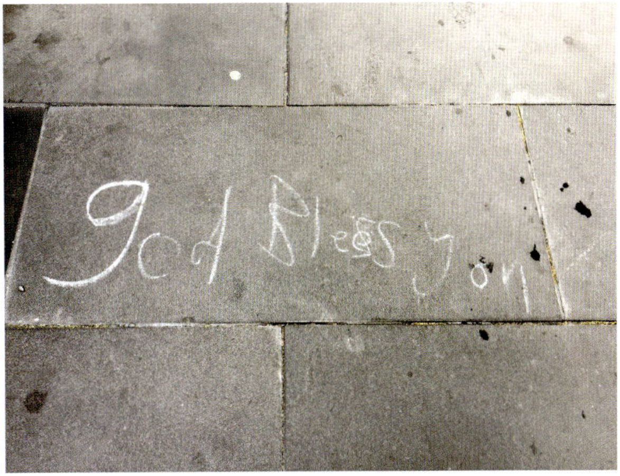
God Bless you

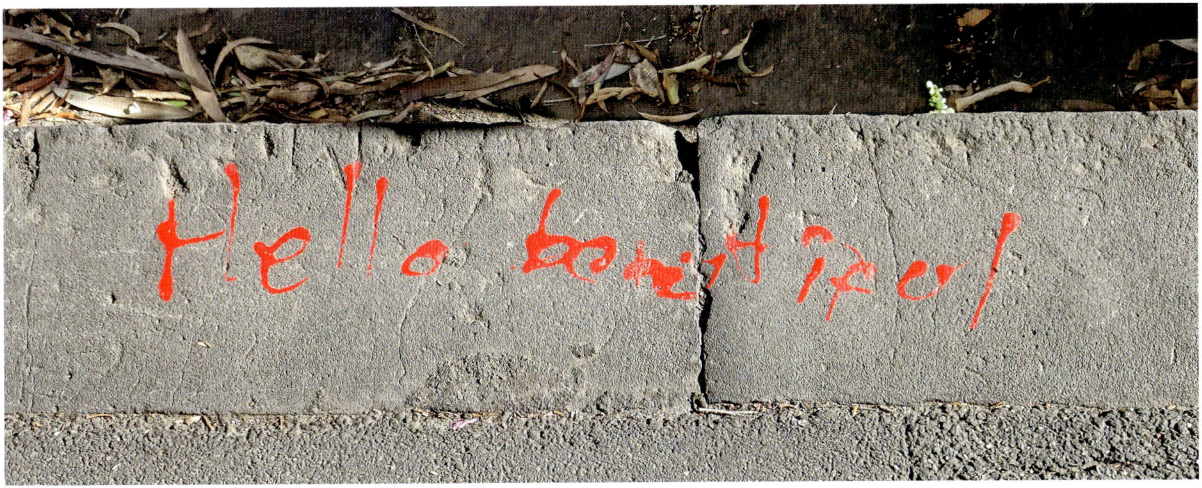
Hello

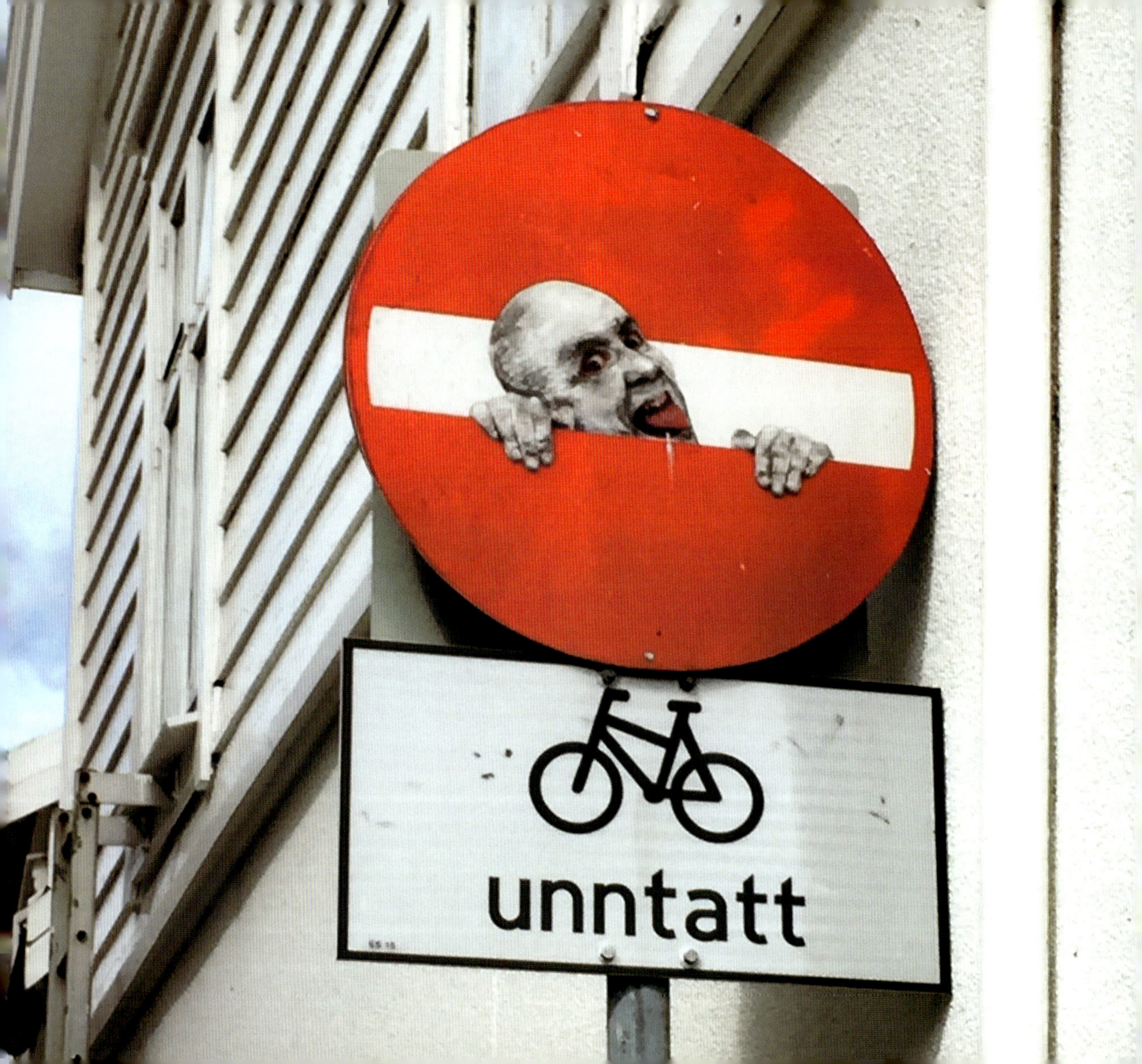
unntatt

Street Sign Interventions

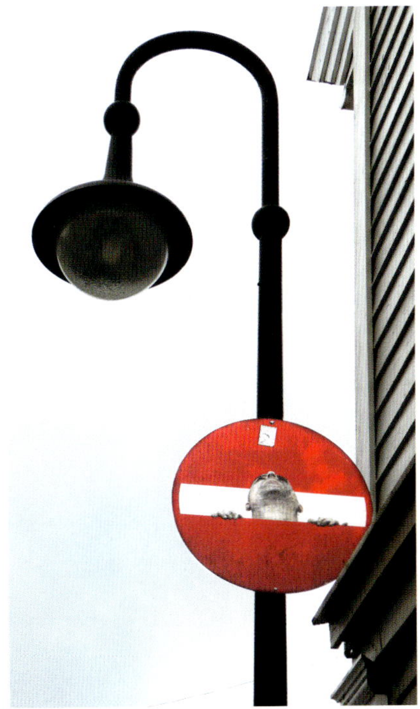

Street signs speak a universal language. The colours and messages of instruction and caution are instantly recognisable in whichever country they are found. As traffic warnings, they are a symbol of authority; they demand obedience. So it's with thought and care that artists intervene by adding to, or adjusting, the message.

Changes can be minor, but they can be potent because they're not authorised. Street signs are a perfect avenue for artists who wish to entertain the passerby and inject humour into the routine commute. Turn the page and find a cheeky pooping bird on a No Entry sign.

There are a number of ways to add such interventions. Removable vinyl stickers are used by Clet and Yipi Yipi Yeah. Not strictly legal, they can be attached quickly, under cover of darkness. They may be in situ for a week or five years, depending on the response of the local authorities. Comments can be added by pen and brush, too. Signs can also be created with council approval and use word play to spread a serious message. 'Children should be seen not hurt' (p. 176) was found in the colourful multicultural Bo-Kaap neighbourhood of Cape Town. There are also examples of sanctioned public art, such as the officially commissioned *Word and Way* project by Evangelos Sakaris in Melbourne (p. 179).

Brooklyn-based artist Dan Witz has been sticking his King Baby additions to No Entry signs since 2007. They make us stop and look.

OPPOSITE Dan Witz, *King Baby, Do Not Enter #3*, Stavanger, Norway, 2016

RIGHT Dan Witz, *King Baby, Do Not Enter #2*, Stavanger, Norway, 2016

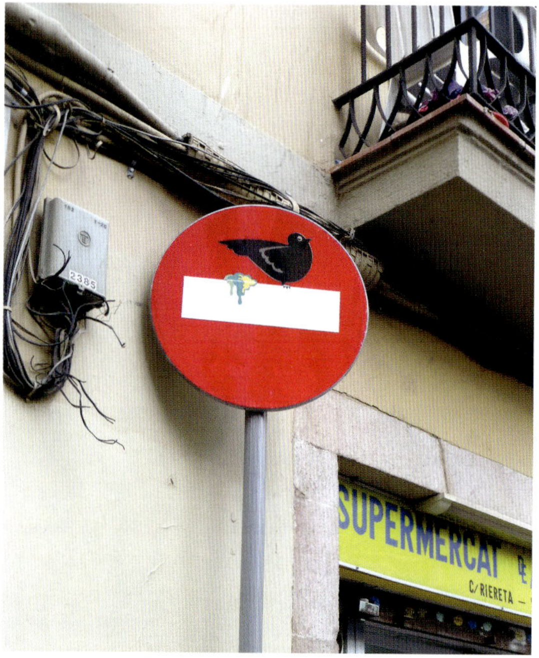
SUPERMERCAT
C/ RIERETA

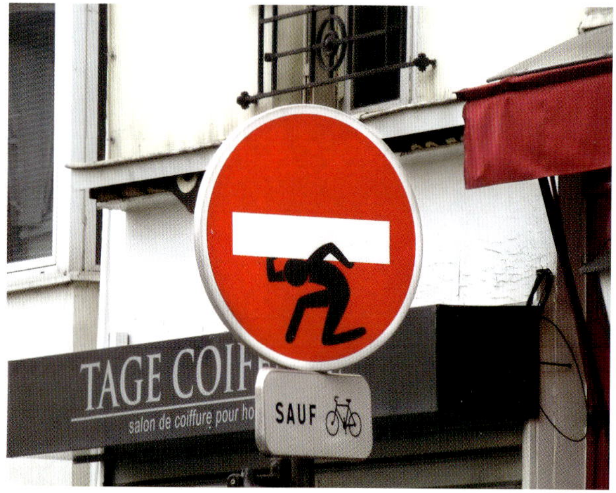
TAGE COIF
salon de coiffure pour ho
SAUF

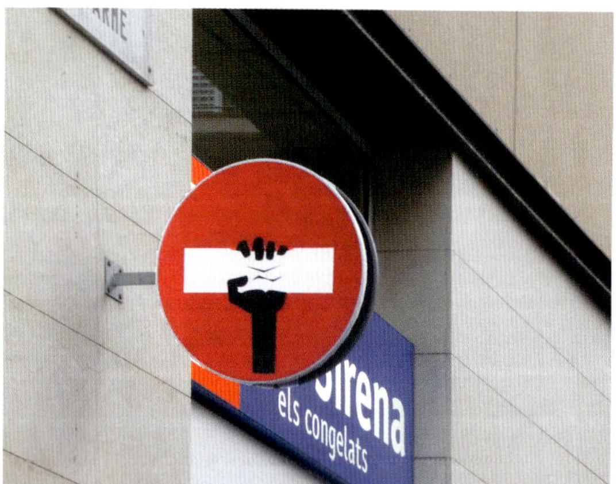
Sirena
els congelats

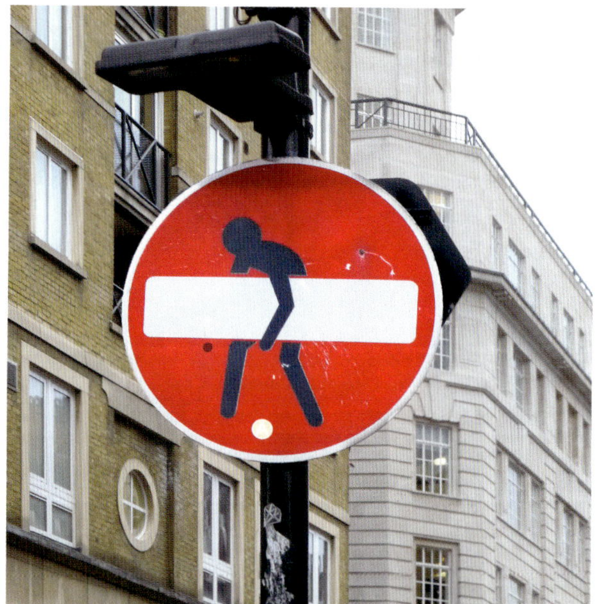

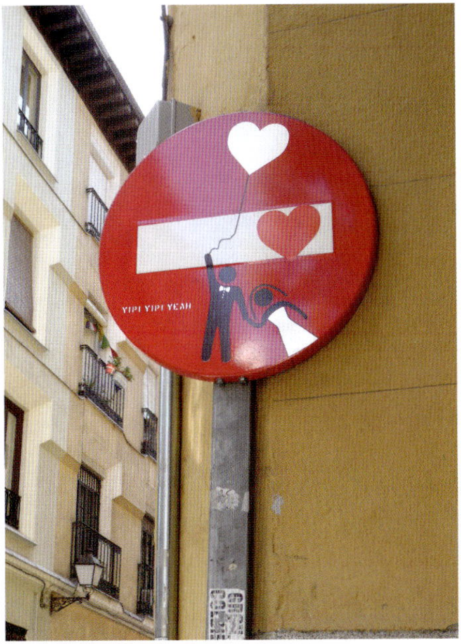

OPPOSITE TOP LEFT Clet, Barcelona, Spain, 2013
OPPOSITE TOP RIGHT Clet, Paris, France, 2015
OPPOSITE BOTTOM LEFT Clet, Barcelona, Spain, 2013
OPPOSITE BOTTOM RIGHT Clet, London, UK, 2015
THIS PAGE, ALL Yipi Yipi Yeah, Madrid, Spain, 2016

DAN Witz (pp. 170 and 171), Clet and Yipi Yipi Yeah find that No Entry signs provide them with great scope for creative modifications without compromising the sign's purpose or function. Their playful additions to a simple white bar on a red ground surprise and delight us.

Clet's silhouetted characters opposite protest against established structures of power in subtle – and not so subtle – ways. He prepares his vinyl stickers before going on a mission and, using his bicycle as a support, applies them in as little as ten seconds before moving on to the next spot. Yipi Yipi Yeah is a team adding humour, and sometimes political views (*End the War Now!*, p. 123), to the streetscape, as seen in the examples on this page.

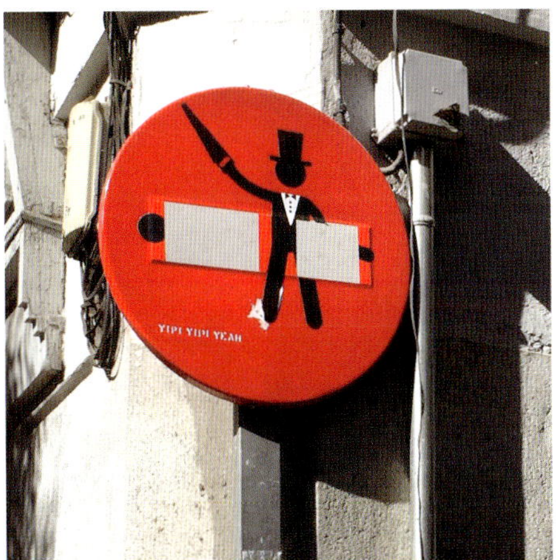

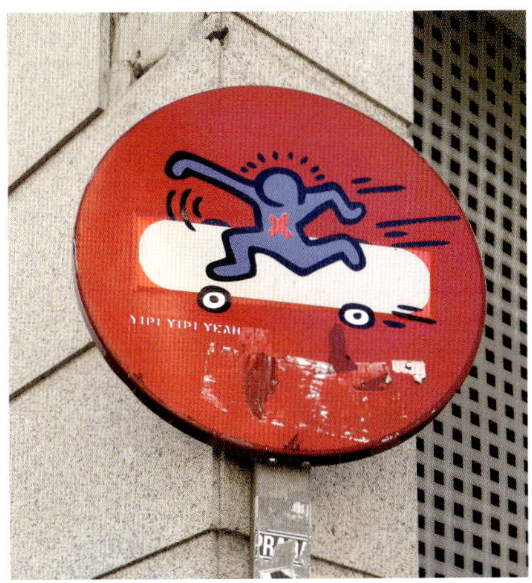

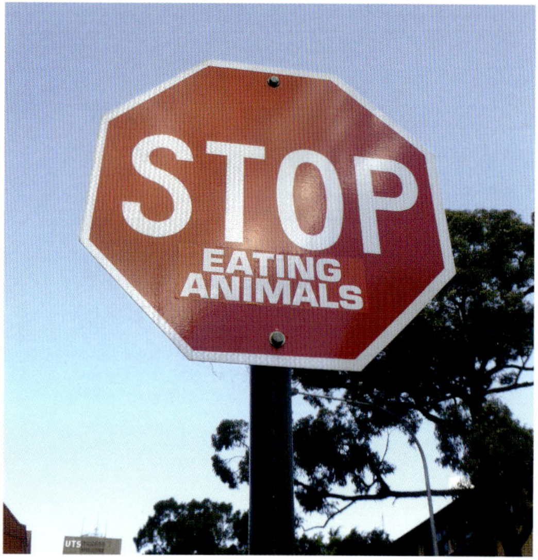

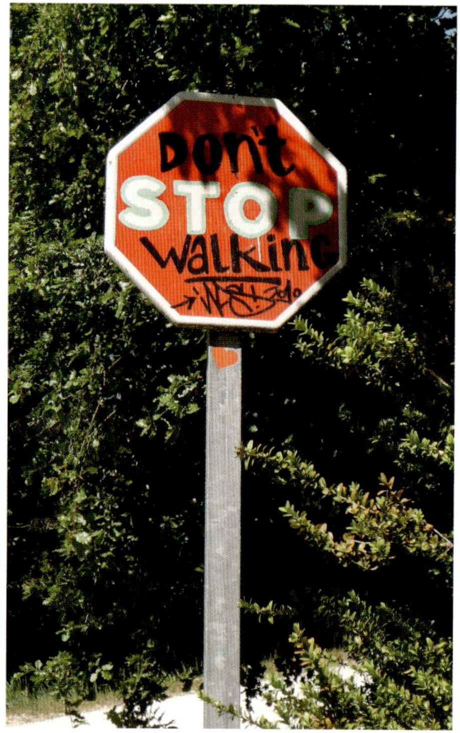

TOP LEFT Unknown artist, Sydney, Australia, 2016

BOTTOM LEFT Unknown artist, New York City, USA, 2018

RIGHT Unknown artist, near Pamplona, Spain, 2011

OPPOSITE Eduardo Kobra, Miami, USA, 2017

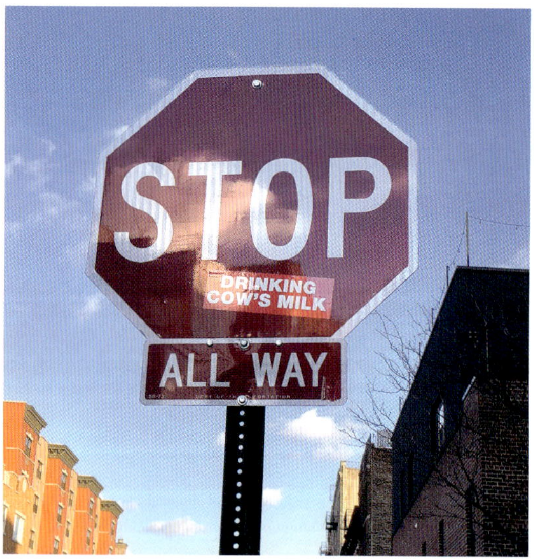

STOP! is such an important injunction in our busy lives that it's not surprising that it's captured the attention of street artists and activists alike. Stop Eating Animals. Stop Drinking Cow's Milk. DON'T Stop Walking – this one on a path of the Camino de Santiago in Spain, a long-distance walking pilgrimage that crosses several European countries.

Brazilian artist Eduardo Kobra is well known for his brightly coloured and patterned portraits that remind us of kaleidoscopes and mosaics. Here we see Yoda, *Star Wars* Jedi Master, as an activist for peace, holding a sign written in the film's iconic font. It highlights the sad fact of war and violence.

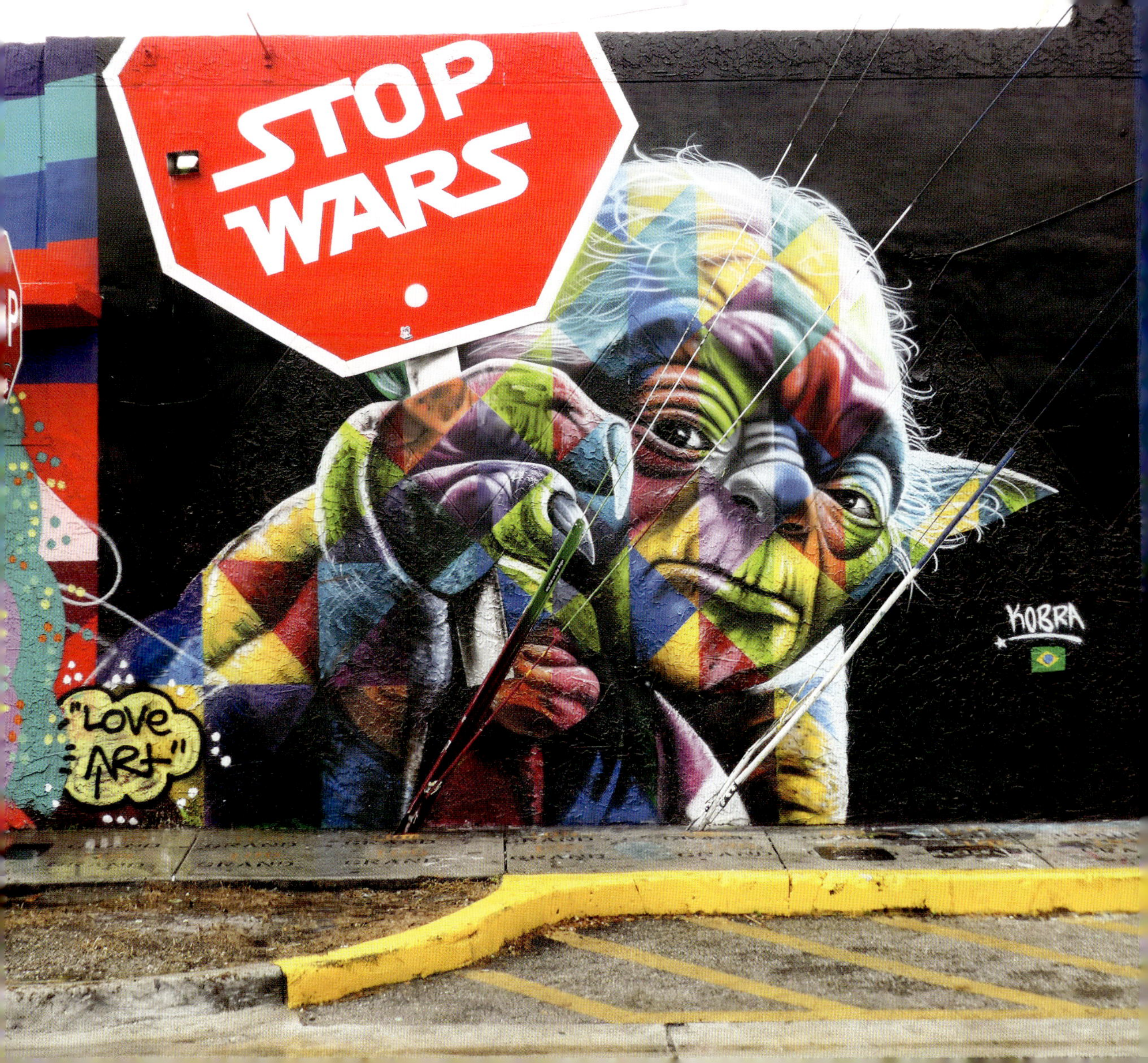
STOP WARS
KOBRA
"LOVE ART"

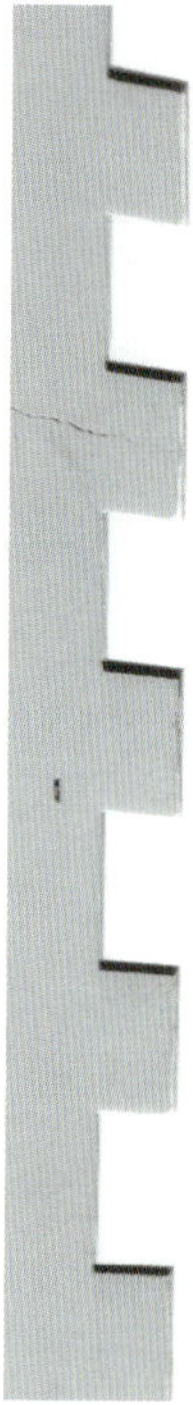

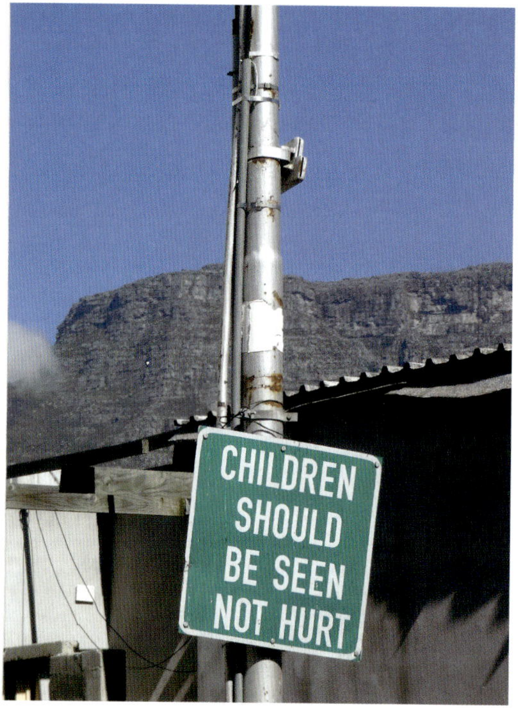

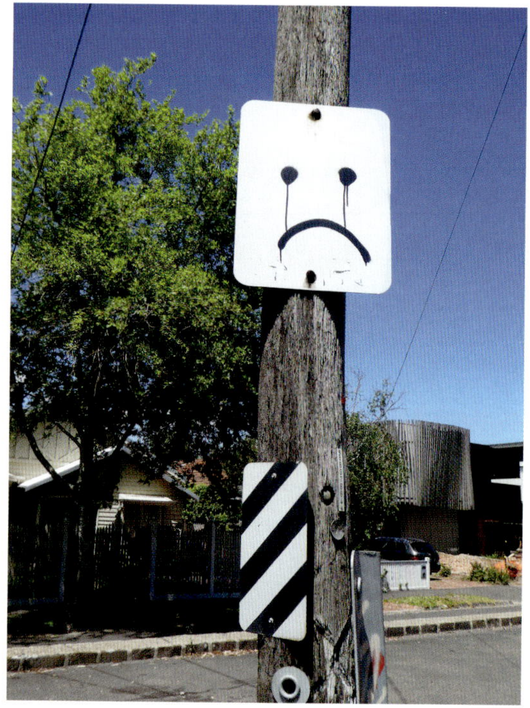

LEFT Unknown artist, Cape Town, South Africa, 2017
RIGHT Unknown artist, Melbourne, Australia, 2017
OPPOSITE LEFT Clet, Barcelona, Spain, 2013
OPPOSITE RIGHT Clet, New York City, USA, 2018

HUMOUR is an integral element of most street sign interventions. The play on words on the sign in Cape Town above left warning drivers to be aware of playing children is a light-hearted response to a safety issue. An unknown artist sprayed a sad face on a faded Neighbourhood Watch program sign in a suburban street.

Clet has installed humorous combinations, opposite, of icon and concept in the additions to the streetscapes of Barcelona and New York. The urban angel with flared wings and the One Way arrow piercing a heart provide a touch of humour for the motorists who notice them.

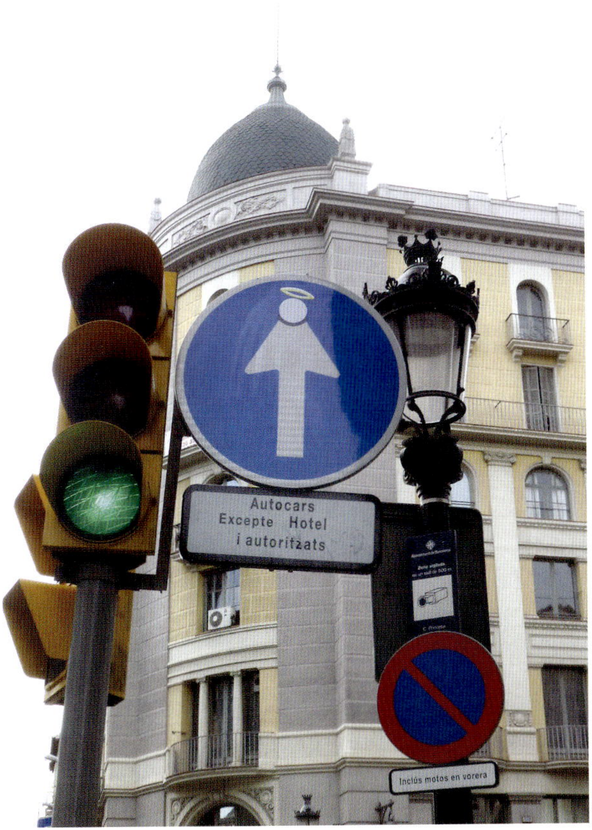
Autocars
Excepte Hotel
i autoritzats
Inclús motos en vorera

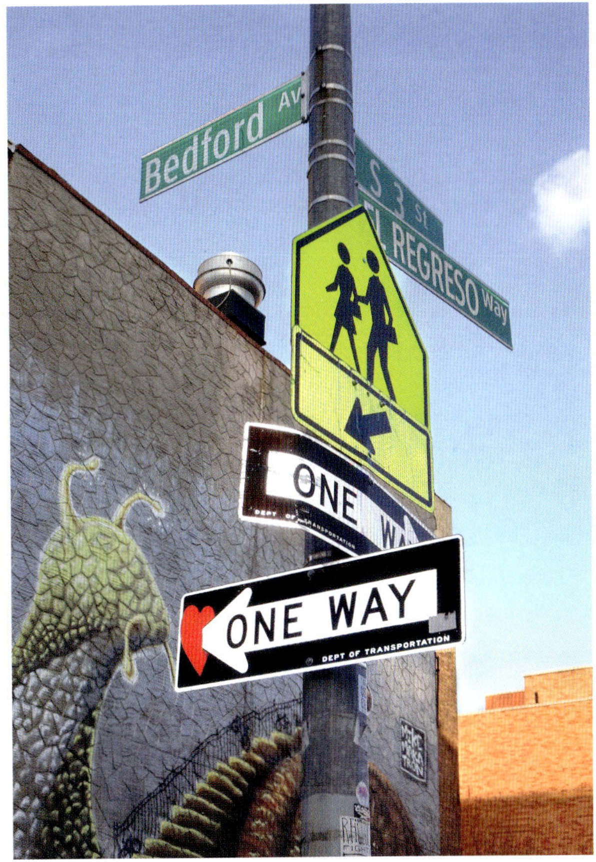
Bedford Av
S 3 St
L REGRESO Way
ONE WAY
DEPT OF TRANSPORTATION

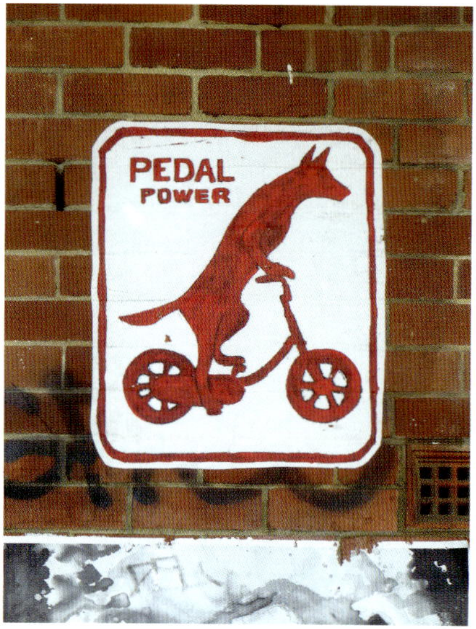

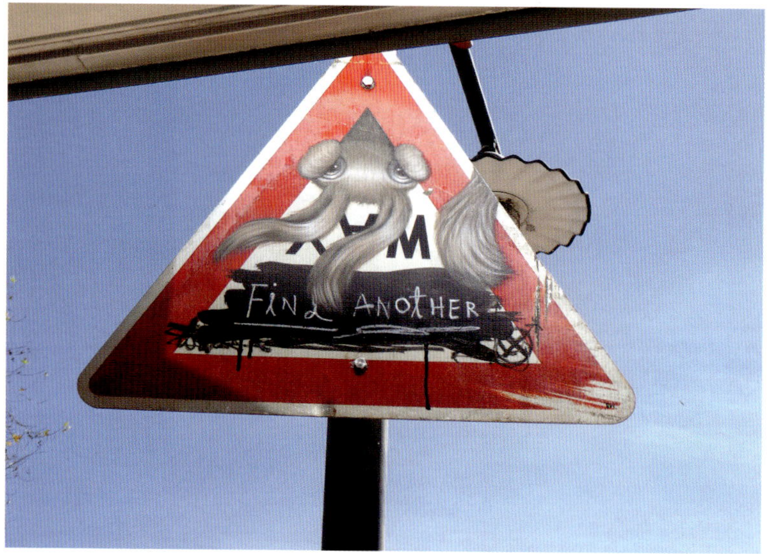

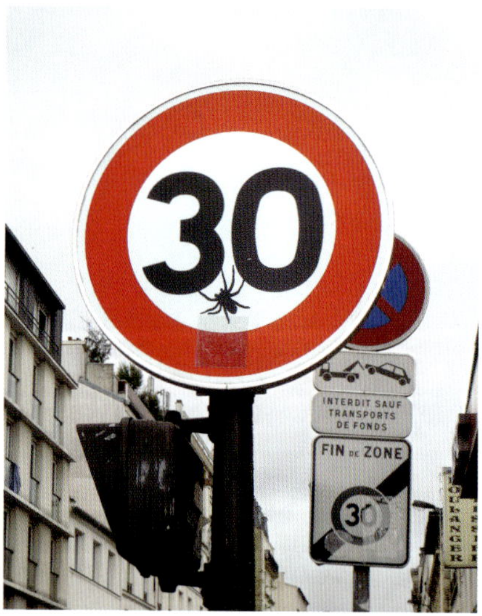

TOP LEFT Unknown artist, Fremantle, Australia, 2014
BOTTOM LEFT Unknown artist, Paris, France, 2015
RIGHT Hayley Welsh, Perth, Australia, 2017
OPPOSITE LEFT Unknown artist, Melbourne, Australia, 2012
OPPOSITE CENTRE Evangelos Sakaris, *Word and Way*, Melbourne, Australia, 2012
OPPOSITE RIGHT Unknown artist, Perth, Australia, 2017

ANIMALS bring humour to the signs on this page – the cycling dingo and the spider are unexpected visitors. One of Hayley Welsh's typically whimsical characters peers at pedestrians from his upside down position on a Give Way sign. In fact, the metal sign itself is upside down – which cleverly echoes the text 'find another way'.

Works from Evangelos Sakaris' officially commissioned project *Word and Way*, installed in 2001–02, can still be found in a narrow laneway between the Greek Precinct and Chinatown in Melbourne. The artist-poet was inspired by the words of ancient Greek and Chinese philosophers, here Lao Tzu, in the text printed on the counterfeit parking regulation signs.

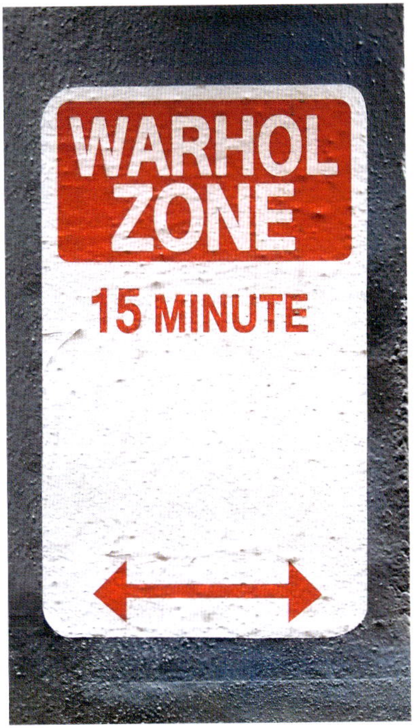
WARHOL ZONE
15 MINUTE

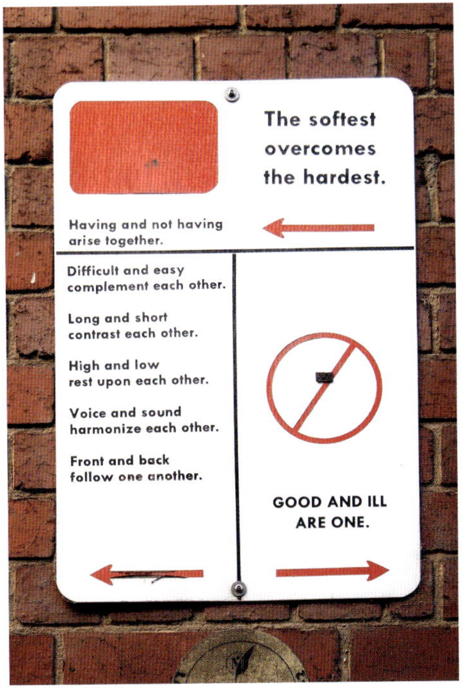
The softest overcomes the hardest.
Having and not having arise together.
Difficult and easy complement each other.
Long and short contrast each other.
High and low rest upon each other.
Voice and sound harmonize each other.
Front and back follow one another.
GOOD AND ILL ARE ONE.

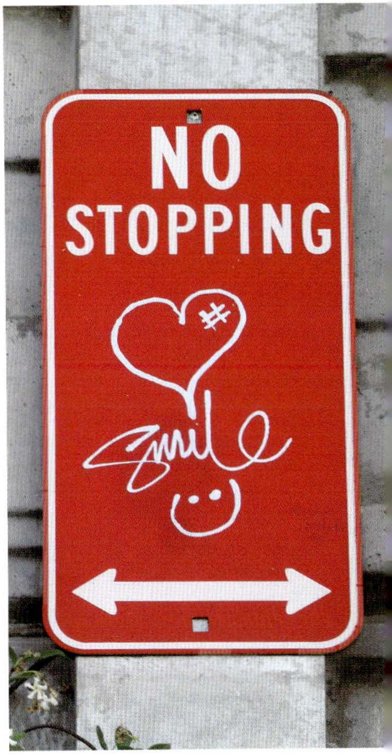
NO STOPPING

List of Artists and Instagram Handles

1AM: @1amsf
281_Anti Nuke: @281_antinuke
Adam Fujita (aka Adam Fu): @adamfu
ADW: @adwart
Amy Peel: @amypeelart
Andrea Riot: @andreariot
Andrea von Bujdoss (aka Queen Andrea): @queenandreaone
Andrew J. Bourke: @andrew_j_bourke
Anna Elizabeth: @annnacat
Astral Nadir: @astral_nadir
Astrotwitch: @astrotwitch
Atle Østrem: @atleostrem
Axel Void: @axelvoid
Baby Guerrilla: #babyguerrilla
Bambi: @therealbambi streetartist
Banksy: @banksy
Barek: @barek_art
Bareket Kezwer: @bkez
Ben Eine: @einesigns
Blu
Boa Mistura: @boamistura
Calm: @thecalm1
cel out: @celout_melb
Cept: @cept_trp
Christian Palmer: @artbypalmer
Christopher Statton
Clet: @cletabraham
CRISP: @crispstreetart
Dan Witz: @danwitzstreetart
David Hollier: @davidhollierart
David Selor: @davidselor
DefyUntruth
D*Face: @dface_official
Dirty Bandits: @dirtybandits
Dolk: @dolklundren
Dolus: @_dolus_
Drasko: @drasko17
drsc0: @drsc0
Eduardo Kobra: @kobrastreetart
eL Seed: @elseed
Elliott Routledge (aka Numskull): @funskull
Ephy
Erin Feller (aka Airy Waters): @airywaters
Ero: @ero_art
Escif: @escif
Eunoia: @eunoia_art
Evangelos Sakaris: @evangelossakaris
Falko One: @falko1graffiti
Fanakapan: @fanakapan
Feik Frasao: @feik_frasao
Felipe Pantone: @felipepantone
fnnch: @fnnch
.frA*: @essegeefra
Gawaa: @lostnomadart
George Rose: @george_rose
Georgia Frances King: @georgiafrancesking
Georgia Hill: @georgiahillbth
Happy
Hayley Welsh: @hayleywelsh
Huge: @hugeart
I'm The Boss: @imthebossartist
in love street art: @inlovestreetart
Jaclyn Rose: @rachmones
Jaeraymie: @jaeraymie
Jason Naylor: @jasonnaylor
Jeremy Novy: @jeremynovy
Jesse Harris: #jesseharris
Jessica Riley: @oh.so.specials
Jimmy Chiale: @jchiale
John Fekner: @johnfekner
Joel Birch: @joeldtd
JPS: @jps_artist
Julie Shiels: @julie.shiels
KAB-101: @kab101ism
Kambeeno: @kambeeno
Karim Jabbari: @karim_jab
Katie Marie Clark: @katie_marie_clarke
Kelly RISK Graval: @riskrock
K-GUY: @cokemoss
Klassy: @klassy_unofficially
La Staa: @lastaa
Lana Hughes: @thisislana_
Lana Milburn: @lunarlana
Latham
Leah Grant: @leah.grant
Loui Jover: @louijover
Louis Masai: @louismasai
Lov3: @edoblov3
Lucy Lucy: @lucylucyone
Lushsux: @lushsux
±MaisMenos±: @maismenos
Maser: @maserart
Matthew Wong: @iamthewong
Mau Mau: @maumauart
Meek
Megan Wilson: #clarionalleymuralproject
Michael Agzarian: @whatafizza
Michelle's Scriptures: @michelles_scriptures
Mike Eleven: @mike.eleven
Mitch Demko: @mitchdemko
Morgan: @morganart
Morley: @official_morley
Mr. Never Satisfied: @dis_satisfied
Murals by Marg: @muralsbymarg
myheadsajungle: @myheadsajungle
Nina Sanadze: @nina_sanadze
Norm Kirby: @normkirby
NOTNOT: @notnotcamscott
Oraculo Project: @oraculoproject
Oscar Low: @mroscarlow
Owen Dippie: @owendippie
Peter Drew: @peterdrewarts
Phoenix: @phoenixthestreetartist
Pøbel: @pobel.no
Raul33: @raul33_
Rene Gagnon: @renegagnon
Retna: @ironeyeretna
Ricky Lee Gordon: @rickyleegordon
Rigo 23: #rigo23
Roach: @roachi
Rob Sharp: @robsharp
Robert Montgomery: @robertmontgomerystudio
Rolando Venegas: @rolandovenegas
Rone: @r_o_n_e
Rory Elphick
Ruben Rojas: @rubenrojas
Ryan Callahan: @ryca_artist
Sandra Chevrier: @sandrachevrier
Sarah Masson: @sarahmassonart
Shepard Fairey: @obeygiant
Silent Bill: @ssosva
Sittoula Sitlakone: #sitlakone_art
SLICK: @og_slick
SOMO.PNG
SpY: @spyurbanart
SST Division: #sstdivision
Stampz: @stampz_37
Stohead: @stohead
STRA: @stra.fr
streetPSA: @streetpsa
Stuart
Sunfigo: @sunfigosunfigo
Taosuz: @taosuz
TeneT: @tenet_ovb
Therese Refvik (aka Tref): @tref.no
Tim Bowtell: @timbowtellart
Tom Dean: #tomdean
Trek Thunder Kelly: #trekthunderkelly
Tristan Eaton: @tristaneaton
Vexta: @vexta
Vitó Julião: @juliao_vito
walden: @wwaallddeenn
Will Coles: @mrwillcoles
Wonderlust: @wonder_fresh
WRDSMTH: @wrdsmth
Yipi Yipi Yeah: @yipiyipiyeah
Zabou: @zabouartist
Zenith: @__zenith____

Acknowledgements

Like much great street art, this book is a collaboration.

There are many people to thank. First and foremost there are the artists and scrawlers who have made this book possible. Their vision, skills, passion and commitment brighten our streets and give us pause for thought in the midst of our daily grind. I speak on behalf of the readers, too, when I say 'thank you'.

I would like to express my gratitude to the team at Hardie Grant Publishing and Explore Australia for their continuing support. Enormous thanks go to Melissa Kayser for her vision of and investment in this ongoing street art project, to Megan Cuthbert for her behind-the-scenes organisation and to Megan Ellis for her patience and efficiency. Above all, I am grateful to Eugenie Baulch, project manager and editor extraordinaire. This is the third project we have worked on together and her professional advice and skills as a wordsmith have contributed much to my pleasure in this adventure.

And then there are my guides. I have been blessed in my travels by the hospitality and passion of many fellow street art enthusiasts. I have walked countless kilometres with these buddies and they have added joy, laughter and local knowledge to each 'mission'. Firstly a big thank you to Sanne Gijsbers (@streetartheerlen) of Heerlen, and co-founder of the website and app Street Art Cities, who so generously showed me around her town and later wrote the foreword to this book. Thanks are also due, and offered cheerfully, to Nick Heard (@heardy67) in London; Tor Ståle Moen (@toris64) in Stavanger; Fernando Alcala Losa (@feralcala) in Barcelona (twice!); Noel Perez (@werewolfone) in Paris (also twice); Fredric Sanabria (@strangefruit_streetart) in Stockholm; Tim Marschang (@streetartantwerp) in Antwerp; Ann Tardiff (@randdomized) in Montreal; Raphael Gonzales (@zurbaran1) and Dave Lee (@pixelatedstreets) in New York City; Wayne Hulley (@streetartjunkie) in Johannesburg; Victoria Gilliand (@streetkiwi) in Dunedin; and Mia Theuns, half of the mighty duo Heronieten (@heronieten), who spent two full days with me in Ostend and Ghent. At home in Melbourne I can always call on the ID expertise of Toby Fairbanks (@allthoseshapes). Thank you all. This book would be much poorer without your enthusiasm, good humour and generous willingness to share.

As always, special thanks go to Des, my long-suffering partner with navigational superpowers. He is always patient and (generally) tolerant of my 'just one more' plea. Thank you.

'Amen' is offered here in the context of emphasising what has been said or written, and is, I think, a fitting closure to this broad exploration of a burgeoning art form and the age-old pastime of scrawling on walls.

Lou Chamberlin
@streetartaustralia

Unknown artist, Melbourne, 2017

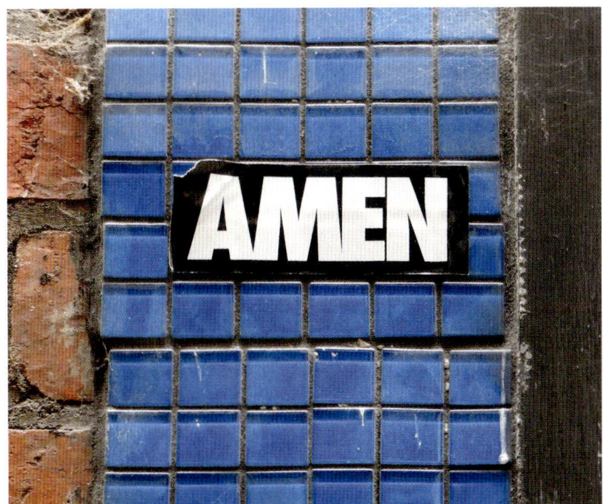

Index

Unknown artist, Melbourne, Australia, 2008

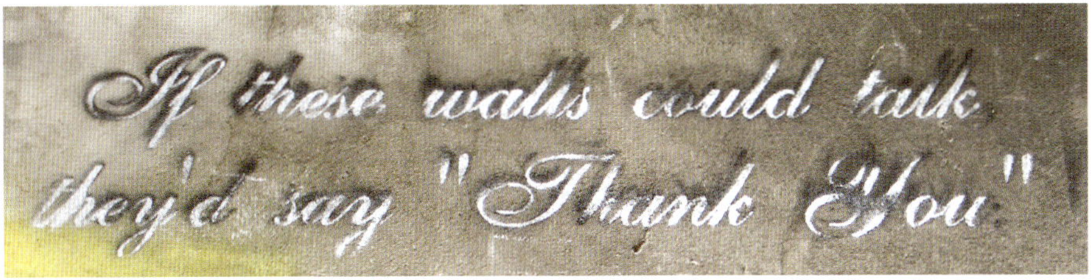

Published in 2018 by Hardie Grant Travel,
a division of Hardie Grant Publishing

Hardie Grant Travel (Melbourne)
Building 1, 658 Church Street
Richmond, Victoria 3121

Hardie Grant Travel (Sydney)
Level 7, 45 Jones Street
Ultimo, NSW 2007

www.hardiegrant.com/au/travel

NATIONAL LIBRARY OF AUSTRALIA

A catalogue record for this book is available from the National Library of Australia

Urban Scrawl
ISBN 9781741176346

10 9 8 7 6 5 4 3 2 1

Publisher
Melissa Kayser

Senior editor
Megan Cuthbert

Project and page editor
Eugenie Baulch

Editorial assistant
Rosanna Dutson

Design
Andy Warren

Typesetting
Megan Ellis

Layout
Lou Chamberlin

Index
Max McMaster

Prepress
Splitting Image Colour Studio

Printed and bound in China by LEO Paper Group

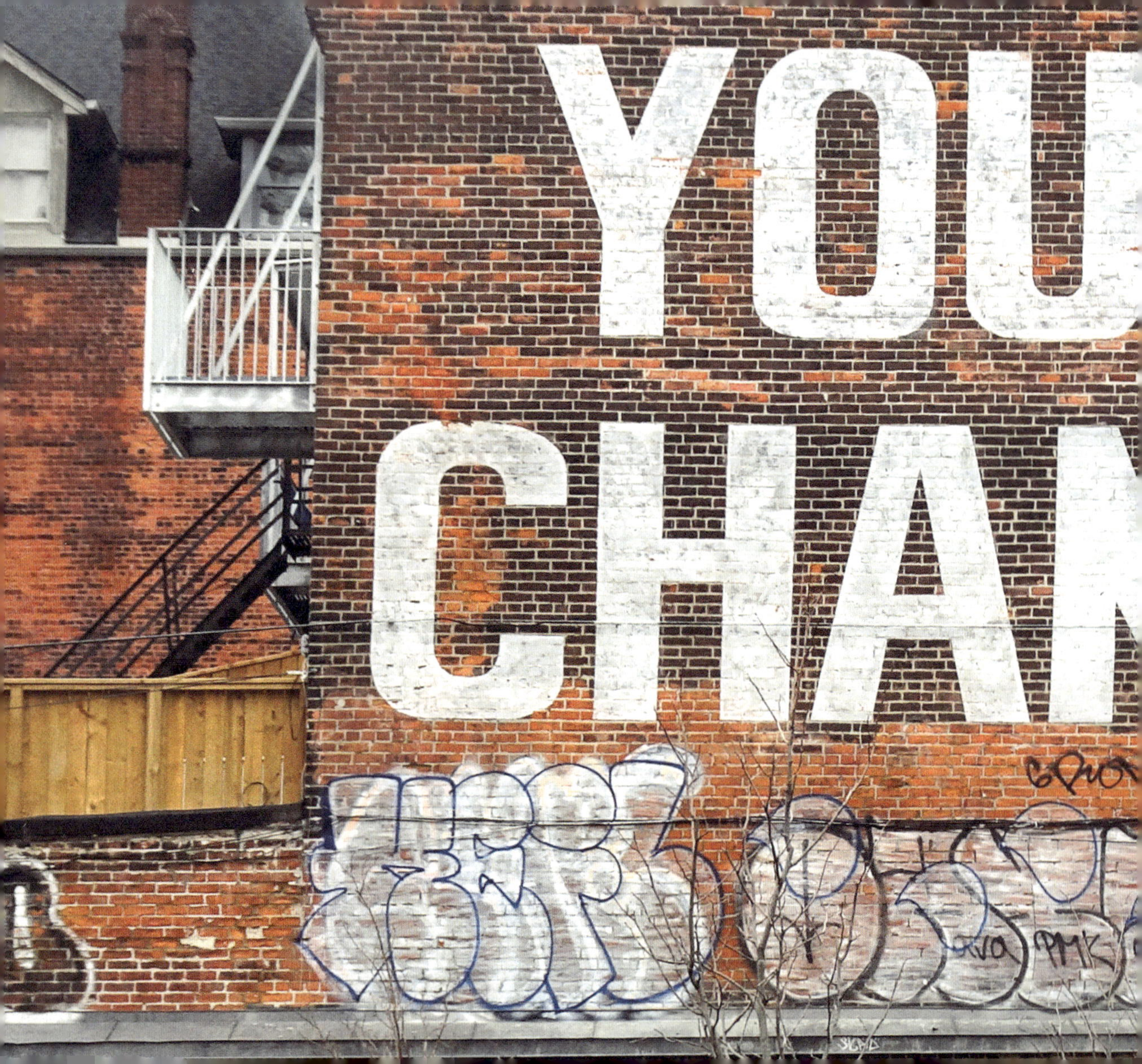
YOU
CHA